JAMES JOYCE AND CINEMATICITY

To my parents' memories of Rhondda chapel lantern shows,
and my long-suffering wife and children

JAMES JOYCE AND CINEMATICITY

Before and After Film

Keith Williams

EDINBURGH
University Press

Edinburgh University Press is one of the leading university presses in the UK. We publish academic books and journals in our selected subject areas across the humanities and social sciences, combining cutting-edge scholarship with high editorial and production values to produce academic works of lasting importance. For more information visit our website: edinburghuniversitypress.com

Edinburgh University Press Ltd
The Tun – Holyrood Road, 12(2f) Jackson's Entry, Edinburgh EH8 8PJ

First published in hardback by Edinburgh University Press 2020

Typeset in 10/12.5 Adobe Sabon by
IDSUK (DataConnection) Ltd, and
printed and bound by CPI Group (UK) Ltd,
Croydon, CR0 4YY

A CIP record for this book is available from the British Library

ISBN 978 1 4744 0248 4 (hardback)
ISBN 978 1 3995 0069 2 (paperback)
ISBN 978 1 4744 0249 1 (webready PDF)
ISBN 978 1 4744 6385 0 (epub)

CONTENTS

Acknowledgements   vi
List of Abbreviations   viii
List of Figures   ix

Introduction   1
1   'I Bar the Magic Lantern': *Dubliners* and Pre-filmic
    Cinematicity   35
2   An Individuating Rhythm: Picturing Time in *A Portrait of
    the Artist as a Young Man*   106
3   'Building-Vision-Machine': *Ulysses* as Moving Panorama   174
Coda: The Media-Cultural Imaginary of *Finnegans Wake*   244
Conclusion: Before and After Film   256

Select Visiography   260
Select Bibliography   267
Index   283

ACKNOWLEDGEMENTS

I am deeply grateful to everyone who helped with this project, especially the anonymous readers of the original proposal and sample chapters; Jeremy Brooker, chair of the MLS for reading drafts and for the privilege of seeing him and Carolyn working their magic live; Mary Cahill and colleagues at the National Museum of Ireland for letting me examine the ash pit slides; Ian Christie who said it sounded like the kind of book he would like to read; Richard Crangle (of the MLS and LUCERNA), for assistance with images; Stephen D'Arcy for kindly inviting me to view the ash pit itself; Sarah Dellmann of the 'One Million Pictures' project; Jeffrey Geiger and Karin Littau, who starting me thinking about cinematicity; the late Mervyn Heard, whose work and performances inspired so many; Onno Kosters and Katherina Hagena for sharing many symposium panels; Matthew Jarron and Steven Gellatly for insights into silent films, Victorian culture and musical accompaniment; John McCourt, for observing that some things are so obvious no one can see them; Luke McKernan, from whom I have learned much in so many ways; Katie Mullin, Cleo Hanaway and the Joyceans at Leeds, for wonderful inputs, academic and sociable; Deac Rossell who probably does not realise yet how a chance conversation would prove so influential on me; Neil Sinyard for unstinting faith and kindness; Nick Wade for enlightening conversations about optical toys and stereoscopy; cohorts of Joyce and cinema students past and future, who provide new ways of thinking about this topic; and colleagues in English, Film, Comics and Art, who listened to my ideas developing with patience and perspicacity; lastly, Dean of Humanities Jim Livesey, for locking me in the writing bunker over the summer until it was finished.

Recent research on Irish visual culture and early film by Kevin and Emer Rockett and Denis Condon has been invaluable, as was the media archaeology of Erkki Huhtamo and Stephen Herbert.

ABBREVIATIONS

EIC	Denis Condon, *Early Irish Cinema, 1895–1921* (Dublin: Irish Academic Press, 2008)
EML	*Encyclopaedia of the Magic Lantern*, ed. David Robertson, Stephen Herbert and Richard Crangle (London: MLS, 2001)
EPVC	*Early Popular Visual Culture*
IiM	Erkki Huhtamo, *Illusions in Motion: Media Archaeology of the Moving Panorama and Related Spectacles* (Cambridge, MA: MIT Press, 2013)
JJQ	*James Joyce Quarterly*
MiTD	Olive Cook, *Movement in Two Dimensions: A Study of the Animated and Projected Pictures which Preceded the Invention of Cinematography* (London: Hutchinson, 1963); repr. as vol. 3 of Stephen Herbert (ed.), *A History of Pre-Cinema* (London: Routledge, 2000)
MLP&MPS	Kevin Rockett and Emer Rockett, *Magic Lantern, Panorama and Moving Picture Shows in Ireland, 1786–1909* (Dublin: Four Courts Press, 2011)
MLS	Magic Lantern Society

FIGURES

I.1 Still from Arthur Robison's *Schatten: eine Nächtliche Halluzination* (1923). Courtesy of BFI National Archive. © absolut Medien GmbH 14

1.1 'Dissolving views apparatus', illustration from Gaston Tissandier, *Popular Scientific Recreations in Natural Philosophy, Astronomy, Geology, Chemistry, etc. etc.* (London: Ward, Lock, 1885), p. 159. Jeremy Brooker's personal collection 37

1.2 Slide from *What are the Wild Waves Saying?* Ian and Daphne Mackley Collection, digital image by David Elsbury 46

1.3 'He sleeps! he sleeps!'. Slide 6 from *Dan Dabberton's Dream* (York and Son, Bridgewater, c. 1887). From the illuminago collection, by kind permission of Ludwig Vogl-Bienek 81

1.4 'On one of the beds lies the body of a middle-aged Woman'. Slide 16 from *Dan Dabberton's Dream* (York and Son, Bridgewater, c. 1887). From the illuminago collection, by kind permission of Ludwig Vogl-Bienek 82

1.5 'Spectre Drama at the Polytechnic Institution', *Illustrated London News* 42, 2 May 1863, p. 486. Reproduced by permission of the National Library of Scotland 87

2.1 'Horses, gallop; thoroughbred bay mare; Annie G'. Plate 626 from Edweard Muybridge, *Animal Locomotion* (1872–85). Science Museum/Science and Society Picture Library (no. 10667598)   110

2.2 'Muybridge's Zoopraxiscope, 1880'. Science Museum/Science and Society Picture Library (no. 10318976)   111

2.3 'Homme vêtu de noir avec des points blancs et des bandes blanches pour l'analyse chronophotographique de la locomotion'. Bibliothèque nationale de France   116

2.4 'Analyse chronophotographique de la marche'. Bibliothèque nationale de France   116

2.5 'Lucien Bull with his high-speed camera, Paris, 1904'. Science Museum/Science and Society Picture Library (no. 10306330)   119

2.6 Still from F. W. Murnau (dir.), *Der letzte Mann* (1924). Courtesy of BFI National Archive, reproduced by kind permission of the Friedrich-Wilhelm-Murnau Stiftung, Wiesbaden, Germany   129

3.1 'A Section of the Rotunda, Leicester Square, in Which Is Exhibited the Panorama', in Robert Mitchell, *Plans and Views in Perspective, With Descriptions of Buildings Erected in England and Scotland* (London: Printed at the Oriental Press, by Wilson & Co. for the author, 1801). Reproduced by permission of the National Library of Scotland   180

3.2 Poster for 'Chas W. Poole's New Myriorama and Trips Abroad'. © The British Library Board c01517-01 Evan.2475   194

3.3 Screengrab from Sagar Mitchell and James Kenyon, *Trade Procession at Opening of Cork Exhibition* (1902). Reproduced by kind permission of the BFI   219

3.4 Still from Walther Ruttmann (dir.), *Berlin: Sinfonie einer Großstadt* (1927). Courtesy of BFI National Archive, reproduced by kind permission of Eva Riehl   225

INTRODUCTION

The way things are, it would seem as if cinema was fifty years behind the novel.

André Bazin in 1961[1]

JOYCEAN 'CINEMATICITY'

James Joyce is widely recognised as the most cinematic of Modernist writers. At the conclusion of the 1933 *Ulysses* obscenity trial in the US, this virtually acquired the status of a legal judgement by the Honourable John M. Woolsey:

> Joyce has attempted—it seems to me, with astonishing success—to show how the screen of consciousness with its ever-shifting kaleidoscopic impressions carries, as it were on a plastic palimpsest, not only what is in the focus of each man's observation of the actual things about him, but also in a penumbra zone residua of past impressions, some recent and some drawn up by association from the domain of the subconscious. He shows how each of these impressions affects the life and behaviour of the character which he is describing.
>
> What he seeks is not unlike the result of a double or, if that is possible, a multiple exposure on a cinema film which would give a clear foreground with a background visible but somewhat blurred and out of focus in varying degrees.[2]

Woolsey not only compared *Ulysses'* 'screening' of consciousness to moving multiple exposures on film, but also invoked an optical toy – the kaleidoscope –

a predecessor to film's dynamically protean imagery. Following Soviet director Sergei M. Eisenstein's view in the early 1930s,[3] André Bazin equated Joyce with the future of cinema, by arguing that he achieved 'ultracinematographic' things on the page which film had still to catch up with in the 1960s. Both deemed Joyce 'ahead of the game' because he seemed to emulate or even outdo what screen techniques achieved both during his lifetime and long after he died in 1941.

However, born in 1882, Joyce's eye and imagination were in fact trained by the rich optical culture of the late Victorian era. Its highly developed and interdependent 'visual literacy' and 'literary visuality' help to explain Joyce's creative receptiveness to film when it arrived in the mid-1890s. Thus Joyce, like his 'low-modern' elder H. G. Wells, was instrumental in extending the classical principle of *ekphrasis* – verbal imitation of visual modes such as painting, sculpture or architecture (real or 'notional')[4] so that audiences might 'visualise' them without seeing them directly – into the age of moving photographic images, broadcasting and telecommunications, by playing on and extending aspects of the common visual culture of his youth.[5] Hence Joyce's work can be seen as a response to the emergence of what Errki Huhtamo in *Illusions in Motion: Media Archaeology of the Moving Panorama and Related Spectacles* (2013) calls a 'media-cultural imaginary' that characterises modernity and in which convergent forms of moving image technologies and entertainment practices played a shaping role.[6]

'EDUCATING THE EYE'

Jonathan Crary has argued that the inception of visual modernity did not stem from experimentation with non-representational form in Post-Impressionist art from the 1880s as is often assumed, but rather from experimental optical devices developed from the early nineteenth century and their wider impact on popular consciousness.[7] This meant that seeing was no longer regarded as neutral perception, but as a subjective and mobile activity, dependent on the body, on perspective, attention and even artificial manipulation. The object of study became vision itself, with all its variables. This is typified by the public mission of Scottish physicist David Brewster, inventor of the kaleidoscope, who also improved the stereoscope and was a photographic pioneer. Brewster's hugely influential *Letters on Natural Magic* (1832) stressed that the eye was the leading sense organ for obtaining knowledge of reality, but that susceptibility to deception was inherent in its very mechanism. Hence 'educating the eye', teaching how vision worked and could be manipulated or augmented, was both a scientific and moral imperative.[8] Brewster and his contemporaries were fascinated by optical illusions that demonstrated the eye's functioning, but also fallibility. Whether they arose from natural phenomena such as 'Brocken Spectres' and mirages, or were artificially induced by magic lantern shows such as the phantasmagoria or by optical toys exploiting 'persistence of vision', many were described and explained in Brewster's *Letters*. This became a kind of handbook offering, as Iwan Rhys Morus puts it, 'an evidential context for the technologies of the eye that proliferated throughout the nineteenth century' and a sceptical method for examining sensational spectacle and devising 'strategies for disciplining vision'.[9] Morus argues that John Henry Pepper's directorship of London's Royal Polytechnic Institution, founded in 1838, epitomises the enactment of Brewster's mission, which provided 'a language and a set of practices . . . to teach audiences how to witness and appropriately frame scientific spectacle'.[10]

The Polytechnic remained at the forefront of that mission for the rest of the century, combining science with shrewd showmanship through the latest visual wonders and influencing how they were exhibited and explained across Britain. Phenomena such as reflection and refraction, binocular and peripheral vision were all accounted for, but perhaps most intriguing was so-called 'persistence of vision'. This effect, whereby the retina retains 'after-images' for approximately one-twentieth to one-fifth of a second after objects casting them are removed, was first scientifically described by Peter Mark Roget in 1824. It revolutionised optics by exposing a delay in human perception – that seeing was a process unfolding in time. Hence after-images filled temporal gaps, allowing series of stills to be perceived as a continuous stream. Although Roget's theoretical model of this perceptio-cognitive 'eye-con' was eventually challenged by phenomenology, persistence of vision remained the standard explanation for cinematicity throughout Joyce's youth.[11] The illusion was explored by a variety of optical or 'philosophical' toys. These were designed to demonstrate aspects of the mechanics of vision through different experiments. They proved that what we see is partly 'out there' in phenomenal reality, but also 'in here' in relations between retina and brain. In showing that vision was part-physiological, part-psychological, optical toys proved that it was capable of manipulation. Their pleasurable effects meant that they also became highly profitable mass-market devices that were instrumental in the development of Victorian moving image culture and the creation of film. Pepper, responsible for perfecting the most successful spook illusion of the nineteenth century at the Polytechnic in 1862, even explained sightings of 'real' spectres as instances of 'that quality or natural property of the eye by which it retains the image of any object presented to it'. Ghosts were simply '*lingering* impressions' on retina and mind.[12]

Drawing on this context, Crary has demonstrated, both etymologically and historically, that being an 'observer' never means perceiving the world neutrally, with an 'innocent' or merely organic eye, but occupying a subject position that is contingent, mediated and therefore ideologically inscribed. Indeed he regards Victorian optical toys as 'disciplinary techniques', 'recoding' the eye's activities 'to heighten its productivity and prevent its distraction', in the interests of an incipient capitalist modernity.[13] Mary Ann Doane also associates these devices with what she calls the 'emergence of cinematic time' long before the Lumière brothers' 'Cinématographe' was patented in February 1895.[14] Experiments in persistence of vision were a driving force in science and philosophy, part of the contemporary obsession with the perception of time and its representability, which led to 'animal locomotion' and 'chronophotographic' studies with high-speed cameras and, in turn, their key role in the invention of the Lumières' machine for projecting 'moving' photographic images on film.[15]

Optical toys created a set of conditions in which marvellous manipulations of vision were paramount, eventually leading to today's mediated culture, as Steven Johnson argues in *Wonderland: How Play Made the Modern World.*[16] As other historians have also shown, the Victorians were fascinated by moving or 3-D illusions. As Kate Flint puts it, 'together with the marvels of scale produced by the telescope and the increasingly domesticated microscope, [they] served to challenge, at the level of popular perception, the quality of observations made by the naked eye'.[17] Similarly, Huhtamo writes of a positive Victorian 'frenzy of the visible' (*IiM*, p. 192), fed by multi-stranded media in which influential periodicals such as the *Illustrated London News* aimed to 'keep continually before the eye of the world a living and moving panorama of all its actions and influences'.[18] Hence by mostly looking forward to the period *after* the patenting of the cinematograph, scholarship has neglected the influence that the key decades leading up to its invention had on Joyce's ekphrastic engagement with the Victorian media-cultural imaginary. Richard Ellmann famously argued that 'We are still learning to be James Joyce's contemporaries, to understand our interpreter.'[19] It is usually assumed that Ellmann was referring to catching up with the significance of writing so ahead of its time. The alternative implication is the need to think ourselves *back into* Joyce's formative historical context in order to appreciate his preternaturally creative response to it.

Joyce was fascinated by the education of the eye, relishing optical novelties and showmanship from an early age. His childhood friend Brendan Gallagher recollected a present given to him at North Richmond Street, where Joyce's family moved in late 1894. This was also the location of 'Araby', from *Dubliners* (1914), whose protagonist, by contrast, fails to bring a back a souvenir of its romantic attractions. (These were in fact far more spectacular than Joyce's story makes out and had a key impact on the cinematicity of his fiction.) As Ellmann recounts, '[w]ith a mysterious air', Joyce revealed a red cardboard box, with hinged front and concealed rollers and 'cranked before Brendan's stage-struck eyes a lordly sequence of coloured pictures of the Port of Southampton, the pyramids of Egypt, and other splendours'.[20] This may have been a miniature 'moving panorama', a peepshow version of large-scale spectacles taking Victorians on virtual journeys around sights of the world, or even a 'roller stereoscope', with its added illusion of three-dimensional imagery. The moving panorama evolved from the original circular and immersive entertainment patented in 1791.[21] Whatever its precise identity, this portable 'moving picture' device representing wondrous elsewheres highlights how the concept of cinematicity has deeper and broader roots in Joyce's life and work than his engagement with its manifestation in projected films.

INTER-MEDIALITY IN MOVING IMAGE CULTURE

Film would never have progressed beyond its primary function for visual recording, but for interaction with other media entertainments. André Gaudreault's argument that it evolved as an inter-medial phenomenon – from technological forms, cultural genres and practices that both preceded and overlapped with it – has shaped new approaches to cinematicity and media archaeology in general. Gaudreault stresses 'the fundamentally *polymorphous nature* [. . .] of the Cinematograph which would basically have been, in the first years of its existence, no more than one incarnation of the cultural series "*projections lumineuses*"'.[22] Thus it is a priority to reveal the wider interactions that determined film's development and their influence on Joyce's work.[23] This cross-fertilisation is avouched as much in Ireland as elsewhere, by the diverse venues, events and entertainment programmes in which early films were exhibited. As Denis Condon notes in *Early Irish Cinema, 1895–1921*: 'Although the variety theatre and charity bazaar were particularly important exhibition spaces for film shows, moving pictures were also shown at business premises, trade shows, lecture halls, pantomimes, and concerts, as well as featuring in film-based entertainments.' Although film's advent in Ireland 'has some unique aspects, it also shares key features with Britain, continental Europe and North America'.[24] Consequently, Joyce's creative relationship with film, to be properly understood, has to be reinflected through the same matrix.

Kevin and Emer Rockett's study, *Magic Lantern, Panorama and Moving Picture Shows in Ireland, 1786–1909*, demonstrates in encyclopaedic detail that from the eighteenth century at least:

> there were already huge numbers of people in Ireland, from all classes, regularly enjoying proto-cinematic experiences through such entertainments as the presentation, from 1786, of transparent paintings, which through various lighting and sound effects, gave the illusion of the passage of time . . . the magic lantern, which though initially limited to simple slide projection, offered from the early nineteenth century, narratively integrated, sophisticated shows that ranged from the gothic or romantic to the melodramatic as well as the morally didactic; the immersive large scale paintings known as panoramas, which adapted by theatre, especially pantomimes, also developed into a range of related entertainments that combined aspects of the transparency of diorama,

the lantern show and mechanical elements (and even actual automata) to produce dramatic moving images or narrative sequences; and *tableaux vivants*, or theatrical posed static representations of paintings, statues and events. Without these entertainments, many developed by Irish inventors and pioneers, whose contributions have not always received international recognition, not only would cinema's moving-pictures have been unimaginable, but so, too, would the cinema space itself and the circulation of film. (*MLP&MPS*, p. 12)

Indeed, far from being a scientific and cultural backwater as sometimes thought, by the mid-1890s Dublin was as primed for the coming of film as other major Western cities, and many of the media and entertainments from which it gestated are referenced and explored in Joyce's work.

PLAYING WITH PERSISTENCE OF VISION

Although the idea of moving images seems inherently contradictory, that paradox flourished in many forms before 1895. Olive Cook, in her classic study *Movement in Two Dimensions* (1963), argued that the 'true perspective' in which to understand film's coming is as another expression of 'the homely popular fantasy' of bringing pictures to life, stretching back to ancient times and deriving 'something from each of its predecessors'. Though possessing 'neither texture nor substance' in manifestation through light (unlike painting or theatre), cinema's subsequent evolution has also been inevitably shaped by new technological developments and processes,[25] mechanical, electronic and now digital, in myriad mobile and multi-platform guises. Moreover, if cinematicity denotes the Victorian cultural desire to conceptualise and represent the world in terms of moving, photographic images, culminating in the Lumières' apparatus, media archaeology affirms that that sense of movement was already emergent in many other forms in Ireland as elsewhere.[26]

Well before Roget, Patrick or 'Patrice' D'Arcy (1725–79), an Irish member of the French Académie des sciences, laid the foundations for research into persistence of vision through optical toys (see *MLP&MPS*, pp. 149–50). These eventually included Joseph Antoine Ferdinand Plateau's 'Phenakistoscope'; Michael Faraday's chromatic 'Faraday Wheel'; Brewster's kaleidoscope; William George Horner's 'Zoëtrope'; and the 'Thaumatrope', credited to John Ayrton Paris,[27] though sometimes to Roget himself. After the invention of rival forms of photography in the late 1830s by Louis-Jacques-Mandé Daguerre and William Fox Talbot, the phenakistoscope in particular became instrumental in the race to construct an apparatus for projecting naturalistic moving images. In her study of Baudelaire's 'media aesthetics', Marit Grøtta argues that because they allowed sight to be radically altered, optical toys also had a radically transformative effect on how writers thought about the visual field and the broader mediation of reality. They 'came to serve as metaphors for different forms of perception, and eventually came to represent a specifically *modern* sensibility'.[28] Optical toys are crucial not just to Baudelaire's works, but to Modernists such as Marcel Proust and Thomas Mann, and consequently to how Joyce presents consciousness conditioned by technologically produced moving images. In the 'Ithaca' episode of *Ulysses*, Bloom recollects watching the world outside become cinematised in his youth by the magically distorting effect of a window with 'a rondel of bossed glass of a multi-coloured pane'. Joyce's description evokes optical toys such as the phenakistoscope, with figures animated around the rim of its spinning discs, or the turning patterns of a kaleidoscope, but also looks forward to the kinetoscope's peepshow film views of busy city traffic, which could be slowed down or speeded up by its crank: 'he had often sat observing ... the spectacle offered with continual changes of the thoroughfare without, pedestrians, quadrupeds, velocipedes, vehicles, passing slowly, quickly, evenly, round and round the rim of a round and round precipitous globe'.[29] Similarly, by an auspicious coincidence that would have appealed to Joyce's fascination with optics and wordplay, but also mythological parallelisms (epitomised by his Daedalus archetype in *A Portrait of the Artist as a Young Man* [1914–15]), the zoëtrope or 'wheel of life' was originally called the 'Daedalum' by Horner. Patented in 1834 for animating image sequences such as flying birds, the zoëtrope became one of the most common and influential optical toys.

Partly because of such trends, experiments in cinematicity moved inexorably towards the point where a mechanical device 'could convincingly represent empirical reality in motion', as David A. Cook puts it.[30] However, Joyce was intensely aware that cinematicity itself neither began nor ended with the cinematograph. Similarly, introducing a recent collection of essays that takes a comparative historical approach, Jeffrey Geiger and Karin Littau define 'cinematicity' not as a property exclusively inherent to the apparatus and institution which became cinema in the early twentieth century, but as a set of evolving characteristics shared by moving images across a whole inter-medial ecology of technologies and forms. They break down the usage of the term into 'two broad but perhaps also broadly opposing tendencies':

> The first, which might be seen as a more traditional use, employs cinematicity to suggest the cinematic properties which are unique to cinema itself. In this sense, cinematicity relates to film aesthetics, cinematography, theatrical projection and ... to what the unique properties of cinema might bring to other art forms. But a second use of the word ... stresses the ways that cinematicity might help express the sense of cinema as dynamic, interconnected and interrelated not only with those media it most closely resembles, but with a broad range of art forms

and expressive modes, even those that came before the watershed year of 1895 and that are likely to outlive the photochemical era of celluloid film projected to an audience in a movie theatre. So, true to the metamorphic nature of language, cinematicity develops and changes over the years, and now might encompass a wide array of scholarly approaches, from examining the phantasmagoric imaginations of writers and philosophers in the eighteenth century to the changing modes of perception due to high-speed rail travel in the nineteenth century to the holodeck imaginary of the future.[31]

In this sense, the cinematograph can be historicised as one particular and contingent outcome.

Cinematicity itself has in turn already mutated far beyond the specific photochemical materiality and consumptive modes of film-based projection, through a rapidly developing host of other media – including television, computers, tablets, iPhones, games consoles and VR devices – which feed in and out of each other. Thus, from a twenty-first-century digital perspective, film increasingly appears an 'intermediate technology' that is being superseded, rather than being cinematicity's ultimate form. Moreover, the ekphrastic techniques of Modernists such as Joyce tell us much about how cinematic forms evolved and remediated one another and their critical role in shaping the common media-cultural imaginary of his time and after. My research confirms that the cinematicity of his literary method was never solely a response to the cinematograph: it was imaginatively primed and nourished through the connective tissue of an already sophisticated moving image and projection culture, imbued with a sense of 'things to come'. Alongside optical toys, this comprised 'shadowgraphy', the magic lantern, panoramas and dioramas, instantaneous photographic analysis, as well as peepshows based on Thomas Alva Edison's 'Kinetoscope' film viewer. Many of these influenced, overlapped and continued to coexist with projected film in Ireland for some time. Virtually all their attractions are referenced in Joyce's fiction. Their effects are also emulated and critiqued in its pages, with a flair for ekphrastic cinematicity that surpasses other Modernists.

Edison's kinetoscope (patented in 1891) built on Eadweard Muybridge and Étienne-Jules Marey's instantaneous photographic anatomisations of movement, before its principle was in turn adapted for projection after Charles-Antoine Lumière realised its potential. The 'Cinématographe' itself – a combined film camera, projector and printing device – was finally created by his sons Auguste and Louis, thus giving birth in 1895 to cinema as a distinct industry based on the public projection of moving photographic images.[32] Edison aimed to produce a 'home entertainment machine' (anticipating the television set), in which moving pictures illustrated his sound recording device, the Phonograph (patented in 1878). The Mutoscope (a hand-cranked rival of Edison's electrically powered peepshow) is the only device for watching photographic moving pictures explicitly named in *Ulysses*, which is set in 1904, even though what we familiarly call cinema was already nearly a quarter of a century old when it was published in 1922. Hence we need to be more 'Janus-faced' in examining Joyce's influences before 1895 as well as after. This book makes the case that by only looking forward into the twentieth century and its post-cinematograph avant-gardism to explain Joyce's Modernism, we neglect the contribution made by the period in which he grew up and its common media-cultural imaginary as a shaping force in his work.

NARRATIVE MONSTRATION

Cinematicity is key to Joyce's narrative methods. Gaudreault makes a distinction between what he calls 'monstration' (showing) and 'narration' (telling) in the relationship between moving screen images and spoken or written words through the audio-visual practices carried over from lantern shows. The lantern lecturer morphed into the 'film explainer' who interpreted (and sometimes vocalised) silent pictures through their patter, before the technical perfection of synchronised dialogue through the optical soundtrack in the mid-1920s.[33] Film explainers certainly presented early Dublin screenings, interacting with both films and audiences. Diarist Joseph Holloway witnessed one such 'cicerone' being made subject to 'any amount of playful banter' in November 1897.[34] Hence what may be disorientating about Joyce's emulation of visual methods of storytelling consists in a deliberate silencing of any 'meta-narrative' voice, equivalent to the lantern lecturer or film explainer's commentary, guiding us through his ekphrastic visuals, because of his famously impersonal literary technique. This requires a more challenging creative interpretation from the reader to process Joyce's images and is, therefore, closer to Gaudreault's monstration than conventional narrative. Similarly, Spiegel argues that Gustave Flaubert's *Madame Bovary* (1857) provided Joyce with a literary model for basing exposition and character development on visualisation of action through subjective focalisation rather than omniscient commentary, through an impassive style of 'showing' rather than 'telling'. As a consequence, Spiegel suggests that a characteristic of post-Flaubertian narrative is its demand for active rather than passive readership, encouraging our own interpretation and analysis rather than presenting them pre-packaged. In effect, he suggests that modern readers must 'think with their eyes', echoing Stephen's phrase in *Ulysses*' 'Proteus' episode, because 'the words that convey the concretised narrative refer the reader to objects in the external world. The words have been chosen to make him grasp the subject largely by means of visual images.'[35] Hence Hugh Kenner and David Hayman conceived the idea of the Joycean 'Arranger' to describe his readers' impression of an almost invisible agency at work behind the highly visual narrative structures of *Ulysses*, particularly through its orchestration of sub-sections and the implied links between them in 'Wandering Rocks'.[36] If this general tendency in Joyce and its hypostasis in that episode is not fully identical with Gaudreault's filmic monstration (and its descent from earlier practices), then there is a least a suggestive convergence between the two on grounds of inter-medial resemblance.

By *Ulysses*, inter-mediality between Joyce's narrative style and cinematic techniques was so synergetic and pervasive as to attract enthusiastic attention from film-makers themselves. Most famously, in the late 1920s Eisenstein became convinced that the 'stretch of tension' (to borrow Dennis Potter's phrase)[37] between words and images in *Ulysses*' interior monologues furnished a template for more creative use of the newly synchronised soundtrack.[38] However, even after documentary evidence of Joyce's early film-going is taken into account, Spiegel's 1976 claim, that almost any of *Dubliners*' stories (written 1904–07) seem to feature 'innumerable angles of vision and sequences of literary montage far more bold and original' than realised in contemporary films, still stands up.[39] Though too dismissive of the levels of sophistication in film's pioneering decade, Spiegel is right to detect a continuing lag between Joycean literary cinematicity and film-making just as acute in *Portrait* or in *Ulysses*, granted that by the latter's publication the medium had developed 'a very rich and expressive vocabulary' of techniques.[40] However, paradoxically, the major reason for Joyce's prescience consists not so much in the alleged belatedness in film's progress as narrative medium, as in his creative response to storytelling methods in the visual culture that gave birth to it.

'LIFE TO THOSE SHADOWS'[41]

There is a distinct awareness in Joyce's fiction of the appeal of moving images, reaching back into the prehistory of film's eye-conning illusion. Joyce makes frequent reference to cave-like spaces in which shadowy animations are displayed, reworking Plato's archetypal media parable (based on Greek shadow puppetry) in numerous contexts; similarly implying both emulation of and wariness about the modern age of mechanised moving images.[42] Joyce's earliest writings show an ambivalent fascination with the suggestive play of light and shade, with lenses, frames, screens and projection effects. According to his brother Stanislaus, Joyce composed a series of sketches called 'Silhouettes' (some time between 1893 and 1898, that is, when he was no younger than 11 or older than 16) at Belvedere College. The first,

> like the first three stories of *Dubliners*, was written in the first person singular, and described a row of mean little houses along which the narrator passes after nightfall. His attention is attracted by *two figures in violent agitation on a lowered window-blind illuminated from within*, the burly figure of a man, staggering and threatening with upraised

fist, and the smaller sharp-faced figure of a nagging woman. A blow is struck and the light goes out. *The narrator waits to see if anything happens afterwards. Yes, the window-blind is illuminated again* dimly, by a candle no doubt, and *the woman's sharp profile appears accompanied by two small heads, just above the window-ledge, of children wakened by the noise.* The woman's finger *is pointed in warning.* She is saying, 'Don't waken Pa.'[43] [italics mine]

Effectively based on a revealing form of back-projection, Spiegel argues that 'in its optical invention and treatment of time and space, the passage is presented in a mode that could only be described as cinematographic'.[44] Certainly, as imagistic narrative it is as striking as anything in late nineteenth-century fiction. Similarly its focus on implied alcoholism and domestic abuse parallels the themes of countless magic lantern and early film shows about the 'Social Question'. According to Spiegel, Joyce's sketch contains in embryo all the written analogues of 'camera-eyed' visualisation and narrative form characteristic of his more mature work, particularly 'the subjective nature of the seen object and the fragmentation of the visual field'. Also notable are Joyce's observer's framed and limited viewpoint, determining the contingent appearance of shapes moving across the 'screen'; temporal condensation between phases of action; the strikingly cinematic synecdoche of heads outlined in profile, severed from bodies by the window-ledge, as well as the 'close-up' of the pointing finger. We might add a sense of ambiguous alternation between two-dimensionality and stereoscopy, as Joyce also began playing with effects of depthlessness and palpability characteristic of projected images. Moreover, the potentially voyeuristic alienation pervading the whole scenario anticipates Joyce's characteristic mode of vision; not just because of the 'oblique separation' between viewer and action, but because of the event's 'remote and enigmatic quality' presented in the form of 'opaque' but animated surfaces.[45]

Spiegel takes this as confirmation that Joyce was cinematic 'in his literary procedure before the cinema'. Thus 'Silhouettes' shows precociousness (individual and historical) in its distinctly visual 'concretised form'.[46] However, Spiegel's argument requires significant qualification in terms of film's prehistory and Joyce's saturation in late Victorian visual culture. Through his narrator watching a private altercation publicly 'projected' against a nighttime blind, Joyce self-consciously rendered his sketch's action as a sequence of moving images in 'shadowgraphic', dumbshow-like display. Joyce could possibly have seen projected film shows from April 1896 when barely 14 (see below for Dublin's first screenings), but shadow animation was itself a proto-filmic entertainment dating back at least to eighteenth-century Europe, when the vogue for silhouette pictures coincided with the importation of *Ombres chinoises* or 'Chinese shadow' puppet shows via Turkey. Moreover, from the fifteenth century, silhouette images were placed over apertures for projection in 'shadow lantern' shows.[47] By the nineteenth century, shadow entertainments given by wandering 'Galantee' showmen were common on Britain's streets. They were also performed by stretching sheets across Punch and Judy booths lit from within (*MiTD*, p. 79). The projection of large-scale silhouettes for theatrical backgrounds dates from the early nineteenth century, and they were later colourised, using gelatine (*EML*, pp. 277–9). Similarly, cut-outs mounted on glass were projected, particularly for comic or caricature effects. The Victorians consequently patented numerous 'shadowgraph' systems using specially adapted lanterns,[48] and 'silhouette slides' furnished sophisticated transformative, moving and even panoramic effects.[49]

Symptomatically, forms of revealing shadowgraphic *ekphrasis* were also deployed in turn-of-the-century popular texts. For example, in *Living London* (1902), a panoramic documentary study edited by George R. Sims that raised consciousness about social conditions, there is an entire section called 'Behind the Blinds'. This alludes to watching moving shadows from the street below, effectively projecting the private dramas of a cross-section of citizens cinematically, rendering them transparent to the observer: 'For us to-day, as we wander through the great city, that fourth wall must also be removed from its ordinary place. Only then can we become privileged spectators of the *vie intime* of London – the life behind the blinds.'[50] The section includes both Sims's description and an illustration of a bobby on his beat watching moving figures screened in the window of a dying woman for the sign of her final passing, like Joyce's boy narrator at the beginning of *Dubliners'* 'The Sisters'.[51]

In *belle époque* Paris, technological innovation led to a blossoming of the shadow play. As Phillip Dennis Cate explains, photomechanical relief-printing made it possible to reproduce high-contrast black-and-white images easily and cheaply. This enabled Henri Rivière to create a system for moving silhouettes mounted in rows at multiple distances from the screen, with scenic backgrounds painted in different colours on glass. The effect produced tonal variations and a three-dimensional impression of action in receding planes.[52] Le Chat Noir was Montmartre's world-famous 'Théâtre des Ombres'. Popular shows included Rivière's burlesque biblical fantasy, *La Tentation de St Antoine*, remediated in trick film format by Georges Méliès and sometimes compared to the fantastic visions of *Ulysses'* 'Circe' episode; and *Pierre Pornographe*, based on the *Commedia del Arte*, a satire of censorial hypocrisy which would have appealed to Joyce: high-minded civic guardians arrest Pierrot for painting Columbine naked, while plotting to seduce his model themselves. Le Chat shows were created by leading artists including Caran D'Ache and attended by writers such as Paul Verlaine.

Although it closed in 1897, other Théâtres des Ombres sprang up which might have caught Joyce's eye during his Paris sojourns of 1902–04. One striking 1910 shadow play, *Ulysse à Montmartre* (at La Lune Rousse), modernises Homer's epic twelve years before Joyce by depicting Ulysses' adventures in Paris's red-light district. It was riddled with deliberate anachronisms, upsetting the status of classicism in French culture. A collaboration by Dominique Bonnaud, Numa Blès and Lucien Boyer, it stemmed from the anti-establishment 'Fumiste' movement, anticipating Dada and Surrealism in provocatively incongruous and *risqué* imagery. *Ulysse à Montmartre* reincarnates Homer's seductive Sirens as prostitutes, and Circe, his man-transforming witch, as their corpulent brothel *madame*. Although there may be no direct evidence of influence on Joyce's 'Circe' chapter, which reworks Homer in a similar context, parallelism with the themes and methods of this moving image narrative, based on phantasmagoric animation, is culturally symptomatic.[53]

Perhaps recognising affinities with their new medium, Louis Lumière entrusted the cinematograph's February 1896 London debut to Félicien Trewey, a magician specialising in shadow shows. In November 1896 Trewey was also responsible for Dublin's first truly successful film programmes, in terms of both technical standards and box office (*MLP&MPS*, pp. 223–4). Although cinemas superseded shadow venues (Montmartre's were all closed by 1923), their methods and forms were remediated by film. In the 1920s they gave rise to sophisticated 'silhouette cartoon' series, such as Pat Sullivan and Otto Messmer's *Felix the Cat*, and even feature-length animations, such as Lotte Reiniger's exquisite Arabian Nights fantasy, *Die Abenteure von Prinz Achmed*. Shadowgraphy also lies behind the equivocal play between light and shade, presence and absence, flatness and depth that permeates German Expressionist cinema. As Cook put it, such films were conspicuous acknowledgements of the underlying continuity between shadow shows 'and the cinema that ousted them' (*MiTD*, p. 80).[54]

Dubliners' opening story, 'The Sisters', famously starts with a boy narrator's nervous expectation of a flickering shadow effect similar to Joyce's first 'Silhouette'. He constantly watches 'the lighted square of the window' from across the street for the terminal sign of his priestly mentor's condition: 'If he was dead . . . I would see the reflection of candles on the darkened blind for I knew that two candles must be set at the head of a corpse' (*Dubliners*, p. 3). There are numerous silhouetted figures and moving shadow effects in other *Dubliners'* stories too.[55] *Portrait* is also riddled with allusions to the shape-projecting fire shadows of Plato's cave. In *Ulysses*, Joyce reworked his juvenilia's method and motifs in terms of the key features and components of film projection. In 'Nausicaa', newsboys announcing the racing results in the evening editions run '[b]y screens of lighted windows' (13.1173), Joyce playing on their ambiguity as blinds and negativised projection surfaces again. In 'Ithaca', Stephen watches Bloom's actions from outside No. 7 Eccles Street in a 'discrete succession of images' framed by 'transparent kitchen panes' (17.109–12). Later, they both gaze at Molly's bedroom window, with its single 'visible luminous sign': a paraffin oil lamp, its 'oblique shade projected on a screen of roller blind supplied by Frank O'Hara, window, blind, curtain pole and revolving shutter manufacturer 16 Aungier street' (17.1174–7). As Austin Briggs has pointed out, this passage suggestively itemises the key mechanical components then necessary for cinema proper (particularly through terms such as 'revolving shutter').[56]

Joyce's sustained interest in moving silhouettes converges strikingly with tendencies in Expressionist films such as Arthur Robison's *Schatten: eine Nächtliche Halluzination* (1923) (figure I.1), its English title, *Warning Shadows*, echoing the hand gesture that closes Joyce's first 'Silhouette'. *Schatten* has much in common both thematically and technically with *Ulysses*, based as it is on a psychologically suggestive shadow play around a husband's jealousy complex, projected by a mischievously mesmeric travelling showman, thus visualising the repressed contents of the husband's unconscious as two-dimensional moving images. At one point phantom cuckold's horns are grafted

Figure I.1 Still from Arthur Robison's *Schatten: eine Nächtliche Halluzination* (1923). Courtesy of BFI National Archive. © absolut Medien GmbH.

on to his head from the shadow of a hunting trophy on the wall, just as they are on Shakespeare's in 'Circe' by cleverly superimposing two separate visual planes: '*Stephen and Bloom gaze in the mirror. The face of William Shakespeare, beardless, appears there . . . crowned by the reflection of the reindeer antlered hatrack in the hall*' (15.3821–4). A coloured French lithograph illustrating a magic lantern show from 1835 uses a similar visual pun, alternating foreground and background. It also comments on projection's role in creating phantasmagorias of possessiveness and forbidden desire. A couple stand before a screen watching the projected image of a goat, which makes the husband appear to be wearing its horns. A liftable flap reveals the cause: a handsome officer concealed in the lantern cabinet, kissing the wife's hand.[57] Shadow play effects remained important throughout Joyce's career: they recur in several passages in *Finnegans Wake*, which also link them with film and the new medium of television.

MAGIC LANTERNISM

More than shadow plays, however, one particular strand of Victorian cinematicity was crucial to the development of projected film: the magic lantern, the subject of my first chapter. It was used for purposes of entertainment, instruction and persuasion in myriad ways and at every social and intellectual level. Charles Musser has explained cinema's evolution as the 'history of screen practice', arguing that it was 'a continuation of and transformation of magic lantern traditions in which showmen displayed images on a screen'.[58] From this long view, 'Screen practice always has a technological component, a repertoire of representational strategies and a cultural function – all of which are undergoing constant interrelated change.'[59] As Ludwig Vogl-Bienek and Richard Crangle elaborate, 'If we can side-step the technological distinctions . . . and look instead at a set of continuities of practice in spectators viewing images on screen, we come closer to a practical understanding of the art of projection in its contemporary contexts.'[60] In this sense, lantern practice was also a key influence on cinematicity in Joyce. By uncanny coincidence, in February 2013 archaeologists from Ireland's National Museum excavated a large cache of lantern slides from the ash pit of the Joyce family house described in chapter 5 of *Portrait* (see Chapter 1 for detailed discussions). Albeit turning out not to belong to the family but to a Presbyterian missionary who moved in afterwards, these slide sets nonetheless constitute substantial circumstantial evidence. They demonstrate how literally embedded and controversial pre-filmic projection practices and genres were in the common media-cultural imaginary of Joyce's youth and in such close proximity to him.[61]

Despite the fact that his first major publication appears to 'bar' the lantern's influence in its one explicit reference in *Dubliners*' 'Grace', Joyce nonetheless alludes to lantern motifs, genres and techniques in other stories (continuing to do so in *Portrait* and *Ulysses*). Indeed, the lantern's presence helps explain key aspects of innovations in *Dubliners* which make its style appear modernistically cinematic before film developed equivalent techniques. Using examples from contemporary slides, Chapter 1 demonstrates the fundamental part that lanternism played in Joyce's ekphrastic method, not least in numerous projection effects and intrusions of detached pictures from one context into another as multi-layered images, but also in 'dissolving views' transitioning in space, time and consciousness. Indeed, far from Joyce 'barring' its influence, devices from lantern shows shed light on one of *Dubliners*' mysteries: how Joyce appears to use 'flashback' form in numerous stories several years before the technique's first achievement by film editing. Magic lantern slides often signified 'multi-spatiotemporality', superimposing or inserting images to visualise the thoughts or fantasies of characters in the main scene. They presented dynamic narrative transformations in photographic 'life-model' sets, which are the immediate predecessors of feature films. It is therefore likely that Joyce also innovated his own literary equivalent to filmic flashback from the parallel influence of lantern techniques.

The lantern also had a reputation as a 'technology of the uncanny',[62] especially for phantasmagoria shows that materialised moving spooks, pioneered by itinerant continental magicians and established in Dublin by the early 1800s. Joyce evokes the phantasmagoria for the memorably uncanny vision that climaxes *Dubliners*' final story. This verbal 'dissolve', in which a shadowy ghost world replaces mundane reality, displays a sense of how the magic lantern passed effects on to film as its successor technology. Thus Chapter 1 shows that *Dubliners* both references film's active inheritance from the lantern, but also anticipates its own narrative futures. Such symptomatic remediations reflected in Joyce's own cinematic style reached maturity in *Portrait* and *Ulysses*.

'PICTURING TIME'

Chapter 2 focuses on how Joyce intensified the literary emulation of the visual analysis of movement, one of the primary technological drivers that created the medium of film. Modern writing and scientific enquiry shared a preoccupation with fixing transient moments for inspection. Virginia Woolf likened *Ulysses* to a slow-motion film anatomising movement more accurately than the naked eye. But she also noted that Joyce simultaneously extended such analysis into the perceptual and cognitive processes of the subject apprehending it. Effectively, Woolf traced Joyce's cinematic vision back to the cultural 'epiphany' of Eadweard Muybridge's instantaneous photographic 'animal locomotion studies', and their influence on the development of film. Similarly, Joyce's notion of 'epiphany' has affinities with the camera's defamiliarising technological gaze, especially the methods by which photography made hitherto unnoticed phenomena visible. As explained in *Stephen Hero* (Joyce's aborted second version of *Portrait*):

> By an epiphany he meant a sudden spiritual manifestation, whether in the vulgarity of speech or of gesture or in a memorable phase of the mind itself. . .
>
> – Imagine my glimpses at that clock as the gropings of a spiritual eye which seeks to adjust its vision to an exact focus. The moment the focus is reached the object is epiphanised.[63]

Hence Chapter 2 investigates Joyce's own visually anatomising tendency as it evolved through *Portrait*'s three different versions. The mobile, camera-eyed focalisation and 'montage' structure of his finished novel are rooted in speculations about an experimental method for picturing a mind developing over time that are framed in visually dynamic terms in Joyce's first version, the 1904 autobiographical sketch, 'A Portrait of the Artist'. Its proposed method was finally achieved in the novel itself (serialised 1914–15). If *Portrait* constituted a breakthrough into sustained 'stream of consciousness' form, it was also synergetic with key aspects of visual culture and technology that gave birth to film.

The 1904 'Portrait's' tropes point towards a psychological purpose and 'moving' interior form that Joyce lost track of in *Stephen Hero*. Their cryptic metaphors – 'the past . . . implies a fluid succession of presents, the development of an entity . . . to liberate from the personalised lumps of matter that which is their individuating rhythm . . . the curve of an emotion' – actually recall Muybridge's animal locomotion studies and the 'Chronophotographie' of his contemporary Étienne-Jules Marey. Muybridge and Marey captured transitory phenomena with the enhanced vision of the camera, materialising time by mechanical means and recomposing action as a series of related moments, in order to apprehend its reality more accurately. Muybridge's photographic sequences anticipate the filmstrip, and his 1879 patent 'Zoöpraxiscope' eventually animated their consecutive stills into a genuinely 'fluid succession of presents'. Similarly, Marey's overlapping shots of gymnasts against opaque backgrounds effectively liberated the 'individuating rhythm' of a moving body from separate moments, making it visible as an abstract curve rising and falling in space.

Thus in his first attempt at *Portrait*, Joyce hypothesised literary means for picturing the psycho-sensory movement of a consciousness developing over time, equivalent to how rapid photography dissected and recomposed physical motion, using its experiments as guiding metaphor. Chapter 2 shows how Stephen's 'mobilised virtual gaze' and the interiorised 'rhythm' of his mind are based on imagistic association which continuously overlaps present perceptions and past memories, tracing a timeline that pushes dynamically towards his vocational future as an artist. This rising and falling pattern marks out both recurrent personality traits and adaptive responses to crises. It is simultaneously the underlying topic and form of Joyce's novel, taking the cinematicity of his work into a radically new phase.

Moving Panoramas

Chapter 3 deals with another visual entertainment comparable to the lantern in terms of cultural impact. The panorama's moving forms have received a fraction of the attention afforded film's other predecessor media, but they are arguably just as influential on Joyce's writing. As Alison Byerly and others have pointed out, the panorama 'was deeply implicated in the changing perceptions of time and space' marking the passage of the Victorian into the modern age.[64] Moreover, as Huhtamo notes, panorama showmen also displayed and explicated moving images, albeit without relying on projection, and the frames across which their painted images scrolled are not usually considered screens (*IiM*, p. 12). One reason moving panoramas have slipped through the cracks in the history of screen practice is their sheer lack of physical preservation. This was due to their liminal status 'between academic painting and architecture, popular visual spectacles, and the emergent mass culture' (*IiM*, p. 10). Their enormous canvases were considered particularly disposable, being either displayed to the point of disintegration or dissected and repurposed as stage backdrops and wall hangings. While the originally upmarket circular panoramas were in oils in the academic tradition, their moving successors were produced in distemper, the staple medium of cheap fairground attractions and popular theatre. They were not designed to impress aesthetically, but to turn quick profits, motion and added attractions offsetting lack of refinement (*IiM*, p. 11).

Recent media archaeology has redressed this neglect by excavating the moving panorama's lost history. The original panorama catered to the public desire for increasingly lifelike and elaborate attractions, which implied a kind of visual mastery over a given location, but also shaped and transmitted Britain's imperial worldview from centre to periphery and back, through a kind of teleportation. The first was opened in 1793 by Irishman Robert Barker, who both coined the term and patented its technique of production and exhibition. These detailed and hyper-realistic paintings, housed in circular viewing galleries known as rotundas, usually depicted famous cities, sublime landscapes or battles, giving viewers the virtual sensation of immersion in a surrounding scene. However, their static structure quickly gave way to moving forms. Most featured auditoria in which viewers sat (unlike the circular panorama's central platform on which they perambulated) watching long paintings on vertical rollers scrolling across a 'window' as increasingly spectacular 'moving picture' events (*IiM*, pp. 6–7). They were fundamentally a narrative medium, dependent on both scripts and performance. They became a ubiquitous and thriving entertainment, meaning that Joyce almost certainly attended some, as references and effects in his fiction, challenging their status as a colonial medium in various ways, confirm.

Both their disposability and innovations align moving panoramas with modernity's emergent *Zeitgeist*. Their attempt to capture a world in motion anticipates Impressionist painting and rapid photography. Moreover, they incorporated a variety of 'dioramic' effects that transformed and animated their images. Their dissolution of boundaries between word and image by the inclusion of narration (together with sound effects and music) converged with trends in lanternism and typified the modern desire for the multi-media synthesis of the arts that led to film. The panorama's evocation as metaphor – persisting even today – testifies to a cultural significance beyond the life of the medium itself. Consequently, Huhtamo historicises a third category developing alongside its immersive and moving forms: the 'discursive panorama'. This refers to the panorama as figure of speech or to written and imagined panoramic representations (*IiM*, p. 15). Consequently, 'its intensive discursive life' also contributed to the emergence of modernity's 'media-cultural imaginary' (*IiM*, p. 332), which Joycean cinematicity both plays on and critiques. This was particularly the case in *Ulysses*, which laid down a kind of critical template for representing the modern city that remains enormously influential in both panoramic fiction and film.

Crucially, Huhtamo identifies three distinct phases in the textual figuring of panoramic perception and form. Chapter 3 demonstrates how they fed into Joyce's multi-levelled strategy for representing the city and brought together previous strands of his literary cinematicity. Huhtamo's first phase occupies the high vantage point of the original panorama's imaginary *tour d'horizon*; the second involves stepping down into the 'moving panorama' of street-level experience (*IiM*, p. 340).[65] Baudelaire's literary *flâneur* is thus a key transitional figure in this inter-medial creativity, helping drive the discursive panorama into its next phase. The *flâneur* strikingly anticipates the mobile film camera's ability to simultaneously visualise the potential alienation of the modern city, but also its dynamic patterns and collective interdependencies. Moreover, just as the representation of mechanised locomotion became prominent among panoramic novelties, the discursive panoramic observer saw the spectacle of life passing through train windows, electric trams or motor cars, in a form remediated in filmic 'phantom rides'. Within this shift there is a markedly proto-Joycean sense of narrative movement at street level, using focalising characters as mobile 'camera-eyes'.

Hence Huhtamo's third and final phase in the typology of discursive panoramas helps explain how Joyce's strategy went further: combining mobilised, street-level immersion with intensely subjective focalisation. In the late nineteenth century, intellectuals also began figuring perception and memory as a kind of proto-filmic, continuously moving panorama. This converged with the concept of the 'stream of consciousness', eventually adopted to designate experimental techniques that presented subjectivity in Modernists such as Joyce. However, the idea of consciousness as continuous imagistic flow had already been formulated by Shadworth H. Hodgson in 1865. Hodgson went on to describe 'the great stream or moving panorama of a Subject's consciousness, as it retreats into the past of memory from any given present moment'. Hence the images passing in front of *Ulysses*' characters and shown replaying in their internal vision are variously suggestive of moving panoramas, lantern shows or even early films.

Similarly, Huhtamo traces an inevitable switch from panorama to cinema screen as the leading metaphor for consciousness after the invention of the cinematograph. Joyce's monstrative literary practice reflects this shift in inter-medial discursivity. The triple level method by which *Ulysses*' moving panorama combines an implied 360-degree panoptic overview of Dublin life with mobilised street-level immersion and intensely subjective, psychological focalisation through individual characters matches the phases of Huhtamo's discursive panorama. However, it also takes the process forward into the film age, as will be examined in detail in Chapter 3, focusing on 'Wandering Rocks'. *Ulysses*' central episode creates an impression of late colonial Dublin in its concrete totality as built, but also *lived and thought* environment, simultaneously presenting the perceptions and flows of consciousness of the citizens inhabiting and interacting with it. This makes *Ulysses* an equally influential model for Modernist urban 'psychogeography' in both fiction and film.

CODA

Chapter 3 is followed by a Coda that challenges how *Finnegans Wake* (1939) has been recently regarded as marking the – then functionally blind – Joyce's final turn away from film, as both cultural medium and ekphrastic narrative model, in his last experimental text. It has been argued that *Finnegans Wake*'s logos-focused method is more like radiophony than cinematicity, in which words, voices and languages rather than images and film techniques continuously shuffle, layer, clash and blend. This radical exploitation of aural and semiotic multiplicity as its principal drive sometimes appears closest to a criss-crossing of wireless broadcasts on heterogeneous frequencies. Nonetheless, *Finnegans Wake*'s creative process and preoccupations continued to be Janus-faced in relation to the history, present and future of moving images. In fact, it represents a further stage of Joyce's experimental *ekphrasis* and relationship with a common media-cultural imaginary, now expanded by broadcasting in *both* aural *and* visual dimensions. Hence section 2 shows that far from splitting with cinematicity's roots, *Finnegans Wake* both continues to creatively 'retrofit' film's predecessor technologies while engaging with its emergent successor in the form of early television.

In Joyce's self-reflexively 'palimpcestuous' text, words, characters and scenes constantly overwrite each other, shifting back and forth, but also displaying ongoing engagement with the legacy of shadow plays and lantern techniques. Dissolving views can be regarded as 'visual palimpsests', one picture shimmering through the outlines and interstices of another. Arguably, Joyce's quest to devise and refine their verbal equivalent could be seen as reaching its hypostasis in *Finnegans Wake*. Its creative processes are based on the principle of 'verbal dissolves', a textual but also distinctly ekphrastic tissue, shimmering between motifs, characters, spaces and times. Through this, linguistic forms and meanings continually morph in and out of each other, like the multi-layered images in dissolving views and their legacy in filmic cross-fades and superimpositions. Joyce carries this process into the technological future by subversively mixing different broadcasts at a time when television itself was limited to experimental networks, although its potential global reach and power was already being debated. Indeed *Finnegans Wake* constitutes one of the few extended literary engagements with pre-war television outside science fiction. With an imagination saturated by forms and effects of visual media since childhood, though with eyesight too dim to make out what was passing on screens big or small, *Finnegans Wake* shows that Joyce remained capable of visualising moving pictures in the projection box of his mind and ingeniously translating their possibilities into words in its 'moving dream panorama'.

BEFORE THE VOLTA: EARLY FILM SHOWS AND GENRES IN DUBLIN

Before focusing on the magic lantern in Chapter 1, it is vital to understand how and under what conditions film finally arrived in Joyce's home city to appreciate how his interest in cinematicity emerged from the broader media-cultural matrix of his youth. This eventually led to his own practical involvement with the new industry and his sole concerted attempt at a comeback from self-imposed exile as one of Ireland's first cinema managers. Joyce made a famous, albeit brief, practical intervention himself in early film's development as a distinct form of entertainment and revolution in visual consciousness in Ireland. He set up the Volta Cinematograph as one of Dublin's earliest cinemas to show continuous programmes, funded by a consortium of businessmen from Trieste where he then lived, to exploit Dublin's relative lack of permanent exhibition venues. Though only running from 20 December 1909 until 16 April 1910 (although there is evidence that screenings continued until June),[66] Joyce's ill-fated venture was the outcome of a long-held fascination with moving picture and projection media, not just the opportunity for a quick profit.[67]

Given Ireland's venerable history of cinematicity in many forms and the role this played in shaping its common media-cultural imaginary alongside the creative aspirations of its writers, it is unsurprising that the Lumières' solution for projecting film excited Joyce's contemporaries. Before the cinematograph arrived in Dublin, reports of its Paris and London debut were raising expectations. The *Evening Telegraph* reviewed its first programme of 20 February 1896 at the Royal Polytechnic, referring to its predecessors among optical toys and moving picture peepshows, but also deeming it 'ahead of the kinetoscope as the kinetoscope was of the wheel of life'. Confessing their inability to describe its 'extraordinary effects', the reviewer applauded that it was no longer necessary to screw the eyes up into 'two tiny holes'. Instead, comfortably seated in darkness, whole audiences simultaneously witnessed an illusion so virtual that it 'appears to be looking through a window at something actually occurring in the next street'.[68] Condon infers that the reference to the 'wheel of life' concerns the zoëtrope (*EIC*, p. 43); alternatively, the Rocketts identify it as the phenakistoscope or even stroboscope (*MLP&MPS*, p. 218), but it might also be Thomas Ross's 'Wheel of Life' lantern (see Chapter 1). What is indisputable is the review's explicit identification of the cinematograph as the culmination of a series of devices progressing towards a totally convincing representation of reality in motion.

Similarly, the *Irish Times* review of the Dublin debut of 'living pictures', a mere two months later on 20 April 1896 at the Star of Erin Theatre of Varieties, Dame Street (later the Empire Theatre),[69] stressed how the technology remediated and combined characteristics of its predecessors. It compared its plenitude of motion to the shifting views of a kaleidoscope, its 'figures brought out in relief with the aid of magic lantern'.[70] Though there were problems with picture clarity according to the *Irish Independent*, it also underlined the device's superiority over Edison's peepshow, simultaneously assuming public familiarity with Muybridge's zoöpraxiscope which animated animal locomotion images, as projected at his Dublin lectures in February 1890:

> [A] little disappointment was experienced in connection with the display of the cinematographie [*sic*]. This instrument is undoubtedly capable of accomplishing great things, but it seemed to be out of order, and the pictures which it showed were much below the level of excellence which the kinetoscope or the zoopractiscope [*sic*] have already showed to music hall audiences.[71]

Technical glitches resolved, Irish papers were as impressed by the new medium's virtualism as those in France and Britain. The *Freeman's Journal* marvelled at how '[t]his very wonderful instrument' projected 'with absolute correctness in every minute detail animated representations of scenes and incidents which are witnessed in everyday life', so that the 'effect is simply startling'. It also confirmed actualities such as *L'Arrivée d'un train* caused audiences to doubt the evidence of their senses, like their Paris and London counterparts (albeit exaggerated accounts of panic are one of film's foundational myths). The oncoming locomotive appeared 'so realistic that for the moment one is almost apt to forget that the representation is artificial. The exhibition is altogether of the finest kind ever seen in Dublin.'[72] The *Evening Telegraph* agreed that this was done 'with such fidelity as to induce a momentary belief in the actuality of the spectacle'.[73]

The effect of vicarious immersion in events happening elsewhere in space and time was equally impressive, according to Joseph Holloway's diary entry about screenings at the Star in November. Despite intermittent blurriness, 'Incidents such as cavalry charges, bathing scenes, trains arriving, live before you for some minutes as if you were taking part in them.'[74] The *Irish Times* particularly highlighted projected film's ability to capture urban scenes with a new kind of vividness that remediated urban moving panoramas:

> Street scenes in the vicinity of the Houses of Parliament in London and elsewhere were with the aid of the magic lantern reproduced in a marvellous form, showing all the varied life of the great metropolis, with its hansom cabs, omnibuses, bicycles, and all the moving population.[75]

No doubt such enthusiastic reactions quickened Joyce's precocious aspiration towards rendering everyday life through ekphrastic moving images (stemming from his juvenile 'Silhouettes'). Joyce's fiction emulated film's virtually stereoscopic and immersive simulation of reality, but also its potential for expanding to a similarly panoramic impression of Dublin's urban milieu.

'ALL THE VARIED LIFE OF THE GREAT METROPOLIS': JOYCE AND EARLY IRISH ACTUALITIES

Dublin saw itself on screen among its earliest shows. As was company policy, the Lumières' Irish operative, Felicien Trewey, was filming as early as 1896 during his tour to exhibit their improved cinematograph in November–December. His crew shot many scenes and events, expanding their catalogue of local actualities, none of which survive. According to Condon, Dublin actualities were first shown at the Star in early 1897 (*EIC*, p. 2). *Traffic on O'Connell Bridge*, Dublin's oldest extant film record, dates from that year in another Lumière production. The shot is taken from O'Connell (then Carlisle) Bridge. It triangulates the monument to Daniel O'Connell, 'The Liberator', in the foreground (right), head cropped out of frame; the General Post Office portico, profiled in the middle distance (right); and the imperialistic Nelson's Pillar thrusting up in the central distance (see *MLP&MPS*, plate 107). This image captures symbolic landmarks that resonated in Irish history, but that were equally resonant in Joyce's fiction.[76] This is partly because of Joyce's encyclopaedic cataloguing of Dublin's 'street furniture', as *Stephen Hero*'s definition of epiphanic seeing terms it (p. 189), but also because his literary techniques emulate the dynamism, plasticity and adventitious detail of photo-cinematic space, effortlessly alternating between panoramic and close-up views at street level, but also including the internal 'image-track' of his protagonists' streams of consciousness.

There was certainly enormous fascination with seeing the city and its daily routines anew in living pictures. Holloway's diary records 'local views' at the Empire Theatre in November 1897 by improved Lumière 'Triograph' being 'warmly received'. These included the fire brigade at Stephen's Green and 'Traffic on O'Connell Street', but also 'views taken from the train of Blackrock Park and Sandymount', effectively early 'phantom rides' passing locations familiar to Joyce from childhood and, in the case of Sandymount, frequently represented in both *Portrait* and *Ulysses*.[77] Some local actualities simply shot random and anonymous human and vehicular movement on the streets, recording the visible patterns of modern, mass life; others recorded specific events such as processions. As such they extended the forms for mediating the city in panoramas and lantern tours. Sagar Mitchell and James Kenyon, who filmed extensively in and around Dublin in 1901–02, continued the Lumières' visual mapping through the phantom ride form. (For the significance of Mitchell and Kenyon's surviving films in relation to the mobilisation of the gaze and panoramic techniques in Joyce's fiction, see Chapters 2 and 3.) The camera's defamiliarisation of the details of everyday life or of cultural and political rituals, putting them on screen in living pictures that made them visible in new ways, has clear affinities with Joyce's scrutinising of telling contingencies in both commonplace experiences and choreographed public events, capturing unexpected epiphanies through his literary lens.

THE PHOTOPLAY IN DUBLIN

The appeal of recordings of actuality – film's initial novelty in its 'cinema of attractions' period – was quickly superseded by the exploitation of its potential for marvellous kinds of optical self-display and for presenting extended fictions. From 1898 the rising popularity of 'photoplays' (with roots in photographic 'life-model' lantern slides) prompted changes in venues and programmes, driving the emergence of a more 'dynamic type of exhibitor' (*MLP&MPS*, p. 239). One notable mode – combining optical exhibitionism with narrative fantasy – was particularly well represented in turn-of-the-century programmes. Joyce scholars recognise that pioneering stop-motion trick films by Méliès and others have striking affinities with and likely influence on the phantasmagoric transformations in 'Circe', *Ulysses*' most cinematically experimental chapter. Recent research confirms that Joyce did not need to wait until his first extended Paris sojourn in 1904 (when he stayed close to Méliès's Star Films theatre) to be enthralled by these, as had been previously assumed (*MLP&MPS*, p. 360, n. 75).[78] He had had ample opportunities at home several years before.

In April 1900 a Cinderella pantomime film was shown at Dublin's Rotunda. If this was Méliès's *Cendrillon* (1899), rather than G. A. Smith's less technically elaborate *Cinderella* (1898), then, at five separate scenes across 150 metres of footage, it would have been one of Ireland's earliest screenings of 'fully plotted multi-scene narrative fiction' (*MLP&MPS*, p. 240). From 1899 Poole and Young's Rotunda seasons also featured trick film fantasy in Myriorama shows. These included Méliès titles such as *La Lune à un mètre* (1898) (in which an astronomer dreams that an animated moon descends through his observatory window, greedily devouring its contents); his twenty-shot *Le Rêve de Noël* (1900) (in which magical events occur in a child's bedroom and at a cross-section of locations across town on Christmas Eve); as well as trick films by others, such as Smith's *Aladdin and the Wonderful Lamp* (in which wishes are instantly fulfilled). Ambitious historical and topical features by Méliès, such as *Jeanne D'Arc* (1900) and his *L'Affaire Dreyfus* (1899), an early 'faction' campaigning against the internationally notorious case of antisemitic scapegoating – a key theme of *Ulysses* – were also shown at the Rotunda and Lyric, alongside Méliès's adaptation of Defoe's shipwreck classic, *Les Aventures de Robinson Crusoe*, at the Empire in April 1903 (*MLP&MPS*, p. 241). Stephen visualises himself as Dumas's hero, *The Count of Monte Cristo*, similarly stranded on a desert island after escaping wrongful imprisonment. Most significantly, the biggest draw of Irish Animated's late 1902 season was Méliès's masterpiece, *Le Voyage dans la lune* (*A Trip to the Moon*). This burlesqued the science fiction of Verne and Wells and was the world's most technically ambitious film to date. Advertised at Dublin's Tivoli Variety Theatre as 'absolutely the most amazing, interesting, amusing and weird living picture ever put before the public', it was also screened at the Rotunda in January–February 1903 (*MLP&MPS*, pp. 245–7).

Ireland's first home-grown photoplays date from 1905, but were relatively simple structurally and made after Joyce's final departure into exile the year before. What the Rocketts call Ireland's 'first complex fiction film', Kalem's *The Lad from Old Ireland*, was not released until 1910 after Joyce's brief return to open the Volta (*MLP&MPS*, p. 251). This was a migration narrative and hence, like many early films, remediated a genre familiar from magic lantern and moving panorama shows. The hero (played by director Sidney Olcott) 'makes good' in the US, and then returns home to save his sweetheart from eviction (see *EIC*, pp. 153–4 and plates 105–6). Olcott's modernisation of an archetypal theme is aligned with the *Odyssey*'s *nostos* structure of exile and return, to similarly save wife and homeland from usurpers. Hence it also converges with Joyce's reworking of Homer's epic as *Ulysses*' key intertext.

THE CREATION OF 'CINEMA' IN DUBLIN: A VISUAL REVOLUTION

As the Rocketts argue, partly because of prestigious features, by the early 1900s a 'showdown' was taking place in modes of exhibition between films as another attraction on variety bills and in hybrid entertainments such as Myrioramas, and programmes as attractions in their own right. This eventually led to specialist premises, converted for projection such as Joyce's Volta or even purpose built (*MLP&MPS*, p. 242). This new phase effectively created the institution known as cinema, making picture-going what A. J. P. Taylor called 'the essential social habit' of the first half of the twentieth century.[79] An early sign of this transformation was an unprecedented run of Rotunda shows by Thomas-Edison Electric Animated Pictures (December 1901–May 1902) (*EIC*, p. 71; *MLP&MPS*, p. 242). Irish Animated Photo Company's takeover by James Taylor Jameson (of the whisky dynasty) consolidated the Rotunda's position as Ireland's 'most important film screening location during the 1900s' and Jameson's as its first significant film entrepreneur (*MLP&MPS*, p. 245 and plate 100). Irish Animated also continued to record local events, featuring them alongside largely imported documentaries, comedies and drama. By 1903 the accompaniment of costumed orchestras and opera singers indicates Irish Animated's distancing from downmarket contexts and appeal to 'respectable' tastes (*MLP&MPS*, pp. 259–60). The Rocketts suggest that the courting of middle-class audiences may explain its relative lack of advertising of features 'in favour of local or foreign actualities' (and occasional comedies) as late as 1909 (*MLP&MPS*, p. 251). However, the idea that the Dublin public were put off by European films (sometimes evidenced to explain the Volta's failure) is contested by Irish Animated's programming in its 1909 Rotunda season. This included continental historical dramas and lasted to within three weeks of Joyce's return seeking premises (*MLP&MPS*, p. 254).[80]

It appears that no exhibitor had yet found a formula to allow the industry to take off as *the* socially inclusive, modern entertainment in Dublin. High levels of poverty may have proved additionally obstructive. Before 1909 there were still no permanent shopfront venues making film-going more regularly affordable, unlike the 'nickelodeons' or 'penny gaffs' proliferating in the US and Britain (*MLP&MPS*, p. 253). However, when the Volta finally opened on 20 December 1909, at least six other venues either had been or still were screening regular programmes. Neither is it strictly true that the Volta was Ireland's first *dedicated* cinema. Condon and the Rocketts concur that this distinction belongs to the People's Popular Picture Palace, opened at Dublin's former Queen's Royal Theatre, Brunswick Street, on 2 March 1908.[81] The Palace screened continuous programmes until January 1909, when its licence lapsed. Accounts include the landmark Irish-Australian feature, *The Story of the Kelly Gang* (1906), alongside melodramas and comedies. Palace programmes also testify to continuities with pre-filmic technologies and practices, being punctuated by 'song concerts' with magic lantern slides. Condon argues that *The Kelly Gang*'s reception proves that audiences were starting to attend particular films rather than just relishing the sheer novelty of living pictures, irrespective of subject or technique; hence, that cinema in Ireland was in transition from the phase of 'attractions' to one of 'narrative integration' that characterised it elsewhere (*EIC*, pp. 3–4, 218–19). The company behind the

Picture Palace – Colonial Picture Combine – evidently spotted the chance to provide the continuous programmes available in English cities, but was unable to supply Irish-related features on a regular basis, its staple being US and British. Nevertheless, the 1,000-seater premises proved that there was sufficient demand for a full-time Dublin cinema well in excess of the Volta's capacity of 400.[82]

Effectively, Joyce aimed to plug the gap left by the Palace. He also strove 'to cater to a broad mixed-class audience' through this democratic new art. The relative cheapness of Volta admission prices indicates this (*MLP&MPS*, pp. 250, 257). Nevertheless, Joyce also failed to find the right formula to bridge cultural divisions in programming policy, perhaps because he had not yet overcome his youthful ambivalence towards Dublin's common people and their tastes.[83] Consequently, the Volta became caught in a dilemma: whether to concentrate on 'upmarket' continental fare or to attract bigger audiences with more American material. Either way, the boom in new premises from 1910 onwards suggests that its failure was not symptomatic of film's lack of appeal to Dubliners, but of a miscalculated strategy by Joyce and his backers.[84]

Joyce fled back to Trieste with acute iritis on 2 January 1910 (a mere day before his managerial contract ended), leaving an Italian deputy with scant knowledge of local tastes and conditions, which probably sealed the Volta's fate. According to John McCourt, while recuperating over two months (in a darkened room with bandaged eyes), Joyce nonetheless stayed closely in touch, 'particularly with regard to programme choices and publicity'. Luke McKernan also concludes that release dates for the bulk of the titles shown before March 1910 indicate that they were dispatched from Trieste in large batches in 1909. This makes it likely that Joyce was personally familiar with the films exhibited and was involved in their selection.[85]

Despite the frustrations of running an actual cinema, there is no doubt that it was more than just a business opportunity, but was bound up with Joyce's long-held and intense fascination with optics and moving images, which remained undiminished.[86] Hence this book explores Joyce's creative response to forms of cinematicity and their role in shaping modernity's media-cultural imaginary – both before and after the coming of film – beginning with the magic lantern.

NOTES

1. André Bazin, 'In Defence of Mixed Cinema', in *What Is Cinema?*, ed. and trans. Hugh Gray (Berkeley, CA: University of California Press, 1967; 2005), vol. 1, pp. 53–75 (63–4).
2. 'The Monumental Decision of the United States District Court Rendered December 6 1933 By Hon. John M. Woolsey Lifting the Ban on "Ulysses"', repr. in the first US edition of *Ulysses* (New York: Random House, 1934), pp. ix–xiv (xi).

3. Eisenstein received a copy of *Ulysses* as early as 1928, but also read *Portrait* a few years previously. For a recent round-up of research on Eisenstein and Joyce, see Keith Williams, 'Odysseys of Sound and Image: "Cinematicity" and the *Ulysses* Adaptations', in John McCourt (ed.), *Roll Away the Reel World: James Joyce and Cinema* (Cork: Cork University Press, 2010), pp. 158–73.

4. John Hollander's historicisation of 'notional ekphrasis' – literary representations of imaginary works of art – supports the argument that some writers have dreamed new forms of visual representation into being on the page. See *The Gazer's Spirit: Poems Speaking to Silent Works of Art* (Chicago: University of Chicago Press, 1995), p. 27.

5. For a brief history of ekphrasis, see Valerie Robillard and Els Jongeneel (eds), *Pictures into Words: Theoretical and Descriptive Approaches to Ekphrasis* (Amsterdam: VU University Press, 1998), especially the Introduction, pp. ix–x.

6. Erkki Huhtamo, *Illusions in Motion: Media Archaeology of the Moving Panorama and Related Spectacles* (Cambridge, MA: MIT Press, 2013), p. 332. Subsequent references to this work are abbreviated to *IiM* and given in parentheses in the text.

7. See Jonathan Crary, *Techniques of the Observer: On Vision and Modernity in the Nineteenth Century* (Cambridge, MA: MIT Press, 1992 [1990]), p. 5.

8. David Brewster, *Letters on Natural Magic* (London: John Murray, 1832), p. 8.

9. Iwan Rhys Morus, 'Illuminating Illusions, or, the Victorian Art of Seeing Things', *EPVC*, 10:1 (2012), pp. 37–50 (41–2).

10. Ibid., p. 37.

11. As Kevin and Emer Rockett recount, persistence of vision was conclusively disproved by phenomenologist Max Wertheimer's *Experimental Studies on the Seeing of Motion* (1912), although the term remains in common usage, especially in film studies. 'Vision happens mainly in the brain (the occipital lobe of the cerebral cortex) and not in the retina. The perception of movement is perhaps best explained by the phi phenomenon which Sigmund Exner's 1875 experiment proved was the reason why "two brief, stationary flashes, . . . [if] not too far away from each other, are seen as a single object in motion".' Kevin Rockett and Emer Rockett, *Magic Lantern, Panorama and Moving Picture Shows in Ireland, 1786–1909* (Dublin: Four Courts Press, 2011), p. 320, n. 95. Subsequent references to this work are abbreviated to *MLP&MPS* and given in parentheses in the text.

12. John Henry Pepper, *A Strange Lecture: An Illustration of the Haunted Man Ghost Illusion* (London: McGowan and Danks, 1863), p. 1; see also Morus, 'Illuminating Illusions', p. 47. Pepper's explanation of the illusion followed in Part 2, 'Ghosts: and How to Make Them'.

13. Crary, *Techniques of the Observer*, p. 24.

14. See Mary Anne Doane, *The Emergence of Cinematic Time: Modernity, Contingency and the Archive* (Cambridge, MA: Harvard University Press, 2002), esp. pp. 1–4.

15. Ibid., pp. 20, 70, 82.

16. See chapter 4, 'Illusion', in Steven Johnson, *Wonderland: How Play Made the Modern World* (New York: Penguin Random House, 2016), pp. 147–85. Alberto Gabriele has also shown how writers from the Renaissance onwards were influenced by pre-filmic

media, such as magic lanterns, philosophical toys and panoramas, in figuring perception and states of consciousness. See Alberto Gabriele, *The Emergence of Pre-Cinema: Print Culture and the Optical Toy of the Literary Imagination* (Basingstoke: Palgrave Macmillan, 2017).

17. Kate Flint, *The Victorians and the Visual Imagination* (Cambridge: Cambridge University Press, 2000), p. 5.

18. Anon., 'Our Address', *Illustrated London News*, 14 May 1842, p. 1.

19. Richard Ellmann *James Joyce* (1959) (Oxford: Oxford University Press, new edn, 1983), p. 3.

20. Ibid., pp. 45–6.

21. For miniature moving panoramas, see *IiM*, esp. pp. 306, 368; for forms of 'roller stereoscope' (often used for narrative sequences and a key influence on mechanisms for feeding filmstrips through viewers and projectors), see Ray Zone, *Stereoscopic Cinema and the Origins of 3-D Film, 1838–1952* (Lexington, KY: University of Kentucky Press, 2007), pp. 16–18.

22. André Gaudreault, 'The Diversity of Cinematographic Connections in the Intermedial Context of the Turn of the 20th Century', in Simon Popple and Vanessa Toulmin (eds), *Visual Delights: Essays on the Popular and Projected Image in the 19th Century* (Trowbridge: Flick Books, 2000), pp. 8–15 (13). Gaudreault's argument about film's dependence on 'other mediums and cultural spheres' for both form and content is elaborated in his *Film and Attraction* (Urbana, IL: University of Illinois Press, 2011), p. 14 and *passim*.

23. Gaudreault, 'The Diversity of Cinematographic Connections', p. 13.

24. Denis Condon, *Early Irish Cinema, 1895–1921* (Dublin: Irish Academic Press, 2008), pp. 25, 74. Subsequent references to this work are abbreviated to *EIC* and given in parentheses in the text.

25. Olive Cook, *Movement in Two Dimensions: A Study of the Animated and Projected Pictures which Preceded the Invention of Cinematography* (London: Hutchinson, 1963); repr. as vol. 3 of Stephen Herbert (ed.), *A History of Pre-Cinema* (London: Routledge, 2000), pp. 135–6. Subsequent references to this work are taken from the reprint edition, abbreviated to *MiTD* and given in parentheses in the text.

26. See, for example, Lynda Nead, *The Haunted Gallery: Painting Photography and Film, c. 1900* (New Haven, CT: Yale University Press, 2008).

27. See John Ayrton Paris, *Philosophy in Sport Made Science in Earnest; Being an Attempt to Illustrate the Principles of Natural Philosophy by the Aid of Popular Toys and Sports*, 3 vols (London: Longman, Rees, Orme, Brown and Greene, 1827), vol. 3, pp. 1–27.

28. Marit Grøtta, *Baudelaire's Media Aesthetics: The Gaze of the Flâneur and 19th Century Media* (London: Bloomsbury, 2015), p. 73.

29. James Joyce, *Ulysses: The Corrected Text* (1922), ed. Hans Walter Gabler with Wolfhard Steppe and Claus Melchior (London: Bodley Head, 1993), 17.498–502. Subsequent references to this work are given in parentheses in the text by chapter and line number.

30. David A. Cook, *A History of Narrative Film* (New York: W. W. Norton, 4th edn, 2004), p. 1.

31. See Jeffrey Geiger and Karin Littau (eds), *Cinematicity in Media History* (Edinburgh: Edinburgh University Press, 2013), pp. 1–18 (8). Geiger and Littau also edited a special issue of *Comparative Critical Studies*, 6:3 (2009), devoted to '"Cinematicity" 1895: Before and After', from the March 2007 Essex University Centre for Film Studies conference.

32. Though generally accepted in film histories, this remains contested. Although the Lumières gave their first public demonstration (to the Société d'Encouragment de l'Industrie Nationale) in Paris on 22 March, Christopher Rawlence argues that cinema was actually invented by another Frenchman, Augustin le Prince, who screened moving pictures as early as 1888 in Leeds; see Christopher Rawlence, *The Missing Reel: The Untold Story of the Lost Inventor of Moving Pictures* (London: Collins, 1991) and his 1989 drama documentary of the same title for Channel 4 Films. English inventor Wordsworth Donisthorpe filed a provisional patent in 1876 for his 'Kinesigraph', a device that printed photographs on a continuous strip and animated them. Donisthorpe proposed combining his apparatus with Edison's phonograph in *Nature* in January 1878; see Stephen Herbert and Luke MacKernan, *Who's Who of Victorian Cinema: A Worldwide Survey* (London: BFI, 1996), pp. 42–3. A Bradford electrical engineer, Cecil Wray, patented a prototype lantern/prism device for projecting kinetoscope pictures on 3 January 1895. Undoubtedly, individuals in many countries were pursuing the same technical breakthrough, including Birt Acres and R. W. (Robert William) Paul in Britain, as well as Max and Emil Skladanowski with their 'Bioskop' in Germany.

33. André Gaudreault, 'Showing and Telling: Image and Word in Early Cinema', in Thomas Elsaesser (ed.), *Early Cinema: Space, Frame, Narrative* (London: BFI, 1990), pp. 274–328 (276).

34. Joseph Holloway Diaries, 15 November 1897: Ms 1794–1797, National Library of Ireland, p. 374; also quoted in *EIC*, p. 41.

35. Alan Spiegel, *Fiction and the Camera Eye: Visual Consciousness in Film and the Modern Novel* (Charlottesville, VA: University Press of Virginia, 1976), p. 25.

36. See Hugh Kenner, *Ulysses* (London: Allen and Unwin, 1980), pp. 61–71, and David Hayman, *Ulysses and the Mechanics of Meaning* (Madison, WI: University of Wisconsin Press, rev. edn, 1982), pp. 88–104.

37. For the role of the 'stretch of tension between sound and picture' in Potter's TV drama, see David Cook, *Dennis Potter: A Life on Screen* (Manchester: Manchester University Press, 2nd edn, 1998), p. 13.

38. According to Gösta Werner, Eisenstein's famous meeting with Joyce took place on 30 November 1929 at the writer's Paris flat, while Eisenstein was on leave from the Soviet film industry to study the new phenomenon of sound film. See Gösta Werner, 'James Joyce and Sergej Eisenstein', trans. Erik Gunnemark, *JJQ*, 27:3 (1990), pp. 491–507, esp. p. 494, the fullest account of the encounter so far.

39. Spiegel, *Fiction and the Camera Eye*, p. 77. Spiegel might have been less astonished if he was more aware of the prescient 'optical speculations' and filmic devices of H. G. Wells's fictions of the 1890s (conspicuously absent from his study). These seemed to outstrip what could be practically realised on screen even earlier. Neglect of more popular 'low' moderns in accounts of inter-mediality

underplays the role of 'middlebrow' forms such as scientific romance as precursors to Modernist cinematicity. Wells laid down many of the parameters they elaborated. See Keith Williams, *H. G. Wells, Modernity and the Movies* (Liverpool: Liverpool University Pres, 2007). Such accounts sustain a lopsided cultural history, as well as missing the crucial role of a common pre-filmic optical culture.

40. Spiegel, *Fiction and the Camera Eye*, pp. 76–7.

41. I am alluding to Noel Burch's pioneering study of early film, *Life to Those Shadows*, trans. and ed. Ben Brewster (London: BFI, 1990).

42. Significantly, during 'the age of the dream palace', it seemed only logical to explain the allegory of the cave in cinematic terms: 'A modern Plato would compare his Cave to an underground cinema, where the audience watch the play of shadows thrown by the film passing before a light at their backs. The film itself is only an image of "real" things and events in the world outside the cinema.' See *The Republic of Plato*, trans. Francis MacDonald Cornford (Oxford: Oxford University Press, 1941), pp. 227–35 and note on 228. For diverse essays elaborating this idea for twenty-first-century media, see Barbara Gabriella Renzi and Stephen Rainey (eds), *From Plato's Cave to the Multiplex: Contemporary Philosophy and Film* (Newcastle: Cambridge Scholars Press, 2007).

43. Stanislaus Joyce, *My Brother's Keeper: James Joyce's Early Years*, ed. Richard Ellmann (London: Faber and Faber, 1958), p. 104. It is also possible that Joyce was influenced by Arthur Symons's poetry volume, *Silhouettes* (1892).

44. Spiegel, *Fiction and the Camera Eye*, pp. 76–7.

45. Ibid., pp. 76–7

46. Ibid., pp. 76–7.

47. See David Robertson, Stephen Herbert and Richard Crangle (eds), *Encyclopaedia of the Magic Lantern* (London: MLS, 2001), p. 16. Subsequent references to this work are abbreviated to *EML* and given in parentheses in the text.

48. The OED online features the following entries:
   '1886 St. Stephen's Rev. 27 Mar. 5/2 At the New Club on Saturday next, Mason and Titus, the American shadowgraphs, who nightly provoke so much laughter at the Oxford, will appear at 11.30 p.m.
   1888 Glasgow Evening Times 10 Sept. 4/3 Prof. Wynne brings his shadow-graph to the Gaiety and Star this week.
   1893 Westm. Gaz. 14 Dec. 4/3 An account of Trewey's famous shadowgraphs.'
   Available at <http://www.oed.com/view/Entry/177218?rskey=DvobhE&result=1& isAdvanced=false#eid> (last accessed 14 October 2010).

49. See diverse examples in Phil Banham, 'Silhouette Slides', *MLS Newsletter* 113 (September 2012), pp. 8–11.

50. George R. Sims (ed.), *Living London*, 3 vols, with over 450 illustrations (London: Cassell, 1902), vol. 1, pp. 273–8 (273).

51. 'Behind the Blinds', in Sims (ed.), *Living London*, vol. 1, pp. 274–5.

52. See Phillip Dennis Cate, 'The Spirit of Montmartre', in Phillip Dennis Cate and Mary Shaw (eds), *The Spirit of Montmartre: Cabarets, Humour and the Avant-Garde, 1875–1905* (New Brunswick, NJ: Jane Vorhees Zimmerli Art Museum, 1996), pp. 1–93 (55, 58–9).

53. William Sayers is sceptical about possible influences on 'Circe': see his review in *JJQ*, 44:1 (2006), pp. 173–6. Joyce did not visit Paris in 1910, although it is possible that he came across the playscript on a later visit.

54. For facsimile documents and images, as well as further discussion of shadowgraphy and film, see Herbert (ed.), *A History of Pre-Cinema*, esp. vol. 2, pp. 151–64, and vol. 3, pp. 47–80.

55. For such effects in 'Araby', 'Eveline', 'The Dead', etc., see Keith Williams, 'Short Cuts of the Hibernian Metropolis: Cinematic Strategies in Dubliners', in Oona Frawley (ed.), *A New and Complex Sensation: Essays on Joyce's Dubliners* (Dublin: Lilliput, 2004), pp. 154–67.

56. See Austin Briggs, '"Roll Away the Reel World, the Reel World": "Circe" and the Cinema', in Morris Beja and Shari Benstock (eds), *Coping With Joyce: Essays from the Copenhagen Symposium* (Columbus, OH: Ohio State University Press, 1989), pp. 145–56 (145).

57. See David Robinson (ed.), *The Lantern Image: Iconography of the Magic Lantern 1420–1880* (London: MLS, 1993), pp. 48, 51.

58. Charles Musser, 'Toward a History of Screen Practice', *Quarterly Review of Film Studies*, 9:1 (1984), pp. 59–69 (59).

59. Ibid., p. 60.

60. Introduction to Ludwig Vogl-Bienek and Richard Crangle (eds), *Screen Culture and the Social Question* (New Barnet: John Libbey, 2014), pp. 1–6 (2).

61. I am grateful to Mary Cahill and her colleagues for inviting me to view the slides and related documentation at the museum's conservation laboratories. For detailed conclusions of the archaeological team regarding dating, purpose and ownership, see Mary Cahill, Andy Halpin, Carol Smith and Stephen D'Arcy, 'Have you Tried the Ash Pit?', *Archaeology Ireland*, 28:1 (2014), pp. 30–4 (34).

62. For Alison Chapman's concept, see Chapter 1 and note 176.

63. James Joyce, *Stephen Hero* (1944) (Frogmore: Granada, 1977), pp. 188–9. Subsequent references to this work are given in parentheses in the text.

64. Alison Byerly, '"A Prodigious Map beneath His Feet": Virtual Travel and the Panoramic Perspective', *Nineteenth-Century Contexts*, 29:2–3 (2007), pp. 151–68 (151).

65. Both Joyce and Benjamin deployed the Baudelairean figure of the *flâneur*, 'whose antecedents can be traced from Edgar Allen Poe and Conan Doyle's Sherlock Holmes on the one hand to Charlie Chaplin's tramp on the other', to visualise and navigate the world of urban modernity, 'explore its possibilities, suffer its shocks and glean advantages from its surprises'. Introduction to Enda Duffy and Maurizia Boscagli (eds), *Joyce, Benjamin and Magical Urbanism*, European Joyce Studies 2:1 (Amsterdam: Rodopi, 2011), pp. 7–29 (18).

66. Programmes have been reconstructed by McKernan up to 16 April 1910, although publicity continued until it was finally sold in June (see 'Appendix: Volta Filmography', in McCourt (ed.), *Roll Away the Reel World*, pp. 187–204). Patterns and programmes of exhibition before the Volta have recently been historicised in greater detail by the Rocketts and in their companion volume, *Film Exhibition and Distribution in Ireland* (Dublin: Four Courts Press, 2011); also by Condon in *EIC*.

67. Film was on Joyce's mind at the most intimate levels. Heyward Ehrlich argues that Joyce's letters to Nora from Dublin shortly before the Volta opened present his erotic reveries as 'short visual scenes', imagining couplings in multiple scenarios and states of undress like brief films and anticipating the instant situational and costume changes of 'Circe'. See Heyward Ehrlich, 'Joyce, Benjamin, and the Futurity of Fiction', in Boscagli and Duffy (eds), *Joyce, Benjamin and Magical Urbanism*, pp. 185–209 (208–9); also Joyce, letter to Nora, 16 December 1909, in *Selected Letters of James Joyce*, ed. Richard Ellmann (London: Faber and Faber, 1975), pp. 190–1. For alternative discussion of the 'dirty letters' in relation to postcard and lantern erotica, see Chapter 1.

68. Anon., 'The Cinematograph: A Startling Invention', *Dublin Evening Telegraph*, 26 February 1896, p. 4.

69. The Empire Theatre of Varieties is mentioned several times in *Ulysses* (also as 'Dan Lowry's music hall', after its proprietor). For example, Lenehan and McCoy pass it in 'Wandering Rocks', noticing the poster for Marie Kendall's headline act (10.495–8). 'Garryowen', the chauvinist Citizen's dog, also wishes to declaim Gaelic epics under 'Lowry's lights' in one of 'Cyclops's' parodies (12.747).

70. Anon., 'Star Theatre of Varieties', *Irish Times*, 22 April 1896, p. 6. There is some doubt whether this debut was by the Lumière cinematograph or the Englishman Paul's rival 'theatrograph' (later renamed the Animatograph). See *MLP&MPS*, pp. 218–19. The Rocketts list the programme on p. 221 as 'typical of the period' (cf. *EIC*, p. 19). For other research on Ireland's first screenings and background to the Volta, see Denis Condon, 'The Volta Myth', *Film Ireland*, 116 (May/June 2007), p. 43; Luke McKernan, 'James Joyce and the Volta Programme', in McCourt (ed.), *Roll Away the Reel World*, pp. 15–27 (an updated version of his groundbreaking article 'James Joyce's Cinema', *Film and Film Culture*, 3 [2004], pp. 7–20).

71. Quoted in Denis Condon, 'Spleen of a Cabinet Minister at Work: Exhibiting X-rays and the Cinematograph in Ireland, 1896', in John Hill and Kevin Rockett (eds), *Film History and National Cinema: Studies in Irish Film 2* (Dublin: Four Courts Press, 2005), pp. 69–78 (70). The Rocketts also note that projection may have been disappointing because of poor illumination (*MLP&MPS*, pp. 218–19).

72. 'The Star Theatre: The Cinematographe', *Freeman's Journal*, 3 November 1896, p. 7. Stephen Bottomore has sifted mythology from evidence in '"The Panicking Audience?" Early Cinema and the "Train Effect"', *Historical Journal of Film, Radio and Television*, 19:2 (1999), pp. 177–216.

73. 'The Cinematographe at the Star Theatre', *Dublin Evening Telegraph*, 3 November 1896, p. 3.

74. Joseph Holloway Diaries, 14 November 1896, p. 106; also quoted in *EIC*, p. 1.

75. 'Star Theatre of Varieties', *Irish Times*, 3 November 1896, p. 6.

76. In *Dubliners*, O'Connell Bridge appears in 'Counterparts' and twice in 'The Dead'; the General Post Office in 'The Sisters' and 'A Mother'; and Nelson's Pillar three times in 'Clay', as the terminus for Martha's tram journeys. In *Ulysses*, the cortege passes O'Connell's statue in 'Hades' (6.249), then the 160-foot-high O'Connell monument in Glasnevin itself (6.641). His monumentalised presence causes Bloom to think of O'Connell as 'a big giant in the dark', making him the stand-in for

Heracles' phantom in Odysseus's parallel visit to the underworld (6.752). The General Post Office is described in 'Aeolus' as a node in the network of communications binding Dublin into the Empire (7.16–19); in 'Ithaca', a bootblack trading under its portico is listed among Molly's alleged lovers (17.2140–1). For *Ulysses*, Nelson's Pillar and the panorama, see Chapter 3.

77. Joseph Holloway Diaries, 15 November 1897, p. 374; see also *EIC*, p. 41.

78. Drawing on Robert Ryf, Thomas L. Burkdall surmises that Joyce first saw Méliès' films in Paris in 1904. See Robert Ryf, *A New Approach to Joyce: A Portrait of the Artist as a Guide Book* (Berkeley, CA: University of California Press, 1962), p. 174; Thomas L. Burkdall, 'Cinema Fakes: Film and Joycean Fantasy', in Morris Beja and David Norris (eds), *Joyce in the Hibernian Metropolis: Essays* (Columbus, OH: Ohio State University Press, 1996), pp. 260–9 (261). The Rocketts also suggest that a film in the Volta's first programme, *The Bewitched Castle*, may have been Méliès' *The Infernal Palace*, because his version of the Faust and Mephistopheles legend screened under the former title in the US (*MLP&MPS*, p. 360, n. 75).

79. A. J. P. Taylor, *English History 1914–1945* (1965) (repr. Hardmondsworth: Penguin, 1975), p. 392.

80. Cf. Rockett, *Film Distribution and Exhibition in Ireland*, p. 21.

81. Ibid., p. 15; see also Condon, 'The Volta Myth', p. 43, and *EIC*, pp. 218–19.

82. Condon, 'The Volta Myth', p. 43.

83. See Rockett, *Film Distribution and Exhibition in Ireland*, pp. 19–20.

84. Ibid., pp. 21–2.

85. Introduction to McCourt (ed.), *Roll Away the Reel World*, p. 4; McKernan, 'James Joyce and the Volta Programme', pp. 23–4.

86. For this reason, the Rocketts' discounting of Joyce's involvement in selecting films for the Volta programmes (and consequently any substantial influence from them on his writing) is debatable (see *Film Distribution and Exhibition in Ireland*, pp. 18–19).

'I BAR THE MAGIC LANTERN': *DUBLINERS* AND PRE-FILMIC CINEMATICITY

JOYCE AND LANTERN CULTURE

As well as being the ancestor of modern projection technologies, the magic lantern was a major strand of Victorian cinematicity. As the *Encyclopaedia of the Magic Lantern* summarises,

> Rather than saying the magic lantern was a straightforward 'precursor' of the cinema, it would be fairer to say that it was the environment into which the moving picture was born, and the medium with which the cinema coexisted for about two decades ... The magic lantern and early cinema also exchanged narratives, visual grammar and personnel. (*EML*, p. 71)

Indeed the cinematograph was, as Steve Humphries and Doug Lear put it, 'only the most sophisticated and successful of a host of late Victorian inventions' related to the magic lantern. The ways in which it both anticipated and prepared the ground for cinema are manifold. When Joyce grew up, the lantern was in its heyday as a public medium and 'almost as common in middle-class homes as television sets are today'.[1] Moreover, in Ireland, as the Rocketts argue, venues and modes of film exhibition, as well as rental practices for titles and equipment, also followed pre-existing patterns set by lanternism (*MLP&MPS*, pp. 255–6). For two hundred years, Irish audiences had already experienced 'a great variety of mass-produced visual representations, both "real" and "magical"' (*MLP&MPS*, p. 20).

Although the actual extent of Joyce's experience of lantern shows is uncertain, he was clearly aware of them. The lantern had a venerable history in Dublin. William Molyneux of Trinity College published one of the first illustrated descriptions of its workings in his 1692 textbook, *Dioptricka Nova*. Molyneux described typical slides as 'Frightful and Ludicrous . . . the more to divert the spectators', anticipating Joyce's critique of it as an instrument for manipulation.[2] By the 1860s Dublin boasted a large cluster of suppliers, slide-makers and distributors around 'the fashionable – middle-class – consumer centre of Grafton Street', linked to concerns in London and on the Continent (*MLP&MPS*, p. 61). One of the most prominent, Robinsons, through an attached 'Polytechnic Museum', clearly had both commercial and scientific aspirations similar to the Royal Polytechnic's for 'educating the eye' (*MLP&MPS*, p. 63). A highlight of Dublin's social calendar was the national Photographic Society's Annual Lantern Exhibition at the Royal College of Science (*MLP&MPS*, p. 65).

As Niamh McCole shows, the lantern was as prominent in Irish visual culture as in Britain's, not just in urban centres, but as a 'regular feature of provincial entertainment programmes', and in its full range of genres: illustrated lectures, scenic and local views, melodrama, comic and trick slides, and so on. Nevertheless, technical sophistication and 'visual literacy' probably lagged in the countryside as the Knock incident suggests (see below). Use of 'multi-unial apparatuses' (with several lenses) also seems to have been less common outside big cities, along with effects such as coloured and dissolving views (see figure 1.1).[3] As a Dubliner, Joyce's chances of seeing the lantern's most advanced capabilities would have been greater. Catalogues and surviving collections (held in the National Library of Ireland's Photographic Archive) of Dublin's most important manufacturer and distributor from the 1870s to the 1910s, William Lawrence of 5–7 Upper Sackville Street, amply confirm this.[4] Lawrence provided a complete service, offering up-to-date equipment and skilled operators.[5]

As a powerful instrument of mass communication, the lantern was used for entertainment, instruction, persuasion and advertisement in diverse ways at every social and intellectual level. According to the National Museum of Ireland team who examined the cache of slides excavated at one of the Joyce family houses, 'None of this was lost on the young James Joyce as he made his way through the streets of Dublin. Lanternism was all around – it could amuse, instruct, and convert; it could change perceptions, shock and titillate.'[6] Hitherto scholars have neglected its importance for Joyce's literary Modernism. As we shall see, he alludes to lantern motifs, narrative forms and techniques in many contexts in *Dubliners* and later fictions. Indeed lanternism helps explain aspects of Joyce's style which seem groundbreakingly cinematic.

Figure 1.1 'Dissolving views apparatus', illustration from Gaston Tissandier, *Popular Scientific Recreations in Natural Philosophy, Astronomy, Geology, Chemistry, etc. etc.* (London: Ward, Lock, 1885), p. 159. Jeremy Brooker's personal collection.

Industrial manufacturing meant increasing democratisation of lantern ownership and use. Toy lanterns were common Christmas presents, used for telling stories, moral lessons and visual tricks.[7] The Rocketts evidence the particular importance of Christmas toy markets to sellers and the sheer variety of slide genres available during Joyce's childhood – historical, geographical, scientific, religious, magical and ghostly (*MLP&MPS*, pp. 64–5). Lawrence's *Illustrated Catalogue* advertises the 'Great Value' '"Boys Own" Series' of toy lanterns, together with 'Dissolving Double Carrier Frame'. 'Comic Tales' available for it (including fairy stories and nursery rhymes) are also listed.[8] Joyce's contemporary, Marcel Proust, recollected childhood bedroom shows in the first volume of *Á la recherche du temps perdu, Du côté de chez Swann* (1913). The narrator reminisces about a lantern

> set on top of my lamp while we waited for dinner-time to come; and, after the fashion of the master-builders and glass painters of gothic days, it substituted for the opaqueness of my walls an impalpable iridescence, supernatural phenomena of many colours, in which legends were depicted as on a shifting and transitory window.[9]

Proust also represents memories and shifts of consciousness from sleep to waking as overlapping or dissolving views. Similarly the 'shadow show' that Stephen hallucinates in *Portrait* is presented like a bedroom lantern performance, albeit with inappropriately adult commentary, as Stephen overhears infirmarers whispering about Parnell's death. As we shall see in Chapter 2, Stephen seems immersed in this 'dissolving view' as he drifts feverishly in and out of consciousness, effectively blurring together with his tragic hero, also the subject of lantern narratives himself.

In *Dubliners'* 'Grace', Joyce cites the lantern directly. Tom Kernan consents to attend a Catholic businessman's retreat, but balks at jiggery-pokery: 'I bar the magic-lantern business' (*Dubliners*, p. 134). Kernan's remark has been taken as hinting at fakery in miraculous apparitions of the Virgin at Knock, Co. Mayo, on 21 August 1879 (allegedly projected on the gable wall of a church by a local priest or police accomplice, with a concealed device). Some historians rationalise the Knock visions as a timely distraction from grievances over land reform, ironically the subject of lantern campaigns too.[10] Joyce connected Knock more explicitly with dubious spirituality in *Ulysses'* 'Circe' chapter: a 'living' photograph got up as a nun refers to the visions while descending from the Blooms' bedroom wall, like a projection miraculously stepping out of the screen (*Ulysses* 15.3434–8).

Knock sheds a revealing sidelight on the importance of lantern shows in Joyce's time. The Rocketts stress that depositions from the official inquiry evidence 'an established shared vocabulary or symbolic visual repertoire', effectively acknowledged in eyewitnesses' attempts to make sense of whatever the mysterious phenomenon was (*MLP&MPS*, p. 75). They testify to the existence of a common media-cultural imaginary, based on iconography from pictures and sculptures remediated by lantern shows, which enabled witnesses to process it. Paul Carpenter steers a similar 'psycho-cultural' hypothesis between antagonistic explanations: even if not actually a projected image, Knock may have been neither miracle nor hoax, but the result of a lantern-conditioned public suggestibility shaping how it was perceived and remembered.[11]

An alternative interpretation is that Kernan, a recovering alcoholic as well as Catholic convert, alludes to lantern shows by campaigning organisations such as the Temperance Movement (for temperance and Irish lanternism, see *MLP&MPS*, pp. 52–7). By mid-century, temperance shows freely capitalised on 'fear of God'-inducing effects from the phantasmagoria for *delirium tremens* scenes representing diabolic agency behind alcohol's temptations.[12] *The Bottle*, an 1847 slide set picturing the ruin of a working man's family by Dickens illustrator George Cruikshank, would become 'the definitive temperance story', as Mervyn Heard puts it, and was also remediated on film.[13] Cruikshank's sequel, *The Drunkard's Children* (1848), particularly controversial for its allusions to prostitution, was projected in Dublin from 1861, although probably more cautiously for that reason (*MLP&MPS*, pp. 55–6). Temperance shows eventually supplemented cartoon or painted images with photographic melodramas using 'life models' (*EML*, pp. 232, 299–30 and discussion below). Lawrence's *Illustrated Catalogue* advertises well-known 'Temperance Tales', 'Each with descriptive Lecture', reflecting this transformation, listing *The Bottle* and *The Drunkard's Children*, but also life-model sets such as *Buy Your Own Cherries – A Tale of Real Life*, *The Gin Shop* and *John Hampden's Home*. Such sets or similar were reworked as early films by R. W. Paul and D. W. Griffith, among others.[14] When Joyce wrote 'Grace', teetotalist practice was typified by Dublin's Total Abstinence Society, which illustrated campaigns with slides (see the poster reproduced in *MLP&MPS*, p. 54). Another *Dubliners*' story focusing on alcoholism, 'Counterparts', contains all the classic elements of temperance shows, albeit featuring greater circumstantial and motivational complexity in its protagonist, Farrington. Thus 'Counterparts' closes on a toxically intergenerational circle of masculine dependency and abuse as he beats his son, rather than temperance's standard moral redemption. 'Grace' can also be seen as parodying stock motifs and outcomes of temperance tales. Moreover, far from 'barring' the lantern's influence, Joyce alludes to its topoi, narrative forms and techniques in many other contexts in *Dubliners* and elsewhere. These seem to have shaped his creative Modernism profoundly if ambivalently, as we shall see.

As its seventeenth-century Latin name *lanterna magica* suggests, the lantern became associated with supernaturalism from its beginnings. Paradoxically, the first published scientific account of its use at the Jesuit College in Rome, in Athanasius Kircher's hugely influential *Ars magna lucis et umbrae* (*The Great Art of Light and Shadow*, 1671), was illustrated by slides of the Crucifixion and Resurrection, but also images of the Grim Reaper and a naked female soul in hellfire, projected by a device concealed behind a partition (see reproductions in *EML*, p. 153). Kircher's book also typifies the key role played by the Jesuits in the development of optical science and technology, as recent research by leading media archaeologists confirms.[15] Largely schooled by the Jesuits himself, Joyce would thus have been exposed to their account of such scientific wonders as handmaids to faith, rather than challenges to it, a view shared by his contemporary Pope Leo XIII, in his enthusiasm for the 'miracle' of photography also alluded to in 'Grace'. However, references to lanternism in *Stephen Hero* suggest that Joyce ultimately reacted with scepticism to Jesuit attempts to reconcile tensions between science and faith. Hence *Stephen Hero* deploys the visual distortions of lanternism as both example and metaphor, highlighting the need for popular enlightenment and the reform of traditional institutions and ways of thinking through educating the eye in the profoundest sense.

Lanternism was widespread in Ireland from the early eighteenth century, predominantly via itinerant showmen. Thus its association with 'being used to frighten and entertain the credulous' was long founded in Joyce's homeland (*MLP&MPS*, p. 17). Consequently, it epitomised the equivocal application of media technology for Joyce: for Brewsterian purposes of education about optics and perception, or for mystification to keep us prisoners of our own illusions, chained up before the 'shadow show' of Plato's cave. Thus, in *Stephen Hero*, Joyce's protagonist directly opposes the lantern's 'transformative and disfiguring' light to the steady and uncompromisingly clinical illumination of modernity:

> – The modern spirit is vivisective. Vivisection is the most modern process one can conceive. The ancient spirit accepted phenomena with a bad grace. The ancient method investigated law with the lantern of justice, morality with the lantern of revelation, art with the lantern of tradition. *But all these lanterns have magical properties: they transform and disfigure. The modern method examines its territory by the light of day* . . . It examines the entire community in action and *reconstructs the spectacle* of redemption . . . here you have the spectacle of the esthetic instinct in action. (p. 167, italics mine)

Vivisection entails anatomising living things with scientific objectivity – in this case social practices and institutions – in the same way that contemporary high-speed photography and early film made it possible to analyse animal locomotion accurately for the first time. Stephen's tropes imply a radical break with phantasmagoric illusions of the past, through a critical aesthetic based on new modes of vision. This might facilitate more authentic observation of the whole 'community in action' and thus 'reconstruct' its 'spectacle', in order to modernise the understanding of individual selves and collective human potentials. The fact that vivisection implies that Stephen's spectacle is 'alive' parallels moving images – early film shows were widely known as 'living pictures'; while the fact that its view is comprehensive – capturing the 'entire community in action' – suggests a democratically panoramic perspective. We should always treat Stephen's undergraduate theorising in context, rather than as definitive statements of his mature author's intent. Nonetheless, this passage foreshadows Joyce's own striving towards a radically Modernist ekphrastic style, drawing both tropes and methods from contemporary advances in optical science and media, of which film was one practical outcome. Hence Joyce critiques an evolving media-cultural imaginary throughout his fiction.

Lantern Cinematicity: Effects of Movement

Joyce's familiarity with the lantern's contribution to the emergence of living pictures suggests that it should be treated as a key context for the development of literary cinematicity in his work. In order to appreciate this, it is important to recognise that imagistic movement of many kinds was central to the lantern's magical appeal. As Martin Loiperdinger stresses, film's own initial attraction consisted in the sheer novelty of its primary 'special effect': the appearance of comprehensive movement. Hence the earliest cinematography manuals represented the filmstrip in terms of continuity, rather than radical difference, as 'a multiple lantern slide', and the apparatus as 'a lantern equipped with a mechanical slide changer'.[16]

Consequently, the ingenious visual 'magic' in lantern shows, like the cinematic effects of optical toys, already constituted a widespread popular aesthetic of wonder for film to inherit and boost in its first phase as an exhibitionistic 'cinema of attractions'. Hence film showcased new capabilities for defamiliarisations of vision, before gradually developing into a medium of 'narrative integration', hiding its artifice under seamless naturalistic illusion achieved by continuity editing, on the model of classical Hollywood.[17] As Hauke Lange-Fuchs demonstrates, from ancient times 'efforts to project pictures have always been connected with efforts to impart movement to the figures'. As early as the seventeenth-century Dutch physicist Christiaan Huygens (sometimes credited with inventing the lantern himself), lanternists devised mechanisms to enable images to move.[18] By Joyce's childhood, countless specialised 'effect slides' had been developed, superimposing moving natural or fantastic phenomena over the main scene, to humorous, spectacular or psychological impact. These included the *aurora borealis*, rainbows, lightning, even volcanic eruptions, as well as thoughts, dreams and apparitions (*EML*, pp. 100–1).

Lever slides employed overlapping glass discs for dynamism – see-sawing boys, doffed hats, and so on; while pivots produced rocking, swinging or oscillation – for sailing ships, trapezes, rippling water, skipping ropes (*EML*, pp. 168–9, 223–4, 280). Windmills and waterwheels revolved through pulley slides; also essential to the chromatrope's 'artificial firework displays' (*EML*, pp. 244–5). 'Rackwork slides' (multiple images set in toothed rings operated by ratchet) became common. Moonrise or sunrise could be simulated (*EML*, p. 198), alongside complex concentric effects, such as shoals of fish swimming in opposite directions simultaneously, and the famous 'vernacular surrealism' of the snoring man swallowing rats. Rackwork also projected orreries of planets orbiting at different speeds (*EML*, pp. 75–6, 247). Slipping slides slid images laterally over one another to create movement or reveal concealed features. Single effects, both naturalistic or magical, included dances or jigs, humans and animals swapping heads, noses extending Pinocchio-like and portraits with eyes following viewers; double effects created movement from either side such as formations of tumbling acrobats (*EML*, pp. 284–5).

Impressions of continuous movement along different axes of the visual field were common. Glass-strip 'panorama slides' (another prominent example of an inter-medial ecology) passed through projectors to traverse land-, sea- or cityscapes, and to show comic chases, processions or other travelling sequences: a popular one, pandering to colonial prejudices as many did, was *Irishmen Pursuing Pigs*.[19] Panorama slides could be cranked vertically to simulate balloon flight or ascents of Mont Blanc (popular subjects of moving panoramas too, as discussed in Chapter 3). By projecting other slides across static panorama backgrounds, Charles I was pursued by Roundheads, animals boarded Noah's Ark, trains rolled across bridges and fleets sailed out (*EML*, pp. 217–18). In the famous set adapted from Irish playwright Dion Boucicault's *The Corsican Brothers* (1880), their duel was enacted by flashing a slide of multiple fencing actions using a 'choreutoscope' (see below), with a second slide keeping the background static. As Humphries and Lear note, such effects brought shows ever closer to comprehensively moving pictures.[20]

Increasingly ingenious combinations expanded lanternists' spectacular repertoire. They sank ships in thunderstorms, and recreated famous battles or conflagrations in extraordinary levels of detail, such as the Jewin Street fire of 1897. One Royal Polytechnic presentation, *The Siege of Delhi*, deployed multiple lanterns simulating bursting artillery shells and horrifying carnage, synchronised with elaborate sound effects.[21] With 'meta-lanternism', 1894's *Gabriel Grub* production (from Dickens's eponymous story in *The Pickwick Papers* [1836–37]) subjected a miserly sexton to a reforming Christmas picture show.[22] It featured fifteen moving effects in a single graveyard sequence alone, including Grub's descent down through the Earth's strata into the goblins' 'showcave'.[23] W. R. Hill, the Polytechnic's animation specialist, devised an equally extraordinary sequence for its 1897 pantomime of *Alice in Wonderland*. Carroll's white rabbit crossed the screen, turned, took out his watch, bending his head to check the time, then walked right off it, 'legs moving in the most natural manner'.[24] By such means, as Deac Rossell puts it, lantern cinematicity edged 'towards ever-faster, smoother, and more elaborate representations of fluid motion'.[25] Consequently, the flickering instability of early cinematograph shows (including its Dublin debut) seemed disappointingly inferior, as noted by Cecil Hepworth (an important figure linking the two media), who dubbed them 'animated palsyscopes'.[26] Henry Walker, comparing the operations of 'the animated photograph and the dissolving view', insisted that the former, though a 'mechanical triumph', required far less artistry and professional skill,[27] whereas lantern shows are closer to 'editing a film live'.[28]

By 1890 Dublin was familiar with virtually every form of slide movement available. Lawrence's *Illustrated Catalogue* inventories extensive 'Mechanical Slides' based on 'Rackwork', including 'Chromatrope Designs', 'A Merry Christmas', the notorious 'Man – Eating Rats', wind- and watermills, figures with 'Changing Faces', 'Telescope with Signs of the Zodiac', and so on. It also mentions 'Lever' and 'Comic Slipping Slides', proudly offering a 'Large Collection to suit full size Lanterns'.[29] A Solomon's advertisement from February 1890 listed a similarly full range of 'Magic, Phantasmagoria and Dissolving View Lanterns', with 'Superior Slides' for 'Frolics, Comicalities, Moving Figures'. Solomon's also offered 'Dioramic effects, astonishing Contrivances, and Illusions, including Ghosts, Acrobats, Magic Visions, and Other Novelties'.[30] Hence expectations about further technological innovations bringing images more fully and convincingly to life were as high in Dublin as anywhere else.

DISSOLVING VIEWS

There was another way in which lantern shows created sophisticated impressions of movement within scenes or transitions between them. This was crucial both to their development as narrative medium and inheritance for film, as well as to Joyce's work. Although dissolving views in their proper form really began in the 1840s at London's Adelaide Gallery and Royal Polytechnic (according to Jeremy Brooker),[31] their principle is often credited to the English slide-painter Henry Langdon Childe, and they may stem from experiments with dual lanterns for moving and superimposition effects in phantasmagorias. Childe reputedly worked for the original phantasmagorist, Paul de Philipsthal or 'Philidor', at London's Lyceum in 1801–03. Philidor may also have produced them during his 1804 Dublin shows.[32] Their development has further possible Irish connections, as discussed below.

Dissolving views created impressive illusions of meteorological, temporal and seasonal transformation, using bi- and (by the 1890s) triunial lanterns with convergent beams. They were also employed for visionary inserts, as in the popular *Soldier's Dream*, where changing views of home hovered above a nostalgic campaigner (*EML*, pp. 89–91),[33] or for projecting elaborate 'thought pictures' in life-model melodramas such as the heavenly visions of *One Winter Night*.[34] Such dynamic techniques influenced filmic dissolves or 'cross-fades'. They created a synthetic space and time by transiting between or mixing images and scenes, in which the 'here and now' and 'then and there', the real and fantastic, bled ambiguously in and out of each other. This visual fluidity pointed forward simultaneously to film and the experimental fiction of consciousness epitomised by Joyce, with its interplay between past and present and dynamic blending of perception, memory and fantasy.

Poet Maria Abdy marvelled at the myriad visual matches, metamorphoses and transitions already in the dissolving repertoire by 1843:

> Are they not wondrous? How the sight
> Revels in changes quick and bright,
> Less like the work of mortal hand,
> Than some gay scene of fairy-land:
> Lo! From our fixed and rapt survey

Object by object melts away,
Yielding their shadowy forms and hues
To merge in fresh Dissolving Views.
The ancient castle seems to shine
Reflected in the clear blue Rhine,
Anon, the proud and stately tower
Becomes a simple woodbine bower;
Swift sailing ships and glittering seas,
Change to the churchyard's mournful trees,
Whose dark and bending boughs diffuse
Shade o'er the dim Dissolving views.[35]

They might also be regarded as 'visual palimpsests', one picture shimmering through the outlines and interstices of another or morphing out of its figures into something else. Arguably, Joyce's quest to devise and refine their textual equivalent reached its hypostasis in the polymorphous wordplay and continuously overlapping scenarios of *Finnegans Wake*.

An Irishman helped to facilitate the rise of dissolving views. Edward Marmaduke Clarke was the son of a Dublin optician, Edward Clarke, who salvaged Philidor's Irish debut by supplying a lantern of his own design after the phantasmagorist lost his crossing the sea. Philidor may have confided the secret of transformational effects to the father. (Edward Clarke devised such a double apparatus for Jacques Alexandre Charles's 1822 shows at Dublin's Sans Pareil Theatre in Royal Arcade.) The son patented his 'Biscenascope' especially for displaying Langdon Childe's dissolve slides by the new 'limelight' gas.[36] London's Royal Polytechnic Institution's purchase of a Biscenascope in 1841 helped establish its tradition of showcasing cutting-edge visual technology (*EML*, pp. 259–60).[37] Its Great Hall and enormous screen – 'the Great Disc' – became Britain's most important theatre for such displays. Hence the former Polytechnic was the logical choice for the cinematograph's UK debut in February 1896.[38]

Lawrence's *Illustrated Catalogue* proves that classic dissolving views were familiar to Dubliners by 1890, listing day, night, moonlight and illuminated sets of 3–6 slides for the Houses of Parliament, the Eiffel Tower, the Bay of Naples, and so on. The Naples set climaxed with 'Vesuvius in Eruption', the bridge of St Angelo in Rome with 'Fireworks', and icebergs with 'Aurora'. There were similarly spectacular touches for a particularly Irish subject: 'Emigrant Ship . . . struck by Lightning. Ship on fire. Rafts put off.' The 'Magician's Cave' went beyond mere natural wonders when 'He waves his Wand and Spirits arise from the Cauldron'.[39] These sets and others like them would have been projected at lectures, theatres, music halls, church-organised children's entertainments and, increasingly, domestic displays.

From Quick-Change Slides to Cinematograph

Lantern cinematicity inevitably progressed beyond trick slides and dissolves. Pioneers experimented with persistence of vision through ingenious modifications. Their aspiration is causally linked to film. Thomas Ross's 'Wheel of Life' lantern, patented in 1871, animated multiple images from rotating disc slides of subjects such as running men or acrobats.[40] In a move spurring Edison and his researcher, W. K. L Dickson, to develop their kinetoscope film peepshow, Eadweard Muybridge brought his 'animal locomotion' stills to life through his 1879 patent 'Zoöpraxiscope', basically a phenakistoscope with a contra-rotating shutter adapted for the lantern. Thus Muybridge animated his photo-sequences by reproducing them as painted silhouettes around the edge of a glass disc, then projecting them, as at his Dublin lectures of 1890 (*EML*, pp. 205–6).

One crucial advance in film was that most lantern devices, however impressive, comprised repetitive and mechanistic movements of selective elements along one or two axes. Conversely, movement in cinematograph images appeared holistic, fluid and 'natural', with random diagonals across receding planes of a background that might also be in motion. Thus reports enthused over the vividness of maritime actualities, such as the Lumières' *Barque sortant du port* or the R. W. Paul/Birt Acres *Rough Sea at Dover*, because of their distinctive mix of familiarity and innovation. Undulating waves and sailing ships had long been common lantern effects, but film added a more complete, more stereoscopic virtualism, mimicking the plenitude and depth of the human visual field in a form which thus appeared, paradoxically, unmediated. Similarly, it superseded the 'looping of time' produced by the action in optical toys such as the zoëtrope or Muybridge's zoöpraxiscope projections, introducing a theoretically endless potential for narrative development, as Esther Leslie notes.[41] Nonetheless, as Rossell emphasises, 'Cinema did not bring motion to the screen; it brought the duration of motion, it brought the elaboration and variation of motion, it brought an unlimited motion of nature, of the natural world, that astonished audiences.'[42]

The marvellously heightened realism of filmic wave motion – as though billows might gush out of the screen – was also highlighted in reviews of early shows in Dublin (*MLP&MPS*, pp. 224–5). Moreover, Irish reporting of the cinematograph's London debut (20 February 1896) was particularly drawn to the virtualism of *La Mer* (*Sea Bathing*):

> [T]he most extraordinary and remarkable scene is the last. You are apparently looking at the sea. The long rollers come tumbling in. A party of bathers run along the springboard and take headers. The waves dash against the rocks and foam flies up in the air, and you expect every moment to see the water pouring into the hall.

Figure 1.2 Slide from *What are the Wild Waves Saying?* Ian and Daphne Mackley Collection, digital image by David Elsbury.

Along with other Lumière actualities, this constituted 'remarkable evidence of what science can do to deceive the senses'.[43] Hence by the time of Dublin's first exhibition of projected film in April 1896, an Irish public 'discourse on the new entertainment already existed' (*EIC*, p. 44). In this context, it seems likely that the young Joyce, familiar with lantern cinematicity in many forms, might have been similarly inspired to raise the ekphrastic virtualism of his own ambitions. Indeed there were anticipations of *La Mer*'s effect of phenomena appearing to intrude into or engulf an audience's sensory space in life-model images such as *What Are the Wild Waves Saying?* In this a bedroom wall dissolves into an immersive picture of waves pouring in, similar to Stephen's fever dream in *Portrait* (figure 1.2).

Mechanising Magic

Actualities, though reproducing movement holistically as never before, quickly lost their fascination as film's potential for 'fabulous and fantastic spectacles in the tradition of its visual forerunners' such as diorama, shadow play and especially phantasmagoria, were exploited (*MiTD*, p. 133). John Arthur Roebuck Rudge, dubbed 'the Wizard of the magic lantern', used a mechanism to instantaneously substitute seven photographic slides in his 1880 'Biophantic Lantern' and animate a man removing and replacing his head in jerky, split-second movements, anticipating a similar feat by the apparition of Bloom's grandfather in one of 'Circe's' fantastic sequences: '*Virag unscrews his head in a trice and holds it under his arm*' (16.2636). Devised with William Friese-Greene (a fellow film pioneer), Roebuck Rudge's visual conjuring clearly anticipates self-decapitating films by Méliès and others, such as *The Man with the Indiarubber Head* (1901) and *The Melomaniac* (1903), acknowledged influences on Joyce's surrealism. It is therefore likely that *Ulysses*' most animated and metamorphic chapter has similarly deeper roots in lantern culture.[44]

A former lanternist like many film pioneers, Méliès frequently acknowledged his professional debt to its themes, motifs and techniques in his distinctively phantasmagoric blend of macabre and burlesque tropes. One Méliès film is even called *La Lanterne magique* (1903), in which it doubles as projector and cabinet of wonders, from which spring high-kicking dancers and a giant jack-in-the-box. In his *Au Pays des jouets* (1908), puppets similarly come to life and screen images with a toy lantern.[45] Indeed as Mannoni argues, the stop-motion principle or 'substitution splice', on which such trick films depended for their wondrous dis/appearances and transformations, was effectively an extension of the magical substitution of lantern images or of instantaneous revelation by unmasking hidden elements within slides. Mannoni instances an 1880 slipping slide in which a book-engrossed philosopher jolts back to matters corporeal when a midwife suddenly presents him with triplets.[46] A similarly popular dissolving view turned a nubile woman into a skeleton; a cautionary 'bacchanalian' version retailed as a temperance set.[47] Exactly the same erotico-gothic motif was reworked by Méliès in his breakthrough stop-motion transformation, *L'Escamotage d'une dame* or *The Disappearing Woman* (1896).

SOUND AND VISION

Besides incorporating live commentary or dialogue, there were other ways in which lantern shows anticipated film's aspiration to sound: music and auditory effects were often integral (*EML*, p. 203), as they would be for 'silent' movie programmes. Lantern shows were a multi-sensory experience, a fact which may have inspired Joyce with his passion for song and audio-visual creativity. Shows were often conducted as participatory 'services of song', as in several sets found in the Fairview Joyce house (see below). They also illustrated popular ballads, promoted new sheet music or featured famous touring performers. From the 1890s 'picture concerts' were enormously popular. They projected images and texts for music hall audiences to sing along to (*EML*, pp. 289–90). Stanislaus Joyce recalled attending London music halls with their father, when they accompanied him on business trips. Joyce was also a great frequenter of Dublin's as an undergraduate.[48] Song slides were also interspersed in early film programmes: Dublin's People's Popular Picture Palace featured them before

Joyce opened the Volta (*EIC*, p. 4). A notice for the Rotunda film programme in August 1906 similarly records that

> An interesting feature is the illustrated songs which are well sung, and the effect is greatly enhanced by the charming coloured slides. Vocal items are also given by prominent artistes, including Miss Durkin and Miss May O'Connor, while the selections played by the orchestral band add considerably to the enjoyment.[49]

Mixing slides into film programmes was the precursor to the 'sing along' film genre. Lantern picture concert repertoires ranged from light opera to the latest popular songs and parlour favourites like 'Love's Old Sweet Song'. Significantly, this is woven throughout the texture of Joyce's Bloomsday, providing a virtual signature tune and point of psychological convergence between *Ulysses*' main characters. Molly first mentions it casually in 'Calypso', as a highlight of the planned concert tour that covers for her assignation with Boylan later that day (4.314). This prompts its chorus to echo ironically in Bloom's thoughts in 'Lotus Eaters' as M'Coy pumps him slyly about their arrangement (5.157–61). Consequently, Bloom meditates on it twice in 'Sirens', while contemplating the thwack of a barmaid's garter against her thigh and the act simultaneously taking place at home which cuckolds him (11.681–2). In 'Nausicaa', Gerty MacDowell alludes to its opening lyrics, as she romantically imagines that her 'dark stranger' (later revealed as Bloom himself) must be mourning 'an old flame . . . from the days beyond recall' (13.666–7). Josie Breen also mentions 'The dear dead days beyond recall' in 'Circe', hinting at what might have been between Bloom and herself (15.455). As *Salvator Mundi*, Bloom is asked to sing 'One of the old sweet songs' by Nosey Flynn in one of its fantastic sequences (15.1720). Similarly, Florry cajoles the loveless Stephen to sing it to her, but he declines (15.2506). In 'Ithaca', Stephen and Bloom discover a music book over the parlour piano left open at this page, among telltale signs of what has transpired that afternoon (17.1307). Finally, Molly, wavering between short-term memories of purely fleshly pleasures with the stud Boylan and the more authentic tenderness of courtship days with Poldy, hears the song's title poignantly drawn out in Doppler effects from passing trains (18.598, 874–7, 896–7).

Appropriately for a Joycean context of projected images with evocative associations, Clifton Bingham's words (to J. L. Molloy's score) chorus with references to seeing 'flick'ring shadows softly come and go' at twilight. Slide number 6 from Bamforth's 1899 life-model set is captioned with Bingham's line, 'Footsteps may falter, weary grow the way'. With the dual temporality typical of many life-model narratives, its image shows a 'Darby and Joan' gazing nostalgically at a couple on a park bench, with a broad sweep of bay and headland in the background. It is uncertain whether the young couple are literally present in the same scene or whether the elderly pair are in fact visualising their counterpart selves at the tenderest moment in their own courtship, as Bloom and Molly separately do in flashbacks to their more explicit consummation on Howth Head, above Dublin Bay.[50] Moreover, Joyce's interest in showing 'opera-phonoscenes',[51] synchronising moving picture and gramophone records at the Volta, though unrealised, had precedents in the lantern shows' integration of music and song. But so too does his counterpart tendency to use evocative snatches asynchronically: as emotional time machines transporting a character's thoughts and feelings from their narrative present into immersive *revisions* of experiences elsewhere and elsewhen (see further examples from *Dubliners* discussed below).

Photographic Virtualism: Defamiliarising the Everyday

From the late 1830s, limelight, a brighter, steadier illumination source than candles or oil, fired by oxy-hydrogen gas and turned up or down on cue, produced the most sharply defined images prior to the invention of electric lightbulbs in 1878. Painted slide images were reproduced *en masse* by transfer printing from the 1820s, but increasingly replaced from the 1850s by photographs (after the introduction of the 'wet-plate' collodion process). 'Grace' suggests how photographic projections stimulated Joyce's fascination with the increasingly powerful virtualism of technological media. Ireland responded quickly to photography's invention in the late 1830s. Its first commercial studio opened in October 1841, appropriately over the Rotunda's main entrance (*MLP&MPS*, p. 47). Moreover, this initiated the transformation of Dublin's central commercial district into what became known as 'the photographer's mile', from the Rotunda and Sackville Street on its north side, across the Liffey to Trinity College, Grafton Street and St Stephen's Green on the south.[52]

It is highly significant that the reference to Pope Leo XIII's poem 'Ars Photographica' (1868), celebrating the camera's miraculous 'hyperrealism' as proof of science's God-given inventiveness, is one of the few facts that Joyce allows the pseudo-learned Martin Cunningham to get right (see *Dubliners*, p. 131, and note).[53] This focuses the story's subtle interplay of motifs of illumination and mystification, mirroring its thematic tensions between scepticism and credulousness. It also suggests how the lantern as proto-filmic medium became a crowd-pulling aid to business-minded piety. The presence of living people, materialised almost tangibly in moving photographs, eventually led to the bizarre theological debate of 1898 after Pope Leo himself appeared before W. K. L. Dickson's camera: did this automatically bless all those who paid to see the resulting peepshow? Was Leo effectively blessing the filming camera itself?[54] Dubliners were able to see Pope Leo in these 'living pictures' at the city's Mutoscope Palace from May 1899, then projected on screen at Christmas 1902 at the city's Antient Concert Rooms in Great Brunswick (now Pearse)

Street (*MLP&MPS*, p. 247; for Joyce and the mutoscope, see below and Chapter 2). Leo XIII's divine photophilia became so famous that Lawrence assembled a special 'Presentation Album' of Irish views in his honour.[55] Photography certainly gave ultra-mimetic enhancement to moving and projected images, just as Joyce's early fictions stretched the boundaries of literary naturalism as never before in extraordinary ekphrastic precision and detail. As Donald F. Theall and others have shown, Joyce's sense of the technological evolution in the recording, duplication, projection and animation of photographed images extends all through his work into the pioneering days of television broadcasting in *Finnegans Wake*.

As well as alluding to photography's magnified and projected form as lantern slides, *Dubliners* is characterised by awareness of its temporal and ontological ambiguity and the proliferation of its images in everyday public and private life. Photographs of the living, exiled or dead are given a prominent role in fraught domestic contexts as triggers for moments of existential crisis: as capsules for absent presences, emotional attractors, or portals into personal pasts, which are themselves often presented like rapid sequences of lantern slides. Eveline's dilemma between duty and escape is visualised when her wandering eyes are arrested by the photograph of an emigrated priest, 'yellowing . . . above the broken harmonium beside the coloured print of the promises made to Blessed Margaret Mary Alacoque' (*Dubliners*, p. 25). Details of photographs are often scrutinised with an intensity sharpened by seeing images blown up beyond life-size. In 'A Little Cloud', on returning to his mean terrace – after being tantalised by Gallagher with glimpses of an alternative life as a glamorous foreign correspondent – Chandler's eye catches his wife's photograph, highlighted by a lamp. He scans it close up, 'pausing at the thin tight lips' and noting the 'pale blue summer blouse'.[56] This prompts his flashback to a scolding for extravagance in buying it, before cutting back to the present in which he gazes 'coldly into the eyes of the photograph', meeting their equally frosty, simulated response. The flashback contrasts with Chandler's lingering mental after-images of continental Jewesses' 'dark Oriental eyes' evoked by Gallagher, before Chandler finally reduces his wife to a virtual synecdoche by asking himself, 'Why had he married the eyes in the photograph?' (*Dubliners*, p. 63). After she returns to find that he has upset their baby, Joyce repeats the close-up motif, with the difference that Chandler now lacks the courage to confront her eyes as they glare back in reality: 'Little Chandler sustained for one moment the gaze of her eyes and his heart closed together as he met the hatred in them' (*Dubliners*, pp. 64–5).

Photographs play a similar role for Joyce's focalising character in 'The Dead'. 'Panning' round his aunt's parlour, Gabriel's eyes alight on a photograph of his mother, appropriately pointing out something in a picture book to his brother as a child. This acts like a portal, though a troubling one, into

Gabriel's own past. He plunges back into another rapid sequence of recollections resembling slide tableaux or short film scenes: his mother's 'sullen opposition to his marriage'; a flashback to her disapproval of his wife Gretta as 'country cute'; a contrasting one of Gretta nursing his mother through her 'last long illness' despite their differences (*Dubliners*, pp. 146–7).

Dublin was also a highly photographed city and images of its streetscapes were easily remediated in lantern shows. The prolific output of Lawrence's photographer-in-chief, Robert French, would become so intimately associated with Joyce in cultural memory that it was used to 'resurrect' the Dublin of Joyce's time in Kieran Hickey's *Faithful Departed* (1968); the photographs were used similarly, for Ireland from Parnell's death in 1891 up to the First World War, in Hickey's second film, *The Light of Other Days* (1972).[57] Justin Carville has recently explored the historical significance of Lawrence's photographic mapping of Dublin's cityscape during a period of increasing challenge to British rule, from the opening of its 'Great Bazaar and Photographic Galleries' in March 1865, until its destruction during the 1916 Easter Rising, which also damaged many of the central imperial landmarks that Lawrence mediated:

> Lawrence's photographs of the city refracted back to the viewer the cultural and political complexities of its modernity. Images of modern transportation (motor cars and electric trams) and the city's vibrant commercial life were juxtaposed with the photographic visualisation of the imperial streetscape with its monarchical and colonial statuary, as well as photographs of the emerging monuments to nationalist leaders that increasingly began to appear on the city's streets from the mid-nineteenth century.[58]

Lawrence's stock, much of which was repurposed as lantern slides, reflected how Dublin's streetscape was both contested and changing at a pivotal time through its key monuments and buildings, just as Joyce's work does.

Documentary 'real-life' slides were frequently projected by campaigning organisations to publicise facts about 'the Social Question', as the Victorians called it, and the conditions they sought to reform, but everyday subjects of work and leisure were also commonly screened and seen with new fascination. Projection revealed and magnified details of the most mundane realities with startling impact.[59] A report on an 1890 meeting of the Photographic Society of Ireland indicates that lanternism was also making marginalised or neglected aspects of Dublin life similarly visible in new ways:

> On the 22nd May this society concluded the winter session by a public lantern exhibition in the theatre of the Royal College of Science. There was a large attendance. During the evening two hundred and twenty

slides were passed through the lanterns by Mr. J. Carson, C.E.; they were described by the secretary, in the absence through illness of Professor J. Alfred Scott. A large number of the slides were made from negatives used in hand cameras, those causing most amusement having reference to street life in Dublin, particularly in some of the slums of the city.[60]

According to Vogl-Bienek, this report typifies the development of the lantern's potential, in terms of approaching 'the social environment by the most modern optical means of the time', but also in screening its problems to large and influential audiences: the seating capacity of the College's lecture theatre was over 500, albeit reactions on this occasion may have lacked appropriate moral concern.[61] Nevertheless, the report testifies to how portable cameras were increasingly taking photography onto Dublin's streets and into under-represented areas, bringing the results back for projection. Published in the *Optical Magic Lantern Journal and Photographic Enlarger* in June 1890, it was no coincidence that the report was succeeded by advertisements for portable cameras with ambiguous implications for visual representation and control: one shows a camera operated by a woman, suggesting a potential challenge to patriarchal perspectives on reality; another displays 'The "UNIT" Detective Hand Camera', underlining its potential for 'candid' or forensically revealing shots, but also covert surveillance and policing.[62]

The *Optical Magic Lantern Journal* ran a whole series of articles about using 'Hand Cameras for Obtaining Slides for the Lantern' in 1890–91. Portable cameras and projected photography undoubtedly contributed to training the modern visual sensibility exemplified by Joyce's notion of epiphany, with its photographic tropes and effect of camera-eyed focalisation as a truth-revealing process. Moreover, as Vogl-Bienek notes,

> The art of projection firmly established the screen as a cultural locale that integrates virtual realities into public performances. No previous medium had a comparable potential for the visual . . . re-presentation of distant realities or fictions . . . Large-scale projections mediate impressive experiences which can be shared by a great number of people. They easily evoke the impression of being witness to the events, or at least support a belief in realistic representation. This belief was even stronger when the images were created with the aid of photography.[63]

Photographic slides effectively made lantern shows into a simulacral medium anticipating the newsreel or 'topicals' of early film, particularly when reporting charismatic, sensational or controversial subjects such as royal jubilees and processions, natural disasters or rail crashes, colonial wars, the latest 'unwomanly' stunts of suffragettes or indeed the evictions publicised by Irish

Nationalists. Technological progress shrank the gap between real events and 'representation-as-perception' both ontologically and temporally, a condition of apparent immediacy emulated and challenged by Joyce, with his paradoxical method of presenting phenomena from ultra-mimetic, but also intensely subjective points of view. By 1900, for the first time, mass audiences in Dublin, as elsewhere, were regularly seeing life-size and increasingly moving projections of events only days after their occurrence. Photographic lanternism similarly covered the 'newsworthy' in sport, theatre and even early film itself, forming a gateway into modernity's cult of stardom and celebrity.[64]

MODELLING FROM LIFE

Another entailment of photography was that from the 1870s lanternists began projecting fictions in similarly virtual form through 'life-model' melodramas, with costumes, elaborate props and specially built sets (see *MiTD*, pp. 101–19). Individual images were hand-coloured, although this was eventually automated by chromo-lithographic contact printing. Modes could also be creatively mixed: *Gabriel Grub*'s goblins set against naturalistic backgrounds are outstanding examples of combining photographic with painted images to insert the fantastic into 'real life' or vice versa, just as mixing graphic animation and live action would do in early film, and foreshadowing Joyce's mixture of naturalism and fantastic animation in 'Circe'.[65] Moreover, as Cook comments,

> The application of photography to the manufacture of narrative slides and the introduction of living models endowed the projected image with a more vivid human interest, a form of realism more readily intelligible to the unsophisticated, and a wider emotional range than it had been so far able to command. They coincided with the publication of a stream of verse and fiction, prompted, as were most of the slides, by the social conditions of the period, the pressing question of poverty and its attendant evils, drunkenness and depravity. (*MiTD*, pp. 102–3)

By the end of Victoria's reign life-model melodramas were a leading popular entertainment, often transcending the mediocre ballads and novels on which they were based in technical innovation and documentary impact. Local amateurs (often proprietors' families or staff), rather than professional actors, posed in dramatic tableaux to provide greater naturalism. They were, effectively, the 'soaps' of the age.[66] James Bamforth and Co. was an influential pioneer of this mode from the 1880s. Bamforth duly made the transition to film, producing comedies based on its own lantern narratives as early as 1899 in its Holmfirth studios (albeit not going into regular production until 1914–18).[67] Both these and classic seaside postcards in cartoon format (which still retail today) were developed from the company's lantern stock. David Francis gives an extensive list of films probably shot from pre-existing life-model narratives by Bamforth and other pioneers such as R. W. Paul, James Williamson and G. A. Smith.[68] There was a similar migratory pattern among Irish slide-makers and exhibitors. Horgan Brothers of Youghal, for example, bought a film camera around 1896 for taking Lumièresque actualities that are among the first Irish-made films (*EIC*, pp. 207–8).[69] By the late 1890s, Lawrence, like its principal Dublin rivals, was adapting too and selling cinematographs (see *MLP&MPS*, note to plate 57).

In 'Ithaca', Stephen watches Bloom's actions from the street outside in a 'discrete succession of images', framed by windows (17.108–9). Although the chapter's analytic mode arguably presents these images like one of Muybridge's photographic locomotion studies of anonymous human subjects carrying out everyday actions, they also resemble a life-model sequence minus any linking commentary to render the individual frames into an explicit narrative flow: 'Reclined against the area railings he perceived through the transparent kitchen panes a man regulating a gasflame of 14 CP, a man lighting a candle, a man removing in turn each of his two boots, a man leaving the kitchen holding a candle of 1 CP' (17.109–12).

Various life-model modes were available in Dublin before Joyce reached his teens. Lawrence's 1890 *Illustrated Catalogue* listed 'Amusing Tales Each with Descriptive Lecture . . . Photographed from Life', including: 'Marley's Ghost', a set of twenty-four from *A Christmas Carol*;[70] 'Mary, the Maid of the Inn', based on Robert Southey's Gothic poem;[71] 'The Life Boat'[72] and 'The Signal Box'[73] by the social reformer George. R. Sims, author of 'Christmas Day in the Workhouse'; and many other ballads adapted by slide-makers such as Bamforth and York and Son, and, in due course, remediated by early film-makers.[74] It seems only logical to assume that there would be many more available for Joyce to see as he grew into his second decade. Bamforth's attracted a great deal of press attention. It was noted that by 1900 the firm was producing around 600 new life-model stories a year and carrying stock of around 2,000,000 slides.[75]

As Joe Kember observes, 'the staging, customing, and gestural language of life model lantern slides could deliver a great deal of information to audiences, and early film-makers familiar with these techniques tended to translate these to moving pictures'.[76] Hence life-model slides were a transitional phase between theatre's fourth-wall conventions and cinematic space-time. Not only did they anticipate film in the way the actors' poses resembled stills from moving narratives caught in *media res*, they could also capture action with the split-second dynamism of instantaneous photography by Muybridge or Marey. In LUCERNA (the Magic Lantern online resource run by the Universität von Trier and now taken over by Exeter), slide seven from *Curfew Shall not Ring Tonight* (York and Son, in/before 1888) shows the heroine swinging on the church bell-rope like a trapeze to prevent it ringing the time for her lover's hanging.[77]

In *The Matron's Story* (Bamforth and Co., 1890), slide two exploits 'composition in depth' to snapshot (a term also coined in this period) its protagonist in the foreground angrily flinging a hymn-book, caught in mid-air hurtling towards its startled target – a clergyman at the rear of the chapel.[78] Some experiments were exactly half-way stages between life-model narratives and feature films. In 1893–94, for example, US writer Alexander Black created 'picture plays' such as his 250-image story about the intrepid female reporter *Miss Jerry* (Blanche Bayliss), by taking location shots with actors sequenced into visual dramas. Influenced by Muybridge's projected animations and Edison's kinetoscope, Black projected frames at the rate of four per minute: fast enough to suggest associative links, but as yet too slow for full persistence of vision.[79]

There was another, less edifying attraction to the unprecedented realism and virtual bodily presence of life-model narratives. Even if not intentionally titillating (though some showings at less respectable venues certainly were), they laid the foundations for the 'anonymous intimacy' and voyeurism that film built on by giving apparently privileged glimpses into the lives of others, oblivious of audiences observing them in the darkness. As Heard and others evidence, the lantern is the only large-scale entertainment medium before projected film known to have ventured into pornography, most likely shown at men-only 'smoking concerts' and as 'fluffing' material in brothels, a practice extended by screening films in the same venues (as a frequenter of brothels in Dublin and the Continent, Joyce probably saw examples in both media). A case reported in *The Times* (20 April 1874) resulted in the confiscation of over 100,000 photographs and 5,000 lantern slides from one studio alone. Erotic figures may have been added to scenes by dissolving views or by having clothes subtracted from them. Colonial peoples were often photographed in revealing native costumes, while posed scenes from erotic classical myths carried the alibi of high culture. Ever shorter exposures meant that sexual action, like any other, could be captured in *media res* or as proto-filmic action sequences.[80] Photographic eroticism in lantern slides made its remediation by projected film both inevitable and rapid. Commentators such as Maxim Gorki realised that the appeal was inherent even before the cinematograph had been turned to that purpose. As he noted of Moscow's first film programme, 'I do not yet see the importance of Lumière's invention [overall] but no doubt it is there.' However, he was certain that innocent actualities would 'soon be replaced by others of a genre more suited to the general tone of the Concert Parisien. For example, they will show a picture entitled: "As She Undresses", or "Madam at her Bath", or "A Woman in Stockings".'[81]

Considering Joyce's fascination with mediated gazing, with the double-edged scopophilia and ethics of looking (already marked in *Dubliners* by projection imagery in stories such as 'Araby' and updated to moving image peepshows in *Ulysses*' 'Nausicaa'), it seems reasonable to assume that some measure of this derives from the virtual bodily presence and 'candid' action represented in life-model narratives. It has been recognised that there are strong affinities between self-reflexive 'Peeping Tom' themes in early film and the voyeuristic preoccupations of Joyce's protagonists; similarly, that his fiction becomes particularly inter-medial with silent comedy. One of Chaplin's first films combines these two strands through the lantern's agency, effectively acknowledging its own roots in the appeal of its predecessor and gestatory host. Keystone's *The Star Boarder*, from March 1914, features Chaplin alongside Gordon Griffith, who plays a mischievous little boy. The boy secretly snaps compromising situations among boarding-house lodgers, creating uproar when the evidence is screened by lantern.[82] In a darker way, *Dubliners*' 'The Boarding House', in which Bob Doran is trapped into marriage after a moment's indiscretion with his landlady's daughter, deals with similar anxieties about surveillance and public exposure in a morally censorious but hypocritical city. Joyce's technique also renders his boarding-house front effectively transparent, as if the reader were able to see private actions occurring in different spaces simultaneously, like juxtaposed lantern slides or film shots, rooms with their fourth walls removed so that we gaze into them unimpeded, rather than merely seeing shadows on blinds.

Photographic slides were often tinted in translucent shades to create dramatic contrasts or highlight 'epiphanic' details. Natural colour photography had been demonstrated to the Royal Institution by Scottish physicist James Clerk Maxwell in 1861, combining images from lanterns fitted with red, green and blue filters.[83] Photographic dissolves switching from monochrome to early colour gave rise to wonderful transformations, such as bouquets bursting into polychromatic splendour or landscapes illuminated by sunrise (*MiTD*, p. 95). Dublin 'Analyticon' shows also incorporated colour photography. It is possible that Joyce invokes such effects in Gabriel's defamiliarised vision of Gretta on the stairs in 'The Dead'. He does not initially recognise this strangely rapt figure because her clothing is rendered monochromatic in the hallway darkness, until he mentally imbues colour back into the picture and realises who she is:

> He was in a dark part of the hall gazing up the staircase. A woman was standing near the top of the first flight, in the shadow also. He could not see her face but he could see the terracotta and salmonpink panels of her skirt which the shadow made appear black and white. It was his wife. (*Dubliners*, p. 165)

Joyce was also aware of the binocular nature of vision and its enhancement by hand-held stereoscopes, used for viewing photographic cards three-dimensionally. Stereo-views were popular in Ireland from the 1850s long into the twentieth century. Lawrence ran a lucrative sideline in stereoscope cards, often repurposing slide images (the National Library of Ireland has over 2,800 surviving stereo pairs produced by the firm). The 'Stereopticon' became a common American synonym for the lantern itself from the 1860s, especially after the first photographic projections. The term both alluded to the stereoscope and the effect of almost palpable prominence and depth in large-scale projections, particularly following increased brightness through limelight, although most slides were monoscopic.[84] Moreover, actual stereoscopic projection, via photographs taken from dual-lensed cameras, also took place in Dublin. The Modern Marvel Company projected such 3-D images in autumn 1898 at the Rotunda, using 'that wonderful product of the nineteenth century, the Analyticon'. According to the *Dublin Daily Express*, it produced 'marvellous' effects 'in bold relief and giving a realistic appearance to objects and pictures projected on the screen'.[85] Analyticon shows also incorporated 'Colour photography and beautiful Dioramic Effects'.[86] They were widely advertised in mixed programmes with the cinematograph and reported as drawing 'extremely large audiences'.[87] The Analyticon depended on special glasses like 3-D film, according to the *Freeman's Journal*: 'The result is accomplished by a peculiar mode of presenting two pictures, which are viewed through instruments called analysers.'[88] Later lantern patents aspired beyond 3-D to total visual immersion, extending the panoramic principle of enveloping audiences in scenes themselves. The 'Electric Cyclorama' demonstrated in 1894 used multiple lanterns suspended in chandelier formation to surround spectators with a 360-degree projected environment (*EML*, p. 103). Strikingly imagistic effects of projection, depth and immersion in Joyce's fictions coincide very suggestively with this modern media tendency towards totalising virtual reality. That convergence would become fully mobilised in the 'camera-eyed' style of *Portrait* and its cinematic presentation of both space and time, then extended to the city-wide moving panoramism of *Ulysses*, which ranges freely around the public and private space of Dublin.

USES AND GENRES

By 1901 when Victoria died, the lantern had become one of the most widespread and effective media in history. The Queen herself had been continually and extensively screened through it, making her one of the first 'media monarchs', in both a modern technological sense and in terms of the organised shaping of her public persona.[89] Practically every film genre – travelogue, documentary, newsreel, alongside various kinds of feature – can be traced to lantern predecessors. This inevitably included mediating Ireland and Irishness, albeit not necessarily from an indigenous point of view. LUCERNA alone lists well over forty surviving titles that include the terms 'Ireland' or 'Irish' produced in England (and occasionally Scotland) between 1883 and 1913, and there were certainly many others. These comprise examples of numerous genres and types of production: comedies, virtual 'tours', politics and, above all, songs.

Lanternism had what Ine van Dooren calls a 'chameleonic' ability to absorb and amalgamate other media 'through re-production, re-editing and re-presentation' of their materials and techniques.[90] It acted as a common medium across classes, simultaneously leaving its mark on all forms of culture. On stage, Joyce could have seen shows as a regular feature of music hall variety bills (likewise important for early film shows), but also in 'legitimate' theatre and opera (*EML*, pp. 83, 300–1). Reciprocally, lantern shows remediated theatrical modes, practices and motifs. However, they became most widely associated with popular subjects such as legends, folktales and proverbs. This was unsurprising, given that many early lanternists, such as the itinerant Savoyards of the eighteenth century, were of limited means and had little formal education themselves. In a symbiotic evolution between form and content, shows often featured pantomime subjects, while pantomimes incorporated lantern-based magic (*EML*, pp. 115–16). Lanternism's key role in popular culture and crowd-pleasing showmanship was consequently passed to film, but also its contrasting aspiration towards aesthetic status.

Art Nouveau in the 1890s – the first modern design style – initiated a vogue for projecting images on to live stage performers, sparked by the American Loïe Fuller's shape-shifting Serpentine and Butterfly 'skirt dances' at Paris's Folies Bergères (similar routines were recorded for Edison's kinetoscope and seen in Dublin; *MLP&MPS*, pp. 158–9; *EIC*, pp. 19, 27).[91] The lantern allowed Fuller to make a distinctively modern moving spectacle of herself (described by Stéphane Mallarmé as a 'phantasmagoria of dusk and grotto'),[92] presaging how film would incorporate, eroticise and bring a new kind of planetary fame to performing bodies through mass-reproducibility, as Bloom relishes by risqué mutoscope peepshow in 'Nausicaa'. This had a consequent influence on Edison and Dickson's choice of subjects for their earliest film loops. Other live acts used lanterns for rapid changes of background scenes or 'moving wallpaper'. 'Pose slides' projected transformations of costume and appearance onto performers in blank garments and masks or even onto statues. They thus anticipate both the instantaneous scene transitions and character metamorphoses in 'Circe' and may be an earlier source of influence on Joyce than the stop-motion trick films which remediated and elaborated their quick-change techniques.[93]

Education: Elsewheres and Elsewhens

The lantern was also a serious instrument of scientific demonstration and public education. Projected enlargements from microscopes date from the eighteenth century. By Joyce's youth, modified lanterns demonstrated a whole spectrum of experiments and processes in optics, physics, biology, chemistry, astronomy, magnetism and electrics, though often with effects as much sensational as edifying (see *EML*, pp. 159, 269–72; *MLP&MPS*, pp. 58–60).

Verity Hunt has investigated the lantern's centrality to the nineteenth-century project of 'educating the eye', especially for middle-class children:[94] hence Brewster's own endorsement in the popular manual, *The Magic Lantern: How to Buy and How to Use it, By 'A Mere Phantom'* (1866). The physicist noted that 'The Magic Lantern, which for a long time was used only as an instrument for amusing children and astonishing the ignorant, has recently been fitted up for the better purpose of conveying scientific instruction.'[95] Such demonstrations were designed to enthral with the wonders of 'natural magic' and gradually reveal the processes behind them as products of science rather than the occult. But clearly they also set the conditions for a media-cultural imaginary both material and internalised. This sometimes resulted in traumatic effects when tensions between sensory impact and rational explanation remained too powerful or unstable to be easily resolved. Such was Harriet Martineau's case.

In her autobiography, Martineau recollected her terror at a phantasmagoria show that she saw around the age of five. A slide of Minerva and her owl materialised her 'nightmare dreams' with such hallucinatory virtualism that she shrieked and hid her eyes.[96] In *Household Education* (1848), Martineau recognised that early training of the senses is vital because of the primacy of vision to childhood itself: 'life is for them [children] all pictures. Everything comes to them in pictures.'[97] Nonetheless, her phobia about lantern shows persisted into her teens, to her secret 'shame'. Despite coming to understand the optics behind projection, when overseeing a group of younger children she still fainted before 'a dragon's head, vomiting flames'.[98] As Hunt puts it, Martineau both 'supports *and* complicates' Brewster's 'unequivocal message that an optical education can transform mystification to rationality'.[99] As we shall see, Joyce also figures childhood as a phase when the faculties of vision and thought are being shaped so intensely and ambivalently by technologically produced images that this can be both creative and distressing for his characters, especially Stephen in *Portrait*.

The lantern's influence is reflected in the imagistic features of *Dubliners'* stories of schooling, as well as *Portrait*'s modernisation of the *Bildungsroman*, the traditional form for novels of education and self-development. The German word *Bildung* even derives from *Bild*, 'image' or 'picture'.[100] Lantern use was both synchronic with, and instrumental in, the expansion of institutional education.[101] Though its attraction, in this context, 'lay in its ability to pass off instruction as entertainment' (*EML*, p. 99), educators with more sober aspirations attempted to shed the associations with sensationalism by renaming it the 'optical lantern'. Explanatory commentary was an integral part of lanternism's *modus operandi*, a function passed on to the 'film explainers' of silent cinema.[102] Slides were accompanied by speakers and (increasingly) professional lecturers, the term 'illustrated lecture' dating from the later nineteenth century (*EML*, p. 143). Sets were hired or purchased with accompanying scripts, enabling showmen and (more often than hitherto realised) women[103] to pass as 'professors' on any subject, or recite stories and verses illustrated (*EML*, p. 165). Educational use ranged through schools and church halls, to Mechanics Institutes and learned societies (*EML*, p. 191).

During the fantastic trial in 'Circe', photographic geography slides illustrate Bloom's property in the Jewish homeland 'at Agendath Netaim in faraway Asia Minor'. They bring the distant close with a mirage-like, out-of-focus shimmer: '*The image of the lake of Kinnereth with blurred cattle cropping in silver haze is projected on the wall*' (*Ulysses* 15.986–7; italics in original). Throughout *Ulysses*, Bloom has many visions of exotic locations. Similar views of the Middle East and Holy Land would have been common by 1904.[104] Painted geography slides were exhibited from the start of the nineteenth century, but their role in the Victorian boom in virtual tourism to exotic elsewheres (for those unable to afford the real thing) was boosted by photography from the late 1850s. This meant that 'audiences saw for the first time actual scenes of faraway places throughout the world, rather than artists' impressions' (*EML*, pp. 125, 232). This boom coincided with the high point of European colonialism and its technological appropriation of other lands, peoples and cultures, in both literal and imagistic senses. Joyce's fellow Irish – 'semicolonials' in relation to Britain's project as *Finnegans Wake* puns it[105] – were alternately audience for, and subject to, this same process. This meant that geography and history slides, especially concerning Ireland itself, were inevitably politically charged (for examples, see *MLP&MPS*, pp. 60–1).

Film's exoticism and ability to bring the faraway tantalisingly close thus catered to an appetite for elsewhere already whetted by panoramas and projected photography's illusory transportations, as suggested by the title 'Araby'. Similarly, in 'An Encounter', the truants' pulp-fiction fantasies may have been stimulated by Western sets.[106] The cowboy slide genre was remediated in one of film's earliest genres, dating at least from Edwin S. Porter's 1903 *Great Train Robbery*, made two years before Joyce composed his story. The narrator of 'An Encounter' also mentions his pubescent taste for 'American detective stories' featuring 'unkempt fierce and beautiful girls', not unlike Black's *Miss Jerry*. (LUCERNA also confirms that detective yarns and crime stories were adapted for the lantern.) Indeed, yearning for 'real adventures . . . sought abroad' (*Dubliners*, pp. 11–12) was intensified by what *Finnegans Wake* would dub the 'reel world' (64.25–6). The potential inauthenticity and risks of this kind of media-stimulated wish-fulfilment and escapism fits neatly with *Dubliners*' running theme of adolescence endangered by adult corruption and deceit. Thus the allure of simultaneously expanded horizons and experiential possibility is figured in the hilltop panorama in 'An Encounter' of 'the spectacle of Dublin's commerce' in the port far below. For the narrator, this allows 'geography' to 'gradually tak[e] substance under my eyes', exactly like a new slide in a biunial lantern coming into focus, while the hitherto restraining image of 'school and home' fades out (*Dubliners*, p. 14). That sense of adventure is shockingly undermined when the boys encounter not a cowboy hero or female sleuth, but a pervert who may be a defrocked priest.

Many lantern travelogues were presented as thrilling vicarious train trips, sea voyages or balloon flights, laying the simulatory basis for early film's 'phantom rides',[107] but also highlighting their inter-mediality with moving panoramas of similar subjects. Arguably, *Dubliners*' motoring story, 'After the Race', is Joyce's literary emulation of this kinaesthetic illusionism, satirising semi-colonial Ireland's distinctly second-hand thrills as a 'backseat passenger' in European modernity.[108] With inter-medial cross-fertilisation typical of the time, lantern travelogues overlapped with moving panorama shows, typified by the Poole Brothers' touring 'Myrioramas': their eclectic programmes were also billed as 'dioramic excursions', incorporating such armchair visiting as 'Venice in Dublin' (1892),[109] which may have prompted the Orientalist bazaar, 'Araby in Dublin', held two years later. Myrioramas were famous in Dublin, as alluded to by Joyce.

Nor did indigenous slide manufacturers fail to map Ireland's photogenic potential. Lawrence specialised in extensive views of rural beauty spots and cities. From 1878, it advertised sets and readings under the collective title *Ireland in the Magic Lantern*, 'graphically describing in an interesting and amusing manner all the points in the tours, and enabling the most inexperienced to conduct a trip round Ireland' (*MLP&MPS*, p. 61).[110] By 1890 Lawrence's catalogue (published under the same title) listed 1,129 views featuring every Irish county, with accompanying lectures on history and topography.[111] One 1894 lantern lecture toured *The Lakes of Killarney and Glengariff, via Cork and Bantry*, overlapping with the rail trip that Stephen undertakes with his nostalgic father in *Portrait*, which also evokes moving train panoramas and filmic phantom rides. A typical script for Lawrence's *Lantern Tours in Ireland* opened with a 'guide's address', co-opting the audience's imagination as virtual travellers:

> Ladies and gentlemen. The heading of our programme indicates the style of expedition, on which I ask you to accompany me this evening. Were I an adept in the wizard's craft, I should not hesitate to transform my audience – for the time being – into a tourist party; but lacking the magic powers (save in my lamp), I have to ask you to imagine yourselves my travelling companions for the present. My task is to place before you this very intellectual assembly of sights and scenes of a country which, if not as sunny, is, in many chapters of its scenery, as fair as any country in the world.[112]

As Condon notes, success 'hinged on the lecturer's dramatic powers' and 'ability to bring the images to life'. In due course projected film would also become a standard element of travel lectures, 'making the virtual tour' one of its earliest genres (*EIC*, p. 125). Lawrence's *Illustrated Catalogue* also ranged further afield, listing additional 'Lecture sets with descriptive readings' of English regions, together with 'Foreign' views including 'Voyage Round the World', 'Wanderings in Paris', Rome, Switzerland, Greece, America, and so on.[113]

Perhaps the (literal) zenith of Victorian virtual tourist experience was reached by the pioneering aerial photographer Cecil Victor Shadbolt, whose work clearly drew on vicarious flying experiences afforded by balloon panoramas (see Chapter 3). From 1882 to 1892, when he died in a balloon crash, Shadbolt conducted lantern shows from projected views of London and Paris, including landmarks taken from above such as the Crystal Palace and Eiffel Tower.[114] No doubt such innovative modes and their defamiliarising angles of vision stimulated Joyce's *Wanderlust* and Daedalian desire to escape the imprisoning labyrinth of Irish culture, or at least to reimagine it from a radically modernising, critical perspective. Lantern tours may also have influenced Joyce's repurposing of Homer's *Odyssey* as the topographical elsewhere on to which he maps his modern Ulysses' epic journey around Ireland's capital. Like geographical dissolving views, the features of Homer's mythic Mediterranean scenes shimmer in and out of parallel actions and locations around 1904 Dublin. (LUCERNA also lists several surviving sets remediating Ulysses' adventures through classical paintings, including the Cyclops, Circe and his homecoming to his wife, Penelope.)

There was complementary traffic to projected 'elsewhens', simulating the past more vividly than ever before. Historical lantern slides initiated virtual 'time-travel' (a cultural topos and technological mode of visualisation emerging across many media in this period, shared with Wells and other scientific romancers).[115] There was a particular boom during Joyce's schooling, on all sorts of subjects, sometimes incorporating photographic models and sets that resurrected the past ever more vividly (*EML*, p. 137). Lawrence's 1890 catalogue alone included no less than seventy-seven slides of key figures in Irish history. Such images could be skilfully threaded together into audio-visual narratives linking past and present, as the Rocketts note (*MLP&MPS*, p. 70). McCole has researched the many Irish examples shown in the peak years of 1897–98, produced by Lawrence and more radical sources, to remediate key historical events including the centenary of the 1798 rebellion.[116] Lanternism inevitably represented a conflicted history from both Unionist and Nationalist perspectives. In its photographic form, it constituted a new kind of documentary eyewitness, offering representations as though immediate perceptions of past or current events themselves. It also played a midwifing role at the birth of modern celebrity and political culture, arousing 'parasocial' relationships through its virtual presentation and contact with the famous and powerful. Politicians mediated by lantern included legendary figures in the Home Rule movement. Charles Stewart Parnell's vast phantom projects metaphorically over the political ironies of *Dubliners'* 'Ivy Day in the Committee Room', as well as hovering above Stephen's boyhood milieu in *Portrait*. Lawrence's 1890 catalogue also has to be considered against the backdrop of Nationalist campaigns, although it is unclear whether the proprietor was a staunch sympathiser or simply cashing in on another lucrative subject.[117] Parnell recurs as Stephen's political icon in *Portrait* from Dante's first mention that the green-backed brush in her press represents him, but he was also projected in slide portraits marketed by Lawrence along with prominent colleagues in the Irish Parliamentary Party.[118] Another Dublin firm, Mayne's, even manufactured a lantern biography of Parnell, possibly distributed by Lawrence with the leader's blessing, in recognition of its potential value to the cause.[119] Michael Davitt – another icon in *Portrait* from the first sight of Dante's red-backed brush – also featured in lantern sets alongside other Land League activists.

The mediated 'afterlife' of such figures, through the lantern's methods of photographic virtual presence and 'episodic' storytelling, bolstered their prominence in public memory, as reflected in their formative role in the media-cultural imaginary of Joyce's fictionalised self. 'Living Statuary' was a popular subject of artier photographic slides, and topical projections of celebrities taken from life also became a kind of portable waxworks, just waiting for film to endow its tableaux with the final appearance of animation: early film shows often began with a still image suddenly cranked into life, to the astonishment and delight of audiences. Appropriately, one of Dublin's earliest and cheapest programmes (projected by Animatograph, Paul's rival to the cinematograph) took place at the World's Fair Waxworks at 30 Henry Street in May 1896 (see *EIC*, pp. 39–40; *MLP&MPS*, p. 223), a venue that impresses Bloom regarding 'the infinite possibilities hitherto unexploited of the modern art of advertisement' (*Ulysses* 17.579–81). Still photographs apparently coming to life are also common in Joyce's fiction, as we shall see.

LANTERNISM AND RELIGION

Perhaps even more prominent than the lantern's role in politics was its role in missionary Christianity at home and abroad. 'Legitimate' spiritual use (as distinct from phantasmagorias and *séances*) expanded vastly, since late Victorian organised religion and popular education were closely interlinked (*EML*, pp. 250–1). Middle-class missionaries used lanternism to impress the 'natives' of darkest inner-city Britain, but also to display their conditions of poverty, child labour and slum housing to mobilise public opinion.[120] Although adopted with evangelical fervour by bodies such as the Temperance Movement and Salvation Army, by the late nineteenth century even the Anglican establishment and the Catholic Church were employing lanternism to spread rival gospels (*EML*, pp. 185–6). The Church Missionary Society set up a Lantern and Loan

Department in 1881, to exploit its conversionary power through the Church Army and its children's temperance wing, the Band of Hope. Countering Protestant campaigns, the Catholic Truth Society published many slide lectures on 'English Martyrs', 'English Church History', 'Catholic Hymns', 'Catholic Foreign Missions', 'Joan of Arc', 'Mysteries of the Rosary', 'The Stations of the Cross', and so on. The lantern was used to visualise biblical stories and conversion dramas, as well as illustrating sermons and prayers. Given increasing use for religious purposes in general, it is possible that 'Grace' alludes to its employment on retreats such as that which Kernan's friends take him on. If so, it is even more ironic that the 'Nausicaa' episode of *Ulysses*, whose 'Meaning' is 'Projected Mirage' and principal 'Organ', the eye (according to the Linati Schema), is also set during a service for a Catholic men's temperance retreat. Lantern shows may similarly have been aids to repentance for younger sinners, as at the school retreat that terrorises Stephen in *Portrait* with graphic visions of hell. Certainly, as the Rocketts note, by the 1860s the lantern had already 'become a staple in entertaining children not least in church-organised activities', even if records are more plentiful in relation to Protestant usage (*MLP&MPS*, p. 57). According to Condon, it was therefore only logical that temperance fêtes would also be a venue where Dublin's poorer children would see their first film shows (*EIC*, p. 22). By the end of the century, Irish lanternism was illustrating missionary lectures, proselytising and fundraising as much as anywhere else in the British Isles. Interestingly, the Catholic Truth Society's lantern lecture *Shrines of Our Lady* (1896) omits the controversial Knock apparitions in its presentation of Marian sites, although it includes Lourdes (which Joyce conflates with Knock in 'Circe').[121] However, that may be because its principal purpose was to demonstrate that Catholic pilgrimage remained as significant at English shrines as mainland Europe's.

The 'McBratney Hoard'

With extraordinary synchronicity, while I was researching this book a significant cache of lantern slides with a religious purpose (well over 200) were discovered in the ash pit of one of the Joyce family houses in Fairview, Dublin 3, by its owner Stephen D'Arcy in October 2012. The Joyces lived at No. 8 Royal Terrace (now Inverness Road) from 1900 to 1901, declining fortunes necessitating removal from one rented property to another. The house and locality are recalled in *Portrait* as Stephen walks along back lanes to University College and hears female patients wailing over the wall of St Vincent's Lunatic Asylum.

Stanislaus makes prominent mention of the ash pit, recalling how the Joyce children unearthed an edition of the gospels and a song-book.[122] Afterwards, their father joked, 'Have you tried the ash pit?', whenever anything was lacking. As archaeological and documentary data gathered by the National Museum team eventually confirmed, this hoard does not constitute a 'smoking gun' regarding direct evidence of Joyce's familiarity with lanternism; nonetheless, it adds significantly to a mass of circumstantial evidence that lantern practices were (literally) embedded in the culture of his time and in intimate proximity to him. As Jeremy Brooker, current chair of the MLS, put it to me, sometimes it is not the needle which matters, but the whole haystack.

Identification was a laborious process among jumbled examples of production, subjects and narrative forms, though with frequently tantalising Joycean resonances. Some were immediately recognisable as scenes from the life of Jesus, such as the Three Kings of the Epiphany, the source of Joyce's key aesthetic theory and calendrical setting of 'The Dead', or the miraculous feast at Cana. Others represented hymns and carols, such as 'Jerusalem the Golden' referenced in 'Circe' (15.1544 and 1271–3). Some sets were less easily identifiable, while others survived as random scenes with themes relating to morality and the Social Question, particularly the dangers of alcoholism and idleness. Labels indicated that some were procured from Lizar's, the well-known supplier of optical equipment in Glasgow and Belfast, but also Mason's of Dublin's Dame Street. Key online resources, such as the websites of LUCERNA and the MLS, have helped identify other titles.

Although the archaeologists' consultation with scholars (including Kevin Rockett and myself) revealed Joyce's fascination with pre-filmic media, they eschewed hasty conclusions. Rental records indicate that the Joyces quit 8 Royal Terrace by August 1901. In 1918 it was let to Thomas McBratney, who had been living next door at No. 10 from 1907. The 1911 Census revealed that McBratney (a Scot with Northern Irish roots) was a Presbyterian evangelist. Given the slides' religious and moralistic nature, he proved the most likely owner. The 1901 Census showed McBratney already working in Athlone as a 'colporteur' or distributor of religious tracts, before moving to Dublin as a lay preacher. The Presbyterian Historical Society of Ireland in Belfast yielded detailed information about McBratney's role in its Mission and accounts recording annual expenditure on slides and projectors.

How likely is it that Joyce, raised a Catholic, encountered lantern services by preachers such as McBratney? The answer is at least a possible yes. The Mission's stated purpose was to convert Catholics. Perhaps somewhat exaggeratedly, service reports note success in drawing large numbers of Catholics 'singing hymns most heartily', but also sporadic animosity. McBratney spent sixteen years touring fairs and markets, wherever he could gather a crowd, building a formidable reputation.[123] One photographic slide in the cache shows a provincial street scene during fair day, a rare example documenting contemporary Irish life, but also the kind of occasion that colporteurs targeted. Meetings were also held at Dublin's Custom House and Phoenix Park, locations familiar to Joyce. Though McBratney died in 1921, his family resided at Royal Terrace until the 1930s. His collection was most likely dumped during a clearout.

Significantly, the excavation revealed sets of late nineteenth- and early twentieth-century production coinciding with Joyce's youth and the temporal setting of virtually all his fiction before *Finnegans Wake*. Though often incomplete, they represent a range of genres from a typical evangelist's repertoire, including masterly hand-painted scenes from *Pilgrim's Progress* (based on David Scott's illustrations originally published in 1851).[124] This set (or one similar) was well known in Dublin. Solomon's, of 19 Nassau Street, advertised *Pilgrim's Progress* in its 1861 Christmas list. It was shown regularly at church and school events during the 1870s, remaining in circulation well beyond (*MLP&MPS*, p. 64). The set's form and usage indicate how seriously Bunyan's emphasis on 'Eyegate' and 'Eargate' was treated by evangelists through the adaptation of his work for lantern shows and other media (see Chapter 3 for moving panoramas on the same subject). Joseph Livesey, the father of teetotalism (insisting on total abstinence rather than temperance's moderation), advised following Bunyan's metaphors for campaign strategies, stressing the collaborative impact of words and images in new forms of mass communication which lantern shows epitomised.[125]

One of the ash pit's most illuminating life-model sets is *In His Steps*, subtitled 'What would Jesus do?' This follows a typical pattern of remediation from popular tracts and fiction. The message of American Charles M. Sheldon's 1896 book of the same title (a 30,000,000 bestseller) was particularly influential in the transatlantic Revivalist Movement at the turn of the century. *Ulysses* references Revivalism prominently in the historical figure of Alexander J(ohn). Dowie, the Scottish-born US evangelist, who liked to play the part of a modern Elijah, even dressing in biblical robes for photographs, and was also associated with international lantern campaigns.[126] Although Dowie never in fact visited Ireland (another key fact that Joyce strategically ignores so as to make a point), the handbill that Bloom receives in 'Lestrygonians' advertises a Revivalist meeting featuring Dowie under his Old Testament alias. Americanised 'Revivalise' is also one of the contemporary forms of English parodied in 'Oxen of the Sun', particularly its climactic paragraph, which references Dowie and his persona once again. In a parody of sectarian hysteria, a phantasmagoric materialisation of Dowie also bears witness against Bloom as his false messianic rival in 'Circe', denouncing him as 'the white bull mentioned in the Apocalypse. A worshipper of the Scarlet Woman' (15.1757–8).

The ash-pit set of *In His Steps* is a typical Revivalist narrative, produced between 1897 and 1904. It may correspond either to a service of song by Bamforth (forty-eight slides, 1899) or one by an unknown maker (twenty-nine slides, n.d.), listed on LUCERNA. *In His Steps* visualises the moral regeneration of a small town, after its complacent pastor is shocked by the death from starvation of an unemployed man during his sermon. The Revd Henry Maxwell realises the gulf between lip-service to Christian ideals and putting them into practice. The pastor inspires a cross-section of citizens (personifying key political, economic and cultural institutions) to pledge to make future decisions according to the principle: 'What would Jesus do?' They set about fighting the standard evils comprising 'the Social Question' (the target of many lantern campaigns): poverty, bad housing, drink and sexual immorality, as concentrated in the slum quarter, 'the Rectangle', aiming to build New Jerusalem on Earth. The full set ends with Maxwell experiencing a 'waking vision' of things to come. This is presented ekphrastically in the accompanying reading like a cross-sectional sequence of lantern pictures of Maxwell's acolytes achieving their local objectives, each prefaced by the phrase, 'He saw . . . '. Moreover, the spectacle expands into a panorama of worldwide missionary triumph. The vision fades, only to be climactically replaced by the millenarian image of Christ's Second Coming. Sheldon's swelling rhetoric clearly echoes lanternism's technical vocabulary and effects as successive images dissolve in and out of each other, ending with a final visual match to his title:

> He thought *he saw* the motto, 'What would Jesus Do?' inscribed over every church door, and written on every church member's heart. *The vision vanished. It came back clearer than before,* and *he saw* the Endeavour Societies all over the world carrying on their great processions . . . And *when this part of the vision slowly faded, he saw the figure of the Son of God* beckoning to him . . . *And the figure of Jesus grew more and more splendid.* He stood at the end of a *long flight of steps* . . .[127] [italics mine]

The whole ensemble of recitation, slides and music would have worked symbiotically as a typically portentous 'multi-media' live performance. It is thus also noticeably steeped in the kind of revelatory and millenarian imagery that Joyce parodies in *salvator mundi* Bloom's vision of 'New Bloomusalem' (*Ulysses* 16.1541–9) and the 'mockalyptic' End of the World which balloons out of Stephen's fracas with the Tommies (16.4660–715).

Also of Joycean resonance are stunning hand-coloured photographic slides from *Home! Sweet Home!* These correspond to another life-model set of forty-seven by Bamforth from 1892, performed as a musical service, from Mrs O. F. Walton's novel *Christie's Old Organ* (1874).[128] They are thus associated with the popular 1823 song (lyrics by John Howard Payne; melody, Sir Henry Rowley Bishop) mentioned twice in 'Sirens'. Significantly, Bloom reflects on the distracting emotional power of sentimental music as a modern Odysseus navigating his way through Dublin's psychological hazards towards his own *nostos* with Penelope's avatar, Molly, at No. 7 Eccles Street (11.1051 and 1258–9). In *Christie's Old Organ*, 'Home! Sweet Home!' plays recurrently to express the hero Christie's yearnings for lost family life. It is a typically mawkish life-model narrative about a street orphan who inherits the instrument of a dying barrel-organ grinder, which functions as a kind of emotional time machine for himself and others. Growing up to become a scripture reader, Christie re-encounters Mabel, the girl whose family showed him Christian charity in his destitution while he was busking outside their house. Mabel finally helps Christie find the 'home, sweet home' of his own that he always quested. Notably, the full set (as listed by LUCERNA) contains several effect slides in which organ music evokes flashbacks to Christie's mother's deathbed. As the accompanying text reads:

> A few months ago little Christie had a mother, and this was the last tune she sang. *It brought it all back to him: the bare, desolate room, the wasted form on the bed,* the dear, loving hand which had stroked his face so gently, and the sweet voice which had sung that very tune to him. *He could hear her even now . . .* [italics mine]¹²⁹

Less nostalgically, though in similar terms, Joyce refers to the tune of a street organ evoking memories of a dysfunctional home life in 'Eveline':

> She remembered the last night of her mother's illness; *she was again in the close dark room* at the other side of the hall and outside she heard a melancholy air of Italy. The organ player had been ordered to go away and given sixpence. She remembered her father strutting back into the sickroom saying:
> – Damned Italians! Coming over here!
> *As she mused the pitiful vision of her mother's life laid its spell* on the very quick of her being – that life of commonplace sacrifices closing in final craziness. (*Dubliners*, p. 28, italics mine)

Just as in a further slide Christie is requested not to disturb the house where another mother lies dying, Eveline's father rages against the organ grinder outside in his distress at his wife's demise. Maternal associations with a favourite song (insensitively trilled by Buck Mulligan in the present) also trigger Stephen's bitter-sweet flashback to the scene of his mother's deathbed in the first interior monologue of *Ulysses*:

> A cloud began to cover the sun slowly, shadowing the bay in deeper green. It lay behind him, a bowl of bitter waters. Fergus' song: I sang it above in the house, holding down the long dark chords. Her door was open: she wanted to hear my music. Silent with awe and pity I went to her bedside. She was crying in her wretched bed. For those words, Stephen: love's bitter mystery. (1.247–54)

In another slide, as Christie and the clergyman comfort the dying organist, the old man contemplates being 'washed white with the blood of the lamb', before entering paradise, paralleling the slogan of the Revivalese flyer thrust into Bloom's hand (8.10–11). Moreover, like *In His Steps*, the set and accompanying text display a sophisticated visual self-reflexiveness surprisingly common even in the most tear-jerking life-model narratives. Climbing the stairs to their garret, after the doctor informs him that 'Old Treffy' has just a month left to live, Christie has a vision of a desperate future back on the streets after the kindly organist passes away. Condensed into mere instants in the diegetic present, the vision appears as real as a succession of lantern images rapidly projecting before his eyes: 'And in the minute which passed before Christie reached the attic, he saw as in a sorrowful picture, what life would be to him without Old Treffy . . .'[130]

Understandably, there are numerous biblical slides in the cache, including Belshazzar's Feast just before the moving hand projects onto the wall, (Joseph's?) carpenter's workshop, the birth of Jesus, Mary and the infant on the donkey during the flight into Egypt, Jesus and the Apostles, the Sermon on the Mount (?), baptism, Satan's temptation of Christ on the mountain, Pontius Pilate, visions of angels and Jesus appearing in the clouds, and so on. Many remediate classical paintings, but also, symptomatic of the media-cultural imaginary in formation at this time, they feature photographically vivid details representing the world of classical antiquity, in the city, the desert and at sea, with which Joyce's Modernist narratives, especially *Ulysses*, would so intimately cohabit. One unidentified slide of an Arabian camel rider even evokes the exotic cover imagery of the guide to the 'Araby in Dublin' charity bazaar, on which the eponymous *Dubliners'* story is based.

A very different set from the ash pit is in cartoon-strip form. Set in a train carriage, it matches that cited on the MLS website as *A Railway Story with a Moral* (eight slides, in/before 1888), created by Alfred Pumphrey and credited with originating in the *Boy's Own* paper. The story is summarised in Walter Welford and Henry Sturmey's contemporary lanternist's *Handbook*: 'Two men quarrel about the window, one wants it open and the other shut, till eventually both tumble out of the door.'[131] The Band of Hope catalogues it as 'An amusing story with a moral, showing the necessity of bearing and forbearing', clearly endorsing it as suitable for the child audiences that the Band targeted.[132]

More secularly, by the 1880s some of the first serial comic-strip characters, notably the subversive anti-hero of the immensely popular *Ally Sloper's Half-Holiday*, featured in slide stories in similar format, thus typifying lanternism's transitional role in the strip's evolution into the genre of animated cartoons (the Sloper trick slides even contain animated effects, which foreshadow this).[133] Ally Sloper is mentioned in *Ulysses* along with other cartoon characters. In 'Scylla and Charybdis', Bloom is compared to the disreputable Sloper's Jewish sidekick, Ikey Moses, by Buck Mulligan (9.607). In 'Circe', Punch Costello morphs into a goblin 'with receding forehead and Ally Sloper nose', Sloper's Mr Punch-like, red, alcoholic's proboscis being his defining feature, in cheerful defiance of temperance strictures (15.2152). Sloper reappears in *Finnegans Wake* (29.26). *Ulysses* also mentions a popular stereotype of Irish ineptitude from Samuel Lover's 1842 comic novel, *Handy Andy*, also projected in strip-like sets. Bella Cohen's animated boot threatens Bloom in 'Circe' as he nervously tries to lace it up: 'If you bungle, Handy Andy, I'll kick your football for you' (15.2824).[134] Additionally, *Ulysses* references the American strip-cartoon character 'Dusty Rhodes', an archetypal down-and-out who survives all sorts of vicissitudes and influenced Chaplin's creation 'the Tramp', the most famous character in silent film and vital for the creation of Bloom as comic hero. In 'Oxen of the Sun', Dusty Rhodes appears in a mackintosh (14.1526). In 'Circe', he is itemised by the papal nuncio as one of Bloom's migratory Jewish forebears (15.1864–5), signalling the pedigree of remediated cartoon characters for Joyce's own comic hero.

'PERCOLATING UP': LANTERNISM AND MODERNISM

As the McBratney hoard's 'mixed programme' exemplifies, lantern shows, whether religious stories, comic tales or sentimental melodramas, were integrated with spoken verse, prose and song. Interplay between words and images was always central. Such narratives are also valuable historical documents. They negotiated with the tastes, desires and situations of popular audiences, but also screened the social and economic conditions that they endured, albeit usually offering emotional palliatives or spiritual consolation rather than radical reform. Notable exceptions include versions of *Christmas Day in the Workhouse*, from Sims's poem campaigning against the cruel hypocrisy of withholding 'outdoor relief' under the Victorian Poor Law (Lawrence's catalogue lists several titles remediating works by Sims). In the 1890 Bamforth set, Sims's 'Pauper John' is shown protesting against an institution that smugly expects the old man's gratitude for a hot dinner once a year, having allowed his wife to starve to death the previous Christmas because she refused to enter it and be separated from him. The present-day framing narrative gives way to a sequence of slides visualising Nance's demise in their garret though flashbacks. Sims's ballad also provides evidence of lanternism's use of a 'speaking picture' technique in which reciters on stage 'lip-synched' the dialogue of characters on screen.[135] It was also remediated in several early film versions, albeit with its radicalism gradually toned down.

The preoccupation of life-model sets with aspects of the Social Question overlaps noticeably with core issues addressed by the naturalistic and socially critical aspects of *Dubliners* – the dangers of poverty, exploitation, alcoholism, moral cowardice, traumatic loss of innocence, dysfunctional marital relationships, entrapment in domestic abuse, all exacerbated by Ireland's semi-colonial condition. Contemporary commentators enthused about the level of artistry sometimes achieved through the techniques of visual narration innovated by life-model pioneers:

> All the parts are made to tend to a dramatic whole, each picture dependent on the other and all the details illustrative of the complete work; the same characters recur again and again, moved in different tableaux with varied passions, one moral running through all; the beginning finding its natural climax in the end. (Redgrave, quoted in *MiTD*, p. 101)

Thus life-model narratives were not only film's immediate predecessors as a form of entertainment; as Cook points out, they also employed many cinematic devices that we have mistakenly come to think of as peculiar to film, particularly flashback, dynamic close-ups, vernacular surrealism and merging states of consciousness (*MiTD*, pp. 101–2).

For Marsh and Francis this raises a key question about the evolving creative relationship between screen culture and 'literature', with particular implications for understanding popular influences behind 'highbrow' innovations such as Joycean Modernism: 'why did visual story-telling . . . combining the projection of images with vocal narrative and sometimes music – develop to such a high degree in Britain, in the last quarter of the 19th century?'[136] They point to the Victorian passion for narrative painting and the prioritising of visual modes of communication by reformist movements; but also to the extraordinary visual imagination and multi-media adaptability of popular writers such as Dickens and Sims. Consequently, 'Lantern slide propaganda flowered into screen stories that required ever finer and finer psychological choices and visual breakdown of critical action – like the decision to reach for the bowl of cherries on the bar counter' in the Revd James Kirkton's *Buy Your Own Cherries*. Hence the old assumption 'that "high" literature inspired the development of screen language and screen culture' seems increasingly challengeable by new research. Evidence indicates influence flowing the other way too, suggesting an alternative conclusion that inverts traditional hierarchies: 'screen culture did not trickle down, but percolated up'.[137] In various slide adaptations of Kirkton's text from the 1870s to the 1920s (Lawrence's *Illustrated Catalogue* confirms at least one circulating in Dublin in 1890), the psychologically pivotal moment works exactly like a Joycean epiphany by radically defamiliarising an everyday, seemingly inadvertent gesture that prompts a moment of intense reflection. The drunkard, having reached for the pub landlady's fruitbowl without thinking and been rebuked, suddenly realises he could afford to share such home comforts with his neglected family if he changed himself by staying sober. Discussing life-model slides as one of the principal attractions of multi-media programmes at large-scale Salvation Army-organised events for children in the 1890s and 1900s, Karen Eifler points out that Miriam Hansen's argument that classical Hollywood constitutes the first exposure of the masses to a technically innovative, industrially produced 'vernacular modernism' can be challenged by evidence of the widespread impact of film's predecessor medium. Borrowing Hansen's criteria, she demonstrates that lanternism had already 'opened up hitherto unperceived modes of sensory perception and experience' for vast numbers of people.[138]

Slide juxtaposition could also be used for a kind of proto-montage to draw critical associations or contrasts between acts or situations separated 'in space, time or the social complex', as Storm Jameson put it in the 1930s, a key decade for modern, inter-medial documentary culture.[139] However, the slogan 'Socialism on Screen' actually goes back to 1892 in the context of Social Democratic Federation magic lantern shows displaying 'shots from the camera at the old order of things'.[140] During that decade, the campaigner from the socialist *Clarion* newspaper, William Palmer, toured the UK in his professional alias as 'Whiffly Puncto' with an agitprop lantern show, *Merrie England*, based on Robert Blatchford's 1893 bestseller. Palmer alternated slides depicting extremes of wealth and deprivation, to (in Bottomore's words) 'create a visual dialectic to counter gross inequality and the status quo'.[141] This strategy gave rise to socialist camera clubs and photo-agencies supplying lantern images of a similar type, and even a periodical, *The Deadly Parallel*, taking its name from their practice. An advertisement for such hard-hitting slides in 1907 summed this strategy up: 'Everywhere you go in the world's richest city, you meet life's "deadly parallels." Sumptuous wealth on one hand: abject poverty on the other. These two great contrasts are presented most forcibly by London's two great classes of unemployed – the exploited poor, the idle rich.'[142] Lantern shows based on taking the camera out on the streets, thus going beyond the studio-bound realism of life-model slides, also deployed a kind of proto-montage to construct a cross-sectional panorama of contemporary urban society, as in the Riley Brothers' *Street Life: Or People We Meet* (c. 1887), comprising over fifty slides of different social scenes and professions. Its intention was 'to bring you face to face with a number of people' by virtual means, 'some poor, others by no means wanting in this world's goods – who claim no relationship with each other, but who, collectively, give life, animation and colour to the gloomy streets of our great cities and towns'.[143] Such images, aggregating into the spectacle of what *Stephen Hero* calls 'an entire community in action', had their equivalent in Joyce's fictional cross-sections of citizens in *Dubliners* and in 'Wandering Rocks', *Ulysses'* most cross-sectional chapter. The principle was extended through the ironic juxtapositions of film montage in agitprop cinema between the world wars, which also figure prominently in the Big City documentary genre (see the detailed comparison with Joyce's use of a kind of critical parallel editing within and between sections of 'Wandering Rocks' in Chapter 3).

The popular verse and fiction that lantern melodramas were based on also cautioned against moral perils and social vices familiar to Joyce's Dubliners, highlighting the gender factor by frequently featuring wives or orphaned daughters at the fulcrum of domestic crisis and at the mercy of tyrannical and drunken fathers like Eveline's. Such narratives included *White Slaves of London* (Chatham Pexton, twenty-four slides, c. 1894), from Fannie Eden's mawkishly sub-Dickensian novel of 1887.[144] This cross-sectioned the plights of a tenement's inhabitants – among them two young seamstresses struggling to stay respectable and keep house while caring for a mother crazed by her own life of similarly repetitive toil. Similarly, *Poverty's Pupil*, by L. E. Tiddemann (1908),[145] epitomised tracts addressed specifically to working girls like Eveline and likewise featured the motherless daughter of a feckless inebriate, vulnerable to ruination (see *MiTD*, pp. 104, 106–7). Such adaptations presented clear-cut moral choices both to characters and audiences, but usually (with honourable exceptions such as Sims and Puncto), rather than radically challenging the causes behind the conditions that put them at risk of falling, they rewarded the impregnably virtuous or newly repentant with closing visions of Heaven alone. Conversely, Joyce deliberately leaves the psychological and social complexity of his heroine's ultimate fate unresolved: whether Eveline remains trapped by her sense of duty as good Catholic daughter, or risks eloping to Buenos Ayres (a contemporary byword for trafficking into prostitution) and expanding her life chances. Hence Joyce throws the burden of judgement back onto his readers' sense of social injustice and desire for reform. As Mullin has shown, the subtext of 'Eveline' problematises the contemporary moral panic about 'white slavery' and generalised fears about the corruption of Ireland's youth by foreign seductions. Similarly, tracts warning about the dangers posed to unprotected young women were common at the time. Illustrations from one, Clifford G. Roe's *The Horror of the White Slave Trade* (1911), posed life models in a cautionary episodic 'faction' that illustrated the tactics used to entrap vulnerable girls seeking romantic escape. Hence its sequential images are exactly like slide sets accompanying lantern lectures and indeed may have been projected in this format at public talks.[146]

LITERATURE AND LANTERNISM

Although the lantern's staple sources were popular texts (which thus reached even the illiterate poor), by the mid-1890s its ambitions had swelled to epic historical fictions such as Lew Wallace's *Ben Hur: A Tale of the Christ* (1880) (with or without copyright permission). LUCERNA lists an 1895 painted set of seventy-two slides by Riley Brothers, including the chariot race scene which would become the visual climax of successive stage and Hollywood adaptations.[147] Clearly such slide remediations were the immediate predecessors of the one-reeler 'pocket epics' screened at the Volta, such as *Nero: A Sensational Story of Ancient Rome* (Italy, 1909) and *Quo Vadis or the Way of the Cross* (USA, 1909). Thus they may also have piqued Joyce's interest in reworking ancient classics in startlingly modern, inter-medial mode earlier than film could have done. (*Ben Hur* remained unfilmed until Harry T. Morley and Sidney Olcott's 1907 adaptation, according to the IMDb. Nevertheless, classical themes were instrumental to the development of early film narrative, according to Christie.)[148]

However, cinema proper was nearly twenty years old when Joyce published his first major work in 1914. This returns us to the question: why does *Dubliners* invoke such an apparently 'outmoded' technology, albeit one that passed on so much to film and continued to coexist with it for at least two decades as a major cultural medium? Arguably, just as *Ulysses*, which takes place in 1904, references the mutoscope peepshow rather than cinematograph or bioscope, *Dubliners* references lantern shows (as does *Portrait*, which covers 1882–1902) because they were still more common and influential in the late Victorian and early Edwardian Dublin in which its stories were mostly written and set than film had become. Most of *Dubliners* was composed by 1904–05 and even its last story, 'The Dead', by 1907. This may, therefore, simply confirm another aspect of Joyce's scrupulous historical and psychological accuracy. At this time, lanternism, far from being anachronistic, would have played a greater part in the lives and media-cultural imaginary of Dubliners such as the characters he describes.

Of course, this does not necessarily discount possible influence from early film on *Dubliners*' narrative techniques. However, clearly any Dubliner around 1904 (fictional or actual) would likely have had more limited experience of film shows than that accumulated by their author, who reconstructed that year in his subsequent fiction up to and including *Ulysses*. Although 'living pictures' were first projected in Dublin on 20 April 1896, at the Star of Erin Theatre of Varieties, the Volta Cinematograph, opened by Joyce in December 1909, was nonetheless one of Ireland's first to exhibit continuous programmes in a specially adapted building. This fact requires that we consider how much of the *cinematicity* in Joyce's presentation of his Dubliners, how they think and visualise their world, might derive from technologies and entertainment practices remediated by film. Only thus can we properly appreciate the richness and creativity of his methods in their 'connectivity' with the inter-medial cultural ecology of his time.

'HER IMAGE CAME BETWEEN ME AND THE PAGE': FRAMING,
PROJECTION AND SUPERIMPOSITION IN *DUBLINERS*

There are many specific ways in which lanternism is evoked in *Dubliners*' techniques, themes and leitmotifs. Frequently Joyce's images have a 'detached' quality, often intruding from one context into another through effects similar to projection, framing and even superimposition. In particular, they suggest that the lantern played a key role in developing Joyce's Modernist method for focalising subjective consciousness. In 'Araby', for example, the protagonist-narrator constantly peers through grubby window panes and letter boxes and under drawn-down blinds. (Stephen is also a watcher behind blinds – see *Portrait*, p. 62, for example.) The story contrasts socially and visually constricted spaces with the potential for imaginative escape into its eponymous elsewhere: both a real bazaar and an imaginary portal into more expansive vistas with the virtual appeal of exotic geography or magical 'Arabian Nights' slides. (Eastern fairy tales were regular attractions in children's programmes, especially those offered by bodies such as the Band of Hope, but probably others too.)[149] Similarly, the opening image from Bamforth's 1897 ten-slide song set *The Holy Shrine*, on LUCERNA, carries the visionary caption, 'Methought I was in Araby, within a fair palace'. As Denis Condon, Stephanie Rains and Katherine Mullin have shown, the latest visual technologies and moving image entertainments were among the main attractions of the series of giant charity bazaars launched by 'Araby in Dublin' in May 1894, inevitably making them a logical venue for some of Ireland's earliest film shows a few years later and a much greater influence on Joyce's work than a cursory reading of his deflating motif in the story 'Araby' would suggest.[150] The bazaars also included spectacular innovations in slide projection. The 'Ierne' Old Ireland-themed bazaar of May 1895 featured 'an outdoor lantern display of a character hitherto unattempted in Dublin'.[151] At 'Cyclopia' in May 1896, a giant magic lantern 'tower' projected slides a prodigious 150 feet on to the largest outdoor screen yet seen in Ireland, at 30 feet square (outdoing outdoor shows in Dublin for political agitprop, as discussed below).[152]

Similarly, in Joyce's story, the tension between repressive circumstances and visionary projection comes to be focused on the adolescent narrator's awakening sexuality through his continuously recollected and magnified image of Mangan's sister. As the boy watches her obsessively, Joyce deploys a phrase that neatly severs her outline from external vision and imprints it in his memory like a photograph: 'I kept her brown figure always in my eye' (*Dubliners*, p. 20). This results in superimposition effects comparable to the face of the dead priest haunting the boy in 'The Sisters', hovering between private pleasure and morbid distraction: 'At night in my bedroom and by day in the classroom *her image came between me and the page* I strove to read' (*Dubliners*, p. 20; italics mine). Such phantasmagoric techniques were remediated for psychological effects in early film. A perfect match to 'Araby' occurs in René Clair's *Le Fantôme du Moulin Rouge* (1925). In this the protagonist Julien Boissel is similarly distracted by the detached image of his unobtainable lover's face appearing multiple times over documents he strives to concentrate on. Thus *Dubliners'* imaginative economy is marked by projecting ekphrastic visions over 'background' views in layering effects. They continuously disrupt diegetic unities of space, time and scale, breaking into other contexts as 'high resolution' pictures, sharply separated from their surroundings to an almost hallucinatory degree, like glowing photographic slides or inserts.

With the girl's highly charged image in mind, the narrator awaits his uncle's return for pocket money to visit Araby. As he gazes through yet another window frame at her house front opposite, there is a further superimposition effect. The same image blots out the building, as though projected (Joyce's synonymous verb is 'cast') over its frontage like an outdoor lantern show such as Cyclopia's or lantern agitprop on central Dublin's streets by Nationalists:[153] 'I may have stood there for an hour, *seeing nothing but the brown-clad figure cast by my imagination*, touched discreetly by the lamplight at the curved neck, at the hand upon the railings and the border below the dress' (*Dubliners*, p. 22; italics mine). Who can say whether the enlarged image does not stem from Joyce's actually seeing slides projected in hugely magnified form against Dublin's buildings. Photographically precise repetition of close-up details from their one direct encounter (described on p. 21) – hand grasping railing spike and lace fringe of petticoat – together with the implicit personification of the light source highlighting them – 'touched discreetly' – intensifies the original scene's implicit eroticism and gives the acts of looking and remembering virtually haptic qualities, as if the boy's eye were reaching out into the image to grasp the object of his desire. Indeed this suggestively three-dimensional quality also recalls the peepshow illusionism of hand-held stereoscopes or even perhaps large-scale stereoscopic projection in Analyticon shows. Certainly, exactly the same image is 're-projected', to borrow Stephen's term from *Portrait*, against different backgrounds by Joyce. Simultaneously, our gaze is directed to features rendered particularly suggestive by its enlargement, like a lantern showman pointing out details, but withholding explicit comment, throwing the burden of interpretation back on the audience. Joyce thus innovated a cinematic template for representing modern subjectivity and its unconscious susceptibilities by simultaneously presenting both *what* and *how* his focaliser sees – in both external and internalised senses – using strategies dependent on the contemporary media culture from which film also gestated.

FLASHBACK IN *DUBLINERS*

Other devices from magic lantern narratives shed further light on techniques in *Dubliners*. For example, Joyce's masterly use of 'flashback' in numerous stories several years before the earliest surviving examples through film editing is probably influenced by the chronological shuffling in lantern shows. Eveline's dilemma is structured around 'cuts' within the young girl's memory between contrasting moments. Analepsis and prolepsis have ancient pedigrees as literary tropes, but Joyce's extraordinary narrative economy thus compresses Eveline's whole emotional prehistory and inner psychological struggle – between daughterly commitment and desire to escape – into a few pages.

Eveline experiences flashbacks: to her recent meeting with Frank ('How well she remembered the first time she had seen him', *Dubliners*, p. 27); their subsequent courtship and her father's interdict ('I know these sailors chaps', p. 27); and back to the present, as Joyce focuses fading light on the matter, literally, in hand: farewell notes to her father and brother ('The white of two letters in her lap grew indistinct', p. 27). Then comes a contrasting flashback to older, fonder memories of her father larking at a picnic with 'her mother's bonnet' (p. 27), betokening intensifying vacillation. Divergent recollections visualise Eveline's self-division – monstration or 'showing' doing away with narrative commentary or 'telling'. This is exacerbated by a street organ (musical evocations of memory were common in lantern shows, as *Christie's Old Organ*, discussed above, exemplifies), triggering a further reminiscence. Here Joyce's grammar appears to mimic a photo-filmic 'eternal present' (the medium's abolition of narrative tenses), a device ever more frequent in later stories, but arguably derived as much from the 'virtual presentness' of past action represented by flashback in life-model slides as from cinema proper: 'She remembered the last night of her mother's illness; *she was again* in the close dark room at the other side of the hall and outside she heard a melancholy air of Italy' (*Dubliners*, p. 28; italics mine). The blacked-out 'close dark room' emphasises how Eveline seems incarcerated in the metaphorical projection box of her own memory. Her will changes emotional polarity again in a summative recollection of the fate that she fears repeating, presented like a rapidly substituted slide sequence or 'accelerated montage': 'As she mused the pitiful vision of her mother's life laid its spell on the very quick of her being – that life of commonplace sacrifices closing in final craziness' (*Dubliners*, p. 28). This last picture deflects Eveline back to her *matinée* image of Frank and their planned elopement. Following an ellipsis, Joyce's third-person narrator then 'flashes forward' (*prolepsis*) to Dublin's dockside station, though whether to Eveline's actual or imagined near future is deliberately unclear for the conscience-stricken girl, fearing the 'sinfulness' of her desires and the honourabless of Frank's intentions.

It seems perfectly possible therefore to describe the story's structure as cinematic shuffling of diegetic continuity. However, that places Joyce ahead of the game in terms of what film had actually achieved to date. 'Eveline' was written in 1904,[154] but the first true filmic flashback – achieved by editing together shots from different 'times' – is often attributed to *After Many Years*, Griffith's 1908 adaptation of Tennyson's monodrama, *Enoch Arden*. Griffith cuts from a desert island shot of his shipwrecked sailor kissing a locket, to a medium close-up of Enoch's wife with outstretched arms on their porch at home, contracted from a wider shot shown before he departs at the beginning.[155] Griffith subsequently elaborated the flashback into a trademark narrative device, especially for psychologically determining moments and moral dilemmas such as Eveline's.[156] It could be argued, therefore, that Joyce anticipated, rather than was influenced by, such film practices.

However, Maureen Turim's specialist study confirms that the flashback's evolution is 'tied to other devices in the narrative arts'.[157] From the 1860s, influenced by the development of composite photographs and scene-within-scene stage sets,[158] lantern slides often signified multiple spatio-temporality by superimposing or inserting images-within-images, visualising characters' thoughts, memories or fantasies. Thus slide-makers constructed a synthetic space and time from segments of photographed realities – as film would also do later – and with surprising sophistication. It is important to grasp that lanternism's innovative techniques were not confined to or derived from a cultural avant-garde, but were used in sets dramatising popular verse and song, as in the following examples. Bamforth's 1898 set for the ballad *Robin Adair* in LUCERNA shows Robin's abandoned fiancée slumped at home in the foreground, while the back wall of her room dissolves into memories of dancing with him at the ball where they first met.[159] Similarly, Bamforth's *The Scent of the Lilies* (1903) opens with olfactory association – an old man sits forlornly in his parlour, flowers in hand, as above him appears a vision of his lost youthful self and dead love meeting on a summer riverbank, before the course of their ill-starred passion is shown retrospectively. Bamforth's *What Are the Wild Waves Saying?* (1898) depicted a proto-surreal dream time. It is based on a ballad mentioned in 'Sirens', which Bloom recollects while watching barmaids holding a shell to their ears to hear the 'singing' of the ocean (11.945-9). In this context, it evokes the deadly song of the sirens, which lured ships on to the rocks in the *Odyssey*. The ballad was inspired by an incident in Dickens's *Dombey and Son*, and the slide shows a storm-tossed sailing ship apparently crashing through the bedroom wall of a sleeping brother and sister (see further commentary and reproductions in *MiTD*, pp. 102, 106, 109, 113 and facing p. 116). In Stephen's fever dream about Parnell's death in *Portrait*, undulating shadows projected by firelight similarly appear to dissolve the infirmary wall into a vision of his own maritime funeral.

Bamforth and Co. championed this highly inventive type of life-model narrative, but its example was widely reported and followed by others. If, as Griffith famously asserted, film techniques enabled directors to 'photograph thought',[160] that process was already well underway in lanternism. Moreover, the literary source of Griffith's allegedly breakthrough flashback, *Enoch Arden*, had already been adapted several times for the lantern, at least once as a photographic life-model set.[161] Even lantern narratives that lacked ambitious dissolves or composite photo-techniques implied space-time shifts between episodic images. These could be projected out of strict chronological sequence, or displayed as multiple strands of action unfolding simultaneously in different places, the showman's commentary suturing them diegetically.

Other technical and thematic details point to lantern narratives in 'Eveline'. Joyce's heroine is also situated against open curtains before a window. Like so many of *Dubliners'* focalising protagonists, she is a watcher through a mediating frame, Joyce foregrounding vision on several planes at once, as lantern narratives often did. Eveline's window evokes scenes from her past and possible future as if screened within it. Intriguingly, *The Curtain: Or, A Peep into the Future* (sixteen slides, in/before 1897), manufactured by T. J. and W. F. Piggot, used its internal framing motif at a meta-level to reveal elaborate *two-way* space-time shifts on to other scenes. The subtitled moralising verse accompanying it (c. 1894) describes a mysterious screen on which the heroine's whole past and future existence appears in a succession of views, fading in and out as its drapes rise and fall. In one slide, a girl in white muslin stands in the foreground gazing at her future self's moonlit wooing by an athletic beau (see description and illustration in *MiTD*, p. 103 and facing p. 116). Another slide shows the same girl reminiscing over a cosy childhood scene before her present crisis, captioned, 'All happy then . . .' (*EML* p. 100). Such methods were widely emulated, and it is tempting to speculate whether Joyce saw *The Curtain* or something generically similar in structure and theme.[162]

Moreover, as Turim puts it, '[i]n all probability the earliest flashbacks in film used this image-within-image technique' derived from lantern and theatre, rather than edited cuts in time.[163] In Dickens and Wilkie Collins's collaborative melodrama *The Frozen Deep* (1856), for example, a polar explorer sees a vision of his fiancée back home in another set revealed at the rear of the stage. The theatre undoubtedly prefigured techniques for subjective vision scenes that would be made easier by composite photographic techniques. This entailed a doubling of images, by which the past could be located in the background of the pro-filmic scene, through slides, rear-projection or double-exposure by matting. Such techniques were common by 1902–03 (indeed Méliès was already using them by the turn of the century, though usually for fantasies). Examples clearly demonstrating this stage-connection include Ferdinand Zecca's *Histoire d'un crime* (1901), which famously features a robber's guilty dream depicting what led him to murder. This was created by building a second set into the back wall of his prison cell, so that it appears to hover above him, just like insert images in the popular lantern set *The Soldier's Dream*. In Edwin S. Porter's 1903 film *Life of an American Fireman* (itself remediating lantern narratives on the same subject), the hero is shown sleeping while his premonitory dream about disaster appears to the right as a similar circular insert. Among increasing numbers of feature films screened in Dublin around the time Joyce wrote his stories was James Williamson's *Remorse* (also 1903). Significantly it was also adapted from a play in which a murderer frames another man, but repents in court after seeing an insert vision of injustice (for Dublin screenings of *Remorse*, see *MLP&MPS*, p. 249). Hence as Turim concludes,

> If such vision sequences were as common as they appear to be, based on surviving films of this period and on accounts of films of this period, one suspects flashbacks as well as dreams were indicated by such techniques in the early cinema – particularly in British, French, and American films where we have evidence of these inserted images.[164]

It also seems possible that Joyce drew on similar strategies from lantern shows for effects which paralleled or anticipated shifts in temporality and consciousness depicted on film.

LANTERNISM IN 'THE DEAD'

Lantern spatio-temporal shuffling may have contributed to the cinematicity of other stories too. As if in homage to this, Edna O'Brien's 'Lantern Slides', her 'sequel' to 'The Dead', reworks Joyce's sequences of flashbacks and flashforwards into memories and thoughts as 'rapid succession[s]' of lantern images rather than alluding to film or television techniques as might be expected in 1990. O'Brien uses deliberate cultural anachronism to satirise a post-colonial, 'Celtic Tiger' Ireland very different from Joyce's time. O'Brien's narrator tells us that 'a hundred lantern slides ran through their minds', as her characters review their predicament.[165] In Joyce's original story, before Gretta shatters Gabriel's misconception that she shares his ardour through simultaneously reliving their passionate courtship in her own mind, Joyce sustains his focaliser's emotional trajectory through a rapid sequence of illuminated memories with associative jumps in space and time, as Gabriel continues to project his own feelings onto Gretta on their way to the hotel: 'Moments of their secret life together burst like stars . . .' – a breakfast love letter, a romantic rail journey, a winter outing (see *Dubliners*, p. 168). It is worth noting again how the existential immediacy of Joyce's phrasing parallels the 'eternal present' of photographic temporality as presented in both life-model slides and film. Gabriel's present excitement gives the impression that he '*was again* in a cab with her, galloping to catch the boat, galloping to their honeymoon' (*Dubliners*, p. 169; italics mine).

Conversely, after Gretta's revelation, Gabriel attempts to backtrack and analyse what triggered his fatal delusion that led to the 'riot of emotions' she has just quelled. Joyce presents Gabriel's sobered retrospection on the evening in similarly condensed flashback. This also prompts readers to review their first impressions of the narrative's events more critically and dig deeper into Joyce's subtext:

> From whence had it proceeded? From his aunts' supper, from his own foolish speech, from the wine and dancing, the merry-making when saying good-night in the hall, the pleasure of the walk along the river in the

snow. Poor Aunt Julia! She too, would soon be a shade with the shade of Patrick Morkan and his horse. He had caught that haggard look upon her face for a moment when she was singing . . . (*Dubliners*, p. 175)

And in ironic contrast with the elated sequence of courtship memories that caused Gabriel to visualise a scene of rekindled passion at the hotel, he then flashes forward to a very different future – the inevitable family regathering for his aunt's funeral: 'Soon, perhaps, he would be sitting in that same drawing-room, dressed in black, his silk hat on his knees . . .' (*Dubliners*, p. 175).

Such personal existential re-evaluation, triggered by involuntary memory, but also anticipating possible futures, was narrated ever more ingeniously in life-model sets. In the Dickens-like *Dan Dabberton's Dream* (York and Son, Bridgewater, c. 1887),[166] for example, a typically incorrigible boozer falls into a morose stupor on Christmas Eve, significantly after resetting the clock. With the protagonist remaining visible in the foreground of each slide, the hearth behind gradually transforms into a visionary frame for 'the theatre of Dan's dreams' (*MiTD*, p. 111; figure 1.3). Dan's past intemperance flashes by in a series of images, as alcohol takes its deadly toll first on his mother, before impoverishing his wife and daughter (figure 1.4). The images then flash forward to their inevitable future of destitution and final tragedy, upon which

Figure 1.3 'He sleeps! he sleeps!' Slide 6 from *Dan Dabberton's Dream* (York and Son, Bridgewater, c. 1887). From the illuminago collection, by kind permission of Ludwig Vogl-Bienek.

Figure 1.4 'On one of the beds lies the body of a middle-aged Woman'.
Slide 16 from *Dan Dabberton's Dream* (York and Son, Bridgewater, c. 1887).
From the illuminago collection, by kind permission of Ludwig Vogl-Bienek.

Dan reawakens on cue back in the present moment in the slide foreground as wife and daughter return home, determined to prevent that shocking vision by reforming himself (for images, see LUCERNA website).

Such moralising tales were produced in great numbers, though what 'Victorian audiences took for granted' in their vividness and narrative dynamism can seem astonishingly modern to our post-filmic sensibility (*MiTD*, p. 112). Again, Joyce's closure in stories such as 'Eveline' and 'The Dead' is much more provisional than the didactic endings of lantern shows, though sharing their techniques. The future of Gabriel's marriage is left open, though with a redemptive hint that his new-found consciousness of universal mortality might have a positive outcome in the longer term if his capacity for empathy and self-awareness genuinely grows.

These Boots Were Made for Talking: Lanternism's Language of Things

The Victorian commentator cited by Cook celebrated another novelty in life-model modes of narration: 'the wonderful way in which all the objects in the picture tend to illustrate the story' (*MiTD*, p. 101). Already in painted sets such as Cruikshank's *The Bottle*, progressive deletion of familiar domestic possessions speaks volumes. By means of successive dissolving views of the same parlour setting, all home comforts gradually disappear, silently recounting the occupants' descent into destitution because of father's boozing.[167] The slide reading for *John Hampton's Home* (York and Sons, six slides, n.d.), one of the temperance narratives stocked by Lawrence under a variant spelling, suggests that the same techniques were reversible to indicate sobriety's material benefits.[168] Objects in lantern shows could thus be used less like traditional theatrical props, instead foreshadowing how close-up details picked out from their surroundings would become metonymically suggestive of characters' motivations and states of mind in films. At the end of 'Eveline', the protagonist is paralysed with indecision at the port barrier. Her posture is an excellent example of how Joyce monstrates and links stories visually by foregrounding leitmotifs with variations, like recurrent symbolic close-ups in lantern slides or films: 'She gripped with both hands at the iron railing' (*Dubliners*, p. 29). As in 'Araby' (and, later, 'Two Gallants'), images of railings simultaneously highlight desire and its blocking; in this case, railings are a final, impassable barrier both to Eveline's body and, more importantly, her mind.

Moreover, in some photographic sets symbolic props displaced human actors altogether in a form of prosopopoeia. For example, magnified articles of clothing told tales about wearers absent from the frame in the Riley Brothers' *A Strong Contrast* (1892). They betray the sobriety or fecklessness of their respective owners: close-ups of two captioned hats in very different conditions shown in successive slides say, 'I am worn by a man who works and thinks'/'And I by one who don't and drinks'; similarly contrasting boots proclaim, 'We guard his feet from damp and dust'/'Like him we are always on the "bust."' Coats and bottles inform the audience in similar ways.[169] Strikingly, the drunkard's casually discarded boots – one left precariously upright, the other collapsed – assume a pose like that noted in Gretta's footwear as Gabriel looks down on her unconscious form at the hotel: 'His eyes moved to the chair over which she had thrown some of her clothes. A petticoat string dangled to the floor. One boot stood upright, its limp upper fallen down: the fellow of it lay upon its side' (*Dubliners*, p. 175). Thus Gretta's drooping boot objectifies Gabriel's mood of sexual and existential deflation, while its counterpart visually matches her emotional collapse upon the bed. Similarly, in 'A Little Cloud', Chandler 'glance[s] nervously' around the marital parlour after returning home from being tantalised by Gallagher, its 'pretty' but 'mean' furniture mirroring his sense of sexual entrapment and thwarted ambition (*Dubliners*, p. 63). Though didactic lantern objects usually spoke in less subtle terms than those monstrated by Joyce, this description nonetheless suggests a technique of visual symbolism avoiding any need for direct narrative commentary on his focalisers' emotional state. Thus *Dubliners* is already characterised by what Alan Spiegel calls 'adventitious details',[170] indiscriminately picked up as if by the camera's eye and indicating a new, epiphanic relation of objects to fiction's narrative drive and semiotic economy. Joyce's close-up details act as silent statements about the crisis in the Conroys' marriage. Paradoxically, even though Joyce presents *what* Gabriel sees as if merely part of the action's objective context captured photographically, *how* he sees it (and what that implies) is specific to Gabriel's consciousness: Gretta's clothes bear the same relation to the utility of objects in earlier fiction as the 'dead, deracinated theatrical prop' does to the dynamically 'animated' film object, in Keith Cohen's terms.[171]

As was recognised by early commentators such as Vachel Lindsay, film appeared to create a new kind of symbolic and affective interchange between people and 'furniture'.[172] However, visualisation of objects in lantern shows may have helped Joyce enrich the surface naturalism of *Dubliners*' style of 'scrupulous meanness' with an emergent form of cinematicity well before it. Griffith called such things, monstrating a character's (often unconscious) thoughts by suggestively arresting their vision, 'objects of attention'.[173] Arguably, both Joyce and film inherited this tendency from the multitude of speaking objects highlighted in lantern images themselves or picked out by showmen. Indeed, in the cinematicity of Joyce's Modernism, objects would become increasingly 'vocal' in ways that monstrated human feelings and dilemmas, climaxing in the literally talking animated boots, buttons, fans, bars of soap and so on encountered in 'Circe's' phantasmagoria. Joyce's writing became ever more finely tuned to the living quality of psychologically 'overdetermined' things seen in close-up.[174]

'The Sisters' adds weight to the hypothesis that Joyce's camera-like eye for tellingly contingent details was sharpened by life-model slides. Its boy narrator is distracted from proper solemnity in his priestly mentor's darkened laying-out room by indecorous details in Nannie's dress, betokening the self-sacrificing neglect of a life dedicated to her brother's vocation. These details are picked out by light diffracted from the lace end of a blind with directorial precision: 'I noticed how clumsily her skirt was hooked at the back and how the heels of her cloth boots were trodden down all to one side' (*Dubliners*, p. 7). Seeing incongruities in photographically enlarged form had psychological impact. In *Robin Adair*, according to Cook, the seducer's splendid evening dress clashes with his glaringly cracked boots (*MiTD*, p. 109; see also the set in LUCERNA). Whether this detail resulted from an amateurish continuity error or a tight wardrobe budget, it speaks volumes in a context of betrayal by dashing idols with symbolic 'feet of clay'. Similarly, 'The Sisters' confronts readers with an unsettling subtext which overdetermines every image, but is never fully uncoverable. The cheerless 'empty fireplace' into which the characters stare in silence at the end (*Dubliners*, p. 7), obscurely conscious that something is being repressed, evokes Joyce's obsession with the shadow show of Plato's cave, which similarly distracts his prisoners from seeing clearly by the light of day. Perhaps rather backhandedly, it also evokes the role of fireplaces in lantern slides as frames-within-frames for projecting a character's innermost thoughts in conversion narratives such as *Dan Dabberton's Dream*. Consequently, Joyce's readers are faced with having to fill in the story's ultimate visual void themselves. Hence Joyce's defamiliarising close-ups of everyday actions or things, with their suggestion that seemingly random gestures or perceptions may be unconscious Freudian 'parapraxes' leading to epiphanies,[175] were monstrated in ways paralleling the lantern's methods of visual storytelling and how they would be pushed further by film.

Joyce and the Phantasmagoria

One lantern tradition in particular converges with critical ambivalence towards its magical appeal in *Stephen Hero* and 'Grace'. It became particularly associated with apparent supernaturalism, as Heard and others historicise. By Joyce's time, it had a venerable reputation as what Alison Chapman calls a 'technology of the uncanny',[176] especially for the 'phantasmagoria' (from Gk. *phantasm* + *ageirein*, 'gathering of ghosts'). The term was coined in 1792 by the German/ Brabantine entrepreneur and 'natural magician' Philidor for his 'rational entertainment', as he described it. Following Enlightenment anti-clerical principles, Philidor promised to simultaneously demonstrate and unmask the tricks of self-proclaimed sorcerers and occult societies to revolutionary Paris.[177] However, the materialisation of moving spooks on concealed gauze roller-screens or swirling smoke was made particularly famous by the Belgian showman 'Robertson' (Étienne-Gaspard Robert). Robertson refined the phantasmagoria's techniques from 1798, effectively professionalising the itinerant lantern show as a new form of mass entertainment, projected in darkness to maximise audience suggestibility, a practice maintained into the film era. At the ruinous Convent des Capuçines (symbolising the deposition of Catholicism's *ancien régime*), Robertson used back-projection by wheeled 'Fantascope', breaking with traditional itinerant shows by concealing the apparatus of projector and screen. This enabled spectres and decapitated heads to spontaneously hover towards audiences, recede and diminish, rise from the earth, turn and disappear back into it, walk in and out of walls and so on, so that startled audiences reputedly struck at them with walking sticks.[178] The phantasmagoria fashioned 'a complete gothic, theatrical experience' (*EML*, p. 228), immersing every sense, but also making audiences doubt the evidence of their senses and the infallibility of vision. Despite the rationalist alibi that shows were based on the new wonders of science, phantasmagorists effectively profited from the persistence of ambiguity through their mixture of terror and forbidden thrills. This tension survives into twenty-first-century entertainment media, exploiting the same 'divided consciousness' in audiences between uncanny and sceptical responses.[179]

Philidor's original phantasmagoria reached Dublin's Little Theatre, Capel Street, on 23 January 1804;[180] appropriately, the same street and exactly a century before Bloom's recollection of visiting the mutoscope parlour in 'Nausicaa' (the chapter's 'Meaning' is also 'Projected Mirage' according to *Ulysses*' Linati Schema).[181] Rival versions with improved and added attractions were performed at various Dublin venues until 1819 at least, and its cultural influence extended throughout the century (see *MLP&MPS*, pp. 40–2). Though rapidly booming in major cities of Europe and the Americas, the phantasmagoria dwindled into a stock routine of travelling magicians and provincial interludes and was eclipsed by dissolving views. Nonetheless, it indicated lanternism's coming of age and demonstrated 'the true potential of the prodigious device in education, propaganda, natural science and pure entertainment', a potential realised in Ireland as much as elsewhere.[182]

In the phantasmagoria's wake, 'Pepper's Ghost' (conceived by civil engineer Henry Dircks in 1858, but perfected at London's Royal Polytechnic by its director, John Henry Pepper)[183] became the most famous and widely imitated spook illusion (see figure 1.5). Bloom alludes to it in 'Lestrygonians' with casual familiarity, while thinking about crucifixes glowing 'miraculously' by

Figure 1.5 'Spectre Drama at the Polytechnic Institution', *Illustrated London News* 42, 2 May 1863, p. 486. Reproduced by permission of the National Library of Scotland.

phosphorous: 'Wake up in the dead of night and see him on the wall, hanging. Pepper's Ghost idea' (*Ulysses* 8.19–20). Similarly, in the parody *séance* in 'Cyclops', Dignam's spirit materialises out of thin air, complete with prismatic 'halo' effects:

> In the darkness spirit hands were felt to flutter and when prayer by tantras had been directed to the proper quarter a faint but increasing luminosity of ruby light became gradually visible, the apparition of the etheric double being particularly lifelike owing to the discharge of jivic rays from the crown of the head and face. (12.338–42)

Using a concealed lantern, Pepper reflected moving images of actors or skeletons (manipulated by assistants below stage) on to glass sheets angled to be invisible to audiences. Later showmen incorporated alternating convex and concave mirrors to increase or diminish their size.[184] Pepper's Ghost was first employed in an 1863 Polytechnic show inspired by another Dickens tale of Yuletide conversion, *The Haunted Man* (1848), whose protagonist interacts with his own spectral double.[185] This established the Polytechnic as the factory for a kind of modern ghost industry. The Polytechnic's subsequent epic lantern entertainments, such as *The Siege of Troy* (1877), incorporated ghost appearances among its succession of Homeric tableaux.[186] In shows such as *Metempsychosis* (1879) (a reincarnation principle referred to many times in *Ulysses*), Pepper created related illusions, as in his version of the popular stage act *The Artist's Dream*, in which a lay figure animates and completes the artist's unfinished painting. Pepper even shrank his own image into a champagne bottle, while nonchalantly continuing a scientific lecture.[187]

Such optical tricks were adapted to make people appear and vanish, to change sex, or to metamorphose objects, all of which became stock routines in 'Circe-esque' stop-motion trick films by Méliès and others. In similar mode, the Polytechnic sketch *Curried Prawns, A Dyspeptic Illusion* featured 'a series of extraordinary hallucinations seizing the imagination of an amateur Faust, after over-indulging in the epicurean dish of the title'.[188] *Devilled Crab*, a trick film shown in the Volta's opening programme (probably *Cretinetti ha ingoiata un Gambero*, Italy 1909), was a parallel comic nightmare in which the serial character played by André Deed experiences fantastic after-effects from eating seafood.[189]

Although Pepper toured his 'Strange Lecture' demonstrating the ghost's principles from the mid-1860s, partly to inoculate the public against the wave of spiritualist credulity sweeping the UK,[190] his device was incorporated for wholesale gatherings of supernatural presences in pantomimes, plays and operas, apparently allowing living and dead, the tangible and phantasmal, to intermingle convincingly in ways that anticipate 'Circe's' abolition of ontological and generic boundaries. By the 1910s, it had been adapted for projecting ghosts by cinematograph in live theatre by Oskar Messter in Germany and Cecil Hepworth in Britain.[191] Pepper also toured Ireland himself, presenting his 'ghost lecture' at Dublin's Antient Concert Hall (*MLP&MPS*, p. 49). Poole and Young's ghost drama, combining realistic action with the same projection principle, had already opened at the Rotunda in September 1863, a venue particularly associated with eerie manifestations for Joyce. In *Portrait*, Stephen experiences a phantasmagoric 'dream epiphany' as a consequence of visiting a similar combined diorama and lantern show by Poole and Young at the Rotunda. *The Strange Story*, as the 1863 ghost show was called (possibly echoing Pepper's lecture title), caused a sensation, running until January the following year.[192] It was reviewed in detail by the *Freeman's Journal*:

> The long expected 'ghost', or rather 'ghosts', made their appearance at the Concert Room of the Rotundo [*sic*] . . . preceded by a representation of Gompertz's Panorama of the war in America . . . The ghost, we must say, is a curious and skilful display of the strange effects which can be produced by certain combinations of light and shadow. The story is simply this:– In the days of the *Grand Monarque* a certain Count in his service is tended, after being wounded in an engagement, by a fair young girl. She loves him; he betrays and deserts her. Her brother comes to him, and taunts him with his perfidy. They fight and the Count slays his antagonist. Afterwards in his chamber at midnight, while thinking over these events, the spectral forms of his lover and her murdered brother appear to him. The fair young girl is arrayed in white, the brother presents the same aspect as just before the fatal encounter with the Count. *The interest of the display mainly consists in the rapidity with which the ghostly figures are projected forward from the window into the apartment, and with which they fade out of sight* as the Count attempts to seize them. The story was narrated by Mr. [Washington] Davis, who also represented the Count.[193] [italics mine]

A tragedy of class betrayal like the ballad 'The Lass of Aughrim', which summons Michael Furey's ghost in 'The Dead', it is also striking that Poole and Young's spooks projected in and out of view through a chamber window, like the eerie shaft of gaslight bisecting the hotel room from the street lamp outside in Joyce's tale. A Dublin advertisement promoted *The Strange Story*'s impressive effects of moving, transparent presences fading in and out, 'as exhibiting at the Adelphi Theatre and Royal Polytechnic Institute London'.[194]

Throughout the 1870s and 1880s, the Rotunda continued to feature ghostly touring programmes based on Schiller's *Storm of Thoughts*, Dickens's *The*

Haunted Man and *A Christmas Carol*, as well as performances of Gounod's *Faust* by the aptly named 'Spectral Opera Company'.[195] Phantasmagoric effects were similarly available on Dublin's domestic lantern market. Manufacturers and suppliers such as Robinson's, Spencer's and Solomon's offered them to schools and private parties from the mid-1860s, basing their promotion around the popular instruction manual, *The Magic Lantern: How to Buy and How to Use it, By 'A Mere Phantom'* (*MLP&MPS*, pp. 51–2; and see discussion above). Although 'Grace' eschews the conjuration of holy spirits, Joyce nonetheless evokes lanternism for phantasmagoric visions in 'The Dead', which climactically dissolves and replaces *Dubliners'* meticulously constructed, realist image of the world, suggesting how Joyce reflected this key influence on the media-cultural imaginary of his time.

Spook Raising in 'The Dead'

Written in an Ireland that Joyce felt to be half-paralysed by the dead hand of its own history, *Dubliners* is a deeply haunted text, so replete with absent and unquiet presences that it has been noted that the titles and subjects of its opening and closing stories – 'The Sisters' and 'The Dead' – are virtually interchangeable. The latter is explicitly a Christmas 'ghost story', set on the Feast of the Epiphany (6 January). It is a cliché that epiphany or 'showing forth' is a key concept in Joyce's early work, both epistemologically and technically, but Christmas was also the season when the lantern was in particular demand for supernatural effects, as well as dissolving views of Yuletide scenes. Lawrence's 1890 catalogue confirms that it had the same appeal in Dublin in the trick set *A Merry Christmas*, and life-model narrative *Marley's Ghost*, excerpted from *A Christmas Carol*. This association of Christmas with magical or ghostly projections was quickly passed to film, as evidenced by Rotunda screenings of *A Christmas Carol* (possibly Paul's *Scrooge or Marley's Ghost* [1901]) and (possibly G. A. Smith's) *Santa Claus* in its 1901–02 season (*MLP&MPS*, p. 242). Joyce knowingly arranges his final *mise en scène* in 'The Dead' with effects evoking the phantasmagoria. Due to a power cut, the hotel bedroom is lit only by 'a long shaft from one window to the door' (*Dubliners*, p. 170): a street lamp acts like a projector beam for occult presences, as in Poole and Young's famous show *The Strange Story*, in which accusing spectres were projected through the set's chamber windows. Gretta herself is eerily highlighted from that same source as she glides towards Gabriel, rendered uncanny like a virtual image of the woman he thought he knew:

> – Gretta!
>
> She turned away from the mirror slowly and walked along the shaft of light towards him. Her face looked so serious and weary that the words would not pass Gabriel's lips. (*Dubliners*, p. 170)

This effect intensifies after Gretta confesses, now gazing back distractedly into the same source as if expecting the shade of her teenage lover to materialise from it (p. 173). (Appropriately, Michael Furey was employed at a gasworks, the origin of this eerily intrusive beam, which also parallels the gas-based lime-light of lantern and early film shows.) In an 1894 slide set illustrating Poe's 'The Raven' (by the American master slide-painter Joseph Boggs Beale, also famed for Christmas shows), visions project into the protagonist's chamber through its fanlight, hovering at the end of a similar beam, including a scythe-wielding spectre, and creating a reflexive emblem of lanternism's phantasma-goric history.[196]

Gabriel's visualisation of the 'otherworld' inhabited by his dead rival, towards which he now feels irresistibly drawn, could be said to display a simi-lar sense of how the magic lantern passed on specific effects to film as its suc-cessor 'technology of the uncanny'. Joyce was hardly alone among modern writers in this respect. Gabriel's experience resembles the immersion in simi-larly spectral parallel dimensions, populated by intangible beings, that is visu-alised in H. G. Wells's 'optically speculative' stories of the late 1890s and early 1900s. Wells also plays with the transition from phantasmagoria to film's mov-ing photographic ghostworlds.[197] Famous accounts such as Gorki's of seeing Moscow's first cinematograph show are wider testimony to this mutation in visual culture: though watching Lumière actualities of everyday scenes, Gorki nonetheless felt immersed in a 'kingdom of shadows' eerily doubling the living one of colour and sound.[198] That spectrality of photographic media themselves, in which images of both dead and living meet in equivocal *re*presentation – '[a]re but as pictures' (to quote *Macbeth*) – persists in Virginia Woolf's viewing of newsreel footage of the lost world before the slaughter of the First World War in the mid-1920s, or Graham Greene's observations about the uncanny celluloid afterlife of silent stars deceased or killed off professionally by the soundtrack in the 1930s.[199]

As Gabriel similarly watches Furey's shadowy otherworld gradually materi-alise around him, it is no accident that Joyce deploys a cluster of terms familiar from both lanternism and early movie watching (also found in Wells's sto-ries), and thus part of the evolving technical vocabulary of cinematicity itself. Gabriel's spooks, like figures on the silent screen, have an unstable, 'flickering existence' (*Dubliners*, p. 176). Flickering is associated both with mortality and emotionally charged moving pictures elsewhere in *Dubliners*. In Little Chan-dler's 'Celtic-twilight' vision, for example: 'The glow of the late autumn sunset covered the grass plots and walks. It cast a shower of kindly golden dust on the untidy nurses and decrepit old men who drowsed on the benches; it *flick-ered* upon all the *moving figures* . . .' (*Dubliners*, p. 53; italics mine). In 'Scylla and Charybdis', Stephen defines spectrality in terms of loss of visual definition through fading out: 'What is a ghost? Stephen said with tingling energy. One who has faded into impalpability through death, through absence, through change of manners' (9.147–9). Similarly, Gabriel's self-image is described as 'fading out' into the monochrome 'impalpab[ility]' of the world of the dead; conversely, the substantial world he took for granted is 'dissolving' and 'dwindling' (*Dubliners*, p. 176). Hence Gabriel's awareness of this other dimension, overlapping and gradually erasing ours, resembles the kind of 'mixing' effect that film took over from dissolving views, in which images temporarily occupy the same space, one 'fading up' to gradually oust the other; or the effects of enlargement and diminution causing apparitions to approach or vanish in phantasmagorias. Thus epiphany functions not only ontologically but technically in 'The Dead', not least in this climactic, highly immersive effect of one picture 'showing forth' (as in its etymology) through another, to engulf and supersede it along with any certainties that its apparent reality signified for Joyce's focaliser.

Joyce ends with a poignant montage of snow falling 'general all over Ireland', erasing differences between the living and the dead, again presented in a rapid succession of images not unlike a wintry lantern slide or film tour of the country's geographical highlights. When Thomas-Edison Electric Animated Pictures opened its new season at the Rotunda in March 1902, it was with *A Winter Tour through Ireland* as part of a benefit for Jervis Street Hospital (*MLP&MPS*, p. 243). Moving effects such as snowfall were particularly renowned among the lantern's repertoire of Christmas tricks, produced by projecting through 'roller blinds' on to static background views via a second lens. Light scintillating through tiny perforations in black calico superimposed falling flakes as the blind was cranked,[200] to seasonally twee effect that contrasts starkly with Joyce's unsettling ending.[201]

Thus Joyce ingeniously *re*presents Gabriel's world in a way that is not only ultra-mimetic, like life-model slides or moving film images, but that also, ironically, renders it visually and ontologically indistinguishable from its shadow counterpart, erasing the boundaries between the two (see *Dubliners*, p. 176). His work evokes the magic lantern and its active inheritance in film, but also anticipates cinema's narrative future in the symptomatic transitions of his own style.[202] Hence we need greater acknowledgement of how Joyce's presentation of his Dubliners – how they think and visualise their world in terms of moving images – might derive from forms pre-dating film, in order to appreciate the full richness and ingenuity of his methods and their 'connectivity' with the common media-cultural imaginary of his formative years. Lanternism's ostensibly banned presence in *Dubliners* appears in fact to have been fundamental to the Modernist dynamic of Joyce's writing, which would, paradoxically, continue to outstrip contemporary movies in *Portrait* and *Ulysses* in its creative cinematicity.

Unlike, *Dubliners* and *Ulysses*, *Portrait* mentions neither magic lantern nor early film shows by name, though the influence of the optical culture of Joyce's time is just as crucial to its modernisation of the *Bildungsroman*. For the history of cinematicity in literary form, what is most significant in *Portrait*'s method is how it engages with another crucial link between lanternism and the coming of film: developments in the photographic analysis of animal locomotion and attempts to animate and project their results. The effect of these developments on the perception of Joyce's protagonist and specifically on *Portrait*'s break-through representation of an artistic consciousness developing over time is the subject of my next chapter.

NOTES

1. Steve Humphries and Doug Lear, *Victorian Britain through the Magic Lantern*, illustrated by Lear's Magic Lantern Slides (London: Sidgwick and Jackson, 1989), pp. 170 and 9, respectively.
2. William Molyneux, *Dioptricka Nova* (London: Printed for Benj. Tooke, 1692), p. 181, table 38, figure 2.
3. Niamh McCole, 'The Magic Lantern in Provincial Ireland, 1896–1906', *EPVC*, 5:3 (2007), pp. 247–62 (249).
4. The collection of images from Lawrence's studios, some 50,000 in all at the National Library Photographic Archive, 'represent the most comprehensive record of the country in the period including its landscape, its towns, its people and the key events' (see *MLP&MPS*, note to plate 57). For an overview, see Sarah Rouse, *Into the Light: An Illustrated Guide to the Photographic Collections in the National Library of Ireland* (Dublin: National Library of Ireland, 1998), esp. pp. 54–7.
5. Lawrence's 'Terms of Hire' include a 'Dissolving View Apparatus, consisting of Two Oil Lanterns, Sheet and 100 Slides selected', available 'With Attendance' (i.e. operators). They also offered a 'First-class Oxy-Hydrogen [i.e. limelight] Biunial, and 100 Slides, with experienced attendant'. *Illustrated Catalogue: Magic Lanterns, Dissolving View Apparatus and Lantern Slides* (Dublin: Printed by Leckie and Co., n.d.), p. 15. See also *MLP&MPS*, pp. 66–8.
6. See Cahill et al., 'Have you Tried the Ash Pit?', p. 34.
7. On the popularity of mass-produced toy lanterns from the last quarter of the nine-teenth century, see *EML*, pp. 304–5; also text and illustrations in Humphries and Lear, *Victorian Britain through the Magic Lantern*, pp. 34–43.
8. Lawrence, *Illustrated Catalogue*, pp. 9–11, 13.
9. Marcel Proust, *Remembrance of Things Past*, vol. I, *Swann's Way*, trans. C. K. Scott Moncrieff and Terence Kilmartin (Harmondsworth: Penguin, 1983), p. 9.
10. For the background and contemporary investigations, see (among others) Terence Brown, 'Joyce's Magic Lantern', *JJQ*, 28:4 (1991), pp. 791–8, and *MLP&MPS*, pp. 72–8.
11. Paul Carpenter, 'Mimesis, Memory and the Magic Lantern: What Did the Knock Witnesses See', *New Hibernia Review*, 15:2 (2011), pp. 102–20. The Rocketts con-firm that a vast array of Catholic images, paintings and sculptures were available on slides by this time (*MLP&MPS*, pp. 77–8).

12. For the movement's exploitation of such methods, see Mervyn Heard, *Phantasmagoria: The Secret Life of the Magic Lantern* (Hastings: The Projection Box, 2006), pp. 212–15. George Cruikshank's illustration to Samuel C. Hall's *The Trial of Sir Jasper* (1873) is the definitive (literally) hair-raising image of this kind, showing a student beset by demons swarming from bottles (Heard, *Phantasmagoria*, pp. 218, 294.)

13. See ibid., p. 215. Cartoons of the drunkard's deterioration from the *Bottle* and a poster advertising its 1863 showing through dissolving views (with Cruikshank lecturing) are reproduced on pp. 216–17.

14. Lawrence, *Illustrated Catalogue*, p. 13. Sets range between six and eight slides, all listed as 'Uncolored' [*sic*], though that doesn't necessarily suggest photographic life-model narratives. MLS and LUCERNA list a life-model version of *Buy Your Own Cherries* by York and Son from 1885, available at <http://www.magiclantern.org.uk/> and <http://www.slides.uni-trier.de> (last accessed 15 March 2016). Now relocated to <http://lucerna.exeter.ac.uk>. Griffith made many temperance films, echoing titles and extending themes and techniques from lantern narratives. In 1909, for example, he directed *A Drunkard's Reformation*, in which the protagonist's conscience is triggered by watching his shortcomings mirrored in a staging of Zola's *L'Assommoir*; *The Drunkard's Child*, in which a cripple is rescued from an abusive father by a charitable old man; and *What Drink Did*, which experiments with parallel scenes between parlour and pub, finally joining them together when the drunkard's daughter is shot in a bar-room brawl after being sent to fetch him. For the pivotal role of *A Drunkard's Reformation* in the development of film-editing techniques, see Tom Gunning, *D. W. Griffith and the Origins of American Narrative Film: The Early Years at Biograph* (Urbana, IL: University of Illinois Press 1994), pp. 164–72.

15. See, for example, Siegfried Zielinski, *Deep Time of the Media: Towards an Archaeology of Hearing and Seeing*, trans. Gloria Custance (Cambridge, MA: MIT Press, 2008), pp. 113–57; also Jussi Parikka, *What is Media Archaeology?* (Cambridge: Polity, 2012), pp. 49, 51, 71.

16. Martin Loiperdinger, 'The Social Impact of Screen Culture 1880–1914', in Vogl-Bienek and Crangle (eds), *Screen Culture and the Social Question*, pp. 8–19 (13).

17. See Tom Gunning, 'The Cinema of Attractions: Early Film, its Spectator and the Avant-Garde', in Elsaesser (ed.), *Early Cinema: Space, Frame, Narrative*, pp. 56–67.

18. Hauke Lange-Fuchs, 'On the Origin of Moving Slides', *New Magic Lantern Journal*, 7:3 (1995), p. 10. Heard reproduces Huygens's sketches for a mechanical slide showing a skeleton doffing its skull (*Phantasmagoria*, pp. 34–5).

19. See David Robinson, 'Shows and Slides', in Dennis Crompton, David Henry and Stephen Herbert (eds), *Magic Images: The Art of Hand-Painted and Photographic Lantern Slides* (London: MLS, 1990), pp. 5–8 (6).

20. Humphries and Lear, *Victorian Britain through the Magic Lantern*, p. 21.

21. Ibid. pp. 22–3; and for moving panoramas on similar subjects in Dublin, see Chapter 3.

22. Originally produced at the Polytechnic in 1875. See <https://muse.jhu.edu/article/620257/summary>; also <https://www.youtube.com/watch?v=7tzSj123I4I> for a live performance of the later 'commercial' version (last accessed 9 December 2017).

23. See Deac Rossell, *Living Pictures: The Origins of the Movies* (Albany, NY: State University of New York Press, 1998), pp. 14–15; also Joss Marsh, 'Dickensian "Dissolving Views": The Magic Lantern, Visual Story-Telling, and the Victorian Technological Imagination', *Comparative Critical Studies*, 6:3 (2009), pp. 333–46.
24. Anonymous review quoted in Morus, 'Illuminating Illusions', pp. 43–4.
25. Deac Rossell, 'Double Think: the Cinema and Magic Lantern Culture', in John Fullerton (ed.), *Celebrating 1895: The Centenary of Cinema* (Sydney, NSW: John Libbey, 1998), pp. 27–36 (29).
26. Rossell, *Living Pictures*, pp. 16–17.
27. Henry Walker, 'Animated Photographs versus Dissolving Views', *Optical Magic Lantern Journal Annual and Almanac*, 2 (1897–98), pp. 109–10.
28. I am grateful to lantern accompanist and composer Timothy Didymus for this striking phrase.
29. Lawrence, *Illustrated Catalogue*, p. 14.
30. *Freeman's Journal*, 17 February 1890, p. 5.
31. Jeremy Brooker, *The Temple of Minerva: Magic and the Magic Lantern at the Royal Polytechnic Institution, London 1837–1901* (London: MLS, 2013), pp. 49–54.
32. See Heard, *Phantasmagoria*, pp. 11–12; for Cook on dissolving views, see *MiTD*, pp. 81–99.
33. It was remade as an 1890 life-model effect set in which a wounded soldier has an inset vision of his cottage. See *Illustrated Bamforth Slide Catalogue* CD-ROM, compiled by Richard Crangle and Robert Macdonald for the MLS (London: MLS, 2009).
34. For reproductions of 'thought pictures' from *One Winter's Night*, see G. A. Household (ed.), *To Catch a Sunbeam: Victorian Reality through the Magic Lantern* (London: Joseph, 1979), pp. 24–30.
35. Mrs [Maria] Abdy, 'Dissolving Views', *Metropolitan*, 38:149 (1843), p. 72.
36. *EML*, pp. 10, 71–2; Heard, *Phantasmagoria*, pp. 200, 202; *MLP&MPS*, pp. 42–5.
37. Brooker is sceptical about the extent of Henry Langdon Childe's role in the development of dissolving views at the Polytechnic (*Temple of Minerva*, pp. 49–52).
38. Although now a very different organisation under Quintin Hogg, it was nonetheless instrumental in launching the cinematograph in Britain (see Brooker, *Temple of Minerva*, pp. 152–4).
39. Lawrence, *Illustrated Catalogue*, p. 14. Heard shows a late nineteenth-century, two-part 'dissolve set' of a wizard conjuring imps from the smoke of his cauldron (see *Phantasmagoria*, pp. 174–5, 282). A comparable set of three illustrating Mount Vesuvius dormant, then erupting are on p. 199. Heard's list of Langdon Childe's dissolving views confirms how typical those in Lawrence's catalogue still were (see *Phantasmagoria*, p. 204; also entries in *EML*, esp. pp. 64–5, 89–92).
40. For the 'Wheel of Life' lantern, see Robertson, Herbert and Crangle (eds), *Encyclopaedia of the Magic Lantern*, pp. 321–2; for a visual demonstration, see <http://www.museudelcinema.cat/eng/colleccio_recursos.php?idreg=1653> (last accessed 5 June 2019).
41. Esther Leslie, 'Loops and Joins: Muybridge and the Optics of Animation', *EPVC*, 11:1 (2013), pp. 28–40 (32–3)
42. Rossell, 'Double Think', p. 31.

43. Anon., 'The Cinematograph: A Startling Invention', *Dublin Evening Telegraph*, 26 February 1896, p. 4.

44. See Raymond Newport, 'The Motion Picture Experiments of John Arthur Roebuck Rudge', *New Magic Lantern Journal*, 8:2 (1997), pp. 1–3.

45. *The New Magic Lantern Journal* reproduces the full US catalogue description of *La Lanterne magique* (see 8:4 [1999], p. 13); for *Au Pays des Jouets*, see David Robinson, 'A Film Maker's Magic Lantern Years', *The New Magic Lantern Journal*, 7:1 (1993), p. 11; also *EML*, p. 192. For early cinema's extension of phantasmagoric traditions, especially by ex-lanternists and magicians, see Heard, *Phantasmagoria*, pp. 254–60.

46. Laurent Mannoni, 'Elbow to Elbow: The Lantern/Cinema Struggle', *The New Magic Lantern Journal*, 7:1 (1993), pp. 1–6 (3).

47. See illustrations in Heard, *Phantasmagoria*, pp. 218–19, 294.

48. Stanislaus Joyce, *My Brother's Keeper*, pp. 110, 125. John Joyce took James around parts of London that had Irish communities, but were also famous for cockney music halls, including the Mile End Road, East End and South East London. See Eleni Loukopoulou, *Up to Maughty London: Joyce's Cultural Capital in the Imperial Metropolis* (Gainesville, FL: University Press of Florida, 2017), p. 18; also John Wyse Jackson and Peter Costello, *John Stanislaus Joyce: The Voluminous Life and Genius of James Joyce's Father* (London: Fourth Estate, 1997), pp. 224–6.

49. Anon., 'Living Pictures at the Rotunda', *Irish Times*, 28 August 1906, p. 6.

50. See the image on LUCERNA: The Magic Lantern Web Resource, available at <http://www.slides.uni-trier.de> (last accessed 6 April 2013).

51. See 'Italian Bioscope Company Invades Dublin', *Bioscope*, 23 December 1909, p. 37.

52. See Justin Carville, 'Mr Lawrence's Great Photographic Bazaar: Photography, History and the Imperial Streetscape', *EPVC*, 5:3 (2007), pp. 263–83 (264); also Edward Chandler, *Photography in Ireland: The Nineteenth Century* (Dublin: Edmund Burke, 2001), p. 97.

53. 'Ars Photographica' (1868) was translated by H. T. Henry in 1902:

> Sun-wrought with magic of the skies
> The image fair before me lies
> Deep-vaulted brain and sparkling eyes
> And lips fine chiselling
>
> O miracle of human thought
> O art with newest marvels fraught
> Appeles Nature's rival wrought
> No fairer imaging!

Quoted in James Joyce, *Dubliners: A Norton Critical Edition*, ed. Margot Norris, Hans Walter Gabler and Walter Hettche (New York: W. W. Norton 2006), p. 242. Joyce owned a bilingual edition of *Le Poesie latine di Papa Leone XIII* (Milan: Società Editrice Sonzogne, 1902).

54. See Ian Christie, *The Last Machine: Early Cinema and the Birth of the Modern World* (London: BFI/BBC, 1994), p. 10.

55. See William Lawrence, *Ireland in the Magic Lantern: List of Photographic Lantern Slides* (Dublin: Printed by the Freeman's Journal, 1890), p. 26.

56. It is unclear whether the photograph is hand-tinted (like many at the time) or if Chandler is simply remembering the blouse's colour.

57. See also Kieran Hickey (ed.), *The Light of Other Days: Irish Life at the Turn of the Century in the Photographs of Robert French* (London: Allen Lane, 1973).

58. See Carville, 'Mr Lawrence's Great Photographic Bazaar', p. 266.

59. See examples in Humphries and Lear, *Victorian Britain through the Magic Lantern*, pp. 85-107; see also below for 'photographic magnification' in *Dubliners*.

60. Anon., 'The Photographic Society of Ireland', *Optical Magic Lantern Journal and Photographic Enlarger* (June 1890), p. 8.

61. See Ludwig Vogl-Bienek, 'A Lantern Lecture: Slum Life and Living Conditions of the Poor in Fictional and Documentary Lantern Slide Sets', in Vogl-Bienek and Crangle (eds), *Screen Culture and the Social Question*, pp. 34–63 (36–8).

62. Anon., 'The Photographic Society of Ireland', p. 8.

63. Vogl-Bienek, 'A Lantern Lecture', p. 35.

64. Humphries and Lear, *Victorian Britain through the Magic Lantern*, p. 153; see also pp. 145–57 for diverse news slide examples.

65. See illustrations in Heard, *Phantasmagoria*, p. 242; also on LUCERNA website.

66. Humphries and Lear, *Victorian Britain through the Magic Lantern*, p. 60. For a detailed comparison between themes and settings of British TV soap and Bamforth's *The Drink Fiend*, see Ken and Judy Fortune, 'Modern History: *Coronation Street* – the Inheritance', *New Magic Lantern Journal*, 5:1 (1987), pp. 2–3. The text and images from *The Drink Fiend* are reproduced in Household (ed.), *To Catch a Sunbeam*, pp. 52–61.

67. A docudrama about Bamforth's switch into film production, *Holmfirth Hollywood*, dir. Steve Webb, was first broadcast on BBC 4 (6 June 2006).

68. See David Francis, 'Magic Lantern Slide Influence on Early Films', *MLS Newsletter*, 9 (January 1984), p. 6.

69. See also Nicholas Andrew Miller, *Modernism, Ireland and the Erotics of Memory* (West Nyack, NY: Cambridge University Press, 2002), pp. 108–9.

70. LUCERNA lists an 1884 life-model set by York and Son. See <http://www.slides.uni-trier.de> (last accessed 15 March 2015).

71. LUCERNA lists a life-model set by York and Son in/before 1888.

72. LUCERNA lists several sets on this or related themes.

73. LUCERNA lists several life-model sets of *In the Signal Box*: by York and Son (1886); Bamforth and Co. (1889). *Christmas Day in the Workhouse* was also adapted into a life-model set by Bamforth (1890); MLS slide reading no. 90111.

74. Lawrence, *Illustrated Catalogue*, p. 14. For the importance of lantern adaptations of Sims's work to social reform, see *MiTD*, pp. 104–5; also *EML*, pp. 237, 290, 299; Joss Marsh and Francis Davis, '"The Poetry of Poverty": The Magic Lantern and the Ballads of George R. Sims', in Vogl-Bienek and Crangle (eds), *Screen Culture and the Social Question*, pp. 64–81.

75. See Willie Anderson, 'Life Model Studies: I – A Peep behind Some Scenes', *The Photogram*, 6 (February 1899), pp. 46–8 (48); also 'Life Model Studies: no. II - The Models Themselves', *The Photogram*, 6 (March 1899), pp. 76–8; Philip Reynolds, 'Sentiment to Order', *The Harmsworth Magazine*, 5:28 (1900), pp. 337–43 (343); Alfred H.

Saunders, 'Prominent Men in the Lantern World: New Series, No.1. Mr James Bamforth, of Holmfirth, Yorks', *The Optical Magic Lantern Journal*, 13:151 (1902), pp. 7–9 (7) (also reproduced in *The Illustrated Bamforth Slide Catalogue* DVD).

76. Joe Kember, *Marketing Modernity: Victorian Popular Shows and Early Cinema* (Exeter: University of Exeter Press, 2009), p. 1. Kember discusses life-model sets and early film in detail on pp. 149–55.

77. See LUCERNA (last accessed 20 October 2018).

78. In Bamforth's twelve-slide adaptation of George R. Sims's poem from *Ballads of Babylon* (London: John P. Fuller 1880) the image is captioned: 'And picked up a brass-bound hymn-book and aimed at our chaplain's face.' Marsh and Francis also reproduce it in '"The Poetry of Poverty"', p. 70.

79. See Terry Ramsaye, *A Million and One Nights: A History of the Motion Picture* (1926) (repr. London: Frank Cass, 1964), pp. 91–103, esp. p. 93. Also Herbert and McKernan, *Who's Who of Victorian Cinema*, p. 25; Kaveh Askan, 'Alexander Black and the Art of the Picture Play', *New Magic Lantern Journal*, 9:5 (2003), p. 67. Black published it as *Miss Jerry, with Thirty-Seven Illustrations from Life Photographs by the Author* (New York: Charles Scribner's Sons, 1895).

80. See text and images in Mervyn Heard, 'Pearls before Swine: A Prurient Look at the Lantern', *EPVC*, 3:2 (2005), pp. 179–95; also Vanessa Davids, '"Nudes and More" – A Short Description of a Pornographic Lantern Slide Collection', in Richard Crangle, Mervyn Heard and Ine van Doren (eds), *Realms of Light* (London: MLS, 2005), p. 45.

81. Maxim Gorki, 'In the Kingdom of Shadows' (1896), trans. Leda Swan, Appendix 2 in Jay Leyda (ed.), *Kino: A History of the Russian and Soviet Film* (London: Allen and Unwin, 1960), pp. 407–9 (409).

82. See Bill Barnes, 'Charlie under the Baneful Influence of the Magic Lantern', *MLS Newsletter* 115 (March 2014), p. 5.

83. See Basil Mahon, *The Man Who Changed Everything: The Life of James Clerk Maxwell* (Chichester: John Wiley, 2004), pp. 93–4; also *EML*, p. 190.

84. See Zone, *Stereoscopic Cinema*, pp. 73–5.

85. Anon., 'The Modern Marvel Co. – The Analyticon', *Dublin Daily Express*, 3 October 1898, p. 6.

86. Advertisement for the Analyticon, *Dublin Daily Nation*, 10 October 1898, p. 4.

87. 'Concert Room Rotunda', *Irish Times*, 3 October 1898, p. 6; *Dublin Daily Nation*, 11 October 1898, p. 5.

88. 'The Analyticon at the Rotunda', *Freeman's Journal*, 7 October 1898, p. 5.

89. See Jeremy Brooker, 'The Queen on Screen', *The Magic Lantern*, 20 (September 2019), pp. 8–10.

90. Ine van Dooren, 'Our Magic Lantern Heritage: Archiving a Past Medium that Nearly Never Was', in Vogl-Bienek and Crangle (eds), *Screen Culture and the Social Question*, pp. 182–8 (184).

91. For more detail, see the section on 'Surreal Images, Projections and Shadows', in Rhonda K. Garelick, *Electric Salome: Loïe Fuller's Performance of Modernism* (Princeton, NJ: Princeton University Press, 2007), pp. 52–6; also text and illustrations in *EML*, pp. 241–2; Bill Barnes, 'La Loïe Fuller, Serpentine Dancer', *MLS Newsletter* 106 (December 2011), pp. 1, 6–7.

92. Stéphane Mallarmé, *Oeuvres complètes* (Paris: Gallimard, 1945), p. 308.

93. See Mervyn Heard's short monograph on 'Pose Slides, Cloak Slides and Moving Wallpaper', *Dressed in Light: The Ancient Art of Projecting on People* (February 2014), available as a PDF from his website, <http://www.mervynheard.com> (last accessed 4 August 2016).

94. Verity Hunt, 'Raising a Modern Ghost: the Magic Lantern and the Persistence of Wonder in the Victorian Education of the Senses', *Romanticism and Victorianism on the Net*, 5:2 (2006), available at <https://www.erudit.org/en/journals/ravon/2008-n52-ravon2573/019806ar/> (last accessed 7 May 2018).

95. Quoted in *The Magic Lantern: How to Buy and How to Use it, By 'A Mere Phantom'* (London: Houlston & Sons, 1866), pp. 18–19.

96. *Harriet Martineau's Autobiography* (1877), excerpted in Valerie Sanders (ed.), *Records of Girlhood: An Anthology of Nineteenth-Century Women's Childhoods* (Aldershot: Ashgate, 2000), pp. 114–59 (121).

97. Harriet Martineau, *Household Education* (London: Edward Moxon, 1849), p. 228.

98. Ibid., p. 91.

99. Hunt, 'Raising a Modern Ghost', para. 17.

100. 'These facets are also to be found in the etymology of the word Bildung: it contains the word Bild (image) in the sense of "sign" and of "reproduction". As a process, Bildung refers to the "reproduction of a pre-given form" (Gestalt), externally as well as inwardly.' Walter Bauer, Introduction, *Educational Philosophy and Theory*, 35:2 (2003), pp. 133–7 (133), DOI: 10.1111/1469-5812.00014.

101. See the major new study by Sarah Dellmann and Frank Kessler, *A Million Pictures: Magic Lantern Slides in the History of Learning*, KINtop Studies in Early Cinema 6 (New Barnet: John Libbey, 2019).

102. Joe Kember evidences examples of professional instructions to lantern lecturers and film explainers indicating continuities between techniques of live explanation in the two media. See Joe Kember, '"Go Thou and Do Likewise": Advice to Lantern and Film Lecturers in the Trade Press, 1897–1909', *EPVC*, 8:4 (2010), pp. 419–30.

103. For recent research unearthing women's extensive and diverse role over centuries of lantern culture, see *Ladies of the Lantern*, a special issue of *The Magic Lantern*, 16 (September 2018).

104. The MLS slide readings library contains the text to a thirty-slide set dating back at least to 1872, *Travels in the Holy Land* (no. 91924).

105. See James Joyce, *Finnegans Wake* (London: Faber and Faber, 1939), 152.16. Subsequent references to this work are given in parentheses in the text by page and line number.

106. Examples on LUCERNA include *Texan Cowboy: Through South-Western Texas with a Camera* (Valentine and Son, thirty-six slides, 1885); *Western Pioneers and Indian Warfare* (Theobald and Co., lecture with twelve slides, n.d.); *Buffalo Hunting in the Wild West* (maker unknown, c. 1891). Many other Western travelogues are also listed.

107. Humphries and Lear, *Victorian Britain through the Magic Lantern*, p. 60.

108. Joyce took a keen interest in the Gordon Bennett trophy race on which his story is based. His interview with a contestant in Paris was published as 'The Motor

Derby: Interview with the French Champion', *Irish Times*, 7 April 1903, p. 5 The race itself took place on 2 July and was partly filmed.

109. See Frank Gray, 'Engaging with the Magic Lantern's History', in Vogl-Bienek and Crangle (eds), *Screen Culture and the Social Question*, pp. 172–80 (178).

110. Solomon's also advertised 'Scenery in Ireland and all parts of the world: illustrating Science, Tales, the Burmah, Egyptian, Boer, Afghan, Russo-Turkish, Franco-Prussian, and Abyssinian Wars, and other subjects, with lectures of an instructive and highly amusing character', *Freeman's Journal*, 17 February 1890, p. 5.

111. See Lawrence, *Ireland in the Magic Lantern*.

112. The text of 'J.B.C's' lecture tour was published as *Ireland in the Magic Lantern: The Lakes of Killarney and Glengariff, via Cork and Bantry: The Prince of Wales Route* (Dublin: William Lawrence, 1894), p. 5.

113. See Lawrence, *Illustrated Catalogue*, pp. 12–13.

114. Shadbolt's images are the earliest known aerial photographs taken in the UK. See the MLS's electronic newsletter, *New Light on Old Media*, 17 (November 2015), available at <https://us3.campaign-archive.com/?u=74cacf8aa6387a5f8f95664f3&id=9618f02af6> (last accessed 18 November 2017). Shadbolt's slides have also been acquired by Historic England and are viewable at <https://archive.historicengland.org.uk/results/Results.aspx?t=Quick&l=all&cr=Shadbolt&io=True&page=1> (last accessed 26 July 2019).

115. For an overview of the mechanisation of time travel in Victorian scientific romance and its links with cinema, see Williams, *H. G. Wells, Modernity and the Movies*, pp. 2–4 and notes.

116. Niamh McCole, 'Seeing Sense: The Visual Culture of Provincial Ireland, 1896–1906', unpublished PhD thesis, Dublin City University, 2005, pp. 236–7, available at <http://doras.dcu.ie/18053/1/Niamh_McCole.pdf> (last accessed 28 September 2018).

117. See Fintan Cullen, 'Marketing National Sentiment: Lantern Slides of Evictions in late Nineteenth-Century Ireland', in Fintan Cullen and John Morrison (eds), *A Shared Legacy: Essays on Irish and Scottish Visual Art and Culture* (London: Ashgate, 2005), pp. 113–31 (123–4); Carville, 'Mr Lawrence's Great Photographic Bazaar', p. 271.

118. Lawrence's *Ireland in the Magic Lantern* catalogues portraits of 'The Irish Parliamentary Party, 1890', including Parnell as MP for Cork City, on pp. 23–4. Michael Davitt also features in 'Noted Portraits, Past and Present', along with various icons from past Irish history, Emmet, Tone, Egan, etc., ibid., p. 25.

119. See Cullen, 'Marketing National Sentiment', p. 127 n. 49.

120. See the 'Saving Souls' chapter in Humphries and Lear, *Victorian Britain through the Magic Lantern*, pp. 133–43; Lindsay Cox, 'Salvation and the Silver Screen' (on the Salvation Army's 'Limelight Department'), *The Magic Lantern*, 3 (June 2015), pp. 1–5; various essays in Vogl-Bienek and Crangle (eds), *Screen Culture and the Social Question*.

121. *Shrines of Our Lady: A Lecture for Use with the Magic Lantern* (London: Catholic Truth Society, 1896).

122. See Stanislaus Joyce, *My Brother's Keeper*, pp. 113–14.

123. For reports on McBratney's veteran skills and experience, see Cahill et al., 'Have you Tried the Ash Pit?', pp. 13–15.

124. LUCERNA lists many sets of Bunyan's allegory dating from the mid-to-late nineteenth century. York and Son's set of forty-three (in/before 1888) mixes coloured illustrations with life-model scenes.

125. See Annemarie McAllister, 'To Assist in the Pictorial Teaching of Temperance: The Use of the Magic Lantern in the Band of Hope', in Vogl-Bienek and Crangle (eds), *Screen Culture and the Social Question*, pp. 124–34 (127). 'Eyegate' and 'Eargate' are sensory entrances to the city of 'Mansoul' in John Bunyan's allegory *The Holy War* (1682; ebook facsimile, Auckland, NZ: The Floating Press, 2009), p. 23.

126. For Dowie's inspirational role in the life of a lanternist, see John Hyett, 'Never Judge a Man by the Size of his Hat: A Study of the Life and Lectures of an Australian Lanternist', *The Magic Lantern*, 18 (March 2019), pp. 3–6 (3).

127. See the published slide reading, *In His Steps, Or What Would Jesus Do? A Service of Song with Readings from the Popular Story by C.M. Sheldon compiled by Thomas Mitchell* (London: T. Mitchell, n.d.), no. 92038. (Slide titles are referenced from the set on LUCERNA.)

128. O. F. Walton, *Christie's Old Organ* (London: Religious Tract Society, 1874).

129. See the published slide reading text, *Christie's Old Organ, Or, Home, Sweet Home* (MLS no. 91859), p. 4.

130. Ibid., p. 7.

131. Walter D. Welford and Henry Sturmey (compilers), *The 'Indispensable Handbook' to the Optical Lantern: A Complete Cyclopaedia on the Subject of Optical Lanterns, Slides, and Accessory Apparatus* (London: Iliffe & Son, 1888), p. 305 (also on MLS website).

132. *Complete Catalogue of Lantern Slides, Dissolving Views, Magic Lanterns etc.* (London: UK Band of Hope Union, 1891) (F [1] on MLS website).

133. LUCERNA lists thirteen effect slides of various types from Ally Sloper titles.

134. *Handy Andy*, in MLS slide readings no. 90523; images on LUCERNA.

135. See Lydia Jakobs, 'Christmas Day in the Workhouse from Ballad to Film via the Magic Lantern', *New Magic Lantern Journal*, 11:10 (2014), pp. 7–9.

136. Marsh and Francis, '"The Poetry of Poverty"', p. 71.

137. Ibid., pp. 71–2.

138. See Karen Eifler, 'Feeding and Entertaining the Poor: Salvation Army Lantern Exhibitions Combined with Food Distribution in Britain and Germany', in Vogl-Bienek and Crangle (eds), *Screen Culture and the Social Question*, pp. 112–23 (121–2); also Miriam Bratu Hansen, 'The Mass Production of the Senses: Classical Cinema as Vernacular Modernism', *Modernism/Modernity*, 6:2 (1999), pp. 59–77 (65, 72).

139. Storm Jameson, 'Documents', *Fact*, 4 (July 1937), pp. 17–18.

140. Quoted in Bert Hogenkamp, *Deadly Parallels: Film and the Left in Britain 1929–1939* (London: Lawrence and Wishart, 1986), p. 14.

141. For further details about Puncto's strategy and its impact, see Stephen Bottomore, 'The Lantern and the Cinematograph for Political Persuasion before WWI', in Vogl-Bienek and Crangle (eds), *Screen Culture and the Social Question*, pp. 24–5.

142. Anon., *The Deadly Parallel* (October 1907), p. 1; quoted in Hogenkamp, *Deadly Parallels*, p. 16.

143. *Street Life, or People We Meet, a Lecture to Accompany a Series of Photographic Transparencies for the Lantern* (Bradford: Riley Brothers, n.d. [c. 1887?]), p. 4 (quoted in Vogl-Bienek, 'A Lantern Lecture', p. 40).

144. Fannie Eden, *White Slaves of London* (London and Dublin: W.B. Horner, 1887). MLS slide reading no. 91139, in/before 1894.

145. Lizzie Ellen Tiddeman, *Poverty's Pupil, or Jenny's Promise* (London: Religious Tract Society, 1908).

146. Clifford G. Roe, *Horrors of the White Slave Trade: The Mighty Crusade to Protect the Purity of Our Homes* (London and New York: n.p., 1911); see also Katherine Mullin, *James Joyce, Sexuality and Social Purity* (Cambridge: Cambridge University Press, 2003), pp. 72–3.

147. Court action in the US over the concept of visual adaptation of texts set the parameters for subsequent remediations of fiction on film. See Oren Bracha, 'The Image as Trespass: The Riley Brothers' *Ben Hur* Lantern Slides and American Copyright', *The Magic Lantern*, 20 (September 2019), pp. 5–7.

148. See Ian Christie, 'Ancient Rome in London: Classical Subjects in the Forefront of Cinema's Expansion after 1910', in Pantelis Michelakis and Maria Wyke (eds), *The Ancient World in Silent Cinema* (Cambridge: Cambridge University Press, 2013), pp. 109–24.

149. See McAllister, 'To Assist in the Pictorial Teaching of Temperance', p. 131.

150. For the significance of giant charity bazaars in Dublin's inter-medial culture and the increasingly technological nature of their attractions, see Denis Condon, '"Baits to Entrap the Pleasure-Seeker and the Worlding": Charity Bazaars Introduce Moving Pictures to Ireland', in Marta Braun, Charles Keil, Rob King, Paul Moore and Louis Pelletier (eds), *Beyond the Screen: Institutions, Networks and Publics of Early Cinema* (New Barnet: John Libbey, 2012), pp. 35–42; Stephanie Rains, 'Modernity and Consumption in Nineteenth-Century Ireland', *EPVC*, 5:3 (2007), pp. 285–300. Rains amplifies aspects of her argument in 'Joyce's "Araby" and the Historical Araby Bazaar, 1894', *Dublin James Joyce Journal*, 1 (2008), pp. 17–29; also in her *Commodity Culture and Social Class in Dublin, 1850–1916* (Dublin: Irish Academic Press, 2010). Katherine Mullin shows how moving and transformative imagery from bazaar attractions, going back to Araby in Dublin, migrates into several fantastic sequences in the cinematic phantasmagoria in 'Circe', to be played out in symbolic forms meshing with the novel's key themes of 'infidelity, jealousy and trangression'. Katherine Mullin, '"Something in the Name of Araby": James Joyce and the Irish Charity Bazaars', *Dublin James Joyce Journal*, 4 (2011), pp. 31–50 (40–1).

151. See *Dublin Evening Telegraph*, 18 May 1895, p. 8.

152. See Rains, 'Modernity and Consumption in Nineteenth-Century Ireland', p. 294.

153. In one famous stunt on the night of 22 June 1897, James Connolly's Irish Socialist Republican Party in collaboration with the writer Maude Gonne organised an outdoor projection to denounce recent rural evictions, from a window of the National Club in Rutland (now Parnell) Square. Gonne had realised the

strategic impact of photographic slides on her recent international anti-eviction lecture tour. They were screened repeatedly, interspersed with starvation statistics and images of nationalist martyrs, such as Tone and Emmet. Beamed roughly twelve metres across the east side of the square, they materialised at an impressive 4.5 metres in scale as a calculated spoiler against civic celebrations for Victoria's Diamond Jubilee. Typically, the stunt was part of a wider inter-medial battle for hearts and minds, albeit an unequal one. As Cullen shows, the Rutland Square show was far from isolated. Connolly and Gonne were 'following a recent trend in the public use of lantern slides to aid political propaganda' ('Marketing National Sentiment', pp. 116–17). Outdoor projection would also figure during the Boer War. The pro-nationalist *Irish Daily Independent* projected telegrams and images on an outside wall of its offices in central Dublin for several nights from 13 October 1899, literally enlarging pro-Boer coverage in its pages. These included portraits of Boer leaders and sites of notorious British defeats in the first Boer War of 1880–81. They continued for a week until the manager was warned by the Dublin Metropolitan Police that he would be held liable should they cause a riot among the crowds being attracted. Tensions rose particularly high after the *Independent* defiantly projected a loyalist poster calling on Trinity College students to besiege its offices and halt the displays. See Denis Condon, 'Receiving News from the Seat of War: Dublin Audiences Respond to Boer War Entertainments', *EPVC*, 9:2 (2011), pp. 93–106.

154. 'Eveline' first appeared in the *Irish Homestead*, 10 September 1904.

155. There is even some ambiguity about whether this is true flashback at all, or just parallel editing for simultaneity. See the detailed account in Gunning, *D.W. Griffith and the Origins of American Narrative Film*, pp. 110–12 (stills on p. 111). Cf. Scott Simmon's description in Paolo Cherchi Usai (ed.), *The Griffith Project: 1, Films Produced in 1907–1908* (London: BFI, 1999), pp. 143–5; also Don Fairservice, *Film Editing: History, Theory and Practice* (Manchester: Manchester University Press, 2008), p. 69. The OED online records the first use of the term in a filmic context in *Variety*, 13 October 1916, 28/4: 'In other words the whole thing is a flash-back of the episodes leading up to her marriage.' However, it was already in use in both mechanics and physics at the turn of the century, and recent research suggests that Griffith's claim to have invented the device (along with many others) in his famous bulletin advertisement in the New York *Dramatic Mirror*, 3 December 1913, is questionable, although he favoured the term 'switchback' (see Cook, *Narrative Film*, p. 55). Most of Griffith's films survive, but there could have been many other examples from the first decade of the twentieth century which have not.

156. Karl Brown, assistant to Griffith's chief cameraman Billy Bitzer, regarded a decisive analeptic moment in *Judith of Bethulia* (1913) as evidence that the director really could 'photograph thought'. It features the heroine unable to overcome her qualms about beheading the sleeping Holofernes, until she flashes back to his massacre of her people. See Karl Brown, *Adventures with D.W. Griffith* (New York: Farrar, Straus and Giroux, 1973), p. 21. As Cook argues, Griffith went on to stitch numerous psychologically revealing flashbacks into *Birth of a Nation*

(1915), similarly visualising how characters struggle with their past. For example, when Margaret Cameron is proposed to by Phil Stoneman, she immediately remembers the body of her brother at the Battle of Petersburg (*A History of Narrative Film*, p. 70).

157. See Maureen Turim, *Flashbacks in Film: Memory and History* (London: Routledge, 1989), pp. 7–12, 21.

158. Cook gives a brief history of composite photographs, going back to the painter and photographer Gustave le Gray and spreading to England (*MiTD*, p. 113); see also Mary Warner Marien, *Photography: A Cultural History* (London: Laurence King, 2002), pp. 77–8.

159. See the colour reproduction in MLS, *The Illustrated Bamforth Slide Catalogue*.

160. See Cook, *Narrative Film*, p. 87.

161. LUCERNA lists two surviving sets with 'Recitations' and there may have been others. These are Newton and Co., twenty-threee slides (in/before 1888); York and Son, twenty life-model slides (1890).

162. For more information on the Piggotts, see Richard Crangle, 'Some Lesser-Known Life Model Slide Makers, No. 3 – T.J. and W.F. Piggott of Leighton Buzzard', *The Magic Lantern*, 19 (June 2019), pp. 4–7.

163. See Turim, *Flashbacks in Film*, pp. 23–5.

164. Ibid., p. 24.

165. See the title story of Edna O'Brien's collection, *Lantern Slides* (London: Weidenfeld and Nicolson, 1990), pp. 177–215 (215).

166. Published as Revd Frederic Langbridge, *Dan Dabberton's Dream, etc* [service of song] (London: UK Band of Hope Union, 1894), 'Temperance Stories with Song' series, no. 8 (MLS slide readings nos. 90051 and 90052).

167. See Heard, *Phantasmagoria*, p. 215.

168. MLS slide reading no. 91498.

169. See reproductions in Household (ed.), *To Catch a Sunbeam*, pp. 31–2. Text in MLS slide readings no. 92199.

170. Spiegel, *Fiction and the Camera Eye*, pp. 91–2.

171. Keith Cohen, *Film and Fiction: The Dynamics of Exchange* (New Haven, CT: Yale University Press, 1979), pp. 113–14.

172. See Vachel Lindsay, *The Art of the Moving Picture* (1915; rev. edn 1922) (New York: Liveright, 1970), pp. 7–8, 61–3.

173. See Cook, *Narrative Film*, pp. 90, 124.

174. For Joyce's increasing use of objectification (to the point of literally animating commodities), see Keith Williams, '*Ulysses* in Toontown: Vision Animated to Bursting Point in Joyce's "Circe"', in Lydia Rainford and Julian Murphet (eds), *Writing After Cinema: Literature and Visual Technologies* (Basingstoke: Palgrave, 2003), pp. 96–121.

175. For Joyce's interest in Freud's *Zur Psychopathologie des Alltaglebens* (1901) (*The Psychopathology of Everyday Life*), see Richard Ellmann, *The Consciousness of Joyce* (London: Faber and Faber, 1977), pp. 53–4, 109.

176. 'Technologies of the uncanny' denote 'evolving paradigms of psychic influence ... such as telegraphy, electric light, phonograph, radio, the telegraph, and, primarily,

photography. Such technologies were seen to disrupt and confuse the relationship between a whole range of binary terms: subject/other, viewer/viewed, nature/culture, time/space, inside/outside.' See Alison Chapman, 'Mary Elizabeth Coleridge, Literary Influence and Technologies of the Uncanny', in Julian Wolfreys (ed.), *Victorian Gothic: Literary and Cultural Manifestations in the Nineteenth Century* (Basingstoke: Macmillan, 2000), pp. 109–28 (109–10).

177. Heard, *Phantasmagoria*, pp. 84, 93–4.

178. For Robertson's refinements and innovations, see Heard, *Phantasmagoria*, pp. 88–107; see also Tom Gunning, 'Illusions Past and Future: The Phantasmagoria and its Spectres', in *Media Art Histories Archive* (2004), pp. 1–17 (9–10), available at <http://www.mediaarthistory.org/refresh/Programmatic%20key%20texts/pdfs/Gunning.pdf> (last accessed 5 June 2017).

179. Although Robertson claimed 'to destroy the enchanted world' through science, like 'scientific' spiritualists succeeding him in the mid-nineteenth century, he nonetheless offered private *séances* for relatives to commune with their departed (quoted in Gunning, 'Illusions Past and Future', p. 5). For the role of the lantern in relation to allegedly paranormal phenomena, see Marina Warner, *Phantasmagoria: Spirit Visions, Metaphors and Media into the Twenty-First Century* (Oxford: Oxford University Press, 2006), esp. pp. 137–43; see also Simone Natale, 'A Short History of Superimposition: From Spirit Photography to Cinema', *EPVC*, 10:2 (2012), pp. 125–45, esp. 134–9.

180. See Heard, *Phantasmagoria*, pp. 152, 154.

181. See Mervyn Heard, 'Paul de Philipsthal and the Phantasmagoria in England, Scotland and Ireland', Part 2, *New Magic Lantern Journal*, 2 (October 1997), pp. 11–16; see also Heard, *Phantasmagoria*, pp. 172–7. Alternatively (drawing on Robert Monks's research), Katherine Mullin argues that since seedier mutoscope parlours tended to be situated down side streets and in vacant shops, the historical model for Bloom's was more likely one in Parliament Street, just south of the river (see her *James Joyce, Sexuality and Social Purity*, p. 146 and note).

182. Heard, *Phantasmagoria*, p. 165.

183. For the genesis of the illusion, see Jeremy Brooker, 'The Polytechnic Ghost', *EPVC*, 2:5 (2007), pp. 189–206.

184. See *EML*, p. 223; Heard, pp. 227–33. See also Morus, 'Illuminating Illusions', pp. 37–50.

185. *EML*, p. 89; Heard, *Phantasmagoria*, p. 230. Alternatively, Brooker argues that *The Haunted Man* scene was only added to the illusion's repertoire at Easter 1863, when it transferred to the Polytechnic's Great Hall due to sensational success ('The Polytechnic Ghost', p. 193).

186. Ibid., p. 202.

187. See text and illustrations to Hermann Hecht, 'Stage Magic and Illusions', *New Magic Lantern Journal*, 6:3 (1992), pp. 10–13; also Heard, *Phantasmagoria*, p. 233; Brooker, 'The Polytechnic Ghost', pp. 195, 200.

188. See Brooker, 'The Polytechnic Ghost', pp. 200–1 (which also quotes this anonymous review from the *Morning Advertiser*, 1 August 1879, p. 3).

189. See McKernan, 'Appendix: Volta Filmography', p. 188.

190. Brooker, 'The Polytechnic Ghost', p. 202.

191. Heard, *Phantasmagoria*, pp. 260–1.

192. Hudson John Powell, *Poole's Myriorama: A Story of Travelling Panorama Showmen* (Bradford on Avon: ELSP, 2002), p. 36; also *MLP&MPS*, pp. 49–50.

193. 'The Ghost', *Freeman's Journal*, 16 September 1863, p. 3; also quoted in Powell, *Poole's Myriorama*, pp. 36, 38.

194. Advertisement, *Freeman's Journal*, 16 September 1863, p. 1.

195. For details of these touring shows, see Powell, *Poole's Myriorama*, pp. 39–45; also *MLP&MPS*, pp. 50–1.

196. For a reproduction of the spectre slide, see Keith Williams, 'Dubliners, "the Magic-Lantern Business" and pre-Cinema', in John Nash (ed.), *James Joyce in the Nineteenth-Century* (Cambridge: Cambridge University Press, 2013), pp. 215–33 (229); other visions from *The Raven* are reproduced in Terry Borton and Debbie Borton (eds), *Before the Movies: American Magic-Lantern Entertainment and the Nation's First Great Screen Artist, Joseph Boggs Beale* (Bloomington, IN: Indiana University Press, 2015), pp. 29, 78, 104.

197. See Williams, *H. G. Wells, Modernity and the Movies*, pp. 39–42.

198. Gorki, 'In the Kingdom of Shadows', pp. 407–9.

199. See Virginia Woolf, 'The Cinema' (1926), in *Collected Essays*, ed. Leonard Woolf (London: Hogarth, 1964), vol. 2, pp. 268–72 (269). For Greene on the haunted persistence of cinema images, see Keith Williams, *British Writers and the Media 1930–45* (Basingstoke: Macmillan, 1991), p. 112.

200. For technical details of rain and snow effects, see *EML*, pp. 248, 287; on their popularity, see Judith Flanders, *Consuming Passions: Leisure and Pleasure in Victorian Britain* (London: Harper Press, 2006), pp. 311–12.

201. C. Goodwin Norton's famous 'country cottage-scene' incorporated such transformations to depict Christmas dawning (see detailed description in *MiTD*, p. 99).

202. Caroline Henkes demonstrates that remediated traits, specifically phantasmagoric visions, show 'performance practices of the magic lantern were still applied in films around 1910', several years after Joyce composed 'The Dead'. See Caroline Henkes, 'Early Christmas Films in the Tradition of the Magic Lantern', in Vogl-Bienek and Crangle (eds), *Screen Culture and the Social Question*, pp. 96–110 (109).

2

AN INDIVIDUATING RHYTHM: PICTURING TIME IN *A PORTRAIT OF THE ARTIST AS A YOUNG MAN*

A Mobilised Virtual Gaze

Joyce began writing *Portrait* in Trieste in 1907. After it was published in book form in 1916, H. G. Wells championed its shattering of formal moulds as 'a mosaic of jagged fragments that does altogether render with extreme completeness the growth of a rather secretive, imaginative boy in Dublin'. He applauded its abrupt transitions indicating shifts in space, time and consciousness: 'The technique is startling but on the whole it succeeds.' Though objecting to the substitution of dashes for quotation marks, Wells framed this in equally cinematic terms: 'one has the same wincing feeling of being flicked at that one used to have in the early cinema shows'.[1] Other reviewers, while less keen on *Portrait*'s innovations, related them to moving images too. The *New Age*'s reviewer criticised Joyce's 'determination to produce Kinematographic effects instead of a literary portrait', so it seemed 'a mere catalogue of unrelated states'.[2] Consequently, *Portrait* has also long been regarded as a key stage towards the cinematicity of *Ulysses*, as Eisenstein recognised, particularly the subjective visuality of Joyce's interior monologue.[3] While the technique does not yet appear in its culminating (i.e. first-person) form in *Portrait*, the novel nonetheless utilises a wide variety of techniques to visualise Stephen's stream of consciousness and 'unfold the display of events simultaneously with the particular manner in which these events pass through the consciousness and feelings, the associations and emotions, of his chief character', to borrow Eisenstein's terms.[4] More recently, Robert A. Gessner has argued that Joyce's Italian film-going came out strongly in *Portrait*'s flashback, cross-cutting and 'editing of time and space with the intensity and concentration of the camera'.[5] To Spiegel, this means that *Portrait*'s 'temporalised space' comes alive, 'as *process*, developing, changing, infinitely flexible, quick with advances and recessions, expansions and contractions, openings and closings, accumulations and dissolutions'.[6] Similarly, Neil Sinyard considers that the four sections of chapter 1 constitute 'one of the finest examples of montage in fiction'.[7] Hence Stephen's feelings and thoughts are monstrated through ekphrastic images rather than narrative commentary, reflecting the methods of lantern shows and their remediation in silent films to emphasise the primacy of visuality in the novel.

In particular, *Portrait* parallels or even anticipates the use of subjective or 'intra-diegetic' visualisation on film, as recently historicised by Christian Quendler's *The Camera-Eye Metaphor in Cinema*. According to Quendler, the camera-eye is a device for foregrounding phenomenological connections with the subjective perception of the viewer, creating a mediated point-of-view vicariously inhabited by them on screen.[8] This helps 'to identify, demarcate, and illustrate basic elements of cinema', but also 'corroborates an embodied and embedded view of the mind' based on 'functional continuity' with its technology.[9] Certainly, *Portrait* extends *Dubliners*' effect of a cinematically mobile, intra-diegetic 'gaze' to a virtually claustrophobic degree, because Joyce's free indirect discourse mediates every sight (and all other sensory experience) through Stephen's developing consciousness as sole 'focaliser'. Indeed *Portrait*'s themes and method are regarded as elaborating *Dubliners*' first three stories with their anonymous boy protagonists (though switching to an all-but-'invisible' third-person narrator). Both the emergent cinematicity of late nineteenth-century visual culture and Joyce's fiction were predicated on what Anne Friedberg calls a '*mobilised "virtual" gaze*', a characteristic feature of modernity: 'The *virtual gaze* is not a direct perception but a *received* perception mediated through representation [. . .] that travels in an imaginary *flânerie* through an imaginary elsewhere and an imaginary elsewhen.'[10] Spiegel points out that the increasingly radical nature of Joyce's focalisation technique makes his protagonists like intra-diegetic 'camera eyes', rather than characters in the traditional sense of being physically described from an external viewpoint. We generally *see with them*, rather than *seeing them* (except for rare moments of extra-diegetic third-person narrative 'tracking' their position objectively in the present, or when they are observed from another character's equally subjective point of view).[11]

Paradoxically, though Joyce's method seems strikingly cinematic on the page, mainstream film has problems presenting characters solely as 'observing consciousnesses', rather than externally visualised *dramatis personae*, because audiences find this effect challenging over extended periods. Using the 'subjective camera'[12] in a sustained way turns protagonists, in effect, into invisible men (or women), leaving filmgoers with only a retrospective first-person 'voice-over' to identify with after the coming of synchronised sound.[13] Similarly, in *Portrait*, Stephen is almost never described in physical detail, except when remembering experiences or fantasising about future situations. Paradoxically, he becomes corporeally 'visible' in the text *only when visualising* his past selves or imagining those to come, even though our reading experience locates us intimately within his senses and mind. In a typical example (for which readers have to wait until chapter 2), the adolescent's review of his days of preparatory school innocence end with a sudden materialisation of his lost childhood self standing beside him, now described externally for the first time, as virtual, oblivious and detached as a projected photographic image: 'It was strange *to see his small body appear again for a moment*: a little boy in a grey belted suit' (p. 78, italics mine). The same effect of self-visualisation – as if watching a virtual double from another time – occurs under emotional pressure to join the Jesuits. Imagined scenes of Spartan discipline in the novitiate are itemised through the repeated phrase, 'He saw himself [. . .]' (see p. 135 and discussion below).

An instructive method of highlighting the radically cinematic effect of *Portrait*'s focalisation technique is to compare the novel to Joseph Strick's 1977 film adaptation. Strick remains true to Joyce's plot, but treats it largely through classical continuity editing as dramatic action. His film is thus, paradoxically, far less cinematic than its source (or indeed typical Expressionist subjective camerawork near contemporary to it). The fact that Strick no longer focalises events through Stephen's developing consciousness is obvious from the beginning. Instead of gradually unfolding the political context of late nineteenth-century Ireland through his childhood perspective, Strick superimposes surtitles over panoramic rural landscapes to explain it. Thereafter, actors playing Stephen at different ages are almost permanently on screen, and moments when action is focalised through his intra-diegetic viewpoint are exceptionally rare. Even conspicuous opportunities such as Joyce's mimesis of blurred vision (an apparent gift to film-makers, as discussed below) are passed up. Details of phenomena and events are often explicitly conveyed through adult conversations rather than filtered through Stephen's child consciousness: Joyce's visually distinctive infirmary scene, in which Stephen's reaction to news of Parnell's death is visualised through dissolve and morphing effects in fevered hallucinations, is reduced to mere shots of the sick schoolboy in bed, alternating with priests using stage whispers. This lack of unmediated visual access to Stephen's interiority also diminishes the importance invested in key words and images which recur as leitmotifs, meaning that the associative rhythm of Stephen's thoughts and memories no longer has the same dynamic presence in the narrative foreground. However, Strick does belatedly attempt to present the diary sequence from *Portrait*'s final chapter as some kind of stream of consciousness. Joyce's discourse is rendered through images from Stephen's final days in Dublin, coupled with a voice-over by the actor playing his adolescent self (Bosco Hogan), hitherto as a conventionally dramatic role.

PORTRAIT AND (CHRONO)PHOTOGRAPHIC ANALYSIS

What inspired Joyce to develop such a radical method of monstrating Stephen's developing consciousness? Just like *Dubliners*, *Portrait*'s cinematicity is rooted in visual technologies and practices that pre-date film. Alongside ongoing references to lanternism (see below), *Portrait* epitomises literary emulation of visual analysis of movement over time. This was one of the primary scientific drives that led to the creation of film in the first place. Contemporary writing and scientific research using cameras shared a preoccupation with fixing 'decisive' but transient moments for close inspection, a pursuit of great significance to moderns such as Wells and, later, High Modernists such as Joyce. Hence, in Joyce's continuous defamiliarisation of the visual field, Virginia Woolf recognised that *Ulysses* (then being serialised in 1918) was '[p]ossibly like a cinema that shows you very slowly, how a horse does jump'. In referencing horses, Woolf was also tracing Joyce's cinematic tendency back to the 'Eureka' moment in 1878 when Eadweard Muybridge's 'animal locomotion studies' proved conclusively by means of instantaneous photography that all of a horse's hooves momentarily leave the ground in the so-called flying gallop (see figure 2.1). Crucially, Woolf added, 'all the pictures were a little made up before. Here is thought made phonetic – taken to bits.'[14] Similarly, Proust recollected how Muybridge's breakthrough both foregrounded the physiological limits of human perception and led to its manipulation by the 'persistence of vision' though film. In *Swann's Way*, Proust's narrator reflects on his inability to trace the associative involutions of his own stream of consciousness by analogy with the filmgoer's inability to arrest and break down the flow of moving images projected on screen back into its constituent photographic stills: 'I did not distinguish the various suppositions of which it was composed any more than, when we watch a horse running, we isolate the successive positions of its body as they appear upon a bioscope.'[15]

Woolf was comparing the almost uncannily mimetic precision of Joyce's descriptions with how technologically enhanced vision in slow-motion scientific films, following on from Muybridge's analysis, made it possible to record and anatomise natural phenomena in ways impossible for the naked eye to catch. But her next comment noted astutely how Joyce's defamiliarised vision represents both the event observed *and* the subject perceiving and reflecting on it. Woolf implied that Joyce carried out simultaneous vivisection (to echo *Stephen Hero*'s term) of the consciousness behind the vision: 'Here is thought made phonetic – taken to bits.' Indeed, as Stephen observes in *Ulysses*' 'Proteus' chapter, the moving phenomena of the world are contingent because of the conditions under which they are seen – stressing the 'Ineluctable modality of

Figure 2.1 'Horses, gallop; thoroughbred bay mare; Annie G'. Plate 626 from Edweard Muybridge, *Animal Locomotion* (1872–85). Science Museum/Science and Society Picture Library (no. 10667598).

the visible' – and must therefore be 'thought through my eyes', as he strives to process and understand them (3.1–2).[16] This underscores Joyce's own project: to represent consciousness itself through both *what* and *how* his protagonists see and the crucial role that cinematic influences play in this. Similarly, Walter Benjamin also thought that by defamiliarising the processes of vision and its capacity for artificial enhancement, 'The camera introduces us to unconscious optics as does psychoanalysis to unconscious impulses.'[17]

Photographically accurate proof of transitory phenomena constitutes one of Victorian culture's key 'epiphanies', with consequences that influenced Joyce's augmented portrayal of human perception and consciousness fundamentally. But this inter-medial tendency spread back wider and deeper. Foreshadowing Muybridgean photographic analysis, Baudelaire was so fascinated by how the Anglo-French artist Constantin Guys's rapid sketches of horse-drawn carriages, individual bodies and crowds appeared to capture fleeting instants of movement with such striking authenticity that he cited them as epitomising the objective of modern art itself in *Le Peintre de la vie moderne* (1863): 'there is in the trivial things of life, in the daily changing of external things, a speed of movement that imposes upon the artist an equal speed of execution'.[18] Muybridge's animal locomotion studies would begin fulfilling Baudelaire's objective by technologi-cal means. Hence Woolf's reading notes indicate that she was working out how *Ulysses'* cinematic presentation of vision can be traced back to this moment, but also how that process is equally connected with Joyce's presentation of con-sciousness. In the preceding section, Woolf refers to how '[t]he inner thought and then the little scattering of life on top to keep you in touch with reality' were simultaneous in *Ulysses*; also to its 'Queer *jerking* [italics mine] variety of thought'. Her terms thus suggest at once the laterally associative, elliptical move-ment of Joyce's characters' streams of consciousness and the notoriously stutter-ing effect of movement in early filmshows.[19]

Similarly, Joyce's artist friend Frank Budgen recollected him saying that in *Ulysses*, 'the body lives and moves through space and is the home of a full human personality', rendering his protagonists' minds inseparable from their sensations and perceptions at any given moment.[20] For this reason, Budgen thought 'Proteus' contained the best 'word picture' of a running dog yet writ-ten, as if it too were a form of animal locomotion study. In his Dublin lectures of February 1890, Muybridge compared the exact gaits of horses with other animals, including dogs, demonstrating them in animated form through his 'Zoöpraxiscope' projector (see figure 2.2). In the same way that no one had

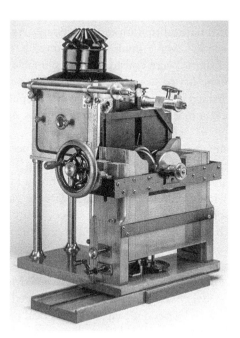

Figure 2.2 'Muybridge's Zoopraxiscope, 1880'. Science Museum/Science and Society Picture Library (no. 10318976).

really seen how a horse gallops before Muybridge, for Budgen Joyce provided a more vividly apprehensible image of how a dog actually behaves as a moving phenomenon in Stephen's visual field than any fiction before:[21]

> Their dog ambled about a bank of dwindling sand, trotting, sniffing on all sides. Looking for something lost in a past life. Suddenly he made off like a bounding hare, ears flung back, chasing the shadow of a lowskim-ming gull. The man's shrieked whistle struck his limp ears. He turned, bounded back, came nearer, trotted on twinkling shanks. On a field ten-ney a buck, trippant, proper, unattired. At the lacefringe of the tide he halted with stiff forehoofs, seawardpointed ears. His snout lifted barked at the wavenoise, herds of seamorse. They serpented towards his feet, curling, unfurling many crests, every ninth, breaking, plashing, from far, from farther out, waves and waves. (*Ulysses* 3.332–41)

Spiegel agrees that this passage is more than just coldly and photographically precise, because Joyce's metaphors also make us simultaneously aware of the manoeuvrings of the mind behind its augmented vision.[22] Although Stephen mentally compares the dog's movements to other quadrupeds – hares, bucks and horses – as Muybridge had also done, this is achieved through tropes as much poetic as biomechanical. There may also be other links with rapid photography's capturing of natural motion in this passage. As Rossell notes, from the mid-nineteenth century, wave images by Gustave le Grey in France and C. A. D. Halford in Britain 'were considered the pinnacle of "instantaneous" photography', in their ability to stop time and reveal the secret patterns of phenomena.[23] Waves remained a common subject of chronophotographic analysis, influencing the earliest subjects of film pioneers such as Birt Acres, as well as the Lumières.

Stephen also compares the perceptio-cognitive processes and effects of organic and photographic seeing shortly after, particularly in relation to depth and perspective as rendered by the 'binocularity' of human vision. He references another optical toy widely available from the 1850s for viewing photographs. The stereoscope or 'solid viewer' (from Greek *stereo*, 'solid', and *scopos*, 'view') was devised in 1838 by Sir Charles Wheatstone to investigate the physiology of vision, whereby we see in depth through convergent images resulting from the slightly different positioning of each eye. Since it artificially recreated the impression of depth so vividly, the stereoscope was redesigned for the mass market by inventors such as Oliver Wendell Holmes and achieved enormous popularity through 'stereo-views'. These 'flat', virtually identical pairs of photographs, taken by twin-lensed cameras, appeared three-dimensional by combination. The stereoscope was also a key influence on effects of virtual tangibility and spatial immersion projected by magic lantern, as at Dublin Analyticon shows, and subsequently on film.[24] In 'Proteus', Stephen takes a hypothetical mental snap-shot; his imagined 'click' possibly referring as much to the locking mechanism of patent stereoscopes as to the camera shutter (as Cleo Hanaway points out). Their double images had to be 'clicked' into the correct focal position for the viewer to appreciate the three-dimensional effect, as alluded to in the fore-ground/background alternation in Stephen's thinking: 'Flat I see, then think dis-tance, near, far, flat I see, east, back. Ah, see now. Falls back suddenly, frozen in stereoscope. Click does the trick' (*Ulysses* 3.418–20).[25]

Stephen's stereo-view, momentarily abstracted from the ineluctably modulating continuum of his visual impressions, also indicates that the relationship between 'frozen' and moving images is equally paradoxical in both Joyce and cinema history. The very first projected films began with still images on screen, before being magically cranked into life to the audi-ence's astonishment as the short reel rushed to its conclusion. Similarly, after the voyeuristic relishing of Gerty Macdowell's choreographed display of leg in Joyce's 'Nausicaa' chapter, Bloom recalls visiting a moving image peep-show, the only explicit reference to a film-viewing technology of sorts in the whole of *Ulysses*: 'Mutoscope pictures on Capel Street: for men only. Peeping Tom. Willy's hat and what the girls did with it. Do they snapshot those girls, or is it all a fake?' (13.351–2). As Gunning points out, Bloom's question – 'Do they snapshot those girls'? – effectively alludes to how instan-taneous photography (widespread from the 1880s following Muybridge's experiments) could 'freeze action in full flight, producing seemingly absurd images of leapers suspended in mid-jump and mid-air, or naughty ladies in mid-kick'. Paradoxically, to assume that the snapshot is 'the exact opposite of a motion picture in which jumps and kicks proceed from start to finish in full arc' actually ignores how it underlies film itself. Technically speaking, it was film's 'necessary antecedent', since filmstrips are actually made up of successive stills, blurred into motion through persistence of vision when passed rapidly through a viewer or projected.[26]

Joyce suggests this paradoxical photo-filmic relation between stillness and motion in several contexts in *Ulysses*. In 'Nestor' Stephen's visual fan-tasy of time rebounding 'shock by shock' (prompted by triumphalist cheers from the games field outside while remembering his own schooling) is pre-sented like a cinematic insert; its rapid sequence of images briefly arrested by the 'frozen deathspew of the slain' like action suddenly freeze-framed in *media res* (2.317). Similarly, in 'Proteus' itself Stephen remembers feel-ing so frustrated by a jobsworth Parisian post office clerk shutting up early that he imagines blowing him apart. Stephen immediately regrets this flash of temper and instantly replays the fantasy in 'reverse'; stopping its action and reassembling the clerk's exploded body unharmed like a filmstrip run backwards: 'Look clock. Must get. *Fermé*. Hired dog! Shoot him to bloody bits with a bang shotgun, bits man spattered walls all brass buttons. Bits all khrrrrklak in place clack back. Not hurt? O, that's all right. Shake hands' (3.185–91).[27] *Cretinetti che Bello!* (1909) or *Too Beautiful!* (shown at the Volta, 3–5 February 1910) is a similar trick film fantasy based on reversing the process of tearing a body to bits. Ladies muster like Maenads driven wild by Cretinetti's sexual magnetism. They finally catch him and rip him apart, only for him to magically reassemble. The scene uses a substitution splice swapping actor for dummy, and then stop-motion animation to reintegrate the body parts. Stephen's onomatopoeic 'khrrrrklak' may mimic the sound of a projector crank suddenly reversed rather than a firearm discharged point blank. Indeed, such playful foregrounding of film's material basis in strips of individual, pausable and reversible frames was one of the chief attractions of early programmes. Though the Lumières' first films consisted of simple actualities less than one minute long such as *Démolition d'un mur*, they quickly discovered (by the sheer serendipity of feeding the reel the wrong way) that cinematic time could run backwards too, so the wall miraculously recomposed itself from rubble (similar effects had already been achieved with Edison's kinetoscope).[28]

THE 1904 'PORTRAIT'

However, Joyce's 'anatomising' tendency – simultaneously visual and psycho-logical and based on the camera's technologically enhanced seeing into space and time – can be traced back much earlier than *Ulysses*. *Portrait*'s distinctive cinematicity is rooted in speculations about a method for representing the pro-cesses of a mind developing over time in Joyce's first version: his brief autobio-graphical sketch of 1904, 'A Portrait of the Artist'. Its cryptic metaphors (long puzzling to scholars) also derive from the context of photographic analysis, especially the *Chronophotographie* – literally 'time photography' – practised by Étienne-Jules Marey, whose work complemented Muybridge's and played an equally influential role in film's development. The sketch's tropes can thus be illuminated by placing them back into this context. Moreover, they point towards an experimental psychological purpose and moving form lost in the inert naturalism of Joyce's much longer second version, *Stephen Hero*,[29] but eventually realised in his published novel. As the 1904 'Portrait's' opening paragraph states:

> The *features of infancy are not commonly reproduced in the adoles-cent portrait*, for, so capricious are we, that we cannot or will not con-ceive the past in any other than its iron memorial aspect. *Yet the past surely implies a fluid succession of presents, the development of an entity of which our present is a phase only.* Our world, again, recognises its acquaintance chiefly by the characters of beard and inches and is, for the

most part, estranged from those of its members who seek through some art, by some process of the mind as yet untabulated, *to liberate from the personalised lumps of matter that which is their individuating rhythm*, the first or formal relation of their parts. But for such as these a portrait is not an identificative paper but rather *the curve of an emotion*.[30] [italics mine]

The unconventional idea of 'features of infancy' still showing forth through 'the adolescent portrait' suggests overlapping images from different places, times or states, like the magic lantern's chronologically shuffling dissolves, inserts and superimpositions referenced in *Dubliners*. However, new leading concepts and dynamically visual phrasing introduced here – 'the past [. . .] implies a fluid succession of presents, the development of an entity [. . .] to liberate from the personalised lumps of matter that which is their individuating rhythm [. . .] the curve of an emotion' – recall other key moments in film's technological prehistory. From the 1860s, new electric shutter mechanisms and instantaneous plates made it increasingly possible to defamiliarise reality temporally; to see the ordinarily invisible. Recording images at 1/1000 of a second or less, they enabled scientists 'to fix attitudes too transitory for the ordinary eye', as Wells put it.[31] Thus Muybridge and Marey inspected moving phenomena in a kind of action replay, but also anticipated the filmstrip. Muybridge may have been the first to break what Ian Christie calls the 'monumental stillness'[32] necessitated by long exposures, through an impression of continuous movement using consecutively arranged batteries of cameras with tripwires, but both he and Marey effectively materialised time by photographic means. Their respective methods sliced up and recomposed continuous action in order to apprehend its dynamic reality more accurately.

Whereas Muybridge segmented action into a series of separate frames, Marey overlapped them. In 1882 he developed a special 'chronophotographic gun' and then a high-speed camera on rails. By 1888 paper roll film, succeeded by celluloid in 1890, enabled extended image strips of black-suited athletes, virtually invisible against ebony backgrounds except for lines of muscular thrust picked out in white (see figure 2.3). Marey's subjects were thus ambiguously 'dematerialised', but with unbounded presence as physical movement. In terms of Joyce's 1904 tropes, Marey effectively 'liberate[d]' the 'individuating rhythm' of a body in motion from shots of separate moments, making its action visible as an abstract 'curve' rising and falling in space (see figure 2.4). Muybridge's work mutually influenced Marey's studies, and both, in turn, influenced Edison's researcher W. K. L. Dickson, whose kinetoscope loop subjects resemble their work closely and whose device finally inspired the Lumière brothers' cinematograph.[33]

Figure 2.3 'Homme vêtu de noir avec des points blancs et des bandes blanches pour l'analyse chronophotographique de la locomotion'. Bibliothèque nationale de France.

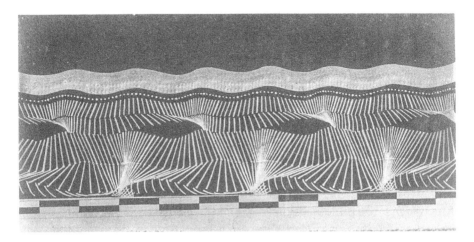

Figure 2.4 'Analyse chronophotographique de la marche'. Bibliothèque nationale de France.

ANIMAL LOCOMOTION STUDIES AND CHRONOPHOTOGRAPHY IN DUBLIN

Muybridge's principal publications – *Animal Locomotion: An Electro-Photographic Investigation of Consecutive Phases of Animal Movement* (1887), *Animals in Motion* (1891), *The Human Figure in Motion* (1901) – aroused enormous interest among writers and intellectuals, as did Marey's chronophotographic survey, *Le Mouvement*, published in 1894 and quickly translated into English the following year.[34] The Poet Laureate, Alfred Lord Tennyson, attended one of Muybridge's prestigious London lectures in 1882, along with leading biologist T. H. Huxley (under whom Wells studied), the Prime Minister William Gladstone and members of the royal family.[35] Photographic analysis aroused similar polymathic fascinations in Dublin. In 1876 Michael Angelo Hayes, founder member of its Photographic Society and fellow of the Royal Hibernian Academy, had already published a pamphlet, *The Delineation of Animals in Rapid Motion*, paralleling Muybridge's research, but quite independently. Hayes's illustrations similarly detailed the exact positions of a galloping horse's legs and were demonstrated by lantern projection and animated on phenakistoscope discs to the Royal Dublin Society in November.[36] Joyce certainly knew about Hayes, listing him in the somewhat ironic context of the roll of 'Irish heroes and heroines of antiquity' in 'Cyclops' (*Ulysses* 12.176, 189).[37] If Hayes had not drowned in 1877, his research would probably have continued. Indeed Muybridge himself acknowledged Hayes's pioneering work and cited the paper that the Irishman read to the Society 'many years before' on his own visit in February 1890.[38]

Muybridge was invited to lecture 'On the Science of Animal Locomotion in its Relation to Design and Art' to both the Royal Dublin Society and the Photographic Society of Ireland, projecting his findings in both still and moving images as reported in the *Irish Times* and *Freeman's Journal*.[39] The *Freeman's Journal* explained Muybridge's methods and what they revealed in great detail:

> As an illustration of his method of investigation we may instance Professor Muybridge's analysis of the gait of a horse. This gait may be either a walk, an amble, a trot, a canter, or a gallop. And each of these different gaits is, of course, the result of a particular mode in which the horse uses its four legs in locomotion. The motion of the legs occurs so rapidly that the unaided eye would be unable to accurately trace the mode characteristic of each respective gait. But the modern developments of the art of instantaneous photography have afforded Professor Muybridge the means of surmounting this defect of the human vision. The duration of one single stride of the horse may be divided into twelve or twenty sub-parts, and instantaneous photographs of each of the strides may be taken by a battery of as many cameras suitably distributed over the parts of the stride.

> In this way a series of permanent pictures are obtained of the successive stages through which the stride has passed, and the whole law of the animal's gait in locomotion becomes apparent.[40]

The report also itemised findings about other quadrupeds, 'as remarkable as they are unexpected' in revealing underlying similarities between them, as well as about secrets of flight:

> Again, it is found that in the course of the flapping of a bird's wing in flight, the primary feathers of each extended wing are standing apart from each other, and that each separate feather undergoes a rotation on its own axis in the course of the flap of the wing exactly similar to the 'feathering' of the oars by rowers in the course of each stroke . . .

Hence Muybridge concluded that this 'rotary motion' provided the necessary uplift for birds such as eagles to soar. Understandably, the report highlighted how '[t]he old dispute about whether a trotting horse ever really leaves the ground completely or not is set at rest'. The *Freeman's Journal* also noted how Muybridge's zoöpraxiscope detailed the running gait of dogs, anticipating Stephen's verbal analysis in 'Proteus'.[41]

Muybridge's device clearly received wide and enthusiastic acclaim and stuck in public memory. When the *Irish Independent* reported on the mixed technical success of Dublin's first projected film programme on 20 April 1896, it acknowledged that the cinematograph was 'undoubtedly capable of accomplishing great things', but compared it unfavourably with both kinetoscope and zoöpraxiscope. The latter's 'excellence', popularised to music hall audiences, meant that 'a little disappointment was experienced'.[42]

Just as Hayes's research paralleled Muybridge's, another Dubliner took a prominent role in chronophotography. Captivated by Marey's work, Joyce's close contemporary Lucien Bull (born in 1876 to a French mother and graduating from the University of Paris's Faculté des Sciences in 1896) attained a permanent post at the Institut Marey in 1902 (the same year Joyce first stayed in Paris). Having served as Marey's personal assistant since 1894, Bull became Marey's scientific heir. Although Marey opposed chonophotographic experiments with film, Bull (working with Pierre Nogues) extended his project through X-ray, microscope and high-speed analysis films after Marey's death in 1904 (see figure 2.5).[43] Chronophotography allowed movement to be scrutinised as an abstract pattern 'developing' in space over time. Dissolving individual identity into curves of poetic dynamism, it anticipated Cubist painting but also Futurism's 'lines of force', and demonstrated how closely innovations in science and cultural forms were interconnected.

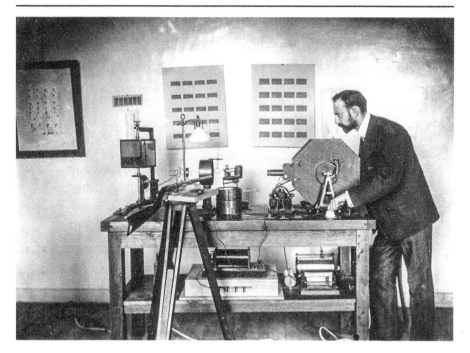

Figure 2.5 'Lucien Bull with his high-speed camera, Paris, 1904'.
Science Museum/Science and Society Picture Library (no. 10306330)

However, could the dynamic and anatomising tendency in Joyce's fiction have been inspired by sources other than Muybridge or Marey's work?[44] As we have seen, the matrix of Victorian cinematicity meant that a sense of movement was emergent in many media. Archie K. Loss argues that dynamism was the most important aspect of Joyce's writing, enhanced by his encounters with Modernist painting on the Continent.[45] It was pervasive not just in Italian Futurist works such as Giacomo Balla's *Dynamism of a Dog Leash* (1911), but also in French Cubist paintings such as Marcel Duchamp's *Nude Descending a Staircase, No.2*, or the Russian 'Cubo Futurism' of Kasimir Malevich's *Knife-Grinder* (both 1912). Moreover, the effect of dynamic painting, Loss acknowledges, 'is, at its most literal, cinematographic – a depiction of successive movements of a figure or object in a limited field of space, the slightly varied forms of hands or feet or wheels suggesting the afterimages of film' and their effects on perception itself.[46] He also argues that dynamic effects in *Ulysses* recall the kinetic 'retinal afterimages' of Futurist paintings. For example, Bloom is described as dashing downstairs 'with a flurried stork's legs' to save his burning breakfast (5.383–4).[47] The Futurists' 'Technical Manifesto' of 1910 specifically referred to persistence of vision, as well as animal locomotion and chronophotographic studies, pushing this cinematic tendency towards rhythmically abstract, geometric patterning:

> The gesture which we would reproduce on canvas shall no longer be a fixed *moment* in universal dynamism. It shall be the *dynamic sensation* itself.
>
> Indeed, all things move, all things run, all things are rapidly changing. A profile is never motionless before our eyes, but it constantly appears and disappears. On account of the persistency of an image upon the retina, moving objects constantly multiply themselves; their form changes like rapid vibrations, in their mad career. Thus a running horse has not four legs but twenty, and their movements are triangular. [italics in original][48]

William S. Rubin also argues that Futurist dynamism was in fact 'a *narrative*, not a *plastic* innovation' and was probably therefore more important for the development of Modernist writing than art.[49]

However, all these instances *post-date* Joyce's 1904 autobiographical sketch. Photographic analysis is therefore most likely the common source (indeed *Nude Descending a Staircase* has been traced back to specific images by Muybridge)[50] and thus a key inspiration in Joyce's early work. Although exposure to Modernist art *after* Joyce's entering permanent exile that year probably helped revive and consolidate structural ideas inchoate in his first version of *Portrait*, these derived from his exposure to the influence of photographic analysis before he finally left Dublin. In that year's version of 'Portrait', Joyce hypothesised a means for simultaneously figuring both physical *and* psychological motion, to present the rhythm of a consciousness developing over time in the same way that instantaneous photography (feeding into film) dissected and recomposed living motion, using such experiments as both technical precedent and guiding metaphor for the project eventually realised in his novel.

Just as *Portrait*'s cinematicity is rooted in this strand of film's prehistory and the expectations it raised, when Edison's kinetoscope was first exhibited in Dublin in April 1895 (shortly after Joyce turned 13), the *Evening Telegraph*'s reviewer drew attention to its scientific basis in the photographic anatomisation of movement:

> The 'Kinetoscope', the latest, and one of the most remarkable inventions of Mr Edison, is at present being exhibited at 68 Dame Street. *The invention is fairly well known, as far as its principle is concerned* . . . By the means of the 'Kinetoscope' photographs of objects in motion, *taken instantaneously*, are reproduced in the same duration of time and in the

same order so that *a practically continuous movement is obtained. The impression produced on the eye is exactly the same as if the figures were in motion in life.*[51] [italics mine]

Commenting on the kinetoscopes exhibited at the Ierne bazaar in May, the *Evening Mail* drew attention both to the marvellous virtualism of their impression of movement and to its plenitude, surpassing the singularity or repetitiveness of action reproduced by the most sophisticated devices hitherto:

> by a mechanical contrivance the film is passed before the eyes with such rapidity that the action depicted is brought out with life-like vividness. Whether the subject be a dancing display, a cock fight, or a wrestling bout a living picture is accurately shown and any scene can be produced, no matter how complex or multitudinal the figures.[52]

A follow-up article explained the mechanism in more detail, going even further back to the familiar principle of optical toys that exploited persistence of vision, such as the thaumatrope (which artificially synthesised separate images into one) and the zoëtrope (which animated them). It also anticipated how Edison's device (through which filmstrips were fed at high speed by electricity) would inevitably be modified for projection and mass viewing:

> The kinetoscope is a thaumatrope on a grand scale, capable by means of photographs from life of producing the most complicated movements. At present the instrument is something like the popular peep-show [i.e. the zoëtrope or phenakistoscope] into which the spectator has to look through a slit at the pictures which are placed within, and being illuminated are passed rapidly before his vision. In time, however, it is likely that the arrangement will be replaced by an optical lantern through which the sliders [i.e. filmstrips] will be passed rapidly so as to produce the same effect on a screen in view of a large audience as is now by means of this box arrangement. The kinetoscope is an object of great popular and scientific interest, and is well worthy of a visit.[53]

Correctly predicting the kinetoscope's fusion with the lantern (already adapted into Muybridge's zoöpraxiscope), the article nonetheless grossly overestimated the standard frame rate of the silent period (14–16 per second), which would give this phase of cinema its characteristic nickname, 'the flickers'.

Accounts of Ireland's first projected film shows also explained the debt owed to technological predecessors. The *Freeman's Journal*'s report on 'The Wonder of Cyclopia: the Animatograph', Paul's alternative to the Lumières' device, followed a similar pattern in May 1896 when it was exhibited at the eponymous bazaar. Under the sub-heading, 'How 'Tis Done', the article explained the new technology in terms of its predecessor moving image devices:

> The wonder is simple of explanation. The Animatograph is but an extension of the principle of Edison's Kinetoscope to enable the pictures to be projected on a large screen capable of being seen by a moderately sized audience. The principle of both is that of the common little toy, the thaumatrope and its improved successors, the padamascope and the zoetrope, or wheel of life. The latter is quite familiar to most people.[54]

It also unpacked the role played by instantaneous serial photography and 'persistence of vision':

> The invention is a pleasing illusion on the optic nerve due to the persistence of vision. During half the time that the spectator is studying the picture with its moving figures there is really no picture whatever on the screen. At a fire a series of pictures are taken in rapid succession on a roll of celluloid film, each exposure being about a hundred and eightieth of a second. From these negatives a series of transparencies or lantern slides are printed on a similar celluloid roll. This roll is placed in a brilliantly lighted optical lantern fitted with special machinery which draws it by a series of jerks in front of the light and the condensers and the pictures are in a succession projected upon the screen, enlarged several diameters as with the ordinary lantern slides . . . The retina, however, retains the image of the brightly illuminated picture during the brief interval that elapses until the next takes its place . . . the eye, unconscious of the illusion, see all the figures in rapid and active motion as in real life.[55]

Finally the article commented on how film projection placed mundane actions under a kind of defamiliarising visual and temporal microscope, so they could be seen in a new way: 'The rapidity of the photographic apparatus enables the most minute movements to be reproduced, such as leaping, running, dancing, and even the movement of the lips in speaking and the varying phases of the expression of the face.'[56]

Indeed, as Dublin's *Evening Mail* recognised within a month of the cinematograph's first public demonstration in Paris, unlike the small-scale subjects of kinetoscope loops (usually short individual performances or actions), the potential of the Lumières' device was proving infinitely greater and more diverse in both space and time for 'reproduc[ing] past scenes, such as processions, ceremonies, situations on the stage, and so on, by means of photography'. Thus it 'paves the way for a new art in the shape of a pictorial retrospect of past events near or remote, so that in future a person will be able to review photographically the actual scenes he may have witnessed in the course of his life, or others belonging to times and places beyond his reach'.[57] This sense of cultural breakthrough, with incalculable potentials, closely parallels Joyce's own innovative method of 'picturing time' through moving images in *Portrait* in several respects. Stephen's developing consciousness is continuously represented through the associative rhythms of perception and memory: scenes he has witnessed occur and recur with concreteness and externalisation that appears both photographically vivid and virtually cinematic.

'A MODERN DAEDALUS'

Besides its initial conception and structure, *Portrait* also references the ongoing development of cinematicity and the role of rapid photographic analysis through its leitmotif. Joyce's epigraph from Ovid's *Metamorphoses* – '*Et ignotas animum dimittit in artes . . .*' – invokes the mythical inventor, Daedalus, who became an artificial 'bird man' in order to escape the Cretan Labyrinth and furnishes *Portrait*'s leitmotif of flight. The Latin translates as, 'So then to unimagined arts he set his mind'; the line continues, 'and altered nature's laws'.[58] By an auspicious coincidence that would have appealed to Joyce's triangulated interests in vision, wordplay and mythological parallelisms, the zoëtrope (classical Greek for 'life' + *tropos*, 'turning') was originally christened the 'Daedalum' in 1834, from the classical Greek for 'skilful' or 'cunningly wrought', the same root as the name of *Portrait*'s mythic 'artificer'. Although its principle goes back at least to second-century China, its modern form was invented by the British mathematician William George Horner. The Daedalum animated sequences of still images by taking advantage of the eye-conning 'persistence of vision' effect.[59] Renamed the 'Zoëtrope' by the American William F. Lincoln (on patenting his mass-manufactured version), it became enormously popular transatlantically from the 1860s. The zoëtrope consists of a horizontally revolving drum, with vertical viewing slots, containing a replaceable strip depicting figures in various stages of movement. As it spins, they spring into jerky, but vivid action. Typical subjects included acrobats jumping through hoops, jugglers, arcing dolphins and (most Joyceanly) gulls skimming the waves (see *MiTD*, pp. 127–8).

The zoëtrope's synonym, the 'wheel of life', was also applied to other patent inventions that exploited the mechanics of vision. The 'Wheel of Life Lantern' was a miniature version of Joseph Plateau's phenakistoscope. By means of a revolving glass disc, it similarly animated sequences of drawings on its rim, but could also project subjects.[60] The Dublin lantern supplier Robinson's promoted this version of the 'Wheel of Life' as the 'new optic wonder' (*MLP&MPS*, p. 52). As we have seen, phenakistoscopes modified by Hayes and Muybridge played a key role in demonstrating animal locomotion in Dublin. The latter's zoöpraxiscope, combining phenakistoscopic discs with a magic lantern projector, animated his consecutive stills into the appearance of a genuinely 'fluid succession of presents', to borrow the evocative phrase from the 1904 'Portrait'.[61] Thence experiments in cinematicity moved inexorably towards a mechanical device that could convincingly represent reality in total motion.

Hence in 1904 Joyce was already staking his claim as a literary experimenter on the crest of a modernity looking out on the twin marvels of moving photographic images and artificial flight. Rapid photography's causal links with aviation design exemplify the fundamental synergy between them: it gave birth to the possibilities of filmic virtual movement on one hand, and helped pioneer powered flight on the other. The French Society for the Encouragement of Aerial Locomotion by Means of Machines Heavier than Air sponsored Marey's chronophotographic anatomisations of bird flight, which furnished the first mechanical prototypes. Orville and Wilbur Wright studied Marey's *The Flight of Birds* (1890), alongside glider-maker Otto Lilienthal's *Bird-Flight as the Basis of Aviation* (1889), for their crucial innovation – cambered wings for uplift and manoeuvrability – applying photography as an essential tool. New short-exposure plates enabled them to capture motion instantaneously themselves, alternating as pilot and cameraman. In turn, 'First flight' captions the photograph witnessing their success on 17 December 1903 at Kitty Hawk, North Carolina, the year before the first version of *Portrait*. Wilbur also piloted the first aerial cinematographer, Félix Mesguich, in 1908, shooting the earliest moving images of the earth from the sky.[62]

Joyce frequently references both natural and artificial aviation in *Portrait*, including Stephen's own visual 'study' of swallow flight (pp. 188–9). Alongside running visual matches with bird forms (ranging from the school bully Heron's beaked profile, to Stephen's triumphant vision of the wading cockle-picker at Dollymount, pp. 64, 144), this suggests Joyce's creative reflection of such pioneering developments. Indeed Joyce had a topical precedent for modernising the Daedalus myth close to home in the genre of 'scientific romance'. In Tom Greer's *A Modern Daedalus* (1885), an Irish inventor discovers the secret that the whole world is questing by studying the mechanics of bird flight and building miniature gliders from dead gulls.[63] Donning his winged flight-packs, a Nationalist air force takes to the sky to attack Dublin Castle, the seat of British rule, bomb the Royal Navy into submission and liberate their homeland, incidentally providing the opportunity for prescient descriptions of moving airborne perspectives (see Chapter 3 for detailed discussion of aerial panoramas in *A Modern Daedalus*). Though Joyce developed more pacifist tactics of literary resistance, he certainly knew Greer's novel and repurposed key aspects of its imagery.

A Cultural Epiphany

Daedalian imagery is just one way in which fascination with the mechanics and potentials of defamiliarised vision is paramount in *Portrait*. It is arguable that Joyce, like Stephen's scholastic hero, Thomas Aquinas, prioritises vision as shorthand for the sensorium as a whole, making sight the novel's leading sense ekphrastically: '[Aquinas] uses *visa*, said Stephen, to cover esthetic apprehensions of all kinds, whether through sight or hearing or through any other avenue of apprehension' (*Portrait*, p. 174). Moreover, seeing in *Portrait* is always presented as more than simply organic. Robert Scholes and Richard M. Kain describe Joyce's notion of epiphany as a kind of snapshot of 'life observed, caught in a kind of camera eye, which reproduced a significant moment without comment'. The young Joyce believed that 'Epiphany could not be constructed, only recorded. But . . . once recorded, could be placed in an artistic framework and used to enrich with reality a fictional narrative.'[64] The tropes of Joyce's famous definition, with its reference to 'the gropings of a spiritual [i.e. more than bodily] eye which seeks to adjust its vision to an exact focus' (*Stephen Hero*, p. 189), hint at photography's prosthetic enhancement of vision and defamiliarisation of objects and phenomena through instantaneous images and close-ups. Hence James Agee, writing in 1946, compared the 'denseness, insight and complexity' of Joyce's literary visualisation techniques to how documentary photographers such as Helen Levitt and Walker Evans 'illuminate and enhance our ability to see what is before us'.[65] Similarly, writing about Muybridge, photographic analysis and its extension into film, Benjamin noted how the camera revealed 'physiognomic aspects, image worlds, which dwell in the smallest things'. It was able to dissect reality in a new way because:

> It is another nature which speaks to the camera rather than to the eye; other above all in the sense that a space informed by human consciousness gives way to a space informed by the unconscious. Whereas it is a commonplace that, for example, we have some idea what is involved in the act of walking (if only in general terms), we have no idea what happens during the fraction of a second when a person actually takes a step. Photography, with its devices of slow motion and enlargement, reveals this secret. It is through photography that we first discover the existence of this optical unconscious, just as we discover the instinctual unconscious through psychoanalysis. Details of structure, cellular tissue, with which technology and medicine are normally concerned – all of this is, in it origins, much more native to the camera than the atmospheric landscape or soulful portrait.[66]

Following Spiegel, Scarlett Baron suggests that Joyce's proto-filmic literary techniques can be traced back to Gustave Flaubert's impassive narrative method. Baron demonstrates how Joyce's interest in optics links Flaubert's own notion of visual examination, to discover 'the essence of an object', with *Stephen Hero*'s quasi-photographic figuring of epiphany. The terms that Stephen uses to describe seeing the ballast office clock mimic the process of a camera focusing on, capturing and fixing the image of an everyday object by isolating it from its phenomenological background – the choice of a clock foregrounding the notion of flash-freezing an instant in time. Baron refers to Joyce's use of such close-ups as 'aesthetic tunnel vision' for creating snapshots of moments in time.[67] She suggests that his method not only allows concentrated scrutiny through precise mimesis, but also, paradoxically, for the object to be rendered significant by presenting it subjectively. Hence both Flaubert and Joyce made use of cinematic methods to align their moving narrative eyes with their protagonists' minds, portraying them in greater depth and vividness through how and what they see.[68]

Nevertheless, in his *Paris Notebook* of 1902–03, Joyce asked himself: '*Can a photograph be a work of art?*' At the time, he replied in the negative because: 'A photograph is a disposition of sensible matter and may be so disposed for an aesthetic end but it is not a human disposition of sensible matter. Therefore it is not a work of art.'[69] Though Joyce distrusted the camera's automatic recording and reproduction of reality, his *Notebook* statement left open the possibility that his own epiphanic snapshots of moments which caught his eye might eventually be edited into narrative contexts which realised their latent potential as art. Similarly, just as individual photographic frames acquire aesthetic value as part of a dynamic flow of images in film, Joyce integrated many of the epiphanic moments he recorded into *Portrait*'s dynamic structure. Hence it is instructive to compare how Joyce eventually went beyond consideration of individual frames into arrangements of multiple images animating into associative patterns through the process of Stephen's thought and memory with Giorgio Agamben's views about photography's inherent temporal ambiguities. Agamben argues that the snapshot's arresting of gestures and actions always implicitly refers beyond its record of an individual moment to the potential series of which it is part. He highlights how this was particularly the case in the context of the dynamism of Muybridgean photographic analysis, as well as in relation to epiphany. Moreover, Agamben extends this into an analogy with Bergson's distinction between conscious recollection and *memoire involontaire*: the single frame's recording function corresponding to 'the recollection seized by voluntary memory', while its gesturing to the instants before and after equates with 'the image flashing in the epiphany of involuntary memory'. Hence, 'while the former lives in magical isolation, the latter always refers beyond itself to a whole of which it is part'.[70] Just as the horse's lifted hooves imply the whole rhythm of its run in Muybridge's projected sequences, so *Portrait*'s individual moments always imply the moving rhythm of Stephen's consciousness, linking and animating them together.

In parallel with Muybridge and Marey's photographic interventions into the development of film, *Portrait* realised a new ekphrastic method of 'picturing time' (to borrow the title of Marta Braun's study of Marey) only speculated about in Joyce's 1904 version: presenting the development of Stephen's consciousness through coordinating present perception, reflection and memory in its cinematic form.[71] Though epiphany is not explicitly named in *Portrait*, Joyce weaves his novel around a number of such symbolic moments, opting for a more satisfyingly dynamic treatment of its principle in action. Consequently, Stephen's undergraduate postulating about 'esthetic emotion' as properly 'static' (p. 172) conflicts with the fundamentally 'kinetic' drive of the text that constitutes him. *Portrait* depends on effects of moving rather than still images for interlinking its epiphanies; the mature writer's practice outstripping his youthful avatar's theories. Nonetheless, the character is 'groping' (to borrow another of *Stephen Hero*'s epiphanic tropes) towards something suggestive of the novel's dynamic rhythm which always subsumes individual moments of experience with an evocative sense of before and after. Note Stephen's concluding use of both the term 'dissolved', redolent of lanternism in *Dubliners*, but also recurring frequently in *Portrait* to evoke associative movement between images (as discussed below),[72] and also 'rhythm' in the following quotation about art's effect on spectators: 'an ideal pity or an ideal terror, a stasis called forth, prolonged and at last dissolved by what I call the rhythm of beauty' (p. 173). Similarly, Stephen's phrase 'the rhythm of its structure' is applied to the basket, exemplifying his definition of the 'integritas' necessary for isolating and presenting objects authentically as if in photographic close-up (p. 178). Moreover, Stephen highlights the term 'image' in relation to each of the three principal literary genres – lyric, epic and tragic – that he discusses (p. 180), as well as describing the process of *ekphrasis* and its vivid effect of *enaergia* just before: 'The image it is clear must be set between the mind or senses of the artist himself and the mind or senses of others' (p. 179).

'ALL THE PICTURES WERE MADE UP BEFORE'

Hence in the course of presenting the individuating rhythm of Stephen's consciousness in its vividly cinematic way, few Anglophone texts pre-dating *Portrait* rival the sustained intra-diegetic focalisation of Joyce's protagonist. This constitutes an effect of seeing phenomena with virtually photographic precision from a single point of view, expanding the impression of a mobilised virtual gaze beyond *Dubliners*' brief narratives.[73] The question of mediated vision is highlighted from the opening page by Simon Dedalus's Cyclopean monocle, foregrounding Stephen's position as sole focaliser with his developing fascinations and susceptibilities. Joyce vicariously immerses us in the infant's sensorium like a moving camera-eye picking out key details: 'his father looked at him through a glass: he had a hairy face' (*Portrait*, p. 5).

Episodically structured like rapid slide substitution or film montage, *Portrait* moves through swift changes between locations and times, though always implicitly sutured by Joyce's stylisation of the un/conscious logic of Stephen's mind with its cumulative sense of before and after. In the preparatory school scrimmage section, displaced from the nursery centre of parental regard, Stephen's intra-diegetic viewpoint becomes literally marginalised, though we continue to share its increasingly alienated slant. Joyce mimics the boy's eyesight like a kind of fuzzy camera alongside the *mêlée*, tracking it across the field:

> The evening air was pale and chilly and after every charge and thud of the footballers the greasy leather orb flew like a bird through the grey light. *He kept on the fringe of his line*, out of sight of the prefect, out of reach of the rude feet, feigning to run now and then. He felt his body was small and weak, amid the throng of players and *his eyes were weak and watery*. (p. 6; italics mine)

Sporting dynamics were a common subject of photographic analysis and the early films it influenced. Local actualities extended this fascination. For example, the 'Dublin Day by Day' series, screened December 1901–May 1902 at the Rotunda, included a rugby match between Trinity College and Lansdowne and the Southern Rovers versus Grocers game for the Cullen Challenge Cup (see *MLP&MPS*, p. 242; *EIC*, p. 70). Perhaps the earliest filmed international football fixture was Mitchell and Kenyon's *Wales v Ireland at Wrexham* (1906). This captured 'remarkable close-ups of the action' and four dynamic goals, despite the limitations of early camera mobility and reel length.[74] Similarly, Joyce presents Stephen's viewpoint with a mimetic precision which narrows in to literally dissect the moving bodies in his visual field as he follows the ball. As Stephen peers downwards through the thicket of flailing legs, Joyce presents a moving synecdoche of lower limbs only, suggestive of cinematic close-ups, but also multiple after-images: 'Then Jack Lawton's yellow boots dodged out the ball and all the other boots and legs ran after' (*Portrait*, p. 6). This characterises how Joyce's simultaneous anatomisation of movement and cognition frames and defamiliarises significant details only, cropping 'shots' into moving parts, detaching legs from bodies or boots from legs by verbal close-up – giving them expressive life of their own. (Stephen similarly imagines stampeding wild creatures to visualise his excitement about getting into University College, p. 139.)

Paradoxically, exact mimesis of vision only intensifies after a cyclist accidentally breaks Stephen's glasses, reinforcing Joyce's virtual impression of sharing his 'hyperopic' condition[75] through effects of distorted proportion and focus, thus anticipating the 'subjective camera' of Expressionist films such as F. W. Murnau's *Der letzte Mann* (1925) (see figure 2.6). The term was coined to recognise the potential for presenting a mobilised intra-diegetic

Figure 2.6 Still from F. W. Murnau (dir.), *Der letzte Mann* (1924). Courtesy of BFI National Archive, reproduced by kind permission of the Friedrich-Wilhelm-Murnau Stiftung, Wiesbaden, Germany.

gaze in such films, convergent with Modernist literary experiments such as Joyce's:

> The fellows were talking in little groups here and there on the playground. The fellows *seemed to him to have grown smaller*: that was because a sprinter had knocked him down the day before [. . .] and his spectacles had been broken in three pieces [. . .].
>
> *That was why the fellows seemed to him smaller and farther away and the goalposts so thin and far and the soft grey sky so high up.* (*Portrait*, p. 34; italics mine)

During lessons, this meticulous simulation is maintained in virtually microscopic close-up. The typography of Stephen's text blurs in and out of resolution as he cranes long-sightedly over it: 'the lines of the *letters* were like *fine invisible threads* and it was only by closing his right eye tight and staring out of the left eye that he could *make out the full curves* of the capital' (*Portrait*, p. 38; italics mine). As with the death notice that opens 'The Sisters' or the newspaper report in 'A Painful Case', when *Portrait*'s focaliser reads, we simultaneously 'see' the text as he does, Joyce now taking the process a stage further. Murnau's film is comparable in using subjective techniques to focalise action through its protagonist's eyes, so that both artists simultaneously monstrate what their characters are seeing *and* feeling as functions of the image. Indeed Murnau admitted being influenced by Joyce's techniques, as well as taking a position on them comparable to Woolf's. As he wrote in 1928 *a propos Der letzte Mann*, 'We have our thoughts and also our deeds. James Joyce, the English [*sic*] novelist, demonstrates this very well in his works. He first picturises the mind and then balances it with the action. After all the mind is the motive behind the deed.'[76] Hence in *Der letzte Mann*, the text of the unexpected letter demoting Murnau's ageing hotel doorman to toilet attendant is only directly visualised on screen after he dons reading glasses. Although the text is initially clear, shock causes the magnified individual letters of the fatal phrase – 'der Grund dieser Massnahme ist Ihre Alterschwäche' ('the reason for this measure is the weakness of your old age') to suddenly fill the screen and oscillate dizzyingly in and out of focus. *Der letzte Mann* is a *tour de force* of such subjective effects representing intra-diegetic visualisation, both naturalistically and psychologically. Just as the doorman's trauma causes individual letters to become illegible blurs, his drunkenness is indicated later by lurchingly rotated camerawork and phantasmagoric double vision, with the faces of the wedding guests around him becoming grotesquely distorted. His whole visual environment, including the inanimate, is reshaped at moments of emotional turmoil. For example, as the doorman sneaks guiltily into the hotel at night to steal back his resplendent uniform (and avoid losing face on his daughter's big day), the whole building appears to rear up menacingly over him, its windows like ghostly eye-sockets glaring, just as the formulae in Stephen's jotter 'morph' into multiple moving eyes indicating his sense of sexual guilt (see below).

Portrait's immersive optical distortion increases when Stephen is victimised by Father Dolan: 'stumbl[ing] into the middle of the class, *blinded by fear and haste*' (p. 41; italics mine). A blurry, virtually monochrome outline of the prefect of studies' features (significantly, also framed by lenses, now conferring authoritarian menace rather than paternal regard or childhood vulnerability) looms over Stephen to summarily convict him of slacking: 'Stephen lifted his eyes in wonder and saw for a moment Father Dolan's *whitegrey not young face, his baldy whitegrey head with fluff at the sides* of it, the *steel rims of his spectacles* and his *nocoloured eyes looking through* the glasses' (*Portrait*, p. 42; italics mine). Thus Joyce mimics Stephen's gaze as if every detail of action and thought were simultaneously presented through moving, intra-diegetic camera.

Symptomatically, Luigi Pirandello's *Si, gira!* (translated as *Shoot!*), one of the first novels about the Italian film industry, also appeared in 1915. It was similarly focalised from the impassively 'camera-eyed' viewpoint of its cinematographer narrator. Serafino Gubbio continually sees through lenses, material or internalised, becoming progressively detached from the immediate impact of physical reality even when filming in a tiger's cage.[77] Joyce had absorbed Frenchman Edouard Dujardin's pioneeringly cinematic 'interior monologue', *Les Lauriers sont coupés* (*The Bays Are Sere*, 1888), which he discovered in Paris in 1903 long before commencing *Portrait*.[78] However, Joyce had also been living in increasingly movie-minded Trieste for a decade by the time *Portrait* was finished. Hence if *Portrait* was not yet cast in the thoroughgoing Dujardinesque grammar of *Ulysses*' interior monologues (which discard even the minimal mediation of *Portrait*'s invisible third-person narrator for completely 'free direct discourse'), Joyce's continuous mimesis of what Stephen sees and feels nonetheless approaches them closely: as, for example, when he braves the rector's office to protest:

> – Come in.
> He turned the handle and opened the door and fumbled for the handle of the green baize door inside. He found it and pushed it open and went in.
> He saw the rector sitting at a desk writing. There was a skull on the desk and a strange solemn smell in the room like the leather of old chairs.
> His heart was beating fast on account of the solemn place he was in and the silence of the room; and he looked at the skull and at the rector's kindlooking face. (p. 47)

In this passage, Joyce simulates eye movements as they alight on 'objects of attention' on a moment-by-moment basis, contracting and expanding his ekphrastic visual field as Stephen moves through corresponding physical spaces. Entering the narrow vestibule, we focus vicariously on Stephen's own hand fumbling for the inner door handle. We share his gaze opening out into the room beyond, with the rector at its centre, followed by its nervous downward flicker towards the forbidding *memento mori* on the desk, before resting on the reassuringly 'kindlooking face'.

Even in the Christmas dinner scene, when adult dialogue and external action take over to almost stage-bound extent, Stephen's 'remembering eyes' (see the discussion of this phrase below) and confused reflections are continuously foregrounded, as when Mr Casey locks horns with Dante:

> Stephen *looked with affection at Mr Casey's face* which stared across the table over his joined hands. He liked to sit near him at the fire, *looking up at* his dark fierce face. *But his dark eyes were never fierce* and his slow voice was good to listen to. But why was he then against the priests? Because Dante must be right then. But he had heard his father say that

she was a spoiled nun and that she had come out of the convent in the Alleghanies when her brother had got the money from the savages for the trinkets and the chainies. Perhaps that had made her severe against Parnell. (*Portrait*, p. 29; italics mine)

At the row's climax it is not so much dramatic action as an apparently adventitious detail that sticks out cinematically. In his shock at witnessing the rational façade of adulthood crack asunder, Stephen literally does not know where to look. Hence the excruciating contrast between the lingering deceleration of Dante's napkin ring, tracked by his gaze, and her explosive exit: 'Dante shoved her chair violently aside and left the table, upsetting her napkinring which rolled slowly along the carpet and came to rest against the foot of an easychair' (*Portrait*, p. 32). The scene and aftermath are recollected telegraphically before Stephen's 'remembering eyes', prompted by related events in other contexts (for example, on p. 58).

PORTRAIT'S 'PHANTOM RIDES'

Joyce's innovative mode of presenting phenomena cinematically goes beyond observing them with a gaze merely mobilised by the body and into effects of mechanised virtual locomotion, in which viewpoint becomes accelerated relative to forms of transport, albeit Stephen never literally takes flight like his archetypal namesake. For example, to block out feverish hallucinations 'projected' against the enclosing curtains of his dormitory cubicle, Stephen shuts his eyes and immerses himself in an imagined scene of departure for the Christmas holidays. Note the temporal paradox of Joyce's past continuous verb phrase 'were rolling', in which this future becomes virtually present through the concrete visualisation of moving details:

That would be lovely: the fellows had told him. Getting up on the cars in the early wintry morning outside the door of the castle. *The cars were rolling on the gravel.*
Cheers for the rector!
Hurray! Hurray! Hurray!' (*Portrait*, p. 16, italics mine)

Indeed Stephen's journeying – real or imagined – is presented kinaesthetically as a kind of 'phantom ride', the fairground-like vicarious travel experience afforded by photographic lantern 'tours' or moving panoramas and extended by early films shot from vehicles. Capturing locomotion, both bodily and mechanical, was key to rapid photographic analysis and its influence on film. Joyce had already featured elaborate virtual motion in *Dubliners*' 'After the Race'.[79] The real event which inspired it was filmed as the *Great Gordon-Bennett Motor Race* and screened by the Irish Animated Photo Company at the Rotunda in summer 1903 (*MLP&MPS*, p. 249). Many films shown at Joyce's Volta similarly featured mechanical transport (planes, cars, ships, etc.) or simulated panoramic tours through natural or architectural spectacles of foreign countries.[80]

Portrait contrives a similar transportive viewpoint through rhythmically repeating details as Stephen's phantom carriage passes through villages – 'The peasant women stood at the halfdoors, the men stood here and there' – then switches transitionlessly into a train interior. Bustling guards' 'keys ma[king] a quick music: click, click, click' match the locomotive's syncopated rhythm, speeding up Joyce's narrative pace. Landmarks and infrastructural fixtures flow past Stephen's framed gaze with rhythmic permutations characteristic of moving panoramas and filmed rail journeys: 'And the train raced on over the flat lands and *past the hill of Allen*. The telegraphpoles *were passing, passing*' (*Portrait*, p. 16; italics mine). In chapter 2, as bankruptcy necessitates cheaper lodgings, Joyce contrives a less exhilarating effect of relative movement 'from the window of the railway carriage' in which Stephen 'sat with his red-eyed mother', as it overtakes removal vans 'lumbering along the Merrion Road' (p. 54). In Stephen's 'night mail' ride to Cork, such kinaesthetic rhythm is intensified. (Interestingly, Stephen's route and destination overlap with scenic lantern tours such as *The Lakes of Killarney and Glengariff, via Cork and Bantry* [1894], slides and text by William Lawrence, which specialised in them. Given the Joyce family's connections with Cork, Mitchell and Kenyon's film *Ride from Blarney to Cork on Cork & Muskerry Light Railway* [1902] might also have attracted their attention.)[81] As Stephen gazes backwards through his apparently still compartment window (a key motif in cinematising the Victorian media-cultural imaginary, as discussed in Chapter 3), the landscape itself is conjured into reverse motion by mechanisation and artificial light. The projective force of this modern visual relativity is perfectly captured by Joyce's verb 'flung', repeated as if the train were unreeling the visible world into place behind it from Stephen's point of view:

> He saw the *darkening lands slipping past him*, the silent *telegraphpoles passing his window swiftly every four seconds*, the *little glimmering stations*, manned by a few sentries, *flung by the mail behind her* and *twinkling for a moment* in the darkness *like fiery grains flung backwards* by a runner. (*Portrait*, p. 73; italics mine)

In another visual match suggesting railway film tropes, birds on telegraph wires sliding rapidly past evoke notes in musical scores.

Seeing with the Eyes of Memory

As Woolf noted about *Ulysses*, in order to create its rhythmic structure, *Portrait* does not simply present an effect of seeing moving phenomena with virtually photographic precision; Joyce focuses simultaneously on cognition and reflection.

Hence *Portrait* also mimics what present perceptions summon from Stephen's inner vision, to present 'thought made phonetic – taken to bits', as Woolf put it. Stephen continuously sees with 'remembering eyes' (p. 190), both in the sense of impressions becoming imprinted, but also new ones being processed through those already stored up. The 'individuating rhythm' of Stephen's developing consciousness is simultaneously *Portrait*'s underlying subject and form, in this reflexive sense. It is narrated not just serially as a 'fluid succession of presents', but as a cinematically associative shuttling back and forth along its chronological axis to fulfil Joyce's 1904 sketch's methodological propositions. Rare interjections by Joyce's third-person narrator foreground this process: 'And he tasted in the language of memory . . . and saw with the eyes of memory' (p. 196).

Hence the protagonist's body and mind in the Modernist fiction that *Portrait* spearheaded tend to simultaneously inhabit 'then and there' as much as the 'here and now' of their ongoing narrative present. Representation of Stephen's interiority is based on imagistic association that continuously 'overlaps' perceptions and accumulating memories, tracing a timeline looping back into Stephen's past, while nonetheless driving dynamically forwards to assert his vocational future as an artist. The rising and falling 'curve' of Stephen's emotional progress inscribes a pattern of recurrent challenges and adaptive responses. Thus *Portrait* added a distinctive new cinematicity to the *Bildungsroman*, revolutionising how the genre 'pictures time' in terms of photographically vivid individual moments, but also how they become choreographed.

Joyce was in Paris in 1903 when Bergson gave his revolutionary lectures comparing human consciousness to the cinematograph's recording process. Bergson began considering instantaneous photography and persistence of vision as analogues for perception and memory as far back as *Matière et mémoire* (*Matter and Memory*) (1896). However, in chapter 4 of *L'Évolution créatrice* (*Creative Evolution*) (1907), 'The Cinematographical Mechanism of Thought', he wrote about how screening a 'living picture' of a marching regiment was dependent on a 'series of snapshots', thrown 'on the screen, so that they replace each other very rapidly' and 'each actor . . . recovers his mobility', through a depersonalising process which first abstracts movement then reconstitutes it.[82] At best, Bergson considered that film recording corresponded solely to perception and cognition in the present, replicating the merely linear and mechanistic sequencing of clock time:

> Such is the contrivance of the cinematograph. And such is also that of our knowledge. Instead of attaching ourselves to the inner becoming of things, we place ourselves outside them in order to recompose their becoming artificially. We take snapshots, as it were, of the passing reality, and, as these are characteristic of the reality, we have only to string them on a becoming, abstract, uniform and invisible, situated at the back

of the apparatus of knowledge, in order to imitate what there is that is characteristic in this becoming itself. Perception, intellection, language so proceed in general. Whether we would think becoming, or express it, or even perceive it, we hardly do anything else than set going a kind of cinematograph inside us. We may therefore sum up what we have been saying in the conclusion that the *mechanism of our ordinary knowledge is of a cinematographical kind.*[83] [italics in original]

Hence Bergson initially rejected cinema, because he felt it highlighted perception in impersonally rational and analytic terms, rather than representing the individual's authentic capacity for living mental evolution in its response to the more fluid interaction between experience and memory.[84] For Bergson, the qualitative experience of time was through a non-linear perspective. Hence his distinction between mere *temps* as mechanised abstraction and psychological *durée réele* ('real duration'), through which time is actually lived, and past and present dissolve into one another. As he explained:

For our duration is not merely one instant replacing another; if it were, there would never be anything but the present – no prolonging of the past into the actual, no evolution, no concrete duration. Duration is the continuous progress of the past which gnaws into the future and which swells it as it advances.[85]

It is interesting to compare Bergson's definition with an observation in Stephen's diary, which seems to comment on *Portrait*'s multi-layered picturing of time as moving structural rhythm: 'The past is consumed in the present and the present is living only because it brings forth the future' (*Portrait*, p. 211). Note the ambiguity of 'past is consumed': not erased by the-here-and-now, but *re*-experienced afresh by continually 'showing through' it in existentially crucial ways, orientating Stephen towards his true vocational future.

Bergson had at least conceded that film might be a helpful model for figuring aspects of consciousness in visual terms, which would be hugely influential in Modernist understanding and representation of temporality. Moreover, *Creative Evolution* evoked film's original recording and replaying functions only, as in early actualities. Only more gradually would the development of dissolves and editing techniques enable its narrative form to correspond more closely to Bergson's interiorised notion of *mémoire involontaire* ('involuntary memory'). This had deeper and more vivid psychological significance though its effect of spontaneous and immersive 'mental time travel' as *durée réele*, rather than being limited to the merely linear temporality of external 'clock time'. Film-makers developed the medium's capacity to rearrange screen space and time according to subjective switches of a character's consciousness. As we have seen, however, filmic space-time fluidity also remediated the methods of lantern shows, which were similarly figured in Joyce's fiction's apparent antici-pations of film, as *Portrait* exemplifies.[86]

Joyce had a copy of *L'Évolution créatrice* in his Trieste library[87] and *Portrait* certainly added a new, cinematised 'fourth dimension' to the subjectivity of the *Bildungsroman*, the traditional genre for novels of education or (self-)develop-ment, by selecting key moments or epiphanies in Stephen's mental evolution, presented as involuntary memories, and editing them together into a structural pattern. As discussed in Chapter 1, the German term *Bildung* derives from *Bild*: image or picture. *Portrait*'s revolutionising of how the genre pictures time nar-ratively thus explains Joyce's ultimate dissatisfaction with *Stephen Hero*: the latter's conventionally linear chrononological structure, largely unanimated by such cinematic features, obscured his original sketch's integral psychological and aesthetic purpose. In *Ulysses*' 'Circe', Stephen would declare his quest for a universal, visual language, in terms echoing Joyce's own 1904 manifesto for Modernist form: 'So that *gesture*, not music not odour, would be a *universal language*, the gift of tongues rendering visible not the lay sense but the first entel-echy, the *structural rhythm*' (15.105–7; italics mine). As Eisenstein recognised in quoting Stephen's remark for the epigraph of his famous 1932 essay on the cinematic qualities of Joyce's fiction, Stephen's quest for a universal monstra-tive language seemed more realisable in film than any visual medium before (although the coming of synchronised dialogue in specific national tongues in the later 1920s threatened to erect new barriers against it).[88] Nevertheless, Eisen-stein's epigraph highlights the significance of the individuating rhythm realised in *Portrait* and enhanced in the interior monologues of *Ulysses* for the subsequent development of cinematicity in both Joyce and film.

RHYTHMIC STRATEGIES

One of the principal challenges thrown up by the radical economisation between *Stephen Hero* and the final version of *Portrait* – Joyce's shift from con-ventional narrative to visual monstration – is that readers must actively connect its 'montage' of imagistic fragments to follow Stephen's underlying perceptio-cognitive rhythm: so much so that *Portrait* appeared formally chaotic to some early reviewers.[89] Readers have to intuit associative processes building up from *Portrait*'s first page. Joyce plunges us straight into a mix of infant sensations and memories, stories and songs.

Almost immediately come swift exchanges between locations and times, though always implicitly sutured by Joyce's stylisation of the unconscious logic of Stephen's mind. Typically, Stephen's transgressive desire to marry the Protestant neighbours' daughter, on which the opening nursery section abruptly ends, is suddenly substituted with a noisy panorama of his prep school games field. Nonetheless, Dante's threat (echoing in Stephen's head as the rhyme, '*Pull out his eyes,/Apologise*') 'laps' by sound match into this succeeding scene: 'The wide playgrounds were swarming with boys. All were shouting and the prefects urged them on with strong cries' (*Portrait*, p. 6). This audio-visual shift immerses us in the thick of a very different moving environment, both dimensionally and socially expanded. It underscores Stephen's ejection from a once-cosy domestic space into a new homosocial one of competition and disciplinary surveillance.

Portrait's 'succession of presents' thus jumps between contrasting moments and locations with the abruptness of rapidly dissolving slide tableaux or even episodic film shots. Scenes are often short and fragmented, but balanced by 'match-cut' effects linking thematically to the next. Similarly, they often cut off before one action has logically finished and plunge into another after it has already begun. One sequence in chapter 2 consists entirely of 'snapshots' marking the family's descent into genteel poverty in successive jumps. Though episodic narrative characterises *Portrait* as a whole, this sequence is abbreviated even by its standards. Each segment begins with verb phrases in the past continuous, achieving the in *media res* impression of an ongoing action captured photographically at a particular instant, but also of Stephen as lone viewer watching a rapid sequence of images in which he takes little part: '*He was sitting* on the backless chair in his aunt's kitchen'; '*He was sitting* in the narrow breakfast room high up in the darkwindowed house'; '*He was sitting* in the midst of a children's party at Harold's Cross' (*Portrait*, pp. 56–7; italics mine). Hence Joyce's wording functions like a series of establishing views, barely orientating us deictically before flashing to the next. Moreover, the impression of Stephen as passive spectator of his own life is particularly emphatic in this sequence, reinforcing the impression of viewing a lantern show or film. All the scenes take place in dark, enclosed spaces with firelight or 'lamp with a reflector' as the sole illumination source, creating projections that 'flickered on the wall' (p. 56). This is enhanced by descriptions of the figures in the rooms gazed into. Rarely are they named or related to Stephen directly, instead being generically characterised as 'a ringletted girl', 'the boy who came in from the street' or 'the old bustling woman'. Their lack of individuation is reminiscent of life-model sets and the early films that succeeded them, whose characters were often social or moral 'types'.[90]

To counter-balance his episodic structure, Joyce employed many methods to keep the individuating rhythm of Stephen's consciousness in view and implicitly unify his text. Just as Marey picked out athletes' lines of muscular thrust in white, highlighting the integral rhythm of pure movement over individual shots of dematerialised bodies, so Joyce highlights motifs and themes to foreground Stephen's developing consciousness through what makes an impression on him and what he recollects. *Portrait*'s 'linguistic palette', for example, is carefully selective, paralleling emblematic touches of colour in life-model sets and early films. Before naturalistic colour stock was invented, photographic slides or individual frames were painstakingly hand-tinted by professional 'retouchers' to foreground significant details. Similarly, on *Portrait*'s first page, Dante's brushes act like symbolic close-ups of 'speaking objects', foreshadowing internecine tensions in Irish nationalism: 'Dante had two brushes in her press. The brush with the maroon velvet back was for Michael Davitt and the brush with the green velvet back was for Parnell' (p. 5). *Portrait*'s opening is famously a kind of overture displaying leitmotifs prominently so that we recognise them in reconstituted or displaced forms as they recur. When Stephen looks at the Earth surrounded by clouds in his geography primer, which Fleming crayons in similar red-green shades, he immediately thinks back to Dante ripping up the brush back that stands for the disgraced Parnell (*Portrait*, pp. 12–13). A parallel transition between Stephen's fever dream in the infirmary and the Christmas dinner scene at home is effected through colour matching the figure of Dante in 'maroon velvet dress with a green velvet mantle hanging from her shoulders', which passes his/Parnell's coffin disdainfully (*Portrait*, p. 22). These emblematic details immediately reconstitute themselves in the next episode's shifted *mise en scène*, morphing into 'A great fire, banked high and red, flamed in the grate and under the ivytwined branches of the chandelier the Christmas table was spread' (p. 22).

Thus, for Stephen, each new experience is filtered through cumulative memories by imagistic association, leading to some epiphanic correspondence (though, as in *Dubliners*, not necessarily in the same way or depth of insight for the character as for the reader). The process is often triggered by sights or other sensations in the present. Such Bergsonian *mémoires involontaires* feature occasionally in surviving chapters from *Stephen Hero*,[91] but were evidently not choreographed into a larger pattern. Memories, reveries and speculations stir, as if spontaneously, at crucial moments, to continually foreground the individuating rhythm of Stephen's feelings and thoughts. Joyce's stylisation of this interactive process constitutes the key breakthrough of the final version, as well as a progression of imagistic techniques in *Dubliners*.

In *Portrait*'s rhythmic repetitions and space-time overlapping, the creative 'editing process' of Stephen's memory is figured like rapidly substituted lantern slides of different scenes and their technical extension into film's accelerated montage. This is a further aspect of the novel's analytic dissection, simultaneously visual and psychological. For example, growing into a troubled adolescent, Stephen strives to recall the experiences of his 'lost' childhood in condensed visions similar to Gabriel's imagistic reviewing of the party at the end of 'The Dead':

> The memory of his childhood *suddenly grew dim*. He tried to *call forth some of its vivid moments* but could not. He recalled only names. Dante, Parnell, Clane, Clongowes. A little boy had been taught geography by an

old woman who kept two brushes in her wardrobe. Then he had been sent away from home to a college. In the college he had made his first communion and eaten slim jim out of his cricketcap and watched the firelight leaping and dancing on the wall of a little bedroom in the infirmary and dreamed of being dead, of mass being said for him by the rector in a black and gold cope, of being buried then in the little graveyard of the community off the main avenue of limes. But he had not died then. Parnell had died. There had been no mass for the dead in the chapel and no procession. He had not died but he had faded out like a film in the sun . . . (*Portrait*, p. 78; italics mine)

Joyce furnishes a similar montage of 'life at Clongowes' reprising leading visual details from this passage, when Stephen re-encounters a master from his primary school sermonising at the retreat (p. 91). The 'slim jim' memory also recurs to the 'reformed' senior schoolboy (p. 132).

Key memories are thus increasingly 'cropped' by Stephen's mental editing process as they recur, both spatially and in terms of duration, but always retaining an effect of recessive impressions behind them. His first tentative flirtation with 'E[mma] C[leary]' on a homebound tram evokes a flashback to an infant moment with Eileen (*Portrait*, p. 58). As Stephen strives to rewrite the tram experience as a poem, Joyce also presents his compositional process as a kind of visual editing: 'those elements which he deemed common and insignificant fell out of the scene. There remained no trace of the tram itself nor of the trammen nor of the horses: nor did he and she appear vividly' (p. 59). The incident compresses into ever shorter 'inserts' when recollected during the Whitsun school play (with E-C herself in the audience to trigger them) and at University College (pp. 64, 187). In this way, Joyce continually foregrounds the selection and compression process of Stephen's visual imagination, typified by phrases such as 'the foul memories condensed within his brain' when he later recollects forays into Dublin's red-light district (p. 97).

'CALLED UP AS IF BY MAGIC': SPACE-TIME SHIFTS IN *PORTRAIT*

Even more than *Dubliners*, *Portrait*'s space-time shifts exhibit the instantaneous materialisation associated with projected images.[92] Many seem conjured up from nowhere like instant lantern pictures: 'A sudden memory had carried him to another scene, *called up as if by magic* . . .' (*Portrait*, p. 65; italics mine). Significantly, whereas Joyce's radical focalisation technique means that Stephen is never physically visible through external description in the present, he experiences memories as if watching his own moving photographic double, with an almost hallucinatory effect of self-externalisation through phrases such as '*He saw himself* sitting at the old piano, striking chords softly . . .' (p. 184; italics mine). Deliberately ambiguous phrasing seems to materialise memories almost palpably, as if projected outside Stephen's subjective consciousness and control. (Cf. Joyce's alternative 's/he was again' formula in *Dubliners*, where the vividness of memory causes past events to be re-experienced immersively, rather than reviewed in this detached manner.)

Significantly, Stephen's undergraduate theorising in chapter 5 connects artistic creativity with capturing, developing and casting living pictures: 'The esthetic image in the dramatic form is life purified in and reprojected from the human imagination' (p. 181). Similarly, *Portrait* builds on *Dubliners'* lantern-like dissolutions of one time or space into another and projection of detached pictures into other contexts, pushing these techniques further. It continuously mixes the outer space of present events with the internalised space of recollection and fantasy, often blurring the boundaries between objective and subjective reality with images so vividly and concretely visualised that they seem to hover ontologically between, making Stephen doubt the evidence of his senses as in some kind of illusionistic show.

Since *Portrait* is simultaneously marked by a fluid succession of presents and this cumulative overlapping between them, images of past moments continuously show through the here and now. Therefore, just as in Marey's overlapping shots of athletes or a reversible film, the abstracted rhythm of Stephen's mental movement can be traced both forward and backward, simultaneously marking change and recurrence. Joyce's increasingly complex pattern of sensory contrasts and matches marks the rhythm of Stephen's consciousness and its rising and falling Daedalian 'flightpath' towards artistic transcendence, cinematically interweaving past, present *and* possible future. In one pivotal example, torn by his senior school director's invitation to join the Jesuits, it is precisely the past showing through the present in this way as involuntary memory that visualises Stephen's unconscious resistance and prefigures his rejection of this 'tempting' offer. As the director talks, Stephen notices that his skull is silhouetted against the window in the waning light (*Portrait*, p. 129). This evokes the time when Stephen appealed to him as the head of his primary school against unjust pandybatting, when the *memento mori* of an actual deathshead was present on the director's desk (p. 47). Objects of attention facilitating temporal transitions by symbolic matches also featured in *Dubliners*, though less frequently and elaborately. The associations dredged from memory by this match induce an irrational sense of suffocation as Stephen exits. In the ensuing passage, Joyce effectively overlaps three separate layers of time, like lantern images or film superimpositions shimmering in and out of one another – interweaving present, past and possible future. Note the instances of *Portrait*'s habitual use of cinematically suggestive terms: 'shadow' implying foreboding, but also recorded or projected picture;[93] similarly, the traversing effect of images moving on slides or filmstrip across a screen in 'passed gravely over', as Stephen imagines the fate awaiting him should he choose unwisely. There is also subtle auditory matching in the gas flames' disquieting 'murmur', suggesting *sotto voce* disembodied speech (compare the effect in the 'shadow show' that Stephen watches in the infirmary, discussed below):

> As he descended the steps the impression which effaced his troubled self-communion was that of a mirthless mask reflecting a sunken day from the threshold of the college. The *shadow*, then, of the life of the college *passed gravely over* his consciousness. It was a grave and ordered and passionless life that awaited him, a life without material cares. He wondered how he would pass the first night in the novitiate and with what dismay he would wake the first morning in the dormitory. *The troubling odour of the corridors of Clongowes came back to him and he heard the discreet murmur of the gasflames.* At once from every part of his being unrest began to irradiate. A feverish quickening of his pulses followed and a din of meaningless words drove his reasoned thought hither and thither confusedly. His lungs dilated and sank as if he were inhaling a warm moist unsustaining air which *hung in the bath at Clongowes above the sluggish turf-coloured water.* (Portrait, p. 135; italics mine)

Stephen's disquiet about the order's repressive discipline initially fixes on an after-image – a detached close-up of the director's bony face like a 'mirthless mask', as if superimposed over the sunset outside. This awakens past traumas nested into one another. Hallucinatory nightmares from Clongowes bleed back into the mind of the Belvedere youth: institutional corridors evoke the imprisoning labyrinth of the Daedalus myth; the 'square ditch' (i.e. open sewer) into which the prep-school boy was bullied, picking up a fever, and the foetid communal bath are conflated into an 'immersive' and powerfully somatic warning from Stephen's unconscious against regressing – hubristically plunging back, like Icarus, into creative suffocation through moral vanity. This is at once mimesis of present perceptions, memories and imaginative processes: a perfect example of *Portrait*'s cinematic monstration. As discussed above, a distinctly Bergsonian observation in Stephen's diary comments on Joyce's multi-layered picturing of time as structural rhythm in this way: 'The past is consumed in the present and the present is living only because it brings forth the future' (p. 211). This passage bears out the ambiguity of 'past is consumed': never erased by the-here-and-now, but *re*-experienced afresh by continually 'showing through' it in existentially crucial ways, orientating Stephen towards his true vocational future. Thus Joyce creates *Portrait*'s distinctive effect of a virtual gaze, moving not just through *physical*, but also *mental* space and time; simultaneously presenting Stephen's perceiving *and* remembering consciousness.

VIVISECTING BODIES

Portrait is riddled not just with episodic shifts and lingering dissolves, but also visually displaced objects and partially recollected impressions, especially in the 'anatomising' form of bodily close-ups. These constantly intrude into other scenes, lacing Joyce's text with recurrent imagery similar to its emblematic colours. The frequency of cropped motifs such as legs and feet (as in the football game discussed above), but especially detached faces, eyes, hands, and so on, is fundamental to how Joyce radically reconstitutes experience through what Stephen sees, remembers and 'dismembers' (to borrow Maud Ellmann's influential term).[94] Spiegel argues that Cranly's head (a particularly recurrent synecdoche) is only one among myriad examples of visual 'racking', truncation and displacement, defining *Portrait*'s space-time as simultaneously psychological, multi-layered and cinematic.[95] As such, Cranly's head also recalls the haunting face of the priest in 'The Sisters', or the 'blow up' of Mangan's sister at the railings blotting out what is physically present before the protagonist's eyes in 'Araby'. As part of *Portrait*'s motific patterning, Cranly's head is also a conspicuous echo of the director's 'mirthless mask', the after-image superimposed on the sunset by Stephen's troubled mind.

Indeed, the recurrent motif of a phantasmagorically projected, priestly deathmask gathers associations in many different contexts. Typically, Cranly's disembodied head appears superimposed on other backgrounds – again blurring mental and external space in Stephen's reveries, corresponding not to what is empirically visible, but to psychological processes. Its first occurrence suggests hesitancy over confiding in his fellow undergraduate about 'unrest and longings in his soul' (*Portrait*, p. 149). Significantly, Cranly's enigmatic features become severed and free-floating after being highlighted during a lecture:

> *Another head than his, right before him in the first benches, was poised squarely above its bending fellows like the head of a priest* appealing without humility to the tabernacle for the humble worshippers about him. Why was it that when he thought of Cranly *he could never raise before his mind the entire image of his body but only the image of the head and face?* Even now *against the grey curtain of the morning he saw it before him* like the *phantom of a dream, the face of a severed head or deathmask*, crowned on the brows by its stiff black upright hair as by an iron crown. It was a priestlike face, priestlike in its pallor, in the widewinged nose, in the shadowings below the eyes and along the jaws, priestlike in the lips that were long and bloodless and faintly smiling . . .
> (*Portrait*, p. 149; italics mine)

In his closing diary, Stephen reflects on this disconcertingly involuntary habit of recalling Cranly's head silhouetted against blank, screenlike surfaces: 'when thinking of him, saw always a stern severed head or deathmask *as if outlined on a grey curtain or veronica'* (p. 209; italics mine). A veronica is a cloth allegedly imprinted with the face of Christ, the most famous example being the Turin Shroud, the kind of proto-photographic 'miracle' that Pope Leo might have celebrated. However, in *Portrait* detached heads always carry associations of coercion and betrayal, especially in clerical contexts. Stephen's out-of-focus close-up of Father Dolan's face (as well as Dolan's treacherously gentle steadying of his hand – the better for hitting it) is similarly repeated as Stephen reflects on cruelty and injustice (pp. 43, 46).

In a strikingly visual passage, facial features of individual Jesuits aggregate and morph, evoking technical continuities between dissolving views, superimpositions and multiple film exposures. Irritated by lesser mortals in his post-retreat *Scheinheiligkeit*, another chain of recollections suggests that Stephen nonetheless suspects at a deeper level that his inauthentic posturing will thwart and deform him in the long run: 'Images of the outbursts of trivial anger which he had often noted among his masters, their twitching mouths, closeshut lips and flushed cheeks, recurred to his memory . . .' (*Portrait*, pp. 127–8). Successive pictures gradually coalesce into a blurry composite of all his masters, which his own face might grow to match. This protean phantasm finally resolves into the complexion and features of one particularly apoplectic individual, blind to his own predicament:

> there followed a mental sensation of *an undefined face or colour of a face*. The *colour faded and became strong like a changing glow* of pallid red brick . . . The face was eyeless and sourfavoured and devout, shot with pink tinges of suffocated anger. Was it not a *mental spectre of the face* of one of the Jesuits whom some of the boys called Lantern Jaws and others Foxy Campbell? (*Portrait*, p. 136; italics mine)

Portrait's motif of detached faces multiplies to monstrate teenage *Angst* about judgemental scrutiny by the collective social gaze. Hence Stephen's view of spectators at the Whitsun play anticipates sinister screen-filling tessellations of bodiless heads and eyes greedily consuming performances in Expressionist films such as E. A. Dupont's *Varieté* (1925) or Fritz Lang's *Metropolis* (1927): 'A few moments later he found himself on stage amid the garish gas and the dim scenery, acting before the innumerable faces of the void.' After the lights go up, this *Gestalt* entity resolves back into clusters of individuals, to Stephen's evident relief: 'through a rift in the side scene, [he] saw the simple body before which he had acted magically deformed, the void of faces breaking at all points and falling asunder into busy groups' (*Portrait*, p. 71). Mention of gaslight and magical deformation simultaneously evokes the transformative imagery of lantern shows and trick films.

To emphasise porousness between external and interior vision, *Portrait* is also studded with close-ups of disembodied eyes: glimpsed, recollected or fantasised about. This compounds Joyce's preoccupation with methods of seeing and being seen – organic, ideological or artificially enhanced – from *Portrait*'s opening sequence with Dante's closing rhyme about eagles pulling out eyes onwards. Joyce foregrounds the notion of mediated vision in his first description of being under parental observation. Instead of merely stating that Mr Dedalus wore a monocle, Joyce creates an impression of distance and scrutinisation from Stephen's infant viewpoint: 'his father looked at him through a glass'. Early interactions with his mother are similarly mediated: dropping him off at Clongowes, her eyes are discreetly veiled, until she momentarily lifts this filter to kiss him goodbye, revealing her tears. That image of long-suffering distress haunts Stephen thereafter: every time he pictures his mother her eyes are red. More phantasmagorically, shapes in the peacock's tail that 'morphs' from formulae in the daydreaming adolescent's maths jotter 'were eyes opening and closing; the eyes opening and closing were stars being born and quenched' (*Portrait*, p. 87). At first, this visualises Stephen's idling sexuality, the tail's movement evoking an erotic fan dance like an orientalist peepshow. However, repetition of the phrase 'eyes opening and closing' undercuts playfulness with horror, creating the impression of being under cosmic observation and judgement instead, which anticipates the reaction that Stephen's furtive activities eventually trigger at the retreat. Similarly, undergraduate reveries about Jacobean courtly seductions focus on 'Eyes, opening from the darkness of desire, eyes that dimmed the breaking east' (p. 196). Other ocular close-ups repel, as when Stephen imagines the parochial outlook of a west coast peasant: 'I fear his redrimmed horny eyes' (p. 212).

Other body parts are also prominently abstracted. Fantasising about priesthood's furtive perks, 'dim scenes of his imagining' include close-ups of 'lips of women and girls' whispering erotic transgressions seen through confessional grilles (*Portrait*, pp. 133–4). *Portrait* later features a 'reverse' point-of-view shot of the same scene, when Stephen jealously imagines 'the latticed ear of a priest' from Emma's perspective as she betrays their intimacies (p. 186). Arguably, such synecdochic motifs – detached body parts and disembodied voices – converge in *Portrait*'s climactic audio-visual match, to express the liberating promise of elsewhere in the rhythmic upbeat closing of Stephen's diary: 'The spell of arms and voices: the white arms of roads, their promise of close embraces and the black arms of tall ships that stand against the moon, their tale of distant nations' (p. 213).

IMPRINTS AND PROJECTIONS

Mentally doodling against the backdrop of a boring lecture, Stephen plays with the term 'projecting' in simultaneously hypothesising and image-casting senses: 'O the dull grey day! It seemed a limbo of painless, patient consciousness through which the souls of mathematicians might wander *projecting long slender fabrics from plane to plane . . .*' (*Portrait*, p. 160; italics mine). Motifs, effects and terms suggestive of projection pervade *Portrait* more than *Dubliners*. For example, a moving beam is cast by a prefect patrolling Stephen's dormitory with a lantern. This momentarily lights up the curtains surrounding his cubicle like transparent screens: 'He peered out for an instant over the coverlet and saw the yellow curtains round and before his bed that shut him off on all sides. The light was lowered quietly' (p. 15).[96] Enclosed in a suddenly blacked-out space, effectively coterminous with the projection box of thought, the feverish Stephen watches an auto-suggestive phantasmagoria comparable to the face pursuing his avatar under the bedcovers in 'The Sisters', or Gabriel's summoning of Michael Furey's shade in 'The Dead'. He recalls the legend of the Marshall, whose moving phantasm materialised to eyewitnesses like a real Pepper's Ghost at the instant of death on a faraway battlefield. Stephen's only way of blocking such eerie images is to overlay them with his contrasting 'flash-forward' to his departure for Christmas.

Also more frequently than *Dubliners*, *Portrait* describes sights 'passing' from experience and imprinting into memory like a photographic recording process, epitomised by Stephen's transcendent vision of the wading girl at Dollymount Strand: 'Her *image had passed into* his soul for ever' (*Portrait*, p. 144; italics mine). The lexical stem 'pass', repeated with different extensions or substituted by synonyms such as 'traverse', connotes not only the impact, but also the duration and movement of images through Stephen's consciousness. Recurrent images in reveries are often connected with the term, as in 'She *passed now dancing lightly across* his memory as she had been that night at the carnival ball . . .' (p. 184; italics mine). Such visualisation of brief, identically repeated actions evokes the gliding movement of figures across the screen in lantern shows as slides passed through the mechanism or of lateral action on film loops (perhaps privately viewed in kinetoscope or mutoscope form). With appropriate ghostliness, back in class after terrorisation by the hellfire sermons, the historic dead '*passed like mute phantoms* behind their veil of names', like silent figures on a long, out-of-focus procession slide or early pageant film (p. 106; italics mine). Similarly, when Stephen hears a servant girl singing, but cannot see her, '*The figure of woman* as she appears in the liturgy of the church *passed silently through the darkness*' (p. 206; italics mine) like a projected religious allegory. Sometimes past experiences recur not as individual moving pictures, but with the episodic sequencing of life-model sets or even film montage: 'Masked memories *passed quickly before him*: he recognised scenes and persons . . .' (p. 132; italics mine). During his interview for the priesthood, there is another suggestive association between 'passing' and visualisation in darkness. Stephen visualises the director's smile in the deepening twilight only as its 'image or spectre . . . *passing rapidly across his mind*' (p. 130; italics mine).

As in 'Araby', sexual awakening is based on the obsessive internalisation of a particular image, not of a friend's sister, but from an illustrated romance in Stephen's bookish case – Alexandre Dumas's *The Count of Monte Cristo*: 'He returned to Mercedes and, as he *brooded upon her image*, a strange unrest crept into his blood.' Exemplifying *Portrait*'s interactivity between inner and outer vision, Stephen seeks the real-life counterpart of her *'unsubstantial image'* (*Portrait*, p. 54; italics mine). Like the memory of Mangan's sister at the railings, Mercedes continually *'traverse[s] the background* of his memory' (p. 83; italics mine), resembling a figure in identical pose or action gliding repeatedly across a screen. Imagining this image coming alive and returning his gaze reverses *Portrait*'s effect of lantern-like dissolves in what Stephen sees: instead he yearns to *'fade into* something impalpable . . . be transfigured' in 'that *magic moment*' (p. 54; italics mine).

Often Joyce's effect is not just of pictures 'passing through' the darkened projection box of Stephen's mind, but – more ambiguously – of them virtually *materialising before his physical vision*, as if cast by some concealed device. Joyce deliberately blurs the boundaries between inner and outer visual space, as with the obsessively recollected image of Mangan's sister intruding between the boy and his books or blotting out her house front in 'Araby'. In *Portrait*, guilt induces involuntary visualisation so compulsive that it suggests the flash-back symptoms of Post-Traumatic Stress Disorder: 'and, *though his eyes were shut fast, he saw the places where he had sinned* and, though his ears were tightly covered, he heard' (*Portrait*, pp. 115–16; italics mine). Similarly, Joyce contrives numerous 'after-image effects', as though impressions stubbornly persisted on Stephen's visual cortex after the things casting them have been physically removed. As discussed, the director's 'mirthless mask' lingers over the sunset; conversely, swallows weaving against the open sky 'soothed his eyes *which still saw the image* of his mother's face', trapped in domestic squalor as Stephen strolls to college (p. 189; italics mine).

Such images, imprinted in and 'reprojected' from Stephen's imagination (to borrow his own term), resemble stereoscopic, virtually tangible pictures, sharply defined against the contexts they burst into. Verb phrases such as 'stood forth', 'started forth', 'sprang up' or 'sprung up' (and variations thereof) recur with them. Fixated on Dumas's Count, 'The figure of that dark avenger *stood forth in his mind* for whatever he had heard or divined in childhood of the strange and terrible' (*Portrait*, p. 52; italics mine). Fantasies about exotic Mediterranean locales manifest with glowing virtualism like travel slides against drab Dublin backgrounds: '*there would come to his mind the bright picture* of Marseilles, of sunny trellises' (p. 52; italics mine). There were silent film adaptations of *The Count of Monte Cristo* as early as 1908, one Italian (dir. Luigi Maggi) and one American (dir. Francis Boggs and Thomas Persons). However, given that lantern adaptations of popular classics ranging from Defoe to

Dickens circulated in late Victorian Dublin, it is not beyond the bounds of possibility that Dumas's story had received similar treatment contemporaneous with when this chapter of *Portrait* is set (c. 1895). James Simonton's Royal Panopticon of Science and Art, at 70 Grafton Street, imported optical devices and entertainments from Paris, Brussels and Vienna (*MLP&MPS*, p. 61).[97]

Stephen eventually imagines entering his hero's picture world as if it were a magic portal he could step through, a well-known self-reflexive topos in life-model slides and early film, from *The Curtain* to Paul and Edison's parodies of naïve cinemagoers. It reached its hypostasis in Buster Keaton's *Sherlock Junior* (1924), in which a dozing projectionist enters the screen along his own beam. Stephen's wish-fulfilment climaxes with seeing his own illumined double in another time and place – as characters in visionary lantern melodramas often did – usurping the Count's role: '*there appeared an image of himself*, grown older and wiser, *standing in a moonlit garden* with Mercedes . . .' (*Portrait*, p. 52; italics mine). *Portrait* is laden with such moments with connotations of involuntary projection and photographic simulation (albeit visual immersiveness and transformation in dioramas may also be influences, as discussed below). For example, during the retreat, the admonishing '*image of Emma appeared before him*'. Like the Knock apparitions of the Virgin, Emma seems so miraculously real and present that '*under her eyes*, the flood of shame rushed forth anew from his heart' (*Portrait*, p. 97; italics mine).

Pictures often spring up instantly from nowhere. For example, when Emma accuses Stephen of being a heretical monk, 'His own image *started forth* a profaner of the cloister . . .' (p. 185; italics mine). Some impressions are even vividly imprinted from other people's experiences. Davin's story of the lonely country woman sticks in Stephen's imagination: 'One night the young peasant . . . *had called up before Stephen's mind* a strange vision' (p. 152; italics mine). The same image is conjured back with sudden impact in another context, exemplifying how Joyce sets going rhythmic associations that overlap different times and places and accumulate significances as they cross-thread his text. The figure of the country woman stands out in relief as a kind of national symbol through linking with others remembered from childhood onwards: the 'woman in the story *stood forth, reflected in other figures* . . . he had seen standing in doorways at Clane as the college cars drove by, as a type of her race and his own . . .' Stephen's associative reverie then 'cuts' back to the narrative present and the impoverished flower-seller accosting him (as the peasant women did Davin), who thus started it up in the first place (pp. 153–4; italics mine). This aggregated image of female suffering projects again as Stephen reflects on the oppressed condition of his 'race' (p. 200). Later, Joyce reverses this process, when Stephen metaphorically smashes E-C's likeness in a jealous rage. His internalised picture of Emma shatters back into associations with other girls previously encountered and brooded on: 'It broke up violently her fair image and flung the fragments on all sides. *On all sides distorted reflections of her image started from* his memory' (p. 185; italics mine). These individual reflections, though narrated sequentially because of the linearity of text, nonetheless convey an effect of exploding outwards, like a multifaceted slide image or film frame splitting into simultaneous actions from different times and places.

Stephen seems to visualise not just his own memories, but those of others as projected pictures with virtually photographic externalisation. In Cork, for example, his father's tales of student roistering, mixing with pubescent frustrations, *'sprang up before him'*. Such visions usurp his present consciousness with a force beyond rational control in vividly moving details. A *risqué* graffito triggers a fantasy in which vanished generations suddenly repopulate the empty anatomy theatre at Queen's College (the location of John Joyce's attempt at medical studies):[98]

> On the desk before him he read the word *Fœtus* cut several times in the dark stained wood. The sudden legend startled his blood: he seemed to feel the absent students of the college about him and to shrink from their company. *A vision of their life*, which his father's words had been powerless to evoke, *sprang up before him out of the word cut in the desk.* A broadshouldered student with a moustache was cutting the letters with a jackknife, seriously. Other students stood or sat near him laughing at his handiwork. One jogged his elbow. *The big student turned to him, frowning.* He was dressed in loose grey clothes and had tan boots. (*Portrait*, p. 75; additional italics mine)

Note the deliberate ambiguity of 'turned to him' – to his fellow student in the past or to Stephen himself? – which suggestively immerses Joyce's focaliser in his own vision. Dioramas, which Stephen refers to in his diary, incorporated ingeniously animated 'change picture' techniques for filling empty spaces such as cathedrals with lively throngs, which could be startlingly immersive and three-dimensional in effect. They were conjured up by illuminating figures painted on the reverse of canvas backgrounds or hitherto invisible gauze screens through hidden light sources and sound effects. The most famous and influential of Daguerre's 'double effect' dioramas, according to Andrew E. Hershberger, was *A Midnight Mass at the Church of Saint-Étienne-du-Mont* (displayed continuously from October 1834 to October 1837).[99] The contemporary journalist Gustave Delville described its extraordinary transformational effect, which seemed to compress time before his eyes:

> At first it was daylight, the nave full of chairs; little by little the light waned; at the same time, candles were lit at the back of the choir: then the entire church was illuminated, and the chairs were occupied by the

congregation who had arrived, not suddenly as if by scene-shifting, but gradually – quickly enough to surprise one, yet slowly enough not to be too astonished. The midnight mass started, and in the midst of a devotion impossible to describe, organ music was heard echoing from the vaulted roof. Slowly dawn broke, the congregation dispersed, the candles were extinguished, the church and the empty chairs appeared as at the beginning. This was magic.[100]

The Inauguration of the Temple of Salomon (September 1836–March 1839) used similarly epic effects.[101]

Though the diorama show proper had declined by the 1850s, the principles of 'change pictures' were incorporated into other entertainments in Dublin, such as the Myriorama referenced in *Ulysses*. Moreover, *Portrait*'s subversive conspiracy between words and projected pictures results in a grotesquely moving after-image that overlays everything that Stephen subsequently sees, summoning desires that he struggles to repress (note the involuntary force of 'sprung up' again): 'But the word [i.e. foetus] and the vision *capered before his eyes* as he walked back across the quadrangle and towards the college gate . . . His recent monstrous reveries *came thronging* into his memory. They too *had sprung up before him, suddenly and furiously*, out of mere words' (*Portrait*, p. 75; italics mine). After entering college himself, a risqué *double entendre* conjures a similar 'Sabbath of misrule' in another lecture theatre. 'His fellow student's rude humour ran like a gust through the cloister of Stephen's mind, shaking into gay life limp priestly vestments that hung upon the walls, setting them to sway and caper.' The figures of staid clerical tutors instantly fill these empty robes, animating in slapstick carnival: 'The forms of the community emerged from the gustblown vestments . . . They came ambling and stumbling, tumbling and capering, kilting their gowns for leapfrog . . .' (p. 161).

Stephen's reviewing of his days of prep school innocence ends with a brief apparition of his lost self standing beside him, oblivious and detached as a projected photographic double in a lantern slide. The vision also foreshadows the outfit worn by Bloom's dead son Rudy in the 'faërie' vision that closes *Ulysses*' 'Circe' chapter: 'It was strange *to see his small body appear again for a moment*: a little boy in a grey belted suit' (*Portrait*, p. 78, italics mine; cf. *Ulysses* 15.4956–72).[102] The same process of self-externalisation, as if watching virtual duplicates framed in another time zone within the main image by insert or superimposition, is deployed when Stephen visualises possible futures under emotional pressure. As noted above, imagined scenes of Jesuit training are itemised through the repeated phrase, 'He saw himself . . .' (*Portrait*, p. 135). Indeed, the *Christmas Carol*-like reviewing of the existential entailments of life choices was common in the multi-layered and spatio-temporally shuffled structures of life-model slide narratives. This was done by similarly presenting a character in the foreground watching photographically multiplied selves in other situations in different planes within the same image or in other slides presented out of chronological sequence. The technique was remediated by film in due course.

VISUAL IMMERSIONS

If projected images hover indeterminately between Stephen's inner and outer vision, their counterpart consists of whole backgrounds appearing and disappearing, enveloping him or fading out according to other switches of consciousness. This also pushes the effect that climaxes *Dubliners* – as one visual environment overwhelms another – much further. In *Portrait* there is frequent 'lapping' between different locations and Stephen's present context, suggestive of dissolving views and their evolution into filmic mixes. Another possible influence stems from visually immersive and transformative effects in dioramic 'change pictures' which shared certain features with dissolving views.

Joyce dissolves subtly from external visual space to Stephen's inner space in a transformative scene in chapter 1. Free-associating deliriously while overhearing the infirmarers' whispering about Parnell's death, Stephen imagines a similar martyr's end for himself. Significantly, the scene begins by refiguring Plato's 'allegory of the cave', with Stephen watching moving shapes cast by firelight behind him on the wall he faces. This reflective illusion quickly turns into another psychological projection effect, with the fire shadows' wavelike rhythm conjuring both the sea and the voices of a lamenting multitude, in which Stephen becomes immersed. It is even possible that Joyce is recalling specific effects from lantern shows such as *What Are the Wild Waves Saying?*, where breakers carrying a storm-tossed ship flood the 'dreamtime' space of sleeping children through their bedroom wall, as if trying to tell them something:

> How pale the light was at the window! But that was nice. The fire rose and fell on the wall. It was like waves. Someone had put coal on and he heard voices. They were talking. It was the noise of the waves. Or the waves were talking amongst themselves as they rose and fell.
>
> He saw the sea of waves, long dark waves rising and falling, dark under the moonless night. A tiny light twinkled at the pierhead where the ship was entering: and he saw a multitude of people gathered by the water's edge to see the ship that was entering the harbour. A tall man stood on the deck, looking out towards the flat dark land: and by the light at the pierhead he saw his face, the sorrowful face of brother Michael.
>
> He saw him lift his hands towards the people and heard him say in a loud voice of sorrow over the waters:

> – He is dead. We saw him lying upon the catafalque.
> A wail of sorrow went up from the people.
> – Parnell! Parnell! He is dead! (*Portrait*, pp. 21–2)

Extreme discontinuity between location and scale is smoothed over by Joyce's consummate visual and auditory matching, gradually adding details which 'morph' one scene into another. Feverish drifting affords an imaginative logic that melts physical surroundings into a very different mental 'inscape'. Note also how the shot/reverse shot effect of seeing the ship from the shore, then viewing the shore from its deck dramatically changes the viewpoint, creating an impression both of relative motion and depth of field in Joyce's moving imagery.

In a reverse example of this kind of transition, after the adolescent's vision of his sinful soul 'flicker[ing] out' against the void, Stephen gradually regains awareness of present surroundings. The sordid 'living picture' of Dublin's back streets through which he is wandering distractedly rematerialises around him:

> Consciousness of place *came ebbing back to him slowly* over a vast tract of time unlit, unfelt, unlived. The squalid scene *composed itself around him*; the common accents, the burning gasjets in the shops, odours of fish and spirits and wet sawdust, *moving men and women.* (*Portrait*, pp. 118–19; italics mine)

Note the word choice 'ebbing back' and 'composed itself', which characterises how Joyce presents phased and apparently autonomous visual transformations in the novel. This vivid suggestion of another sensory environment gradually fading up into full resolution around Stephen also occurs when recalling past events. For example, the riotous premiere of Yeats's *The Countess Cathleen* in May 1899 is conjured up by a snatch of song: 'The verses crooned in the ears of his memory *composed slowly before his remembering eyes the scene* of the hall on the night of the opening of the national theatre' (p. 190; italics mine).

Not only do effects, motifs and terms related to dissolving views and dioramic change pictures occur frequently in *Portrait*, but also allusions to instabilities inherent in both mental and photochemical processes for fixing reliable images in memory or celluloid.[103] On the cusp of adolescence, Stephen visualises his innocent childhood self *'faded out* like a film in the sun' standing beside him (*Portrait*, p. 78; italics mine). Joyce's simile with photographs decaying into indefinition anticipates 'he is noewhemoe. Finiche! Only a fadograph of a yestern scene' in *Finnegans Wake* (7.15). It is repeated a few sentences later to emphasise the precariousness of preserving the authentic past in mind or media. Uncle Charles similarly dwindles into 'an image which had lately been *fading out* of memory' (*Portrait*, p. 73; italics mine).

Joyce uses the highly suggestive phrase 'dissolving moments' to describe Stephen's sacramental ecstasies, which finally cause traumatic flashbacks to scenes of sexual transgression to fade out (*Portrait*, p. 128). Later, to wipe out reveries, the undergraduate erases the 'fantastic fabrics of his mind' by '*dissolving them* painlessly and noiselessly' (p. 135; italics mine). In the Dollymount Strand episode, Joyce embeds another momentary dissolve effect in which the contours of one picture emerge phantasmagorically through another, defying every physical law of space, time and proportion. Musing on Dublin's distant, blurry skyline and troubled history, Stephen imagines that '*the ghost* of the ancient kingdom of the Danes had *looked forth* through the vesture of the *hazewrapped* city' (p. 142; italics mine). Shortly after, Joyce's leitmotif of the Daedalian birdman suddenly shows forth too (invoking epiphany's etymology again) in full visibility, finally confirming the 'nominative determinism' latent in Stephen's surname. An indefinable form hovering in and out of mind from infancy onwards, its image gradually projects with stronger resolution in the foreground of Stephen's life, thus 'fading up' as he grows in self-knowledge and artistic confidence. It is now revealed in the ascendant:

> Now, at the name of the fabulous artificer, he seemed to hear the noise of dim waves and to see a winged form flying above the waves and slowly climbing the air. What did it mean? Was it a quaint device opening a page of some medieval book of prophecies and symbols, a hawk-like man flying sunward above the sea, a prophecy of the end he had been born to serve and had been following *through mists of childhood and boyhood . . .?*' (*Portrait*, p. 142)

Appropriately, it is Stephen's past experience – reduced to mere 'mists of childhood and boyhood' – which dissolves away compared to this numinous revelation about his future. The whole passage is visually fluid, layered and inter-medial, switching between beachside panorama and close-up recollection of leafing through an illuminated manuscript to encounter an enigmatic figure whose full significance finally appears projected against the sky.

Joyce then reworks his sobering ending to 'The Dead', repeating the phrase that describes Gabriel's engulfment by the chilling ghostworld of Michael Furey in his existential meltdown. The final sentence of 'The Dead' begins: '*His soul swooned slowly* as he heard the snow falling faintly . . .' (italics mine). *Portrait* repurposes the same words with exultant contrast as Stephen's subjectivity melts into a very different parallel reality visualising his own unformed creative potentials: '*His soul was swooning* into some new world, *fantastic, dim, uncertain* as under sea, traversed by *cloudy shapes and beings*' (*Portrait*, p. 145; italics mine). 'Swooning' already featured in a very different context to signify the phantoms of adolescent desire which beset Stephen so tantalisingly:

'He stretched out his arms in the street to hold fast the frail swooning form that eluded him and incited him' (p. 84). It is also used in Stephen's first encounter with the prostitute, to simultaneously 'black out' his consciousness and the scene's suggestive eroticism, as he feels pressure on his lips 'darker than the swoon of sin, softer than sound or odour' (p. 85).

CAVES OF ILLUSION: *PORTRAIT*'S CINEMATISED UNCONSCIOUS AND MEDIA-CULTURAL IMAGINARY

As Stephen wonders about the source of his libidinous fantasies in Cork – 'from what den of monstrous images' they project so automatically and irrepressibly (*Portrait*, p. 76) – we might well ask whether *Portrait* effectively explores Benjamin's optical unconscious as a *cinematised* phenomenon. Arguably, this is a leading aspect of Joyce's engagement with modernity's media-cultural imaginary.[104] The year after *Portrait* was first serialised, Hugo Münsterberg, author of one of the earliest academic studies of film, argued that it visualised mental processes more effectively than any medium before. According to Münsterberg's *The Photoplay: A Psychological Study* (1916), film was evolving closer to the 'language of the mind' because of its miraculous ability to rearrange appearance, space-time and action at will; to visualise the impossible as if actual: 'The photoplay tells us a human story by overcoming the forms of the outer world, namely space, time, and causality, and by adjusting the events to the forms of the inner world, namely attention, memory, imagination and emotion.' Film's moving images, albeit photographed from objective realities before the camera, were recomposed to 'reach complete isolation from the practical world through the perfect unity of plot and pictorial appearance'.[105] This might almost be a description of *Portrait*'s own method: both recording phenomena perceived with ultra-mimetic precision beyond any previous degree of naturalism, yet simultaneously orchestrating them according to the subjective rhythm of Stephen's 'attention, memory, imagination and emotion'. However, in this respect, as we have seen, the cinematicity of *Portrait* continues to reflect how film had deeper roots in pre-existing screen practices in the wider media ecology of Joyce's youth.

Moreover, while referencing media forms and techniques pervasively, *Portrait* also updates key philosophical questions posed throughout the history of illusionistic representation. Plato's proto-cinematic 'allegory of the cave' is frequently alluded to in figuring the workings of Stephen's imagination. In *The Republic*, lifelong prisoners are subjected to a show of shadow puppetry which they mistake for a reality that they have never encountered:

> Imagine people living in a cavernous cell down under the ground; at the far end of the cave, a long way off, there's an entrance open to the outside world. They've been there since childhood, with their legs and

necks tied up in a way which keeps them in one place and allows them to look only straight ahead, but not to turn their heads. There's firelight burning along way further up the cave behind them, and up the slope between the fire and the prisoners there's a road, beside which you should imagine a low wall has been built – like the partition which conjurors place between themselves and their audience and above which they show their tricks.[106]

Similarly, echoing the fire shadows on the infirmary wall, when the senior schoolboy stares distractedly into a grate, Joyce provides striking visual matches suggesting Stephen's desire to escape straitened circumstances into new dimensions of creative possibility, but also the dangers of becoming lost in a shadowy labyrinth of naive delusions. In the moving chiaroscuro of the flames, Stephen glimpses whole worlds, through dramatic fluctuations of focus and proportion, but with an underlying threat of entrapment, like Axel Lidenbrock in Verne's *Journey to the Centre of the Earth* (1867): 'He sat listening to the words and following the ways of adventure that lay open in the coals, arches and vaults and winding galleries and jagged caverns' (*Portrait*, p. 56). Stephen's *bricolage* model of Monte Cristo's desert island refuge suggests another parallel between imaginary caves and immersive projections: 'At night he built up on the parlour table an image of the wonderful island cave out of transfers and paper flowers and coloured tissue paper and strips of the silver and golden paper in which chocolate is wrapped.' Stephen finally breaks up 'this scenery, weary of its tinsel', because it fails to satisfy his adolescent stirrings, only to replace it with a shadowy image less palpable and more tantalisingly elusive: the lanternlike 'bright picture of Marseilles, of sunny trellises, and of Mercedes', which now obsesses his thoughts (*Portrait*, p. 52).

Joyce frequently figures Stephen's secretive imagination as a kind of cave or dark chamber (the etymology of camera) screening 'living pictures' in private. However, some threaten to burst its confines and become shamefully visible to others, so apparently concrete and paranoid is his visualisation process. (There is a simultaneously aural dimension to this, in step with contemporary sound-recording technology. Stephen's memory is also figured as an 'echo chamber' retaining and replaying impressions from his past phonographically. For example, 'The echoes of certain expressions used in Clongowes sounded in remote caves of his mind' [*Portrait*, p. 132]). Moreover, this is more than just topical analogy with evolving media. Joyce seems to recognise that human subjectivity is historic and always conditioned by the forms and techniques of the culture in which it takes shape; that, paradoxically, we can be imprisoned within them, but can also be liberated if their influence on our imagination is critically objectified and challenged. Hence, though shocked by the Cork *graffito* 'to find in the outer world a trace of what he had deemed till then a brutish and individual malady of his own' (p. 75), Stephen is prompted to ponder how this correspondence between secret desires and mediated images that he is exposed to comes about. His 'sootcoated packet of pictures' hidden up the chimney flue (p. 97) exemplifies the seedier side of mass-produced photographic postcards in the 1890s through cheap new processes. It also foreshadows Joyce's exploration of the commodification of the erotic by moving images in 'Nausicaa' through the mutoscope, which animated such *risqué* photocards in sequences on a revolving drum through the 'flipbook' principle.[107] The Victorian postcard industry boomed alongside life-model narratives and the beginnings of film in a media ecology with systematically transferable themes, motifs and techniques. As we have seen, firms such as Bamforth and William Lawrence were typically pioneers in creating or dealing in all three.

Joyce thus shows Stephen's maturing critical awareness of how his subjectivity is moulded by such influences from the media-cultural imaginary of his time. Initially, adolescent guilt and frustration breach the boundaries between inner and outer vision, so that they seem in paranoid correspondence: 'By his monstrous way of life he seemed to have put himself beyond the limits of reality. Nothing moved or spoke to him from the real world unless he heard in it an echo of the infuriated cries within him' (*Portrait*, p. 77). However, impressions from the outer world undergo active processing in the 'darkroom' of Stephen's mind, going beyond passive fixing and imprinting of photo-like images in the *Dubliners* stories about adolescent fantasy such as 'Araby'. Hence Stephen 'exulted to defile with patience *whatever image had attracted his eyes. By day and by night he moved among distorted images of the outer world*' (p. 83; italics mine). Nonetheless, Joyce hints that this process does not remain entirely involuntary; Stephen gradually learns to control it to some extent. Certainly, phrases such as 'The images *he had summoned* gave him no pleasure' (p. 196; italics mine) imply degrees of agency, if not literal image manipulation, but also hint at growing weariness with simulations and a desire for more authentic and unmediated human contact.

Significantly, Stephen's recurrent vision of Cranly's priestlike, free-floating head opens a 'strange dark cavern of speculation' (pp. 149–50). Once again, Joyce deliberately echoes Plato's parable, underscoring how his novel is preoccupied with exploring the relationship between the imagistic processes of the mind and technologically modernised, inter-medial forms. Arguably, the sermons in chapter 3 owe some of their graphic terrorism to the tradition of projecting illusions to serve authoritarian agendas, stretching at least as far back as Huygens's disavowed 'lantern of fear', used to discipline both public imagination and individual conscience by depicting the torments of the damned. This practice was still very much alive in Victorian slide shows that adapted phantasmagoria techniques for reformist ends and that may have been shown on religious retreats, as 'Grace' implies. LUCERNA lists three surviving sets based on the medieval vision of Hell: *Dante's Inferno* (seventeen slides, in/before 1888), *Subjects from Dante's Inferno* (in/before 1895) and *The Vision of Hell by Dante Alighieri* (n.d.), from Doré's illustrations. It was also remediated by early film epics such as *L'Inferno* (dir. Francesco Bertolini and Adolfo Padovan, 1911), made while Joyce was living in Italophone Trieste. Significantly, *L'Inferno* was Italy's first full-length feature, screening Dante's concentric Hell through the full range of spectacular special effects then available, including hosts of damned souls tortured by devils according to particular sins, gigantic monsters and a three-headed Lucifer at its centre.

Portrait also elaborates themes and effects from the phantasmagoria tradition already evident in *Dubliners*. As discussed in Chapter 1, the phantasmagoria's ostensible function was 'rational entertainment', enlightening revolutionary France about the deceptions practised through optical trickery, a purpose echoed in *Stephen Hero*'s critical opposition between mystification and modernising clarity of vision. Similarly, *Portrait*'s hellfire sermons can be considered Joyce's most egregious example of manipulation of the media-cultural imaginary by institutions that he sought to expose and demystify through his new form of self-consciously cinematic fiction. The rhetoric of the sermons exemplifies precisely what both Tom Kernan and his author distrust about 'the magic-lantern business'.

In Father Arnall's final sermon, sadistic descriptions of infernal torture climax with the virtual ocular wounding of his captive audience. This anticipates the reflexive visual shock of violated eyeballs in films, such as the opening 'double-take' of Luis Buñuel's *Un Chien Andalou* (1929) or during the Odessa Steps massacre in Eisenstein's *Battleship Potemkin* (1925). While not literally employing a device such as a magic lantern or film projector, Arnall nonetheless commits a form of organised ekphrastic violence upon his audience's emotions and, by proxy, sight. Not only does he show the sinner's body progressively irradiated with fiery pain, organ-by-organ, in a kind of X-ray anatomisation of the living dead,[108] but eyes are his ultimate target: 'The blood seethes and boils in the veins, the brains are boiling in the skull, the heart in the breast glowing and bursting, the bowels a redhot mass of burning pulp, the tender eyes flaming like molten balls' (*Portrait*, p. 102). Significantly, Joyce went on to make 'vision animated to bursting point' the technic of 'Circe', to stress the sheer ekphrastic overload of *Ulysses*' most demonically cinematic chapter. 'Circe' stretches the sense of sight to the point where it similarly threatens to explode altogether in a kind of 'mockalyptic' parody of evangelising rhetorical excess like Arnall's.

As Condon notes, the Irish public (like their counterparts on the British mainland) were bombarded with far more coverage about the new medium of X-rays than the cinematograph when both debuted in Dublin in 1896, albeit the attractions of moving pictures eventually eclipsed X-rays' sensational appeal as their narrative potential developed.[109] However, initially the uncanny properties of X-rays (first exhibited widely to Dubliners at the optically themed Cyclopia bazaar) took greater hold on the popular imagination, at least 'as far as the daily newspapers reflect this'. Effectively, they beat the cinematograph to the title of 'the new photography' at the time.[110] By April 1896, when the cinematograph finally arrived in Dublin, one of the city's scientists was already conducting experimental X-ray investigations into human anatomy after developing his own apparatus. Their ability to render clothes and bodies transparent even led to speculations about using them to see inside the mind, a particularly terrifying thought for conscience-stricken Catholic adolescents such as Joyce and his literary avatar. One comic article in the *Dublin Evening Herald* of 15 March 1896 described how an English photographer allegedly took X-ray pictures of his own thoughts, a very different take on the idea of psychological visibility to Griffith's view that film technique could 'photograph thought' by depicting subjective points of view.[111] Only gradually would the actual physical dangers of X-rays become evident through serious or fatal burns caused by long exposure to their 'invisible fire'. However, it is tempting to think that the effect of X-rays on the body, exposing the skeleton beneath in a hellish vision of a state paradoxically alive beyond death, adds topical force to Arnall's discourse. It would be a perfect example of the latest developments in optical science adding to a long tradition of authoritarian attempts to appropriate technology to discipline the common visual imaginary.

Joyce famously based Arnall's rhetoric on a widely available and gruesomely illustrated guide to Hell. The National Library of Ireland holds a copy with woodcuts depicting the torments of a damned soul.[112] Since the rhetorical tropes of such pamphlets were used on retreats, it is perfectly possible that their illustrations were also projected as lantern slides. Certainly, having absorbed infernal imagery from infancy, Stephen's overwrought state makes his own eye-sockets appear to spontaneously combust on cue (*Portrait*, p. 105). However, it is the phantasmagorically immersive effect on how Stephen sees afterwards that is most striking. This intensifies features of the technical and thematic rhythm that *Portrait* has built up specific to its process of inter-medial visualisation. Paranoid matches project animistically on to mundane objects such as empty clothing, as Stephen 'passed up the staircase and into the corridor along the walls of which the overcoats and waterproofs hung like gibbeted malefactors, headless and dripping and shapeless' (p. 105). Characteristic audio-visual motifs of disembodied heads and detached voices take on a supernatural twist, combining with further Platonic allusions. Stephen hesitates fearfully on the threshold of his room, now transformed into a shadowy cave in which 'faces waited and watched', with 'murmurous voices' filling its 'dark shell' (p. 115).

Certainly, *Portrait*'s frequent representation of visions materialising in, or stemming from, darkened spaces is highly significant to its critique of the media-cultural imaginary. After Stephen's diary entry recollecting his immersive experience at a Rotunda diorama, in which pictures of 'big nobs' were also projected, Joyce plants his climactic cave of illusion reference in the form of a nightmare effectively reconfiguring the show's contemporary media terms. Subhuman figures emerging from Stephen's dream cavern resemble blurry 'spirit photographs' of *Gestalt* beings: 'One does not seem to stand quite apart from another. Their faces are phosphorescent with darker streaks' (*Portrait*, p. 211).[113] Moreover, these trogolodytes are dwarfed by gigantic statues of dead kings, nourished on the 'errors of men' in the form of a perpetual sacrificial fire, its play of light and shadow providing the vault's sole illumination. The trogolodytes' enigmatic appeal to Stephen – 'They peer at me and their eyes seem to ask me something. They do not speak' (significantly 'voiced' in cinematic dumbshow by expression only) – hints at his author's project: to inspire compatriots to liberate themselves through the progressive cinematicity of his fiction, which strove to reveal the machinery, both literal and psychological, behind their entrapment in a cave of illusion serving 'false idols'.[114] Joyce believed that such unconscious forces prevented his fellow Irish from achieving both independent modernity as a nation and their human potential as individuals. Hence the 'uncreated con- science of my race' (*Portrait*, p. 213), which Stephen finally vows to 'forge' on his Daedalian mission, refers to an enlightened ethical consciousness, but also implies the material conditions and media-cultural forms operating against it as *Portrait* represents them.

Thus the individuating rhythm of Stephen's own consciousness, its underly- ing pattern of struggle and adaptive response to repressive challenges, always shows through Joyce's text like the abstract curves tracing the distinctive mus- cular thrust of one of Marey's athletes. In this way, we can view the further advances in ekphrastic cinematicity made in the novel – especially its distinc- tive method of 'picturing time' through subjective perception and memory – as in a direct line of development from his earlier work. *Portrait* both unpacks *Stephen Hero*'s scepticism towards lantern practices, as epitomising 'distorting' projections of the real relationship between subjective self and social institu- tions, and intensifies the creative challenge to such repressive influences implicit in *Dubliners*' themes and techniques.

One of *Portrait*'s most shocking effects of 'cognitive dissonance' induced by guilt reworks a dream vision recorded in Joyce's *Notebook of Epiphanies*, kept between 1900 and 1903. Arguably, the vision's new context and force indicates how much Joyce absorbed from the influence of early film by the time he incorporated it, especially in terms of immersion, kinaesthetics and the expressive power of the cinematic presentation of space. However, the vision also confirms how Joyce's prior imaginative training by the optical culture that gave birth to film primed him to push the epiphany's features further on the page.[115] The passage consists of a 'double-take' anticipating those in horror films, as Stephen falls into fitful sleep after Arnall's final sermon. Seeking refuge from paranoid audio-visual echoes in the fade-out of oblivion, Stephen instantly transits instead into a nightmare of hallucinatory virtualism: '[T]he senses of his soul closed. They closed for an instant and then opened. He saw.' Stephen's vision initially appears silent, but gradually exhibits subtle sound effects as it rotates around him like a 'peristrephic' panorama (see Chapter 3), gradually filling with moving details until he jolts awake:

> A field of stiff weeds and thistles and tufted nettlebunches. Thick among the tufts of rank stiff growth lay battered canisters and clots and coils of solid excrement. A faint marshlight struggled upwards from all the ordure through the bristling greygreen weeds. An evil smell, faint and foul as the light, curled upwards, sluggishly out of the canisters and from the stale crusted dung.
>
> Creatures were in the field; *one, three, six*: creatures *were moving in the field*, hither and thither. Goatish creatures with human faces, hornybrowed, lightly bearded and grey as indiarubber. The malice of evil glittered in their hard eyes, *as they moved hither and thither*, trailing their long tails behind them. A rictus of cruel malignity lit up greyly their old bony faces. One was clasping about his ribs a torn flannel waistcoat, another complained monotonously as his beard stuck in the tufted weeds. *Soft language issued from their spittleless lips as they swished in slow circles* round and round the field, winding hither and thither through the weeds, dragging their long tails amid the rattling canisters. They moved in slow circles, *circling closer and closer to enclose, to enclose*, soft language issuing from their lips, their long swishing tails besmeared with stale shite, *thrusting upwards their terrific faces* . . . (*Portrait*, p. 116; italics mine)

'A faint marshlight' gives this scene the phosphorescent impression of tinted monochrome. It opens with a kind of establishing long shot – 'Creatures were in the field' – panning around the space – 'one, three, six' – then alternating this with zooms in and out of extreme close-up – 'Soft language issued from their spittleless lips as they swished in slow circles round and round the field.' The satyrs' sinister choreography is both Dantean – 'circling closer and closer to enclose' – and dynamically stereoscopic, building a sense of vicarious panic and entrapment. Thus Joyce's climactic close-up of monstrous heads thrusting upwards manages to seem as much 'in your face' as Stephen's through sheer haptic shock.

Joyce's description of these demons as 'hornybrowed, lightly bearded and grey as indiarubber' may be a rare clue allowing some of this passage's cinematicity to be traced, or at least closely paralleled, to a specific film; one particularly likely to have stuck in Joyce's mind, given his well-known phobia about horned beasts. Percy Stow's trick film, *A Glass of Goat's Milk* (GB, 1909) (screened at the Volta on 3–5 February 1910),[116] used location-shooting in a similarly weed-choked field to depict a mild-mannered gentleman's metamorphosis into a demonic satyr. With wonderfully vernacular proto-surrealism, he chases people in circles around the field, butting over trees, buildings and even climactically an omnibus. Punctuating close-ups of his leering face suggest a rampant and knowing libido threatening to burst out of the screen in sheer glee at his one-man 'mockalypse'. The effect of transformation after he innocently drinks the milk – possibly done by inflating crude India rubber 'prosthetic' horns (rather than by dissolve or stop-motion substitution) – seems not only to parallel *Portrait*'s queasily tinted vision, but also to anticipate Bloom's cuckold's antlers and the many animalistic metamorphoses in 'Circe'. Certainly, this passage extends phantasmagoric tendencies in Joyce's earlier work through its uncannily vivid sense of movement and immersion, just as film remediated lantern and moving panorama techniques.

However, the advent of film may not have been the sole factor prompting Joyce's extraordinary reanimation of his original dream epiphany. A new study of French *diableries*, popular from the mid-nineteenth century, shows that these miniature infernos depicting aspects of life in hell were ingeniously modelled in clay, but also converted into coloured stereographic images. These could be viewed by individuals through stereoscopes or projected by 3-D lanterns for large-scale, startling effects, including devilish faces leering outwards from the scene towards the viewer.[117] In their satirical ethos, with burlesque ladies partnering macabre, satyr-like demons, they anticipate the eroto-gothic themes of trick films by Méliès and others. They were also cheekily self-conscious about remediating traditional notions of sin and damnation by the latest visual technology, and their ambivalent impact on both the sense of titillation and fear of public exposure and shame. In *La Photographie de Satan* (*Satan's Photographic Emporium*, 1868), which proudly proclaims 'We operate day and night', a semi-naked couple are snapped by gleeful devils *in flagrante delicto*.[118] *Diableries* were certainly exhibited in London as early as 1860. A report in the *British Journal of Photography* gave a very detailed account of several 'Satanic slides', including an infernal railway train, a devils' ball, Satan's wedding and the Temptation of St Anthony at Shew's in Oxford Street, displayed as stereo views.[119] Though *diableries* may not have been widely shown in Ireland, and their popularity declined from the 1890s, Joyce could have seen some during his first Paris sojourns and certainly saw examples of their filmic successors. Moreover, as discussed above, Stephen's own table-top model of Monte Cristo's cave, which is replaced by adolescent brooding on the 'bright picture' of Mercedes and fantasies of entering its space, suggestively links his 3-D replica with immersive projected images of Dumas's fictional world.

ANTICIPATIONS OF *ULYSSES*

As we have seen, *Portrait*'s media-conditioned stream of consciousness technique builds on the subjective focalisation, lantern-like shuffling of chronology and reprojection of images through memory tried out in many *Dubliners'* stories. However, it also laid the basis for refining such techniques in the interior monologues of *Ulysses*, confirming the latter's position as *the* superlatively inter-medial Modernist text in a world saturated with projected film by the time of its publication in 1922. For example, the most sustained interruption of *Portrait*'s forward narrative drive by flashback typically dilates from an involuntary perceptual 'cue' in the present – an extreme close-up on Heron's mouth. It shares the projective materialisation of *Portrait*'s other visual shifts and use of lantern terminology, instantly transporting Stephen back into the sensory environment of elsewhen, like a psycho-physiological time machine:

> The confession came only from Stephen's lips and, while they spoke the words, *a sudden memory had carried him to another scene called up, as if by magic*, at the moment when he had noted the faint cruel dimples at the corners of Heron's smiling lips . . . (*Portrait*, p. 65; italics mine)

Heron teases Stephen to 'admit' his crush on E-C, simultaneously tapping a cane across Stephen's calf. This propels him back four years to an accusation of 'heresy' and a schoolboy inquisition by Heron's gang to beat another confession out of him. The dilation returns to the present as Stephen realises that his ability to rise above past traumas is a mark of growing maturity, though the past action is still 'replaying' in his consciousness – another conspicuous instance of space-time overlapping and projective imaging: '*while the scenes* of that malignant episode *were still passing sharply and swiftly before his mind* he wondered why he bore no malice now to those who had tormented him' (*Portrait*, p. 69; italics mine). The phrase 'scenes [. . .] passing sharply and swiftly before' is practically formulaic in deliberately suggesting a sucession of rapidly moving pictures like slides or film-shots. The flashback's duration of some five pages clearly anticipates the greater frequency and elaboration of such analeptic and proleptic effects in the interior monologues of *Ulysses*.

There are many other ways in which *Portrait* anticipates specific cinematic strategies in *Ulysses*. Joyce's visual pun on the dripping jar that opens chapter 5 switches scale to match 'topographies' dramatically different in space, time and volume: 'The yellow dripping had been scooped out like a boghole and the pool under it brought back to his memory the dark turfcoloured water of the bath at Clongowes' (*Portrait*, p. 146) The jar symbolises Stephen's come-down to sordid domestic reality again after the closing upbeat of chapter 4 with its expansive vision at Dollymount:

> He rose slowly and, recalling the rapture of his sleep, sighed at its joy. He climbed to the crest of the sandhill and gazed about him. Evening had fallen.
>
> A rim of the young moon cleft the pale waste of skyline, the rim of a silver hoop embedded in grey sand; and the tide was flowing in fast to the land with a low whisper of her waves, islanding a last few figures in distant pools. (p. 145)

Joyce deliberately laps over this lyrical impression of moonlit figures islanded in 'distant pools' to contrast the jar's coagulated residues and their subsequent match with the disgusting communal bath, extending this associative chain of stagnation imagery from the novel's prep school phase. Stephen's high-angle, panoramic view from 'the crest of the sandhill' celebrates new-found freedom, reflecting the soaring possibilities of Joyce's Daedalus leitmotif, while the extreme close-ups of breakfast dregs return us to earthbound claustrophobia and entrapment, making the following scene squalidly deflating. Such ironic match cuts also anticipate key visual puns in 'Telemachus', the opening chapter of *Ulysses*: between Mulligan's shaving bowl on the Martello Tower parapet, the bowl of bile in Stephen's flashback to his mother's sickbed, and the 'bitter waters' enclosed by the bowl of Dublin Bay. The bereaved Stephen gazes over the last, standing near the shaving bowl in the narrative present as *Ulysses'* first full interior monologue begins, transporting him back cinematically to the traumatic scene of her recent death.

Sometimes *Portrait*'s intra-diegetic focalisation (mimicking Stephen's eyesight with ultra-naturalistic precision) shifts into psychologically interiorised effects resembling other Victorian moving image devices which also feature in his later fiction. In chapter 3, distracted by the anticipation of visiting Dublin's red-light district again, Stephen's maths exercise 'morphs' in the fading light into psychedelic forms. They resemble those of a projecting kaleidoscope (the Dublin supplier Solomon's offered one adapted for the lantern with 'marvellous results' from the 1860s [*MLP&MPS*, p. 52]) or perhaps 'Chromatrope' slides which screened rotating multi-coloured geometric shapes, alternating between centrifugal and centripetal patterns. Joyce was familiar with Brewster's immensely popular optical toy, patented in 1817. Brewster coined its name from the Greek: *kalos*, 'beautiful', *eidos*, 'form', *scopos*, 'to see': hence literally 'beautiful-form-seer'.[120] It consists of moving coloured shapes reflected by mirrors set at angles inside a tube, viewed in symmetrical permutations of combination and dispersal. Francis Skeffington recorded Joyce performing a boisterous charade punning on the device's name, by colliding into a partner, then flying apart, in his diary entry of 8 November 1903.[121] This appeared in *Finnegans Wake* as 'Answer: A collideorscape!' (143.28). Judge Woolsey's acknowledgement of cinematic form in *Ulysses* also referred to how it projected 'ever-shifting kaleidoscopic impressions' on the 'screen of consciousness', as if recognising the part that pre-filmic influences played in Joyce's text.

In *Swann's Way*, Proust's narrator similarly recalls staring at 'the shifting kaleidoscope of the darkness' in his childhood bedroom, his imagination populating it with moving after-images.[122] Whether specifically reflecting kaleidoscope or chromatrope, Stephen's formulae certainly animate into elaborately suggestive motifs, dilating and contracting through space and time in step with his free-associating consciousness:

> The equation on the page of his scribbler began to spread out a widening tail, eyed and starred like a peacock's; and, when the eyes and stars of its indices had been eliminated, began slowly to fold itself together again. The indices appearing and disappearing were eyes opening and closing; the eyes opening and closing were stars being born and quenched. The vast cycle of starry life bore his weary mind outward to its verge and inward to its centre . . . (*Portrait*, p. 87)

It is also arguable that this passage's ingenious visual matching aspires to the 'polymorphous plasticity' of early experiments in cartoons, where graphic forms came to life and displayed protean malleability. As I have argued elsewhere, cartoons are an influence behind 'Circe', *Ulysses*' most animated and transformative episode.[123] However, self-reflexive materialisation and quickening of graphic symbols is already rife in *Portrait*, in step with Stephen's sensitivity to language's polymorphic creative potentials. Tempted to join the Jesuits, his prospective title springs forth into projective relief on its own:

> The Reverend Stephen Daedalus, S.J.
> His name in that new life *leaped into characters before his eyes* . . .
> (p. 136; italics mine)

Increasingly *Portrait*'s language acquires autonomous, phantasmagoric life as projective, moving images, becoming a virtually tangible entity. When Stephen contemplates texts by Aristotle and Aquinas, 'the very words themselves . . . *set to band and disband themselves in wayward rhythms*' (pp. 148, 150; italics mine). With similarly cartoon-like synaesthesia, a physics professor's droning voice is seen 'to *wind itself slowly round and round* the coils it spoke of . . .' (pp. 162–3; italics mine). When Stephen composes his villanelle, a 'roselike glow' from his sense of achievement 'sent forth its *rays of rhyme*' and '*liquid letters of speech . . . flowed forth* over his brain' (pp. 183, 188;

italics mine). Thus Joyce figures language itself – the literal medium of his text in its materiality of graphemes and phonemes – as if it had plastic or cinematic properties. Stop-motion animation was used for titling as far back as several Mitchell and Kenyon films, including their panoramic phantom voyage by steamship, *A Trip to North Wales on the St Elvies* (1902), and the comic feature *Diving Lucy* (1903), thus playfully bringing typography to life on screen. However, these early examples are pre-dated by Méliès, who may have used animated titling as early as 1898. The British animator Arthur Melbourne Cooper's *Matches an Appeal*, which paraded formations of animated matchsticks spelling out its propaganda message, may date back to the Boer War of 1899.[124]

Notably, *Portrait* dissects Stephen's perceiving and remembering consciousness by ekphrastic methods which are auditory, as well as visual: Stephen hears with 'the ears of his memory' as well as seeing with its eyes (*Portrait*, p. 190). Just as Joyce laps visual fragments from one time or context into another (to keep the individuating rhythm of his subject's developing mind continuously foregrounded), so he laps aural recollections and associations. This initiates Joyce's 'asynchronous' or contrapuntal use of sound so admired by Eisenstein in its more developed form in the interior monologues of *Ulysses*, when the Soviet director considered Joyce's novel as a model for the creative use of the newly perfected soundtrack, most famously in his essay 'A Course in Treatment' (1932).

Significant though all these techniques anticipating aspects of Joyce's experimentation beyond *Portrait* undoubtedly are, it is Stephen's reference to attending a 'diorama' – a kind of transformative moving panorama show – at the Rotunda that provides the most appropriate segue into analysing new varieties of cinematicity in *Ulysses* itself, but also their ongoing debt to the proto-filmic ecology of late nineteenth-century media. Between *Portrait* and *Ulysses*, Joyce subsumed his alienated would-be artist into the broader perspective of mature citizenship. The panorama originated as an immersive spectacle representing a city within the context of the British Empire. Hence *Ulysses* as a moving panorama which 'examines the entire community in action', as *Stephen Hero* puts it, but also challenges Dublin's 'semi-colonial' subordination in the media of the time, is the topic of my next chapter.

NOTES

1. See H. G. Wells, Review of *A Portrait of the Artist as a Young Man*, *Nation*, 20 (24 February 1917), pp. 710, 712; repr. in Patrick Parrinder and Robert M. Philmus (eds), *H. G. Wells's Literary Criticism* (Brighton: Harvester, 1980), pp. 171–6 (172–3).
2. Unsigned review in *The New Age*, 12 July 1917, N.S. 21:11, p. 254; repr. in Robert H. Deming (ed.), *James Joyce: The Critical Heritage*, 1: *1902–1927* (London: Routledge and Kegan Paul, 1970), pp. 110–11 (110)).

3. See Sergei Eisenstein, 'Sur Joyce', *Change* (May 1972), p. 51.

4. Sergei Eisenstein, 'Achievement', in *Film Form: Essays in Film Theory*, ed. and trans. Jay Leyda (London: Dennis Dobson, 1963), pp. 179–94 (184–5).

5. Robert A. Gessner, *The Moving Image: A Guide to Cinematic Literacy* (London: Cassell, 1968), p. 266.

6. Spiegel, *Fiction and the Camera Eye*, pp. 164–5.

7. Neil Sinyard, *Filming Literature: The Art of Screen Adaptation* (London: Croom Helm, 1986), p. viii.

8. Christian Quendler, *The Camera-Eye Metaphor in Cinema* (New York: Routledge, 2017), p. 124.

9. Quendler, *The Camera-Eye Metaphor*, pp. 5, 3 and 2, respectively.

10. Anne Friedberg, *Window Shopping: Cinema and the Postmodern* (Berkeley, CA: University of California Press, 1993), pp. 2–3.

11. Spiegel, *Fiction and the Camera Eye*, p. 142.

12. 'Subjective camera' was coined for the presentation of intra-diegetic viewpoints in Expressionist silents such as Murnau's *Der letzte Mann* (1925) (see Cook, *A History of Narrative Film*, pp. 103–5).

13. Classic Hollywood's most extended experiment with intra-diegetic visual narrative was *The Lady in the Lake* (dir. Robert Montgomery, 1946), shot as if seen entirely through gumshoe Philip Marlowe's eyes. The effect of Marlowe's absent presence is uncannily like the viewpoint of an Invisible Man (except for brief moments when his image is reflected in mirrors or casts shadows).

14. See Virginia Woolf, 'Reading Notes for "Modern Novels"' (Joyce), 1 volume [April 1918], '*Ulysses* VII, Dark Blue', in New York Public Library Berg Collection (also available in microform, Reel 11, M91). I am indebted to my late colleague, James Stewart (an expert on Woolf's handwriting), for verifying that the key noun is 'horse'.

15. Proust, *Swann's Way*, p. 7.

16. This passage forms a gateway into considering perception and cognition in a seminal volume of bilingual essays. See Fritz Senn, 'Hören und Sehen/Do You Hear What I'm Seeing?', in Ursula Zeller, Ruth Frehner and Hannes Vogel (eds), *James Joyce: 'Gedacht durch meine Augen' = 'Thought through my Eyes'* (Basel: Schwabe 2000), pp. 7–22 (especially 20–1).

17. Walter Benjamin, 'The Work of Art in the Age of Mechanical Reproduction' (1936), in *Illuminations*, ed. Hannah Arendt, trans. Harry Zohn (London: Fontana, 1973), pp. 217–52, esp. 237.

18. Charles Baudelaire, 'The Painter of Modern Life' (1863), in *Selected Writings on Art and Literature*, trans. P. E. Charvet (Harmondsworth: Penguin, 1972), pp. 390–435 (394).

19. Woolf, 'Reading Notes for "Modern Novels"', '*Ulysses* VI, Green'.

20. Frank Budgen, *James Joyce and the Making of 'Ulysses'* (London: Grayson and Grayson, 1934), p. 21.

21. Ibid., p. 54.

22. Spiegel, *Fiction and the Camera Eye*, pp. 113–14

23. Deac Rossell, '*Rough Sea at Dover*: A Genealogy', *EPVC*, 15:1 (2017), pp. 59–82 (67–70).

24. For the stereoscope's relation to photography, see Laura Bird Schiavo, 'From Phantom Image to Perfect Vision: Physiological Optics, Commercial Photography, and the Popularization of the Stereoscope', in Lisa Gitelman and Geoffrey Pingree (eds), *New Media, 1740–1915* (Cambridge, MA: MIT Press, 2004), pp. 113–38. For the stereoscope and cinema, see Zone, *Stereoscopic Cinema*, esp. pp. 76–7.

25. For an alternative view on Joyce and Muybridge, see Louise E. J. Hornby, 'Visual Clockwork: Photography, Time and the Instant in "Proteus"', *JJQ*, 42–3:1–4 (2004/2006), pp. 49–68; also her *Still Modernism: Photography, Literature, Film* (New York: Oxford University Press, 2017), pp. 17, 110.

26. Tom Gunning, 'Waking and Faking: Ireland and Cinema Astray', in Kevin Rockett and John Hill (eds), *National Cinema and Beyond: Studies in Irish Film 1* (Dublin: Four Courts Press, 2004), pp. 19–31 (23–4). For further discussion of the Lumières and photography, see Tom Gunning, 'New Thresholds of Vision: Instantaneous Photography and the Early Cinema of Lumière', in Terry Smith (ed.), *Impossible Presence: Surface and Screen in the Photogenic Era* (Sydney: Power Publications, 2001), pp. 71–100.

27. For detailed discussion of Joyce's familiarity with fantastically enhanced bodies in films and cartoons, see Keith Williams, '"Sperrits in the Furniture": Wells, Joyce and Animation before and after 1910', in Matthew Creasy and Bryony Randall (eds), *Alternative 1910s*, a special issue of *Literature and History*, 3rd ser. 22:1 (2013), pp. 95–110; and Williams, '*Ulysses* in Toontown', pp. 96–121.

28. *Démolition*, recording Auguste supervising workmen on the family estate, was routinely shown backwards. As Ramsaye noted: 'One of the earliest novelty effects sought in the Kinetoscope in the days when it was enjoying scientific attention was in exactly this sort of reversal of commonplace bits of action. It continues today a somewhat hackneyed bit of trick camera work . . . we saw runners backing up at high speed and backing locomotives swallowing their smoke in reverse gear.' See Ramsaye, *A Million and One Nights*, pp. 153–4.

29. *Stephen Hero* was written in roughly 1904–06, though surviving chapters were only published in 1944. Joyce eventually reduced its sixty-three to just five in *Portrait*. The manuscript – covering Stephen's student days only – is over two hundred pages, subsequently condensed into a mere section of *Portrait*'s chapter 5. *Portrait* is thus a mere third as long as the whole of *Stephen Hero* may have been. See 'Composition and Publication History', in James Joyce, *A Portrait of the Artist as a Young Man (1914–15)*, ed. Jeri Johnson (Oxford: Oxford University Press, 2000), pp. xl–xliii.

30. 'A Portrait of the Artist' (1904), in Robert Scholes and Richard M. Kain (eds), *In the Workshop of Daedalus: James Joyce and the Raw Materials for* A Portrait of the Artist as a Young Man (Evanston, IL: Northwestern University Press, 1965), pp. 60–8 (60).

31. Christie, *Last Machine*, pp. 69–70; H. G. Wells, *The King Who Was a King: The Book of a Film* (London: Ernest Benn, 1929), p. 9.

32. Christie, *The Last Machine*, pp. 69–70.

33. Links between series photography and film have been extensively historicised in, among others, Gordon Hendricks, *Eadweard Muybridge: The Father of the Motion*

Picture (London: Secker and Warburg, 1977); Brian Coe, *Muybridge and the Chronophotographers* (London: Museum of the Moving Image, 1992); Rebecca Solnit, *Motion Studies: Time, Space and Eadweard Muybridge* (London: Bloomsbury, 2003); Brian Clegg, *The Man who Stopped Time: The Illuminating Story of Eadweard Muybridge, Father of the Motion Picture, Murderer* (Washington, DC: Joseph Henry Press, 2007); special issue of *EPVC* on Muybridge, 11:1 (2013); Marta Braun, *Picturing Time: The Work of Étienne-Jules Marey* (Chicago: University of Chicago Press, 1992). Herbert reproduces key images and facsimiles of documents in his *History of Pre-Cinema*, vol. 1, pp. 39–217. Tate Britain staged a major exhibition of Muybridge's work, including a demonstration of the Zoöpraxiscope (September 2010–January 2011), with accompanying catalogue: Philip Brookman and Marta Braun (eds), *Helios: Eadweard Muybridge in a Time of Change* (London: Tate, 2010). See also the British Universities Film and Video Council research portal: 'Eadweard Muybridge: Defining Modernities', available at <http://bufvc.ac.uk/gateway/index.php/site/1363> (last accessed 29 July 2019).

34. E. J. Marey, *Movement: The Results and Possibilities of Photography*, with 200 illustrations, trans. Eric Pritchard (London: Heinemann, 1895). This included key images of athletes: 'Fig.41 – Man dressed in black, with white lines and points for the chronophotographic study of the movement of important parts of the body' (p. 60); 'Fig.42 – Images of a runner reduced to a system of bright lines for representing the position of his limbs. (Geometrical chronophotography)' (p. 61). Its final chapter, on 'Synthetic Reconstruction of the Elements of an Analysed Movement', included illustration sections on flying gulls in the phenakistoscope, zoëtrope, etc., as well as Muybridge's zoöpraxiscope and Marey's own 'chronophotographic projector' (pp. 304–18).

35. See Hendricks, *Eadweard Muybridge*, p. 141.

36. See *The Delineation of Animals in Rapid Motion* (Dublin: Royal Dublin Society, 1877); alternatively, see illustration and discussion in Chandler, *Photography in Ireland*, p. 66; also *MLP&MPS*, pp. 150–1 and plates 76–7. Animations of Hayes's phenakistoscope discs are viewable on the National Gallery of Ireland website at <http://doras.nationalgallery.ie/index.php?a=QuickSearch&qsv=Hayes,%20Michael%20Angelo> (last accessed 5 October 2018).

37. *Ulysses* refers to him as 'Michelangelo Hayes'. It is unclear from the context whether this is for his animal locomotion studies, or as painter of panoramic social documentary pictures such as *Sackville Street* (reproduced as a popular lithograph, the original hangs in the Irish National Gallery). Hayes was also city marshall from 1857.

38. Muybridge's tribute to Hayes was quoted in a report of the first of his own lectures to the Royal Dublin Society. See 'Animal Locomotion: The Zoöpraxiscope', *Freeman's Journal*, 13 February 1890, p. 7.

39. For Muybridge in Dublin, see also Chandler, *Photography in Ireland*, p. 89, and *MLP&MPS*, pp. 152–3.

40. See anon., untitled article on Muybridge's lecture to the Royal Dublin Society, *Freeman's Journal*, 17 February 1890, p. 5.

41. Ibid., p. 5.

42. Anon., 'The Star Theatre of Varieties', *Irish Independent*, 22 April 1896, p. 6.

43. For the significance of Bull's work, see (among others) Chandler, *Photography in Ireland*, p. 89; Herbert and MacKernan, *Who's Who of Victorian Cinema*, pp. 29–30; Laurent Mannoni, 'Lucien Bull', in Richard Abel (ed.), *The Encyclopedia of Early Cinema* (London: Routledge, 2010), p. 86; Braun, *Picturing Time*, pp. xv, 206, 344 and *passim*. Bull recollected Marey forbidding staff from attempting film projections of his work, an instruction duly ignored during his annual vacations. See Deac Rossell, 'Chronophotography in the Context of Moving Images', *EPVC*, 11:1 (2013), pp. 10–27 (24, n. 7).

44. Scholes and Kain cite D'Annunzio's 'The Soul of the Artist: Socrates', from *Le Virgini delle Rocce* (1895) as a possible source for the 1904 'Portrait's' strange imagery. D'Annunzio writes of 'the living centre' of Socrates as man and philosopher being 'rhythmically developed' in his work, so that 'he succeeded with a firm hand in describing upon a continuous line the integral image of himself'. See translation in Scholes and Kain (eds), *In the Workshop of Daedalus*, pp. 270–4 (271). In 'The Soul and the Body' (1912), Henri Bergson also urged writers to strive towards 'a particular dancing of the sentence, in making the reader's mind, continually guided by a series of nascent movements, describe a curve of thought and feeling analogous to that we ourselves describe'. Henri Bergson, *Mind-Energy: Lectures and Essays*, trans. H. Wildon Carr (Westport, CT: Greenwood Press, 1975), pp. 37–74 (57). However, Joyce's imagery figures the idea of internal self-portraiture as more visually dynamic.

45. Archie K. Loss, *Joyce's Visible Art: The Work of Joyce and the Visual Arts, 1904–1922* (Ann Arbor, MI: UMI Research Press, 1984), p. 62.

46. Ibid., p. 63.

47. Ibid., pp. 62–4.

48. Umberto Boccioni et al., 'Futurist Painting: Technical Manifesto' (1910), in Umbro Apollonio (ed.), *Futurist Manifestos* (London: Thames and Hudson, 1973), pp. 27–31 (27–8). For the Futurists' distinction between their aims and film's, as developed from chronophotographic anatomisation of motion, see Anton Giulio Bragaglia, 'Futurist Photodynamism 1911', in ibid., pp. 38–45.

49. William S. Rubin, *Dada and Surrealist Art* (New York: Abrams, 1968), p. 33.

50. *Nude Descending a Staircase* is known to be inspired by Muybridge's studies of a woman walking downstairs in *Animal Locomotion*, albeit Duchamp's overlapping images probably owe as much to Marey (see Muybridge, *Animal Locomotion*, plates 128–50).

51. 'Edison's "Kinetoscope"', *Dublin Evening Telegraph*, 4 April 1895, p. 3.

52. 'The Kinetoscope at "Ierne"', *Dublin Evening Mail*, 14 May 1895, p. 4.

53. 'The Mechanism of the Kinetoscope', *Dublin Evening Telegraph*, 6 April 1895, p. 5.

54. 'Cyclopia', *Freeman's Journal*, 20 May 1896, p. 5.

55. Ibid., p. 5

56. Ibid., p. 5.

57. *Dublin Evening Mail*, 27 January 1896, p. 4.

58. Ovid, *Metamorphoses*, viii. 188–9, trans. A. D. Melville (Oxford: Oxford University Press, 1986), p. 177.

59. See 'On the Properties of the Daedalum, a New Instrument of Optical Illusion', *London and Edinburgh Philosophical Magazine*, January 1834; repr. in Herbert (ed.), *A History of Pre-Cinema*, vol. 1, pp. 271–6.

60. The Phénakistocope was invented by the Belgian Joseph Plateau in 1832, albeit others were working on similar discs for animating images simultaneously. For their history and adaptation for projection, see (among others) <http://www.stephen-herbert.co.uk/phenakPartOne.htm> and <http://www.stephenherbert.co.uk/phena-kPartTwo.htm#fn7> (last accessed 4 October 2018).

61. For the Zoöpraxiscope's development, see Amy Lawrence, 'Counterfeit Motion: The Animated Films of Eadweard Muybridge', *Film Quarterly*, 57:2 (2004), pp. 15–25.

62. For detailed history and examples of the Wright brothers' photographs, see especially Walt Burton and Owen Findsen, *The Wright Brothers' Legacy: Orville and Wilbur Wright and Their Aeroplanes* (New York: Abrams, 2003); Ian Mackersey, *The Wright Brothers: The Remarkable Story of the Aviation Pioneers Who Changed the World* (London: Time Warner, 2004).

63. See Tom Greer, *A Modern Daedalus* (1885; facsimile repr. Kessinger Publishing, 2015), pp. 1–2.

64. See Introductory Note to the Epiphanies, in Scholes and Kain (eds), *In the Workshop of Daedalus*, pp. 3–7 (4).

65. See James Agee, Introductory Essay to Helen Levitt, *A Way of Seeing* (Durham, NC: Duke University Press, 1989), pp. vii–xv (viii). Agee's documentary collaboration with Walker Evans, *Let Us Now Praise Famous Men* (1941), was saturated with Joycean influence, not least in foregrounding the subjective revelations of both photographic and literary 'camera-eyes'. See Keith Williams, '"The Unpaid Agitator": Joyce's Influence on George Orwell and James Agee', *JJQ*, 36:4 (1999), pp. 729–64.

66. Walter Benjamin, 'Little History of Photography' (1931), in *Selected Writings*, 2: *1927–1934* (Cambridge, MA: Belknap Press of Harvard University Press, 1999), pp. 506–30 (511–12). For a detailed discussion of the implications of Benjamin's theory that the 'optical unconscious' was opened by camera-eyed vision, see Quendler, *The Camera-Eye Metaphor in Cinema*, pp. 23–6.

67. Scarlett Baron, 'Flaubert, Joyce: Vision, Photography, Cinema', *Modern Fiction Studies*, 54:4 (2008), pp. 689–714 (691).

68. Baron extends her examination of Flaubert's formative influence on Joyce's 'Cinematographic Cuts and Structural Patterns' in her *'Strandentwining Cable': Joyce, Flaubert, and Intertextuality* (Oxford: Oxford University Press, 2011), pp. 49–54, 75–82.

69. Repr. in Scholes and Kain (eds), *In the Workshop of Daedalus*, pp. 52–5 (55).

70. Giorgio Agamben, 'Notes on Gestures', in *Means without End: Notes on Politics*, trans. Vincenzo Binetti and Cesare Casarino (Minneapolis, MN: University of Minnesota Press, 2000), pp. 49–62 (55–6).

71. According to the online concordance to *Portrait*, 'time' (in just about every sense) occurs on 119 occasions, 'times' at least 21; 'memory' 37 times and 'memories' 6. These collocate with 41 occurrences of the verb 'remember', plus other forms

thereof: 'remembered' (22), 'remembering' (4), 'remembers' (5). See <http://www.doc.ic.ac.uk/~rac101/concord/texts/paym/> (last accessed 7 January 2013).

72. There are two occurrences as verb – 'dissolves' and 'dissolved' – and two as adjective – 'dissolving' (including 'dissolving moments' in chapter 4).

73. 'Sight' occurs 17 times; the verb 'see', 83, plus variants – 'saw' (70), 'seeing' (16), 'seen' (28).

74. Dave Berry, 'Mitchell and Kenyon in Wales', in Vanessa Toulmin, Patrick Russell and Simon Popple (eds), *The Lost World of Mitchell and Kenyon: Edwardian Britain on Film* (London: BFI, 2004), pp. 103–12 (106); also David Russell, 'The Football Films', in ibid., pp. 169–80.

75. For the case that Joyce depicts his own condition of long- rather than short-sightedness (as often assumed), see Francisco J. Asaco and Jan L. van Velze, 'Was James Joyce Myopic or Hyperopic?', *British Medical Journal*, 343 (2011), pp. 1–3, doi: 10.136/bmj.d7464, available at <http://www.bmj.com> (last accessed 7 January 2013). Also Jan Leendert van Velze, 'James Joyce on his Blindness', available at <http://deficienciavisual14.com.sapo.pt/r-James_Joyce-On_his_blindness.htm> (last accessed 21 June 2012).

76. F. W. Murnau, 'The Ideal Picture Needs no Titles: By Its Very Nature the Art of the Screen Should Tell a Complete Story Pictorially', *Theatre Magazine*, 48:322 (1928); repr. in Richard McCormick and Alison Guenther-Pal (eds), *German Essays on Film* (London: Continuum, 2004), pp. 66–9 (68).

77. See Luigi Pirandello, *The Notebooks of Serafino Gubbio or (Shoot!)*, trans. C. K. Scott Moncrieff (1915) (Sawtry: Daedalus, 1990). For a detailed discussion of the novel, see Quendler, *The Camera-Eye Metaphor in Cinema*, pp. 71–4; although Quendler neglects to discuss Joyce, he does focus on several key authors whose camera-eyed literary methods were influenced by him, for example John Dos Passos and Christopher Isherwood (pp. 74–92).

78. Although Joyce's acknowledged source for interior monologue, Edouard Dujardin's *Les Lauriers sont coupés*, was published in 1888, Schnitzler employed the form in his story, 'Leutnant Gustl' (first published in magazine form in 1900) (i.e. even before Joyce read Dujardin while staying in Paris in 1903). For Joyce and Dujardin, see Ellmann, *James Joyce*, pp. 126, 665; also the introduction to the English translation of *Les Lauriers sont coupés*, *The Bays Are Sere*, trans. Anthony Suter (London: Libris, 1991), pp. xi–lxvii.

79. For a discussion of this, see Williams, 'Short Cuts of the Hibernian Metropolis', pp. 160–-2.

80. See McKernan, 'Appendix: Volta Filmography', pp. 187–204,

81. For Mitchell and Kenyon's other Irish phantom rides and Dublin panoramas, see Monks, 'The Irish Films in the Mitchell and Kenyon Collection', pp. 75–97. Many are included in the *Mitchell and Kenyon in Ireland* DVD (London: BFI National Film and Television Archive, 2006); see also detailed discussion in Chapter 3.

82. Henri Bergson, *Creative Evolution*, trans. Arthur Mitchell (New York: Henry Holt, 1911), p. 305

83. Ibid., pp. 305–6.

84. Ibid., pp. 368–70.

85. Ibid., p. 4.

86. Mary Ann Gillies gives a detailed reading of Joyce's handling of time in Bergsonian terms in 'James Joyce: Fiction as the Flux of Experience', in her *Henri Bergson and British Modernism* (Montreal: McGill-Queen's University Press, 1996), pp. 132–50, without, however, considering whether a common sense of cinematicity figures in this. For more recent discussions of Bergson, cinematic temporality and Modernism, see among others, Helen Powell, *Stop the Clocks! Time and Narrative in Cinema* (London: I.B. Tauris, 2012), pp. 16-18; also Laura Marcus, *The Tenth Muse: Writing about Cinema in the Modernist Period* (Oxford: Oxford University Press, 2007), pp. 3–4, 138–89, 210–11.

87. See Michael Patrick Gillespie, *James Joyce's Trieste Library: A Catalogue of Materials at the Harry Ransom Research Center, the University of Texas at Austin* (Austin, TX: Harry Ransom Humanities Research Center, 1986), pp. 46–7.

88. 'A Course in Treatment' (1932), in Sergei M. Eisenstein, *Film Form: Essays in Film Theory*, ed. and trans. Jay Leyda (London: Dennis Dobson, 1963), pp. 84–107, esp. p. 84.

89. Edward Garnett, for example, who rejected it for Duckworth, considered it 'formless', failing to recognise that its form was radically different. Edward Garnett, 'Reader's Report', in Deming (ed.), *James Joyce: The Critical Heritage*, vol. 1, pp. 81–2 (81); also quoted in Ellmann, *James Joyce*, p. 404.

90. I am grateful to my former PhD student, Faye Harland, for this insight.

91. See, for example, Stephen's flashback to communal meals at Clongowes prompted by feeling similarly alienated by students at University College (*Stephen Hero*, p. 165).

92. According to the online concordance, 'image' occurs 47 times, 'images', 9.

93. 'Shadow' occurs 14 times; 'shadows', once; 'shadowed', twice.

94. See Maud Ellmann, 'Disremembering Dedalus: *A Portrait of the Artist as a Young Man*', in Robert Young (ed.), *Untying the Text: A Post-Structuralist Reader* (London: Routledge and Kegan Paul, 1981), pp. 189–206. According to the online concordance, there are 128 uses of 'face' and 26 of 'faces'; 79 of 'head' and 9 'heads'; 19 of 'eye' and 173 'eyes'; 26 of 'mouth' and 4 'mouths'; 46 of 'lips'. Also 79 of 'hand' and 71 'hands'; 7 of 'finger' and 31 'fingers'.

95. Spiegel, *Fiction and the Camera Eye*, p. 167.

96. *Portrait* is shot through with lighting effects. According to the online concordance, 'light' occurs 75 times; 'lights', 8; 'lit', 15; 'lighted', 2.

97. Other American adaptations quickly followed: *The Count of Monte Christo* [*sic*] (Challenge Film Company, 1910); *Monte Christo* (dir. Colin Campbell, 1912); *The Count of Monte Cristo* (dir. Joseph A. Golden and Edwin S. Porter, 1913). The last was screened in Dublin long after Joyce returned to Trieste, so an earlier lantern set seems more likely to be an influence (see advertisement for 'Phoenix Picture House', *Irish Times*, 2 June 1913, p. 7). I am grateful to Cleo Hanaway-Oakley for this lead.

98. See Ellmann, *James Joyce*, p. 37.

99. Andrew E. Hershberger, 'Performing Excess/Signalling Anxiety: Towards a Psychoanalytic Theory of Daguerre's Diorama', *EPVC*, 4:2 (2006), pp. 85–101 (92).

100. Gustave Deville, *Biographies des hommes du jour* (1841), quoted in translation in Helmut and Alison Gernsheim, *L. J. M Daguerre: The History of the Diorama and the Daguerretotype* (New York: Dover, 1968), p. 32.

101. See Hershberger, 'Performing Excess/Signalling Anxiety', pp. 93–4.

102. For Rudy and fairy photography, see R. Brandon Kershner, *The Culture of Joyce's Ulysses* (London: Palgrave, 2010), pp. 209–25.

103. According to the online concordance, there are 3 instances of 'fade' as verb, together with 10 of 'faded' and 9 of 'fading'.

104. Benjamin, 'The Work of Art in the Age of Mechanical Reproduction', p. 237.

105. Hugo Münsterberg, *The Photoplay: A Psychological Study* (New York and London: Appleton and Co., 1916); repr. as *The Film: A Psychological Study* (New York: Dover Publications, 1970), pp. 72, 84, and 14–15, respectively.

106. Plato, *The Republic*, trans. Robin Waterfield (Oxford: Oxford University Press, 1998), p. 240.

107. For a recent study of flipbooks and their remediation through mechanised devices, see Wiebke K. Fölsch, *Buch Film Kinetiks: zur Vor- und Frühgeschichte von Daumenkino, Mutoskop & Co.* (Berlin: Freie Universität Berlin, 2011).

108. See Condon, 'Spleen of a Cabinet Minister at Work', pp. 69–78.

109. Ibid., p. 70. Cf *EIC*, pp. 47–53.

110. Condon, 'Spleen of a Cabinet Minister at Work', pp. 71–2.

111. Ibid, pp. 76 and 74, respectively. Andrew Shail has unearthed an example of such claims in the wake of X-rays: W. Ingles Rogers, 'Can Thought Be Photographed? The Problem Solved', *Amateur Photographer* (February–March 1896). Rogers allegedly photographed images retained on the retinae by the last objects placed before them using a 'vacuum camera'. See Andrew Shail, 'Archive Feature', *EPVC*, 8:1 (2010), pp. 91–100.

112. Joyce based much of Arnall's imagery on a translation of the Jesuit Giovanni Pietro Pinamonti's *Hell Opened to Christians* (1688). See James R. Thrane, 'Joyce's Sermon on Hell: Its Sources and Backgrounds' (1960), repr. in Michael Patrick Gillespie (ed.), *Foundational Essays in James Joyce Studies* (Gainesville, FL: University Press of Florida, 2011), pp. 85–124. The Norton Critical Edition of *Portrait* reproduces eight woodcuts depicting the torments of damned souls from the pamphlet version held in the National Library of Ireland (*A Portrait of the Artist as a Young Man*, ed. Hans Walter Gabler [New York: W. W. Norton, 2007], pp. 282–9). Thrane also notes possible influence from a version of such imagery, aimed specifically at children, the Revd John Joseph Furniss's *The Sight of Hell* (Book X of a series published 1856–63), in which the body and skull quiver with fiery torment and flames shoot from eyes and ears ('Joyce's Sermon on Hell', pp. 115–16).

113. See examples of Victorian images with multiple and merging ghostly presences in Clément Chéroux et al., *The Perfect Medium: Photography and the Occult* (New Haven, CT: Yale University Press, 2005), pp. 39, 72.

114. Joyce may also have been alluding to 'Idola specus' or 'Idols of the Cave', an extension of Plato's allegory in Francis Bacon's *Novum Organum* (1620), published in Latin and one of the earliest treatises advocating the logic of modern scientific method. Bacon's idols symbolise how culturally conditioned

biases distort the subject's sense of reality and prevent them seeing clearly. See 'Aphorism XLII', *The New Organon*, in *The Works of Francis Bacon*, 10 vols, ed. and trans. James Spedding, Robert Leslie Ellis and Douglas Denon (Boston, MA: Taggard and Thompson, 1863), vol. 8, pp. 56–349 (77).

115. The original dream epiphany (no. 6 in Joyce's notebook) reads: 'A small field of still weeds and thistles alive with confused forms, half-men, half-goats. Dragging their great tails they move hither and thither, aggressively. Their faces are lightly bearded, pointed and grey as indiarubber. A secret personal sin directs them, holding them now, as in reaction, to constant malevolence. One is clasping about his body a torn flannel jacket; another complains monotonously as his beard catches in the stiff weeds. They move about me, enclosing me, that old sin sharpening their eyes to cruelty, swishing through the fields in slow circles, thrusting upwards their terrific faces. Help!' See Scholes and Kain (eds), *In the Workshop of Daedalus*, p. 16; see also James Joyce, *Poems and Shorter Writings: including* Epiphanies, Giacomo Joyce *and* 'A Portrait of the Artist', ed. Richard Ellmann, A. Walton Litz and John Whittier-Ferguson (London: Faber and Faber 1991), pp. 155–200 (166). According to Ellmann, Joyce completed drafts of the first three chapters as early as April 1908, although he continued to make revisions to the whole manuscript up until 1914 (*James Joyce*, p. 264). Cf. Hans Walter Gabler, 'Introduction: Composition, Text and Editing', in *A Portrait of the Artist as a Young Man*, ed. Gabler, pp. xv–xxiii (xvii).

116. See McKernan, 'Appendix: Volta Filmography', p. 194. For an alternative account of *A Glass of Goat's Milk*'s significance, see Philip Sicker, 'Evenings at the Volta: Cinematic Afterimages in Joyce', *JJQ*, 42–3:1–4 (2004/2006), pp. 99–132, esp. pp. 123 and 130–1.

117. See Denis Pellerin, Brian May and Paula Fleming, *Diableries, Stereoscopic Adventures in Hell* (London: London Stereoscopic Company, 2013).

118. See reproductions of the original model and stereocards in Pellerin et al., *Diableries*, pp. 62–3.

119. Simeon Headsman, Report on 'Satanic Slides', *British Journal of Photography*, 15 August 1860, p. 242.

120. See David Brewster, *The Kaleidoscope: Its History, Theory and Construction* (London: John Murray, 1858), p. 1.

121. See Ellmann, *James Joyce*, p. 53, note.

122. Proust, *Swann's Way*, p. 4.

123. See Williams, '*Ulysses* in Toontown', pp. 96–121.

124. For details, see Berry, 'Mitchell and Kenyon in Wales', pp. 106–7; for Méliès, see Giannalberto Bendazzi, *100 Years of Cinema Animation* (New Barnet: John Libbey, 1994), p. 7. Some commentators argue that Melbourne Cooper's animation dates from the First World War. See Denis Gifford, *British Animated Films 1895–1985: A Filmography* (Jefferson, NC: McFarland, 1987), entry no. 6, p. 4.

3

'BUILDING-VISION-MACHINE': *ULYSSES* AS MOVING PANORAMA

In an 1899 debate on the future of Irish literature, John Eglinton drew attention to the possibility of a national epic reviving the ancient legacy of Homer through the 'concrete . . . poetry' of technology, including the most modern media – the cinematograph and phonograph.[1] Eglinton's vision is so prophetic of *Ulysses* as cinematised, modern epic that it is tempting to think that Joyce read it.[2] Be that as it may, *Ulysses* is just as influenced by the techniques of another pre-filmic visual entertainment – the panorama, which subsumed the modern city and its activities in its epic, 'all-seeing' scope – especially through the moving forms into which it evolved.

Dolf Sternberger, in his classic 1938 study (which Benjamin reviewed and was influenced by in developing his own critique of modernity's media-cultural imaginary), considered the panorama crucial for understanding 'how the 19th century man saw himself & his world & how he experienced history'.[3] Sternberger detected the influence of 'panoramisation' everywhere – in media, technology, travel and narratives of colonialism, evolution and progress – enabling the contemporary Western subject to visualise their dominant place in the world and the whole 'moving spectacle' of civilisation. Alongside actual panorama shows, Huhtamo has historicised the emergence of a 'discursive panorama' as 'figure of speech, writing, or visual representation'. Hence 'Panoramas of the imagination are no less interesting, or real, than the concrete ones' (*IiM*, p. 15). According to the *OED*, the term quickly accumulated richer meanings, such as a 'complete or comprehensive survey or presentation of a subject', evident in titles such as *The Political Panorama* (1801), *The Panorama of Youth* (1806) and *Literary Panorama* (1806). From around 1802 (after Robert Barker's patent expired), it was used for 'an unbroken view of a whole region surrounding an observer'. By 1813 it had acquired a subjective meaning, anticipating its association with the psychological 'stream of consciousness': as a 'continually moving scene or mental vision in which life passes before ones eyes'.[4] As William Uricchio points out, both panoramic practice and its linguistic invocations gradually slipped their moorings from Barker's definition, 'eliding the elaborate framing of an image so as to make one feel on the spot', for the effect of visual teleportation and immersion in general.[5]

Thus the panorama is another important strand in the history of ekphrastic cinematicity. As with literature's synergetic relationship with lantern shows, there was a well-developed tradition of written panoramas before *Ulysses*. Huhtamo and others have excavated many 'imagined by novelists, poets, journalists, scientists, philosophers, and propagandists'. By the late nineteenth century, the moving panorama was repeatedly evoked in myriad contexts, 'ranging from travel accounts to religious tracts and psychological explorations' (*IiM*, p. 19).[6] This gradually transformed it into a topos expressing many things: 'perceptual experiences, changes in the space-time continuum, battles between world views, ideas about the human mind'. Hence, like the lantern's, its 'intensive discursive life' contributed to the formation of the modern media-cultural imaginary, as literary engagements with film and other moving image media continue to do (*IiM*, p. 332).

The panorama's evolution from a spectacle into a mode of perception and set of inter-medial practices bound up with imperialism and urbanism is equally reflected in Joyce's work. Like the original static panorama, *Ulysses* is immersive and totalising in tendency, its implied textual horizons apparently fading into the social, geographical and historical distance; like the moving panorama, it is imagistically mobilised; like the diorama (see below), it is transformative, moving between situations and states of consciousness. *Stephen Hero* anticipates *Ulysses*' panoramic method. Its protagonist voices his conviction that, unlike the illusory projections of past systems of thought, 'The modern method examines its territory by the light of day . . . It examines the entire community in action and reconstructs the spectacle of redemption.' Stephen's statement thus affords insight into Joyce's own expanding project: to create a critical 'moving panorama' of Irish society pivoting around his home city, which highlights its paralysing contradictions, but also its potential for progressive modernisation. In the process, Joyce inevitably referenced and challenged how Ireland's image was mediated under its 'semi-colonial' status within the British Empire through actual panorama shows of his time.

The Circular Panorama: Visual Immersion

Sackville (later O'Connell) Street was already the location of the 1767 'Round Room', with its impressive diameter of around eighty feet. Known as 'The Rotunda' (or sometimes 'Rotundo'), this eventually became one of Dublin's most important venues for visual entertainments, including many forms of panorama and eventually early film shows. Before cinema's dream palaces, the panorama was perhaps the most important hybrid 'building-vision-machine', as Huhtamo calls it (*IiM*, p. 123), for virtual experience of elsewheres in space and time. Significantly, the term (from Greek: *pan*, 'all'; *horama*, 'view') was coined in 1791 by Irishman Robert Barker (1739–1806) to designate his patent procedure for creating giant realistic paintings. Barker's invention became one of the first 'genuinely popular mass pictorial entertainments' (*MLP&MPS*, p. 79). It gave the illusion of a commanding 360-degree perspective stretching to the horizon, thus appearing to immerse spectators in an alternative visual 'reality', as well as being a logical extension of topographic views and mapping. Arguably, Barker's apotheosis of *trompe l'oeil* tradition paralleled the exploitation of individual binocular vision through the stereoscope, a comparable illusion of 'solid seeing', but without peepshow limitations. Using a square frame on a portable mount, Barker captured elevated perspectives on cityscapes and surrounding topographies, initially Edinburgh (where he resided). His apparatus rotated to allow sketching 'frame by frame', anticipating, but also influencing, photographic panoramas and, eventually, filmic *tours d'horizon* or camera 'panning'. The resulting composite painting was hung in a circular framework, using a system of curved lines to prevent distortion and maintain smoothly accurate perspective as the gaze swivelled. Barker's 1787 royal patent, entitled *La Nature à coup d'oeil* ('Nature at a Glance'), stressed its break from fixed Cartesian perspective to make spectators feel 'as if really on the very spot', presenting a scene 'as it appears to an observer turning quite around'.[7] Hence Barker anticipated film's illusion of embodied spectatorship, but also (especially in the panorama's later moving forms) its 'mobilised virtual gaze', which apparently allows us to enter into and traverse the screen's simulatory space at will, as though the camera's artificial viewpoint were grafted on to our capacity to perceive surroundings. Barker stipulated that displaying panoramas in specially constructed circular buildings or 'rotundas' lit from a central dome would cause the distance between vision and representation to virtually disappear. Ever more elaborate foreground scenery and effects became incorporated to facilitate transition from the viewer's actual space to the panorama's simulated one. Panoramas such as *Paris by Night* at London's Colosseum in 1848, which simulated the perspective from a balloon hovering over the Tuileries, were fêted for synthesising 'foreground and background perspectives into a complete illusion of place', as Byerly puts it.[8] It encapsulated 'many of the characteristics that made panoramas satisfying: coherence, uniformity, attention to detail, and the creation of an imaginary space for the viewer to occupy'.[9] A review of Robert Burford's *Summer and Winter Views of the Polar Regions* (1850) typified the sense of being absorbed by a panoramic simulation: 'it is so *real* that an effort is needed to abstract the mind from the scene in the picture to the reality'.[10]

Hence the panorama's vaunted authenticity foreshadowed the 'consensual hallucinations' of film, television, Cinerama, I-MAX and virtual reality simulators, as well as CGI-enhanced theme park rides (*MLP&MPS*, p. 80). Similarly, as Huhtamo notes, experience of such ultra-mimetic verisimilitude is always historically relative to the context of audience expectations. Myriad accounts of dogs leaping into painted waves to rescue the drowning, drunks startled into bombarding advancing enemy fleets with oranges or bumpkins recognising their own dwellings may have been hyped by panorama showmen. However, they undoubtedly anticipate accounts of filmgoers whose senses were similarly overwhelmed on first encountering another medium into forgetting the distinction between illusion and reality. Joyce recalled his over-excited partner exhorting a screen policeman as if witnessing an actual crime at Lifka's travelling Bioscope in Pola in 1904: 'There were a series of pictures about betrayed Gretchen. In the last [act] Lothario throws her into the river and rushes off, followed by rabble. Nora said, "O, policeman, catch him."'[11] Such reactions were rapidly sent up by film-makers such as Paul and Edison. Their *The Countryman and the Cinematograph* (1901) and *Uncle Josh at the Moving Pictures* (1902) (respectively) are thus 'a personified topos' descended from 'all the drunken sailors who raved at panorama shows half a century earlier'. Moreover, this pattern of response evidences how technical features and subjects passed down to film so that the collective imaginary which accumulated around it 'accommodated pre-existing discursive formulas' (*IiM*, p. 79).

IMPERIAL WORLDVIEWS

Panoramas functioned not just like somatic portals looking into other worlds, but as a form of teleportation into other environments through apparently total recreation of places or events. However, they depended on techniques of simulation that acted on observers (in Crary's sense) in carefully calculated and disciplining ways. These placed audiences in subject positions that were mediated and, above all, ideologically inscribed. Panoramas thus functioned 'interpellatively', in Louis Althusser's terms; integrating spectators into a globalising world through literally shaping an imperial worldview.[12] Early panoramas were therefore also visualisations of the principles of British supremacy and political order, as extensively historicised by Denise Blake Oleksijczuk.[13]

The panoramic perspective's comprehensive view reinforced the sense of mastery and appropriation of territory. This made them one of the principal spectacles by which, as David Cannadine puts it, the British 'created their imperial society, bound it together, comprehended it and imagined it'.[14] In a global project 'of unrivalled spaciousness and amplitude', the panorama was key to how the British 'exported and projected vernacular sociological visions from the metropolis to the periphery, and . . . imported and analogised them from the empire back to Britain, thereby constructing comforting and familiar resemblance and equivalancies'.[15] Colonial panoramas were shown in mainland Britain, while panoramas of the 'motherland' mediated Britain to its colonies as the hub from which global civilisation radiated, in what Byerly calls 'a self-referential process of mutual replication'. Especially in moving form as virtual expeditions or journeys, panoramas represented an exaggerated manifestation of an impulse that underlay real travel in the Victorian period: the effort to grasp 'the essence' of places from fragmentary experiences. Their selective synthesis of landmarks – their ideologically packaged tour – defined their subject, at the same time bypassing 'genuine engagement with foreign people or ideas'.[16] Most panoramas offered a key in the form of a guidebook, neatly eliding the difference between being a real traveller and one imagined into being by a journey based on a visual simulation. Hence 'At a time when real travel seemed to offer unlimited opportunities for both personal enrichment and imperialist expansion', panoramic simulation exercised a powerful appeal. Victorian appetite for this kind of *faux* experience 'seems an early sign of the incipient commodification of reality' described by Benjamin and Baudrillard.[17] Though promoted as a new art form, it was in fact indicative of a deeper paradigm shift in the consumption of mediated realities. As Huhtamo notes: 'it was an early manifestation of media culture in the making. Although it was not wired in the sense of broadcasting or the Internet, it was capable of teleporting its audience to another location, and dissolving the boundary between local existence and global vision' (*IiM*, p. 5).

Indeed panoramas controlled audience vision while apparently ceding pleasurable freedom to it. Huhtamo notes ironic parallelism between this 'scopic-ambulatory' emancipation and the guard's position in Jeremy Bentham's Panopticon prison design, which had such an influence on Michel Foucault's theories of surveillance.[18] With its central viewing tower and radiating periphery of cells, each prisoner would be aware that they could be watched at any time by an invisible warder and therefore internalised this gaze to become psychologically 'self-policing'. (As 'disciplinary spectacle', the Panopticon was compared to panoramas at the time.)[19] As Uricchio points out, as well as sharing structural features, they had complementary objectives of control: 'one convincing the viewer that they had visual access to everything that could be seen from a particular vantage-point, and the other convincing the viewed that they

were always being seen'.[20] However, though apparently masters of all they surveyed, the spectator's vision, like the prison guard's, was 'by no means unfet-
tered', as Huhtamo puts it, but was determined by 'concerns lurking behind the
apparently limitless canvas' (*IiM*, p. 5). Designed for mass observation under
an intensifyingly mechanised and regulated modernity, the panorama's privileged vantage point, as Alison Griffith puts it, 'gave cramped urban spectators
a quick hit of immersive spectacle and momentary sovereignty over all they
surveyed, placing them at the heart of a simulated universe', but also incarcer-
ating them in a predetermined way of conceiving that world and their position
within it in capitalist and imperial terms.[21]

It is no coincidence that Barker's first panorama brought Scotland's capital
to London in a reflexive, 'semi-colonial' process. As Byerly writes, 'The fact
that panoramas were often seen as a source of useful information about other
countries suggests that to the Unionist and imperial British, "knowing" another
country meant seeing the major sights of its major cities.'[22] Cities were the panorama's foundational subject, creating a parallel between their virtually immersive experience and the actual one of surveying a city from a central vantage
point such as Edinburgh's Calton Hill or Dublin's Nelson's Pillar.

Panoramas in Dublin

Exhibits housed in rotundas, modelled on Barker's in London's Leicester
Square (see figure 3.1), which opened in 1793, sprang up in Dublin as early
as 1794 with Sackville Street's 'Grand Panorama', *A View of London*. One of
Barker's own canvases (or possibly that of a local rival, Nelson's), it measured
an impressive 285 feet by 45 (*MLP&MPS*, pp. 93–4), mediating Britain's
imperial centre back to its Irish periphery. Just as middle-class Dubliners
experienced 'teleportation' to England's metropolis and paid implicit homage
to it, reciprocally their own environment became appropriated for virtual visiting in views such as *Bay of Dublin*, exhibited at Leicester Square (1807–09).
Dubliners also saw their locality reimaged in subsequent panoramas exhibited in Dublin itself.

Urban-topographical panoramas were soon supplemented by explicitly military subjects. One topical depiction of naval victory created a dramatic viewpoint between rival fleets. Its imperial triumphalism countered the
United Irishmen's attempts to secure Napoleonic aid by sea (*MLP&MPS*,
pp. 107–8). Others followed depicting the battles that defeated their 1798 rising. However, panoramas of subsequent British victories in Egypt, India and
so on were double-edged. Although encouraging collaboration in imperial
expansion after the 1801 Act of Union, they inevitably carried latent remind-
ers of resistance to Ireland's own semi-colonial status. Moving battle panoramas prompted Dubliners to imagine themselves 'in the picture', taking part
in vicarious thrills at pivotal moments in imperial history. They anticipated

Figure 3.1 'A Section of the Rotunda, Leicester Square, in Which Is Exhibited the Panorama', in Robert Mitchell, *Plans and Views in Perspective, With Descriptions of Buildings Erected in England and Scotland* (London: Printed at the Oriental Press, by Wilson & Co. for the author, 1801). Reproduced by permission of the National Library of Scotland.

the appeal of the epic films that succeeded them in the same genre, but also their aestheticisation of violence from spectatorial positions that were thrillingly close to the action, yet immune to the consequences. The Revd Thomas Greenwood's 1830 poem, written after seeing a 'peristrephic' moving panorama (i.e. scrolling between vertical rollers, in a concave, semi-circular form) of the Battle of Waterloo captures this tension between visual seduction and moral unease, describing 'Soft Pity [as] the pageant of horror and death passes by', while conceding that its 'splendid display . . . extorts the applause of the eye'.[23] Joyce was keenly interested in Waterloo and toured the historic site in September 1926 to 'secure details for his description of the battlefield and the Napoleon-Wellington struggle' for chapter 1 of 'Work in Progress', as *Finnegans Wake* was then known.[24] It is also likely that he visited the rotunda which houses the (now recently restored) circular panorama nearby. Although dating from 1912, it was the culmination of many such representations of Napoleon's final defeat and a highly elaborate example of the genre, with *faux terrain* and lifelike figures and props in the foreground. Joyce too seems to have been impressed by its scale and artistry, though appalled by its 'pageant of horror and death'.[25] The archetypal glorification of imperial violence in Homer's Trojan War epic, the *Iliad*, personified by its killing-machine hero, Achilles, clinched Joyce's decision to choose the homebound adventures of his draft-dodging counterpart Odysseus instead as the mythological armature for his own panoramic epic conveying an alternative pacifist message. At the date *Ulysses* is set (1904), militaristic propaganda had just climaxed in the Boer War (1899–1902), just as it had peaked again just before the time of *Ulysses'* publication in 1922, during the First World War. As historians maintain, the Boer War was the first to be fully mediated by modern technologies such as film. Nonetheless, the magic lantern and a contemporary development of moving and dioramic panorama shows, the 'Myriorama', also played prominent roles in reporting it.

PANORAMIC MOVEMENT AND 'CHANGE PICTURES'

In common with cinematic aspirations across nineteenth-century entertainment culture, panoramas quickly developed moving effects that enhanced their illusion of embodied presentation. These often included living figures (human and animal), automata, puppets and elaborate mechanical props in *faux-terrain* foregrounds that boosted their sense of animation and three-dimensionality. Panoramas also became multi-media experiences, incorporating music, transformational lighting and sound effects, lantern projections and so on, anticipating the avant-garde ideal of the *Gesamtkunstwerk* in popular form. As they broke out from the static, circular frame, painted backdrops began to scroll and change too, anticipating film's visual mobility. Helmut and Alison Gernsheim note that both dioramas and moving panoramas were often publicised as 'Grand Moving Pictures'.[26] Charles Musser has explained the emergence of cinema in terms of the 'history of screen practice', arguing that it was 'a continuation of and transformation of magic lantern traditions in which showmen displayed images on a screen'.[27] However, as Huhtamo points out, panorama showmen also displayed and explicated images, albeit without relying on projection and although the frames, across which panorama images scrolled, are not usually considered screens (*IiM*, p. 12.). Hence the silent era's 'film explainers' probably descended as much from them as from lantern lecturers. Joe Kember has investigated the performative role of both lantern lecturer and panorama showman and their legacy for film programmes and genres, as mediators between audience and their experience of 'apparitional space and time'.[28]

Influenced by stage machinery, panoramic canvases could be unwound horizontally, up or down, or even on either side of audiences simultaneously, creating the illusion of travelling across, vertically or even into scenes themselves. As with lanternism, they also developed effects depicting temporal change and naturalistic phenomena. Key to this was invention of the 'Diorama', from Greek *dia*, 'through', and *horama*, 'view'. With Charles Marie Bouton, French scenic painter (and later photographic pioneer) Louis-Jacques-Mandé Daguerre refined the panoramic principle in his 1822 patent Paris Diorama. Still a semi-immersive experience, it added ingenious transformative effects akin to dissolving views and similarly anticipating the epic techniques and topicality of film.[29] Daguerre's fifteen-minute 'double-effect', *The Village of Alagna* (1836), of the 1820 Monta Rosa avalanche, which showed an alpine village engulfed by natural forces, typified the diorama's spectacular animations.[30] The diorama's diurnal, metereological and seasonal changes were based on the principle of multi-layered painting or 'change pictures'. Through gradual alterations in front and back lighting, images in colour wash on the front of semi-transparent screens could be faded out and replaced by ones rendered more strongly in distemper on the reverse. Such effects were elaborated with colour filters, shutters and curtains. Daguerre's original amphitheatre design also mobilised audiences, rotating them on platforms to face different views (usually one exterior, another interior). Thus he claimed to improve on static panoramas, providing a 'complete means of illusion, animating the tableaux by various movements found in nature'.[31]

Like Barker's predecessor, dioramas quickly opened in special buildings across Europe, including in London, Edinburgh and Dublin. Irishman Edward Marmaduke Clarke (as well as developing the biscenascope for dissolving views, incorporated into his 'Optical Diorama') opened London's Royal Panopticon of Science and Art in 1854 especially for housing dioramic displays (*EML*, p. 259; *MLP&MPS*, p. 44). Typical subjects were alpine valleys and cathedral interiors, although later programmes diversified into city views, harbour scenes, biblical subjects such as the Flood, as well as topical events such as disasters, conflagrations and battles. Because their effects were developed in parallel with dissolving views, dioramas were likewise boosted in resolution and impressiveness by the adoption of limelight.[32] However, large-scale transformations could be staged more portably and cheaply by projection, leading to the decline of the diorama proper by the 1850s and the lantern's inevitable rise over panorama shows in general.

Nonetheless, dioramas enjoyed a vogue in Dublin, leaving a profound impression on the city's cultural memory and visual imaginary. Groves's multi-subject 'Animated Diorama' (presented at the Rotunda from February 1839) consisted of cities, landscapes, sea and river views, with numerous human and animal figures 'moving with the greatest precision . . . [and] by the power of Mechanism, display[ing] a perfect imitation of animated nature'.[33] Popular subjects included *Napoleon Bonaparte's Crossing of the Alps* and the *Great St Bernard's Pass*. Groves also animated theatrical subjects, as in *Vision of Shakespeare*, as well as mythological themes. The panorama was already an established news medium, recreating topical events from faraway places as virtual eyewitness experience (in the days before portable cameras and instantaneous photography, publicity claimed that panorama images were based on rapid sketches made on the spot, anticipating location footage). Its dioramic offshoot also mediated news to Dubliners, as with the life-saving heroics of Grace Darling, a similarly popular subject of lantern shows (*MLP&MPS*, pp. 140–1). Dioramas both brought exotic subjects to Irish audiences and mapped their own country in spectacularly animated forms, as in the *Grand National Diorama of Ireland* shown at Dublin's Antient Concert Hall in 1865.[34]

VIRTUAL VOYAGING

As Wolfgang Schivelbusch and Erkki Huhtamo historicise, well before train windows mobilised the viewpoint, contemporary accounts demonstrate that moving panoramas affected how travelling by carriage or sailing ship was experienced, through their aesthetics of perception mimicking modes of transport, so that real passengers began considering their experience as a kind of moving panorama show. Panoramas assimilated successive technological innovations such as air balloons, trains and steamships, which revolutionised the space-time continuum. As Huhtamo puts it, 'Such experiences were simulated by enterprising showmen, who persuaded their audiences that virtual travel was not only a less cumbersome alternative, but even more impressive than the real thing' (*IiM*, p. 84). Circular panoramas featured elevated central platforms, simulating bird's-eye views from buildings, sterns of ships or even balloon gondolas. Similar vantage points were also adopted by moving panoramas, with ever more enhanced illusions of mobility. They were thus another key aspect of the nineteenth-century trend for virtual voyaging, which eventually mutated into film's 'phantom rides', as evidenced by early films shot in Dublin. Moving panoramas mutually influenced similar narrative 'journeys' in magic lantern shows – not only touristic, but also historical and fictional. The lantern's shifting between images was not unlike scrolling between panoramic tableaux of different locations.

Dublin's first exhibition of Marshall's patent semi-circular *Grand Peristrephic Panorama* took place at the Rotunda in April 1815. It displayed life-size, eye-level views along the Thames between Windsor Castle and London Bridge, inaugurating the river journeys that dominated the genre (*IiM*, pp. 66–7; *MLP&MPS*, pp. 121–2). The *Freeman's Journal* published a verse 'Impromptu' indicating how real and virtual travel were becoming interfused in a new kind of technological modernity:

> About travelling Balloons people make a great rout,
> The greatest of journeys in them appear small;
> But at the Rotunda you'll quickly find out,
> How to go 30 miles without moving at all![35]

Marshall's show was evidently a great success, leading to the building of at least three new Dublin pavilions for housing more from 1818.[36] As Byerly notes, such journeys provided the perfect topic for linking disparate scenes 'into a seamless continuum, so that the viewer's experience of them is naturalised as the experience of a real-time journey through an identifiable landscape'.[37] Epic seaborne panoramas were also popular in Dublin. The visiting Prince Hermann Pückler Muskau wrote an account of Marshall's peristrephic *Battle of Navarin* in August 1828, marvelling at shifts in location, perspective and scale and the feeling of being in the position of the Turkish fleet with British warships bearing down.

It is likely that some of Marshall's special effects – transformations, lifelike figures, moving vessels fading in and out of view – were produced by dioramic 'change pictures' or portable lanterns.[38] The felt sense of transportation – of being in two places at once, one static, the other moving dynamically – had a profound and enduring effect, intensifying as nineteenth-century media developed. Arguably, Joyce reflects this in *Ulysses*' characters' own subjective fluctuations between situations in the here-and-now and the then-and-there, as well as alternating narrative parallelisms between contemporary Dublin and spaces of fantasy and myth.

Marshall's peristrephic panoramas also featured awe-inspiring natural scenery in virtually photo-realistic levels of detail and expanding space-time durations. Views could be paused to allow spectators to linger in individual places, as showmen guided them along (*MLP&MPS*, pp. 122–3). There is even evidence that paused scenes in later moving panoramas were cleverly enlarged, so that audiences experienced them close-up as if disembarking from whatever simulated vehicle they were 'travelling' in (*IiM*, p. 196). Such ingenious innovations fuelled the mid-century 'panoramania', as Albert Smith dubbed it, and its vogue for virtual world travel.[39] Smith's hugely popular monologue programmes the *Ascent of Mont Blanc* and *Journey on the Overland Mail* were typical of multi-media programmes that blended panorama and lantern forms, in which, as Byerly puts it, 'a traveller-showman narrated his journey while the sights described appeared and disappeared behind him'.[40]

Transportive panoramas were closely linked to colonisation and emigration, two sides of the imperial process that were of particular significance in Ireland. They seemed so authentic relative to contemporary expectations that panorama-goers were encouraged to treat them as 'pre-familiarisation', before voyaging in reality in the hope of escaping poverty and oppression. Simulated experience of the New World's attractions was epitomised by gigantic Mississippi panoramas at Dublin's Rotunda from 1849, presenting moving, double-sided riverbank perspectives from paddle-steamers. John Banvard's *Panorama of the Mississippi*, shown in 1851, was the highpoint of the river journey genre. Similar panoramas afforded simultaneous views of both sides of streets, canals, railway tracks and harbours, sandwiching spectators between unscrolling canvases, giving the impression of travelling forwards or backwards, fast or slow. As Huhtamo notes, they marked a significant 'shift from prosaic illustrated lectures' towards film's phantom rides and today's VR simulators (*IiM*, p. 201). *Two Hours in the New World* and *Great American Panorama*, shown in Ireland in 1862 and 1872, simulated trans-continental rail journeys through the wonders of US geography and technological prowess (*MLP&MPS*, pp. 145–9). Reciprocally, *Howorth's Hibernica* toured America in the 1880s, combining nostalgic moving views of the Old Country with themed variety acts (*IiM*, p. 264).

Audiences could also traverse strange landscapes with famous expeditions to Africa or the Antarctic, or be tourists in cities such as Rome or Jerusalem (*MLP&MPS*, pp. 125–6). Because the panorama's realism depended on recognising that someone had actually experienced the depicted scene, the presence of an authoritative lecturer as 'tour guide' or narrator was indispensable.[41] Typically, Banvard's 'Panorama of the Mississippi' capitalised on this effect through the charismatic showman himself. As Dickens wrote, 'there he is, present, pointing out what he deems most worthy of notice. This is his history.'[42]

However, countering the panoramic perspective's imperialistic appropriations of elsewhere, writers seized on its alternative, socially critical potential closer to home. Dickens's review of Banvard's Mississippi journey, while affirming the power and authenticity of its representation, was tinged with satire. Dickens concluded by imagining a similar three-mile-long moving panorama through the heart of England to reveal the condition of the nation, pausing at telling details of poverty and exploitation in close-up, rather than skimming past in a picturesque view: 'There might be places in it worth looking at, a little closer than we see them now; and worth the thinking of, a little more profoundly.'[43] As Byerly points out, Dickens's imagined 'panorama of England' became emblematic of what he strove to achieve in the socially comprehensive and investigatory project of his own writing, which had a huge influence on others. Similarly, Dickens often used the persona of a panoramic 'traveller-narrator' in his essays to engage readers on a kind of vicarious journey, especially in *The Uncommercial Traveller*, recognising 'in the secondary or displaced travel experience of the panorama something similar to the insights generated in his own literary travels'.[44]

Appropriately, coronations and civic processions – mobile spectacles in themselves – were common subjects of moving panoramas, as they would be of early films and in *Ulysses*' most explicitly panoramic chapter, 'Wandering Rocks', which tracks the Lord Lieutenant's viceregal cavalcade across Dublin, along with pedestrians, cyclists, cars and trams. (Earlier, in 'Hades', Dignam's funeral cortege provides a comparable mobilised perspective across the city for Bloom through his carriage window.) However, Joyce's modernised, moving panorama follows in the more socially critical mould of Dickens's, deliberately subverting the medium's imperialistic associations without the presence of a controlling narrator, as we shall see.

A DAEDALIAN PERSPECTIVE

The aerial perspective of some transportive panoramas also has particular significance for Joyce's alternative critical view. A surviving 1854 playbill from Dublin's Theatre Royal advertises an ambitiously Vernian 'GRAND BALLOON ASCENT From the Rotundo [*sic*] Gardens', with soaring views over Dublin Bay and beyond as far as Constantinople (see reproduction in *MLP&MPS*, p. 120.). Like vertical panorama slides, mountain and balloon ascents were simulated by scrolling canvases up or down, rather than horizontally as for land or sea voyages (for detailed methods of balloon panoramas, see *IiM*, pp. 114–20). Although Joyce may never have flown above Dublin himself, visitors to its giant charity bazaars certainly had the opportunity to look down on their city in the panoramic perspective simulated by aeronautic panoramas, as at Cyclopia in 1896, which among other defamiliarising visual amusements such as X-rays and Paul's Animatograph featured ascents in a 'captive balloon'.[45] Experiments with visual immersion by film pioneers extended virtual voyaging, as in the 'Stereopticon Panorama' and the 'Cinéorama' balloon flight simulator at the 1900 Paris Exposition (see below). This potentially analytic visual perspective over cities was enhanced by films shot from aeroplanes, as reflected in several shown at Joyce's Volta, such as *Aviation Week at Rheims* and *The Aviator Blériot Showing Flights Over Vienna* (3–5 January and 10–12 March 1910).[46]

Panorama-goers seem to have particularly relished how, as Byerly notes, its totalising perspective 'seemed to make vast urban spaces seem "knowable"'.[47] The view associated with hot-air balloons in particular inspired a new 'Daedalian' perspective on the labyrinthine complex of the modern city, making its geographies, infrastructure and human interactions potentially more comprehensible. The privileged relationship between panoramic scene and stationary spectator became symbiotic with the defamiliarising experience of actual balloon flight. The sense of 'freedom and detachment' prominent in balloonists' accounts reflected their awareness of the mediated perspective created by panoramas. In a triangulation with this, numerous Victorian writers, as Byerly notes, used similar aeronautical perspectives to reposition readers as virtual travellers, 'providing a passport to the fictional world that renders it more realistic and knowable'.[48] Both actual panoramas and discursive evocations of their synoptic views 'seemed to expand the horizons of the Victorian gaze'.[49]

Balloonists often compared landscapes to a moving spectacle below. The social reformer Henry Mayhew invoked panoramic perspective with easy confidence of readerly familiarity with the effects of aerial simulations to render his own sublime view from a moving balloon imaginable to those who had not experienced it directly:

> The earth, as the aeronautic vessel glided over it, seemed . . . to consist of a continuous series of scenes which were being drawn along underneath us, as if it were some diorama laid flat upon the ground, and almost gave one the notion that the world was an endless landscape stretched up on rollers, which some invisible sprites below were busily revolving for our especial amusement.[50]

The paradoxical feeling of hovering perfectly stationary inverted the panorama's illusion of travelling, so the landscape appeared mobilised relative to the balloonist. In 1871 James Glaisher saw London's complete layout, radiating from centre outwards, interconnecting districts, activities and widening horizons in one sweep, presumably not unlike depictions such as 1854's 'GRAND BALLOON ASCENT' panorama from the centre of the Irish capital.[51] Other balloonists described cities transformed into vast 'animated' charts or models, their 'constituent parts' visible as never before.[52] Mayhew conveyed an exuberant sense of understanding London's labyrinthine urban complex with all its moral and socio-economic contradictions, in a new structural as well as aesthetic perspective:

> Indeed it was a most wonderful sight to behold that vast bricken mass of churches and hospitals, banks and prisons, palaces and workhouses, docks and refuges for the destitute, parks and squares, and courts and alleys, which make up London – all blent into one immense black spot – to look down upon the whole as the birds of the air look down it, and see it dwindled into a mere rubbish heap – to contemplate from afar that strange conglomeration of vice, avarice, and low cunning, of noble aspirations and humble heroism, and to grasp it in the eye, in all its incongruous integrity, at one single glance . . .[53]

This perspective complemented the street-level views presented in Mayhew's social study, *London Labour and the London Poor* (1849–50), notable for its geographical specificity and precise locations of particular trades among an encyclopaedic wealth of details. His balloon flight afforded an overview which might seem disjunctive, but also potentially interrelated, like distant views and zoomed in close-ups of the same topography.

Tropes in ballooning narratives epitomised how panoramic perspective became interchangeable with real experience and are another powerful instance of the growth of Huhtamo's media-cultural imaginary. This feedback loop raised awareness of the anatomy of the modern city, opening it up and making viewers feel it might be grasped 'as an organic whole', as Byerly puts it.[54] The balloon panorama was clearly an influential model for imaginative anatomisations of the city's workings for writers such as Dickens. Symptomatically, Cruikshank's frontispiece to *Sketches by Boz* (1836) depicts a balloon ascending over an awestruck crowd, suggesting that Dickens intended 'to present a panoramic overview of the London scene', as Byerly concludes.[55] Dickens also attended *Aeronautikon*, the most influential balloon-panorama of the age, and wrote a detailed account of it.[56] Hence the moving perspective embodied in accounts of balloon journeys and the genre of aeronautic panoramas themselves is paralleled by the characteristic narrative viewpoint of much Victorian urban fiction. David Herman suggests that Dickens's narrators often function in a manner that seems 'to transcend the limits of space and time' and 'individualised point of view'.[57] However, Byerly demonstrates in detail that this 'destabilised, floating, unidentifiable' viewpoint reflects 'the kind of generalised perspective embodied in panoramas'.[58]

Such transportive panoramas and their discursive parallels may also have energised Joyce's youthfully Daedalian aspirations to soar above the repressive conditions of his home city and put them into dynamically modern narrative perspective. Significantly, *A Modern Daedalus*, Greer's fantasy about flying resistance to British rule, frequently features perspectives traversing London and Dublin from above, as well as topographies between. They are figured explicitly as moving panoramas and change pictures, positioning readers as virtual aeronauts.[59] Aerial fantasy had been transformed into the new genre of scientific romances about artificial flight. Greer was developing what writers such as Verne had done before him and others such as Wells would continue, under the same panoramic influences.

This all-seeing view of the city – combining aerial and ground-level views with internal reflection – also clearly matches Huhtamo's three-stage developmental model of the discursive panorama (see discussion below): from elevated vantage point, to street level, to internal flows of consciousness. Moreover, Joyce had abundant precedents for mediated vertical perspective in the development of moving balloon panoramas, like those over Dublin discussed above, as well as pioneering aeronautical photography over Paris and London. As discussed in Chapter 1, Cecil Victor Shadbolt was conducting panoramic lantern tours over the highlights of such cities in the 1880s and 1890s. Similarly, an 1896 Dublin newspaper article, 'Triumphs of Photography', confirms how bang-up-to-date such expectation about aerial mediation was in Joyce's home town. It focused on how film projection technology might eventually combine and enhance virtual immersion and movement familiar from lantern and panorama shows based on ballooning. A month after the cinematograph debuted in Paris and only three before its first exhibition in Ireland, Dublin's *Evening Mail* heralded a patent by Chicago inventor

Charles A. Chase, 'expected to figure on a grand scale at the Paris Exhibition of 1900':

> It may be described as a sort of cyclorama of the sort familiar to us in the cases of 'Niagara' and the 'Siege of Paris', &c, but with real photographs of the scene projected from lanterns suspended from a car in the centre of the hall, and forming a complete circuit round the spectator. The projecting lanterns have diaphragms to give the usual panoramic effects of night, dawn, or gloaming, &c. By combining the kinetoscope of Edison and the cinematograph of Lumière with it, animated figures are added to the streets, and processions, whether of soldiers or civilians, political manifestations, and so on, can be reproduced with vivacity.[60]

Chase had first revealed his design for the 'Electric' or 'Stereopticon Cyclorama' in *The Optical Magic Lantern Journal* in March 1895. His detailed technical article with illustrations clearly shows that he was influenced by pioneers of composite photographic panoramas such as Muybridge, which led to the development of cameras for photographing horizons in a continuous 360-degree 'sweep' by others such as Percy S. Marcellus. Chase's article climaxed with the optimistic claim that 'when the scene is projected upon the screen the floor upon which the spectators stand is run right off into the scene, and it is so real that it seems as if we could step right out into the country viewed'.[61]

Chase's project did not actually progress beyond a demonstration prototype in a specially adapted rotunda. However, it was widely reported, inspiring others to take it further.[62] They included the Lumières' circular projection system for still images, the Photorama.[63] Some results did indeed feature at the Paris Exposition, in media terms 'a gateway to the new century' (*IiM*, p. 306), as the *Evening Mail* predicted. Its many moving panoramas included familiar journey genres, but their significant innovation consisted in incorporating elements of large-scale or immersive film projection, with varying degrees of success (*IiM*, pp. 307–18). Moreover, a common feature was 'vehicular amplification' (in Huhtamo's phrase), attempting to increase their reality effect through auditoria that simulated views from a moving liner (the *Maréorama*), a train (the *Trans-Siberian Railway Panorama*) or views of cities and landscapes from a balloon flight (*IiM*, p. 309).[64] The last – Raoul Grimoin-Sanson's *Cinéorama* – came closest to realising Chase's concept, opting for his circular format and also replacing painted canvas with a battery of ten synchronised film projectors mounted under the basket. Though closed as a fire hazard after a few performances, the *Cinéorama* marked an important moment in 'histories of virtual reality' by attempting to synthesise panoramas and projected moving images, exactly in line with the *Evening Mail*'s predictions (*IiM*, p. 318).[65] However, it is also indicative of the potential of moving aerial perspectives for imagining a panoramic overview of the city that presents it in a critically totalising form, of which *Ulysses* is the primary Modernist example.

Moreover, the *Dublin Evening Mail* article on Chase's prototype had also noted the possibility of a 'new art' emerging from such inventions, allowing us to review a temporally immersive panorama of our life or times recorded and projected with photographic virtualism:

> Lumière's cine-matograph [*sic*] reproduces past scenes, such as processions, ceremonies, situations on the stage, and so on, by means of photography, and paves the way for a new art in the shape of a pictorial retrospect of past events near or remote, so that in future a person will be able to review photographically the actual scenes he may have witnessed in the course of his life, or others belonging to times and places beyond his reach.[66]

Hence long before film developed as a narrative medium, Joyce's Dublin was exposed to a sense of expectation that contextualises the literary cinematicity and photographic precision of his own panoramic renderings of his life and home town.

PANORAMIC PERCEPTION AND JOYCE'S MOBILISED VIRTUAL GAZE

Joyce's fiction seems to reflect the influence of panoramisation in many ways. Simulation of travel had aesthetic, cultural and psychological effects beyond direct experience of the medium itself, leading to a phenomenon which Schivelbusch, in his study of nineteenth-century rail journeys, dubs 'panoramic perception'. In contrast to 'traditional perception', this

> no longer belonged to the same space as the perceived objects: the traveller saw the objects, landscapes, etc. *through* the apparatus which moved him through the world. That machine and the motion it created became integrated into his visual perception; thus he could only see things in motion.[67]

Sternberger also suggested that modern travel and its mediation 'elaborated the new world of experience, the countries and the oceans, into a panorama . . . [I]t turned the eyes of travellers outward, offering them a rich diet of changing tableaux, the only possible experience during a trip.'[68] Schivelbusch traces the evolution of this version of visual experience: from the moving panorama, through the train window, which it often mimicked, and then on to the cinematograph screen. Thus he historicises the stages of 'panoramic perception' through successive technological innovations, their inter-medial cross-overs and the cultural imaginary in which they became embedded. As discussed in Chapter 2,

Stephen's mobilised virtual gaze (though which Joyce focalises *Portrait*) is itself symptomatic of panoramic perception in vivid descriptions 'sped-up' by mechanised travel, presented almost like virtual experiences for the reader. This also confirms the novel's transitional position in a world where visual consciousness had already been transformed by the movement and framing of machinery, but in which the cinema screen was beginning to take that process further, adding its own distinctive features. In *Ulysses*' 'Wandering Rocks' chapter in particular, Joyce orchestrated that process into a cross-sectional moving panorama of a whole city, seen from different mobilised points of view, some pedestrian, some vehicular, which anticipated the Modernist montage documentary films of the later 1920s, as discussed in detail below.

Narrative Panoramas

Moving panoramas led to a significant shift that aligned the form with storytelling media. Breaking the static format meant liberation from immersion in a single place or event into more itinerant, narrative forms with multiple means of expression, as 360-degree curved views were replaced by sequential scrolling ones with multiple locations contained in increasingly screen-like frames or proscenium arches, which might last from thirty minutes to an hour or more.[69] However, As Huhtamo notes:

> Most moving panoramas represented scenes of the real world; the events unfolded on a single plane of reality. Dissolving views were different – they shifted from topic to topic, and between levels of reality, gliding into fantasy and back again. Their transformations followed the logic of dreams rather than rivers, trails, or marching armies. (*IiM*, p. 271)

Hence the respective advantages and limits of moving panoramas and magic lantern shows as rival media led to experiments in their combination. These also pointed ahead towards a yet unrealised narrative medium which might successfully assimilate key features of both, capable of simultaneously representing both actuality and fiction with the same level of hyper-real verisimilitude and creative freedom. The moving panorama's inherent handicaps for visualising fictions may have been a chief factor in its eventual demise as a distinct medium, whereas photographic slide sets could be produced, copied and distributed cheaply and easily to meet growing demand for storytelling through images. Hence 'The step from life models to narrative silent films was short and logical' (*IiM*, p. 364).

Nevertheless, like the episodic and temporally shuffled structures of lantern shows, moving panoramas also anticipated aspects of Modernist form by taking liberties with diegesis. Typically, *Aeronautikon* condensed space-time by omitting journey sections deemed insufficiently spectacular.[70] Along with breaks for scroll changing, often covered up by magnificent 'drop scenes' (like the interior of the Temple of Abou Simbel in Warren and Fahey's 1849 *Grand Moving Panorama of the Nile*), such montage-like manipulations anticipated film editing in their geographical and chronological ellipses, becoming a standard method (*IiM*, pp. 118, 253). As the moving panorama developed into more free-ranging formats, rapid shifts between locations and periods typified its contribution to narrative form, as well as to changing cultural perceptions of the space-time continuum. As Byerly points out, such eclecticism within programmes, as moving panoramas came to feature multiple destinations, corresponds to Foucault's 'heterotopia'.[71] The panorama was both materially real as building-vision-machine and an illusory depiction of multiple, incompatible locations and times. It altered the Victorian audience's sense of their 'own relation to reality' through rapid teleportations to imaginary, but also seemingly embodied elsewheres.[72] Conversely, this increasing desire to visualise the world in a montage-like series of juxtaposed images, epitomised by the Myriorama's mixed 'Dioramic Excursions' in Dublin (discussed below), anticipates the structure of Modernist fiction; again suggesting the key role played by panoramic forms in modernity's accelerating 'media-cultural imaginary', but also Modernist writers' ambivalent response to this globalising process.

SUNSET OF A MEDIUM

Photography was a major cause of the demise of large-scale panoramas and their offshoots. It competed fiercely with their exotic attractions and topical portraiture of events and celebrities. From the 1850s, panoramists responded by using location photographs to enhance verisimilitude in painted images or even incorporated large-scale photographic views into shows. However, every photographic image was potentially duplicable and transferable to rival media of lantern or stereoscope, to be viewed in public projections or even domestically. This was another symptom of the paradigm shift from a manually produced, uniquely 'auratic' image culture to the explosion of mechanically reproduced images, diagnosed as the essential condition of modernity in Benjamin's famous essay. Moreover, large-scale and outdoor projection literally outshone the attractions of panorama shows. Although the sheer size of panoramas and the labour involved in producing them might seem to reinforce their claim to accurate reproduction, they could not be updated quickly enough to keep pace with unfolding events, unlike topical slide sets or films. Handicapped by their dinosaur-like bulk with their enormous canvas rolls, panoramas were ill-suited to survive into the era of mass media, rapid distribution and constant demands for programme changes (*IiM*, p. 280). Reporting on Gompertz's 1859 *Diorama of India* at the Rotunda (which sought to remediate the Raj's imperial image following the upheavals of the Indian Mutiny), the *Irish Times* noted that educationalists would inevitably 'recognise in the Diorama one of the most powerful instruments of their art'. However, history, geography, science, art, and so on were more widely mediated by lantern in Joyce's youth on grounds of portability and cost.[73] Nevertheless, hybrid forms of moving and animated panoramas 'remained part of a variety entertainment package into the twentieth century', often incorporating projected photographs and film among their attractions (*MLP&MPS*, pp. 141–2).

One distinctive form in which panorama tradition continued to flourish into the Dublin of Joyce's twenties was Poole and Young's multi-media Myriorama, a term adopted in 1882 by Charles W. Poole from Greek *myrioi*, 'various', and Barker's ubiquitous suffix.[74] It was eventually employed by all branches of the Poole family's touring entertainment franchise – part topical representation of 'passing events', part 'dioramic excursion' and part variety show, which like lantern bills anticipated the mixed programmes of early film. The formula made Poole and Young the most successful showmen of their type in Britain and Ireland (*MLP&MPS*, p. 144; *IiM*, pp. 287–96). Myrioramas, including those displayed at Dublin's Rotunda, specialised in accelerated virtual tourism, while also reflecting the panoramic ideology that positioned Ireland within the British Empire and endorsed its project,[75] as in their 1886 *Trips Abroad* and 1892 *Sights of the World* (see figure 3.2). The latter featured topical views of 'Venice in Dublin', the Falls of Niagara, 'Darkest Africa', London, Sydney, Australia and the 'British Navy, Past and Present', alongside a moving panorama of Ireland incorporating Dublin views, such as along Dame Street from College Green, and rural ones, such as the Lakes of Killarney. Titles such as 'Venice in Dublin' also underline how this trend for recreating exotic locations was shared with charity bazaars such as 'Araby in Dublin' (which took place two years later), and their interlinked value within a capitalist-colonial economy. They also underline how the period's media attractions overlapped and fed off one another in terms of subject matter and technique, weaving a matrix for cinema's gestation.

Like other panorama programmes, Myrioramas mediated topical events, as in *Trips Abroad* which (after its opening global tour) focused on colonial wars in Egypt and Sudan. Myrioramas also featured fantastic interludes from classical mythology and the phantasmagoria: *Trips Abroad* included a (possibly Homeric) scene called 'Consulting the Oracle', before jumping back to the present for a humorous scene, which visualised a Londoner entertaining friends with ghost stories.[76] Myriorama backdrops also constituted the moving panorama's highpoint, involving up to six scrollable canvases, each around a mile in length and fifteen feet high, with individual pictures up to thirty feet wide. One account of a Rotunda show compared these 'cylinders' to 'the Corinthian columns outside the Bank of Ireland'.[77] 'Stereorama' sets incorporated in Myriorama programmes refined mechanised special effects, simulating storms and battles with real explosions, as in 'The Bombardment of Alexandria',

Figure 3.2 Poster for 'Chas W. Poole's New Myriorama and Trips Abroad'.
© The British Library Board c01517-01 Evan.2475.

recreated from the 1881 Anglo-Egyptian War. A miniature cannon nearly caused a serious conflagration during a Rotunda show.[78] After relishing *Sights of the World* at the Rotunda, a *Kilkenny Journal* reporter filed a rare 'behind-the-scenes' account in July 1892. Despite exposing the illusion's complex workings, the reporter still felt a disorientating sense of being in two very different places at once, boundaries blurred between virtual and real with almost no transition between: '[I]n under ten seconds I had left beautiful Venice, India, and the Lord Mayor's Show, and was out into the cool atmosphere of Sackville-street [*sic*], enjoying the odoriferous breeze of the Liffey.'[79]

The Myriorama also epitomises how late developments in moving panoramas increasingly anticipated Joycean Modernism through their montage-like structure. Unlike the static panorama's all-encompassing, immersive view of city or event, Myriorama shows leapt eclectically between scenes, often zooming in on the anecdotal rather than maintaining distant, impersonal perspectives. They presented brief glimpses into different cultures both through large-scale topical formats and close-up focus on dramatised moments in individual lives. Moreover, realising that the panorama era was waning, Poole and Young made multi-media adaptability their selling point, incorporating film shows as early as December 1896. This was undoubtedly a factor that enabled the franchise to survive for longer and meant that many Dubliners saw their first projected films at Myrioramas.[80] Poole and Young also quickly took advantage of screen magic for promotion. Mitchell and Kenyon's trick film *Poole's Clitheroe* (1901) uses a stop-motion cut to conjure a street crowd of the 'factory gate' genre. One of the Poole brothers appears on screen bowing and doffing his boater theatrically. Then – Hey presto! – he metamorphoses into a worker, amid a crowd leaving a mill, which materialises as a potential audience for his Myriorama.[81] Such mixed entertainments nurtured a cuckoo in the nest, which eventually usurped them. Nonetheless, as with other popular forms such as lanternism, charity bazaar and music hall, film absorbed significant cultural DNA from its host, which it remediated, as reflected in Joyce's work, particularly in his represention of the city in *Ulysses*.

LITERARY PANORAMAS BEFORE JOYCE

As with lantern shows, there was a long and rich history of creative interaction between fiction and panorama forms for Joyce to draw on. Similarly, he would have been influenced not just by actual panorama, diorama or Myriorama shows that he may have seen, heard or read about, but by their wider role as multivalent discursive topos and model for literary form and technique. This was particularly the case in writing which aspired to represent a rapidly expanding urban modernity, mimicking the totalising overview apparently offered by panoramas themselves, but also epitomised, as Byerly notes, by promotional and journalistic descriptions of the panoramas which 'promised a comprehensive and synoptic view of scenes, like the burgeoning London metropolis'.[82]

Significantly, an 1895 article about teaching literary technique highlighted characteristic differences between moving panorama and lantern shows, but also the advantages of combining them in a new form that overcame their mutual limitations. Ellen E. Kenyon recommended that, 'as the story is told, its scenery should be made to pass through the children's minds like a panorama', while employing 'frequent pauses, with closed eyes, to develop the pictures that follow one another in dissolving views', thus making 'the story a living reality'.[83] With her added hint of photography in the expression 'develop the pictures', it is telling that Kenyon's article was published in the very year of the cinematograph, thus coinciding with the birth of the hyper-real medium which eventually succeeded in combining moving panoramic scope with the lantern's sequential close-ups and mimesis of shifts in consciousness. Hence the article was symptomatic of close convergence between the ecology of late nineteenth-century media and the ambitions of modern literary form.

As precedent, moreover, Huhtamo cites numerous writers who combined references to moving panoramas with dissolving views to figure the free-ranging processes of perception, memory and fantasy. In this respect, the panorama seems to have been as important as the lantern for Dickens.[84] However, it was his lesser-known collaborator on *Household Words* who most anticipated Joyce's cinematic stream of consciousness in *Portrait*, with its highly compressed structure of vivid moments fluidly interconnected. J. D. Lewis described the involuntary processes of his own visual imagination in exactly such inter-medial terms in his 1857 memoir:

> the whole panorama of my college life seemed to unroll itself before me. Not, indeed, with such a degree of distinctness as to enable me to grasp even its leading features; but rather as a series of dissolving views, each presenting some point or scene in my career that had unaccountably lingered in the memory, to the exclusion of events of seemingly greater importance.[85]

Inevitably, other writers added photography to the mix for figuring parallel aspirations to a new precision and vividness in capturing fleeting impressions. Typically, as James Stirling also put it in 1857, emphasising the difficulties of fixing the transitory through the long exposures required before instantaneous photography: 'You have to daguerreotype a scene that is at once a moving panorama and a dissolving view.'[86] Consequently, as Huhtamo infers, this 'accumulation and assimilation of media references' in literary contexts 'can be read as a symptom of the gestation process of a media-cultural imaginary' (*IiM*, p. 273.), a modern phenomenon thus already well underway by Joyce's time. Through a continuing process in which we have internalised and become dependent on its criss-crossing forms, this imaginary has now matured into 'a state of being, where media have come to dominate minds to such an extent that they have replaced other reference points. In a way they have turned into a second nature, a "panoramic" simulacrum of the world' (*IiM*, p. 366). Hence in its relationship with the panoramic tradition, Joyce's work reflects a critical phase of this immersive and virtual history, which can simultaneously tell us much both about the evolution of his style and about how we have arrived at our current, 'postmodern' condition.

PANORAMIC REFERENCES IN JOYCE'S FICTION

Although *Ulysses* may be Joyce's most extensive engagement with the evolving form, a kind of moving panoramic perception that activates readers' critical responses is elaborated from *Dubliners* onwards. The case that *Dubliners* is more properly a composite novel – effectively stimulating us to construct an overall picture of the city's paralysed condition by inferring connections between Joyce's cross-section of locations and focalisers – is well established.[87] The airy views sweeping out over Dublin's frozen cityscape imagined by Gabriel in 'The Dead' (nervously evading his audience's expectant gaze before his speech) exemplify the internalisation of panoramic perception:

> Meeting a row of upturned faces he raised his eyes to the chandelier. The piano was playing a waltz tune and he could hear the skirts sweeping against the drawing-room door. People, perhaps, were standing in the snow on the quay outside, gazing up at the lighted windows and listening to the waltz music. The air was pure there. In the distance lay the park where the trees were weighted with snow. The Wellington monument wore a gleaming cap of snow that flashed westward over the white field of Fifteen Acres. (*Dubliners*, p. 159)

Significantly, Gabriel's widening vision pivots around the top of Dublin's 'testimonial' to Britain's 'Iron Duke', at 203 feet the largest obelisk in Europe. This celebrated Wellington's victories against the French, particularly at Waterloo, a battle of great significance to Joyce as we have seen, especially in *Finnegans Wake*. Waterloo, which also cemented British rule in Ireland, was mediated in battle panoramas by Barker and others.[88] In 1816 Marshall's also exhibited a moving peristrephic panorama of it.[89] Though never intended to double as a literal viewing platform, unlike Nelson's pillar, the Wellington monument nonetheless marked a visually commanding but controversial height in central Dublin (as would have been even more the case had the original plans to site it in Merrion Square not encountered opposition from residents). Work began in 1817, but was only completed in 1861 for lack of popular subscription after Wellington's death. Nevertheless, this effect – of Gabriel's imagined gaze roaming freely around and above the city to compensate for his sense of social entrapment – is expanded and ironised at the end in the panoramic sweeps of his stream of consciousness which visualise snow falling general across the whole topography of Ireland, further and further westwards, finally zooming in on the grave of Michael Furey in Galway.

Moreover, each of Joyce's principal fictions, including *Finnegans Wake*, contains at least one explicit reference to panorama shows, effectively historicising the increasingly mobile, transformative and multi-media forms evolving from them. In 'A Little Cloud', while crossing Grattan Bridge, Little Chandler thinks of shabby houses on the distant lower quays from his moving viewpoint as an audience of tramps 'stupefied by the panorama of sunset' (*Dubliners*, p. 55). According to the *Kilkenny Journal*, 'dazzling sunsets and sunrises' were among the most spellbinding change picture effects of Rotunda Myriorama shows in 1892.[90] While Chandler's disdainful metaphor suggests an audience of Dublin's dispossessed goggling at spectacular entertainment mistaken for reality, at another level it inadvertently evokes his own disabling self-absorption as would-be 'Celtic Twilight' poet immersed in a misty-eyed fantasy of Ireland's fading cultural glory, while evading personal and national crises in the present.

Similarly, *Portrait* mentions the same venue (a key location for visual entertainments of all kinds in Victorian and Edwardian Dublin, as we have seen, including film's 'living pictures'),[91] as well as another specific form of panorama show: the diorama. Stephen's closing diary records his attendance at this kind of semi-immersive, moving image entertainment as 'a diorama in Rotunda. At the end were pictures of big nobs. Among them William Ewart Gladstone, just then dead' (*Portrait*, p. 210). His show can thus be dated no earlier than May 1898 (the Liberal Prime Minister died on the 19th of that month). However, 1898 was long after the heyday of Daguerre's transformative improvement on Barker's static panorama, which declined from the 1850s as an attraction in its own right. Nevertheless, 'diorama' or 'dioramic' continued to be used for a whole spectrum of moving shows in marketing and popular parlance. The mixed attractions seen by Stephen suggest one of Poole and Young's Myrioramas or a similar programme. These were widely advertised as 'Dioramic Excursions' after the family adopted their distinctive brand name for all branches of the touring franchise. Daguerre's basic principle was still used for the Myriorama's impressive change pictures, moving action from one scene to another or magically transforming the view without laborious scrolling between cylinders.[92] There was indeed a Myriorama at the Rotunda in Poole's regular annual slot from 15 August 1898, less than four months after Gladstone died (possibly titled *Picturesque Trips Abroad and Latest* events; see ticket reproduced in *IiM*, p. 290). This featured a 'graphic depiction of the Spanish-American War', another colonial conflict on the other side of the world, including the blowing up of the US cruiser *Maine*, and the resulting bombardment of Santiago.[93] Its military spectacle was combined with virtual tourism around the UK – 'the perfect representation of all the beautiful and interesting places in Great Britain and Ireland'[94] – but also between metropolis and frontier – 'London to Khartoum'[95] – where Britain came similarly close to renewed war with imperial rival France during the Fashoda crisis in the Sudan (also represented in Poole's programme). Despite its nationalist leanings, the *Freeman's Journal* praised this 'exceptional entertainment' which 'no one should miss'.[96]

Moreover, surviving records show that the principal attractions of the Myriorama at the Round Room from 8 August 1899 (the year following Stephen's fictional visit) remained emphatically in this tradition, placing Dublin within the context of contemporary imperial networks and events. These included a virtual voyage from 'Cairo to Cape', the charge of the 21st Lancers at the battle of Omdurman in the Sudanese War, the Spanish–American War, the Indian frontier rising, Dargai, together with 'Fine Views of Ireland'.[97] In a typical pattern, according to Kember, Poole's Myriorama of the *Soudan and Egyptian Wars* was toured widely from 1885, then bulked out and topically updated with scenes from the Boer War in 1900.[98] Such propagandism climaxed with *Our Empire*, exhibited at the Rotunda in summer 1901. This Myriorama included a narrative recapping of the Boer War from the beginning, in characteristic hybrid form of variety turns, cinematograph films and moving panorama segments. Reports suggest that audience reactions were sharply divided, but feelings ran even higher in the provinces. A local reporter gave a detailed account when the show transferred to the Theatre Royal, Limerick.[99] Representations of British victories provoked deafening boos and hisses, while performers were assailed with rotten eggs and flour bombs.[100]

The 'pictures of big nobs' that Stephen recalls concluding his Rotunda show might suggest topical lantern images of other British dignitaries alongside Gladstone, or perhaps even royalty. Such pictures seem to have been projected in a format anticipating the newsreel. Lantern lives of Gladstone were also in circulation, including his relationship with Parnell and the Home Rule movement.[101] By 1898 Stephen's pictures may even have been films featuring news footage of the same: films were frequently called 'living pictures' at the time (eventually abbreviated simply to 'the pictures'). Myrioramas were exhibited seasonally in Dublin from the 1880s to the 1900s and included film screenings as early as December 1896. As the Rocketts note, Myrioramas incorporated footage of Victoria's Diamond Jubilee procession at the Rotunda in August 1897 and also exhibited other living pictures there in 1898 (*MLP&MPS*, pp. 230, 239).

The Myriorama's mixed attractions and imperial agenda are particularly suggestive when considered alongside the uncanny 'dream epiphany' that Stephen records in his next diary entry, as if triggered by the involuntary memory of his visit. His 'big nobs' seem to morph into statues of oppressive idols in this symbolic vision of yet another cave of moving shadows (a pervasive motif in *Portrait*), while the 'sub-humans' serving them seem dream counterparts of Myriorama stereotypes of colonised peoples, as in 'Darkest Africa', or even the Irish themselves as 'loyal' but inferior subjects of Empire represented in other views. The trogolodytes' enigmatic appeal to Stephen hints at his author's project: to inspire his compatriots to liberate themselves by means of the demystifying cinematicity of his fiction. This strove to reveal the machinery (both literal and psychological) behind their entrapment in a cave of mediated illusions serving false 'idols', which Britain's panoramic tradition played a key role in creating.

In 'Penelope', *Ulysses*' closing interior monologue, Molly Bloom also recalls the Myriorama by name, less for any memorable attractions in the spectacles unscrolling or transforming onstage than for a random distraction in the auditorium. This casts an ironic sidelight on audience motives for attending shows in disinhibiting darkness, as well as on the question of reciprocal disciplinary vision (which also anticipates film-age habits). Molly witnesses an indiscretion as well as the guilty party's reaction on finding himself the unexpected focus of her attention: 'I met do you remember Menton and who else who let me see that big babbyface I saw him and he not long married flirting with a young girl at Pooles Myriorama and turned my back on him when he slinked out looking quite conscious' (*Ulysses* 18.38–41).[102]

Besides such explicit references to different types of panorama, loaded with contextual ironies, there is a critical sense of the power of technologies mediating the city of Dublin in panoramic but also imperial terms at deeper levels. To appreciate this, it is worth pausing to consider related developments in devices for watching urban environments and populations from above: the camera obscura and monumental viewing tower. Through a system of lenses and mirrors, camera obscuras amplified natural light to reflect a continuous live view of the surrounding area from a swivelling mount atop an observatory down on to a circular tabletop screen. Like an ancestral CCTV system, they thus allowed observers the advantage of seeing without being seen. As Crary argues, in the history of Western visuality, the camera obscura typifies a subject position produced 'according to the model of an idealised observer separated from the object observed', established as an apparently disembodied eye scrutinising the world at a distance.[103] In 1807 a 'Grand Camera Obscura' was erected in an octagonal building at the junction of D'Olier and Westmoreland Streets. This commanded a 360-degree view over the recently renovated heartland of Dublin's Anglo-Irish ascendancy. As the Rocketts note, most camera obscuras and panorama rotundas tended to be sited in the same area, 'on, or close to, either Lower Sackville Street or adjacent to the new bridge on the south side'. Inevitably, this was also where many of Dublin's first cinemas congregated a century later (*MLP&MPS*, p. 14). Moreover, in 1897 the Lumières' cameramen shot some of the first panoramic film footage of the capital's streets and monuments from roughly the same position as the original Grand Camera Obscura (*MLP&MPS*, pp. 15–16). As a viewing device, the camera obscura complemented, and probably influenced, static panoramas. Though outdoing painted virtualism (by relaying constant live movement, changing light and colour), it nonetheless could not rival the panorama's most distinctive feature: the effect of total immersion in an elsewhere produced by an apparently complete perspective of its horizon as the gaze turned.

Although there may be no direct reference to camera obscuras in *Ulysses*, there is nonetheless an implicit sense of an alternative panoramic gaze ranging freely around Dublin, zooming down to a particular street level and character, then moving on elsewhere. But this effect also deliberately challenges the governing view of Ireland's capital as mediated by the panoramic tradition, which placed it in a position of dependency within the British state and global empire. This perspective, though not identifiable with any single focaliser, is strongly implicit in the overall montage of Joyce's most panoramic novel and his famously invisible monstrator who orchestrates it.

Crucially, Sackville Street was also the site of Nelson's Pillar. Erected in 1808 to furnish one of the first monumental viewing towers (pre-dating London's Nelson's Column), it offered an imperially commanding view, in this case both live *and* immersive: it effectively combined the functions of camera obscura and panorama.[104] The Pillar celebrated Britain's 'hero of Trafalgar' by imposing his presence unignorably on the city's central profile. It also afforded Dublin's ultimate 'panoramic experience' from a unionist perspective (*MLP&MPS*, p. 11), until it was belatedly blown up by the IRA in March 1966 (on the fiftieth anniversary of the Easter Rising, which it survived). Nelson's victories were also a frequent subject of naval panoramas by Barker and others, and the Pillar itself became, self-reflexively, a frequent object of mediation in Dublin's panoramic culture.[105] According to Carville, it was the iconic terminus of photographic depictions taken from Carlisle (O'Connell) Bridge down Sackville Street, including landmarks such as the General Post Office and the Rotunda complex in the distance, and served as a kind of visual metonymy for Dublin as imperial city from the 1860s. However, the Pillar's presence gradually lost definition in later stereoscopic views taken by Lawrence's studios from the same perspective. These shifted their clarity of focus to the busy activity of people and vehicles in the foreground at street level, as well as picking out the statue of the nationalist leader William Smith O'Brien instead. As Carville puts it, while the Pillar remains in view at the apex of such images, 'it is placed under erasure by the hazy smudges and tones of the surface of the photographic print', almost as if the 'city's imperial status has been dissolved', like a symbolic premonition of what actually happened to its monumental centre in 1916.[106]

Similarly, in one of the more explicitly satirical scenes in *A Modern Daedalus*, Greer's Fenian aeronaut perches like a disrespectful gull on the Pillar's London counterpart: Nelson's Column in Trafalgar Square. From there, he scopes out a rotating panorama of the very centre of British power, now intimately vulnerable to the possibility of aerial attack for the first time in history, as a new dimension of warfare that transcends maritime dominance is opened up. He notes cheekily that 'the hero's cocked hat afforded ample room to sit and survey the scene beneath'.[107] In a comparably subversive way, Joyce appropriated Nelson's Pillar for his ironically Mosaic glimpse of Dublin in 'Aeolus', mocking its imperial symbolism and outlook in Stephen's anti-climactic 'parable of the plums'. The Pillar first appears at the beginning of the chapter, in its role as marker for the Sackville Street terminus and radial hub of Dublin's new electric tram system (a role frequently foregrounded in photographs and postcards from the time).[108] It thus also implies a panoramic perspective on the city's modern traffic circulation, to be more fully played out in 'Wandering Rocks'. (The Pillar also reappears in one of the phantasmagoric sequences in 'Circe', as the high point from which Bloom hangs miraculously by his eyelids to prove his credentials as Irish messiah and from which 'many most attractive and enthusiastic women . . . commit suicide' in his cause; *Ulysses* 15.1841–3, 1745–8.) In Stephen's parable, a pair of elderly 'Dublin vestals' are so exhausted by climbing the Pillar's internal staircase and so overcome by vertigo as they emerge onto its viewing platform that they fail to appreciate its imperial panorama or pay homage to its crowning statue of the 'onehandled adulterer' towering above them (*Ulysses* 7.923, 1018). Thus Stephen invokes Mosaic imagery to subvert any glimpse of the 'promised land' of Ireland's future as British dominion, suggesting instead its lost chance of peaceful Home Rule, forestalled because of the scandalous fall from on high of another, more recent 'adulterer' – Parnell. Hence instead of enjoying the view, the matrons merely squat down to recover by picnicking, obliviously spitting plumstones through its balustrade.

In 'Aeolus', Joyce prepares a context for this moment of supreme bathos through another reference to moving panoramas in an article aiming to present a similarly rosy overview of the condition of Ireland, derided by the *Freeman's* journalists for its stilted rhetoric. Significantly, the article imagines a mountain-top vantage point like the elevated central platform that audiences occupied in Barker's original shows, inviting us to '*bathe our souls . . . in the peerless panorama of Ireland's portfolio*' (*Ulysses* 7.316-20; italics in original). It then rotates through touristic images of '*bosky grove and undulating plain and luscious pastureland of vernal green*', as if scrolling them successively before an audience. Moreover, the article's sentimentally proprietorial *tour d'horizon* incorporates transformative lighting effects as if through transparent screens like dioramic 'change pictures', as its moving views become '*steeped in the transcendent translucent glow of our mild mysterious Irish twilight . . .*' (7.322-4). The article is thus also a kind of parody of Huhtamo's discursive panorama, reflecting major characteristics of the actual medium as it developed. By foregrounding its influence on the contemporary media-cultural imaginary, even down to the most clichéd contexts, Joyce sets up the conditions for Stephen's subversion of such imperialising viewpoints in his parable.

An influential parallel among subjects depicting life in Britain's colonies during the 'panoramania' of the 1850s was T. C. Dibdin's *Diorama of the Ganges*. This virtual voyage along the Raj's principal river began with a rotating 360-degree view of Calcutta. It was presented as if from the summit of the 165-foot Ochtorloney Column, a comparable imperial landmark celebrating Major General Sir David Ochtorloney, 'hero' of the Anglo-Nepalese War. As this initial sequence scrolled around, the audience's gaze also appeared to swivel above the city from the same point. Such views anticipated and influenced the filmed *tours d'horizon* that became a widespread genre of early urban actualities (discussed in detail below). Ironic parallelism between such set pieces and Joyce's subversion of Nelson's Pillar's similarly commanding perspective is highly suggestive.[109] It indicates his familiarity with the ideological connotations of such viewpoints – actual, in the Pillar's case, simulated, in Dibdin's *Diorama* – which led Joyce to create his alternative anti-colonial overview of his home city in 'Wandering Rocks'. Following the rejection of the commanding view in 'Aeolus', strongly identified with the history of imperial prestige and surveillance, *Ulysses*' central chapter comes emphatically down to earth, countering the governing perspective on Dublin by mocking its key political and religious institutions from multiple, moving and subjectivised viewpoints.

David Spurr also recognises how *Ulysses*' subversion of Nelson's Pillar, among other imperial monuments, deliberately parodies the tradition of totalising panoramic views. These dominated 'everything from urban planning to the great international exhibitions of Paris, London, and Chicago' and were 'symptomatic of a need to render the city as a "closed and unified spatial order" . . . thereby creating the illusion of rational mastery over the aleatory, repressed, and uncontrolled elements of urban space'.[110] Contrastingly, Joyce's visual politics 'are rigorously decentred, presenting a series of local views by a variety of different eyes moving through the streets, not over the rooftops. Imperial monuments thus are seen from ground level and without inspiring the awe intended by their imposing design.'[111] Spurr also argues that the episode's parallel with the mythical 'Wandering Rocks' itself provides an image for how the moving panorama of *Ulysses* dislodges imperialism's 'monumental and archaic architectural forms' from their intended ideological contexts 'in the shifting configurations' of its alternative handling of urban space.[112]

'Wandering Rocks' revolves around the 360-degree rooftop perspective of the chapter's monstrator (always implied, but rarely materialised in explicit descriptions from that high vantage point); 'zooming' down into the immersive and often disorientating presentation of close-up action at street level; always shifting between the individual perspectives of a cross-section of Dublin's citizens, on foot or in vehicles, through brief sections of their interior monologues as focalising characters. Joyce also places the reader in the collaborative, but somewhat challenging position of assembling an alternative panoramic perspective on the city from their response to his narrative fragments or 'montage', as film-makers would call it.

From Pillar, to Street, to Stream of Consciousness

Significantly, Huhtamo notes three distinct phases in the development of perception and topicality in the discursive panorama which anticipate the Modernism of Joyce's narrative strategies in *Ulysses*. The first involved an imaginative stepping down from the high vantage point of the original circular panorama into more mobile modes and terrains which reflected the panorama's own evolution into moving forms. Thus the panoramic observer in literary texts was gradually '"transfigured" from the context of rotundas, stuttering lecturers, and creaking rolls of canvas, and transplanted into great varieties of discursive landscapes' (*IiM*, p. 339). Huhtamo cites mid-nineteenth-century writers who evidence this descent into the 'moving panorama' of street-level imagery. Famously, in 1863 Baudelaire celebrated the paradoxical 'anonymous intimacy' in thus observing modern life from this perspective enjoyed by the *flâneur*, his new kind of artistic urban idler. Baudelaire was consequently a key transitional figure in the inter-medial relationship which constituted the discursive panorama. His *flâneur* represented the restlessly moving, electrically charged panorama of the city from down on its boulevards:

> The observer is a prince enjoying his incognito wherever he goes . . . Thus the lover of universal life moves into the crowd, as though into an enormous reservoir of electricity. He, the lover of life, may also be compared to a mirror as vast as this crowd; to a kaleidoscope endowed with consciousness, which with every one of its movements presents a pattern of life, in all its multiplicity, and the flowing grace of all the elements that go to compose life. It is an ego athirst for the non-ego, and reflecting it at every moment in pictures more vivid [*images plus vivantes*] than life itself, always inconstant and fleeting.[113]

Baudelaire's metaphor – 'a kaleidoscope endowed with consciousness' (invoking another pre-filmic optical toy that fascinated Joyce) – foresees the roving camera's gaze as a prosthetic technological extension of *flânerie*, through how it reflects the excitement and shock of the 'more than living' pictures of city life in all their perpetually changing imagery. As Benjamin argued, this passage was symptomatic of how 'technology has subjected the human sensorium to a complex kind of training'. It anticipated how '[t]here came a day when a new and urgent need for stimuli was met by film. In a film, perception conditioned by shock was established as a new formal principle.'[114] Indeed, Benjamin's line of thinking also has much in common with Dziga Vertov's foundational 'Kino-Eye' manifesto of 1923, which laid the theoretical foundations for the Soviet director's own film panoramas of the modern city.[115]

As Huhtamo notes, epitomised by Baudelaire's kaleidoscope endowed with consciousness, 'Transmuted into a *flâneur* the panoramic observer becomes immersed in the crowd, observing the kinetic sight of countless human beings hurrying past' (*IiM*, p. 340). *The Social Kaleidoscope*, an 1881 collection by George R. Sims, the quintessential 'multi-media' figure of his age following Dickens's death in 1870, exemplifies how that trope was reflected in panoramic popular texts documenting the Victorian Social Question and the city's contradictions:

> Substitute for the fragments of coloured glass the many-hued virtues and vices, passions and peculiarities of mankind, and at every twist of the Social Kaleidoscope we get a glimpse of human nature in a varied aspect. What the arrangement of reflecting surfaces does for the glass atoms, the arrangement of surrounding circumstances forms for the attributes of humanity. It gives them a special form and a dominant colour, and unites them in a series of perfectly dissimilar pictures.[116]

Similarly, as the representation of artificial locomotion became more prominent in moving panoramas, 'the discursive panoramic observer stepped into a vehicle' as well, observing their moving spectacle in accelerated form through the windows of trains, then newer forms of mechanised transport such as trams or cars (*IiM*, pp. 341–2). Within this shift there is a markedly proto-Joycean sense of narrative movement at street level and of using literary focalisers as mobile 'camera-eyes', on foot or in vehicles, which culminated in 'Wandering Rocks'. *Ulysses* famously creates a montage of the city in its concrete totality as built, but also individually lived environment, simultaneously presenting the criss-crossing perceptions and flows of consciousness of the citizens who inhabit and interact with it. This made Joyce's novel an equally influential model for a kind of Modernist, panoramic 'psychogeography' in both literature and film.[117]

Hence a third shift in the typology of discursive panoramas noted by Huhtamo helps explain how Joyce's strategy came to combine an implied overview with mobilised, street-level immersion and intensely subjective, psychological focalisation from multiple viewpoints, thus opening out and socialising *Portrait*'s isolated perspective. In the late nineteenth century, intellectuals began figuring consciousness as a kind of proto-filmic, continuous moving panorama, through which individuals perceived but also remembered sensory impressions that they internalised and replayed. Significantly, this third phase converged with the concept of the 'stream of consciousness', popularised by William James's definition in *The Principles of Psychology* (1890):

> Consciousness, then, does not appear to itself chopped up in bits. Such words as 'chain' or 'train' do not describe it fitly as it presents itself in the first instance. It is nothing jointed; it flows. A 'river' or a 'stream' are the metaphors by which it is most naturally described. *In talking of it hereafter, let us call it the stream of thought, of consciousness, or of subjective life.*[118] [italics in original]

The term was famously adopted by critics to designate techniques presenting subjectivity in Modernist experimental fiction, following May Sinclair's application of it to the style of Dorothy's Richardson's Joyce-influenced *Bildungsroman* sequence, *Pilgrimage*, in 1918: 'It is just life going on and on. It is Miriam Henderson's stream of consciousness going on and on.'[119]

The figuring of consciousness as flow or flux also features heavily in Bergson's philosophy of time. However, its conception as a continuous flow of moving and internalised images had already been formulated at least as early as 1865 by the English philosopher Shadworth H. Hodgson. Hodgson endeavoured (in his words) 'to trace as it were the stream of consciousness and of existence to its source'.[120] He enlisted the moving panorama in developing his theory. For Hodgson (as H. Wildon Carr summarised), consciousness was 'a reflection, it is a looking back on a receding stream' of impressions. This stream moved 'from the present vivid actuality into the past', yet was 'retained in the present as it moves away'.[121] Hence in a very proto-Joycean manner, Hodgson saw consciousness as behaving like persistence of vision by retaining perceived images after their objects were removed; its activity thus flowing in opposing directions simultaneously – present into past, but also past back into present – which are of 'one and the same time duration indistinguishable'.[122] By stressing this visual aspect, Hodgson inevitably considered the active role that media forms and practices play in shaping how the stream's flow was experienced and figured. Hence it consisted not only of present sensory impressions causing feelings in the subject, but (due to memorisation through after-images) of 'represented also; not isolated but in combinations and groups; in fact, a full and varied picture, changing its content from moment to moment'.[123] By 1898 in *The Metaphysic of Experience*, Hodgson had reformulated his concept into 'the great stream or moving panorama of a Subject's consciousness, as it retreats into the past of memory from any given present moment'.[124] Spiegel also calls Stephen Dedalus 'one of the great spectator heroes of modern fiction, refusing to engage in any part of the living spectacle that passes before his eyes'.[125] Hence at different times the images that pass in front of Joyce's characters, but also replay in their consciousness, are variously suggestive of magic lantern shows, moving panoramas or even early films.

Similarly, Huhtamo traces an inevitable switch from moving panorama to film screen as key metaphor for the imagistic flow of consciousness after 1895. Symptomatically, Hodgson too had varied his metaphor by referring to 'that moving picture which sometimes goes under the name of our subjective thought or imagination', thus using a term which could also refer to the panorama's successor medium.[126] Such thinkers even numbered Bergson among them, though he was originally suspicious of such 'mechanistic' analogies. Hence the topos was 'filled with new content that corresponded better with changed technological realities' (*IiM*, p. 351). Joyce's correspondence reflects this further shift in inter-medial discursivity and the common imaginary. In 1906, in a particularly fluid and multi-topical missive from Rome, Joyce noted, 'The Italian imagination is like a cinematograph, observe the style of my letter.'[127] While recovering from eye surgery two years after *Ulysses*, Joyce referred to involuntary memory as a kind of endless interior screening of past life: 'whenever I am obliged to lie with my eyes closed I see a cinematograph going on and on and it brings back to my mind things I had almost forgotten'. Similarly, he described the imagistic flow of his dreams as 'prolonged cinema nights'.[128]

The methods by which Joyce thus orchestrates an implied 360-degree panoptic overview of city life, with mobilised, street-level immersion and intensely subjective, psychological focalisation – reflecting the three principal phases of Huhtamo's discursive panorama, but also taking the process forward into the film age – will be examined in detail in the rest of this chapter.

PANORAMIC ANATOMISATION OF THE CITY

In the moving panorama of *Ulysses*, Joyce gathered such tendencies together into the ultimate Modernist anatomisation of a city and the interactions of Dublin's inhabitants, rendered four-dimensionally open to narrative tracking, simultaneous action and virtually 'telepathic' accessibility by his ubiquitous monstrator. In particular, Joyce's text challenges the subordination inscribed in mediations of Ireland within the tradition of panoramic entertainments, which strove to keep it in a position of semi-colonial dependence or touristic exoticism. By such means, Joyce fulfilled the promise made in *Stephen Hero* to 'examine [. . .] the entire community in action and reconstruct [. . .] the spectacle of redemption'.

Both imperial panoramas and fiction's omniscient narrators are ambivalently connected with the rise of surveillance culture in the nineteenth century and with the internalisation of an all-seeing disciplinary gaze, tending to make imperial citizens complicit in their own surveillance. However, Joyce challenges such processes, rejecting the authoritarian role that panoramic tradition played in the construction of Dubliners as imperial British subjects and, like Dickens or Sims, aiming to arouse a more critical kind of moral consciousness instead. Hence, from the point of view of Huhtamo's developing media-cultural imaginary, 'Wandering Rocks' can be seen most illuminatingly as a moving panorama in which all the painted figures on the city streets have become animated into living pictures. Joyce's camera-eyed monstrator thus follows them not just in their alienated and apparently disconnected *flâneuring* through its labyrinthine background, but even inside the spaces of its *trompe l'oeil* buildings. Joyce's monstrator also tracks them though a kind of telepathic access to their most intimate flows of thought as they interact with urban environment and milieu, rendering this as Hodgson's 'moving panorama of a subject's consciousness'. In *Portrait*, Stephen fears that his thoughts will be exposed by the X-ray-like fires of Father Arnall's rhetoric, which threaten to bore through his eyes and brain; in 'Wandering Rocks' Joyce renders both the houses and minds of Dublin's citizenry transparent, like the 'great glass hive' of future London in Wells's scientific fantasies of surveillance, but to ultimately liberating ends.[129]

Anticipating today's surveillance culture, Joyce's characters are tracked as though wearing electronic tags that reveal their whereabouts at any given time on police monitors. 'Wandering Rocks', like so much of Joyce's fiction, is thus pre-eminently about seeing and being seen. Characters are tailed by Joyce's monstrator, but also by one another and sometimes with sinister intent by covert agents of state. In 'Lestrygonians', Bloom is wary about informants in Dublin Castle's pay: 'Never know who you're talking to' (*Ulysses* 8.441). Paul Saint-Amour argues that the city that Joyce's panorama reveals is thus 'a colonial espiocracy',[130] in which information about citizens under observation is fed to government bureaucrats such as Martin Cunningham, who keep files on their activities. Thus undertaker Corny Kelleher and Constable 57C are seen exchanging 'news' about a 'particular party' (*Ulysses* 10.224–5). However, the moving panorama of 'Wandering Rocks' foregrounds 'the nexus of authority and sight-lines',[131] only to critically deconstruct them through its inter-medial method.

MOVING PANORAMAS AND EARLY FILMS IN IRELAND

In his Prologue to *Living London* (1902), Sims indicated a shift from the tropes of the moving panorama to film in how his text represented the metropolis:

> in these pages there is to be enacted before us a great human drama. In them we are to find a breathing, pulsing panorama of living London. Panorama is hardly the word – cinematograph would be a better one, for it is not a London of bricks and mortar that will pass before our eyes, but a London of flesh and blood.[132]

The numerous short articles of the text, with over 450 illustrations (many wide photographs of street scenes and interior close-ups), effectively follow a cross-section of citizens going about their daily lives, tracking them as if by camera-eye.

Similarly, early film actualities of Dublin effectively took visual cross-sections through the diurnal life of Dublin and its inhabitants, at work, rest and play, building up a kind of composite panorama of the city (*MLP&MPS*, p. 249; *EIC*, pp. 70–1). Exploiting the appeal of such local 'topicals', the Thomas-Edison Electric Animated Pictures programme at the Rotunda for December 1901 to May 1902 included prominent city and regional items as 'Dublin Day by Day' and 'Life in Ireland'. Rebranded the Irish Animated Photo Company, Thomas-Edison expanded its list of 'Local Scenes and Daily Events'. Among those screened at the Rotunda in 1903 were several more resonant of particular subjects and motifs in Joyce's fiction, including the *Great Gordon-Bennett Motor Race*, focus of *Dubliners*' 'After the Race'; film of the Juverna bazaar, comparable to the leitmotif of 'Araby' and to the background to *Ulysses*, as we have seen; a funeral, corresponding to *Ulysses*' 'Hades' chapter; as well as the Lord Lieutenant's garden party and Edward VII's procession through Dublin (*MLP&MPS*, p. 249), both of which resonate strongly with 'Wandering Rocks'. That chapter can be seen as Joyce's cinematically panoramic and subversive response to the propagandist mediation of British state events, as demonstrated below. Similarly, Cecil Hepworth's film of Victoria's controversial visit in April 1900 (recently rediscovered by the BFI) was widely screened across the Empire (*MLP&MPS*, pp. 234–5).[133] The camera's defamiliarisation of the details of everyday life or of cultural and political rituals, putting them on screen in living pictures that made them visible in new ways, has clear affinities with Joyce's scrutinising of telling contingencies in both commonplace urban experiences and choreographed public events, capturing unexpected epiphanies through his literary lens.

As Gunning argues, film extended the treatment of urban subjects by older media, but also, potentially, democratised their approach to mediating the spectacle of the modern city environment and its inhabitants:

> The portrayal of the masses, particularly in the modern form of the crowd, posed a challenge to the traditional arts of painting or literature; the naturalist novel and, successively, Impressionist and Futurist painting partly arose from this challenge. But, as Louis Lumière claimed, the cinematic apparatus could 'represent the movement of the streets, of public places, with truly astonishing fidelity'.[134]

Thus film seemed the perfect medium for panoramic effects of crowd movement through urban spaces, while preserving their contingent particularity as human individuals. As Gunning concludes, film sacrificed 'principles of selection and hierarchy found in traditional images', giving its own 'a democracy of composition that matched the subject'.[135] As Monks notes, before the redis-covery of the lost Mitchell and Kenyon stock, 'subjects relating to Ireland were mainly tourist views, royal visits or spectacular events such as the launch of the *Oceanic II*'. However, their thirty-three Irish actualities show a dramatic difference in subjects recorded at the time. Only about five are without sig-nificant numbers of people, providing a visual portal into aspects of everyday urban life in the early 1900s.[136] Hence, in Monks's view, they confirm how panoramas were ceasing to be merely painted environments or passing scenery from train windows, but were being remediated as 'people in the streets filmed from trams', sometimes unawares. Mitchell and Kenyon's city films thus justify the exhibitor's marketing slogan, 'Come and see yourselves', in more ways than one. 'The viewers became the subjects': ordinary people themselves, 'in processions, leaving factories and churches, at sporting events, in street mar-kets, or exiting trains or trams, were for a short period of history the featured attraction'.[137]

In 1915 Vachel Lindsay named this genre 'the picture of Crowd Splen-dour', in *The Art of the Moving Picture*. However, he also thought that film was as yet 'shallow in showing private passion', in preserving a sense of individual subjectivity against its moving panoramic backgrounds.[138] In this context, it is arguable that Joyce managed to negotiate the contradic-tion between an inclusive impression of Dublin's crowded streets and rep-resenting subjective experience through the imagistic flow of his characters' streams of consciousness which interact with the city environment. 'Wander-ing Rocks' thus both reflects and critiques the transition of urban panora-mas into the new medium, influenced by the fact that many of the first films shot in Ireland were themselves extensions of panorama principles. As was Lumière policy, the cinematograph's producer-exhibitors filmed brief actu-alities of busy streets in Dublin and Belfast, as well as 'phantom rides' from trains in and around such cities.[139] Their Irish films and those of Mitchell and Kenyon afterwards relate very strongly to the panorama. Moreover, as Con-don notes, they present 'an up-to-date city framed in the modern progressive technology of the cinema apparatus. Modernity frames modernity; and the Parisian spectator might see a place at roughly the same stage of develop-ment as his or her own city' (*EIC*, p. 126). That early urban actualities tend to look similar internationally emphasises 'the simultaneity of modernity in many parts of the world', contrasting with 'the unequal development' crucial to the colonial 'tourist gaze' (*EIC*, p. 152).[140] Ironically, the pattern also characterised Irish location features shot by British and US companies, which tended not to show Ireland's cities in the throes of modernisation, but 'a place of picturesque landscape and a whimsical premodern people' (*EIC*, p. 126).[141] This was already marked in many lantern tours and panoramic excursions, which, even while sometimes manufactured in Dublin, were neither focused on contemporary urbanism nor necessarily addressed to home audiences (*EIC*, p. 128).

It is likely that 1897's Irish films were shot by the Lumières' roaming operative, Alexandre Promio, himself credited with originating views based on travelling shots from trams and trains, which remediated the simulated vehicles of many moving panoramas. Out of the twenty-five Irish Lumière actualities shot overall, fourteen are street scenes from Dublin and Belfast, and eleven phantom rides of this type (*EIC*, p. 150). Dublin's Empire Theatre was exhibiting Lumière views of the capital in November 1897, on their technically superior 'Triograph'. Among these was a phantom train ride taking in Blackrock and Sandymount, locations very familiar to Joyce and, in Sandymount's case, frequently represented in both *Portrait* and *Ulysses* (both the 'Proteus' and 'Nausicaa' episodes takes place at Sandymount, focusing on Stephen and Bloom, respectively). In a self-reflexive segue between the virtual and real, the 'Dublin Day by Day' series screened from December 1901 to May 1902 included a tramcar ride from Kingsbridge (now Houston Station) to the Rotunda itself where the film was being watched (*MLP&MPS*, p. 242). Mitchell and Kenyon's stock also includes several examples extending this transportive, but also potentially meta-cinematic viewpoint. Their 1901 *Ride on a Tramcar through Belfast* passes a file of men cycling with sandwich boards advertising the North American Photo Company's own programme at Ulster Hall, which commissioned the film. Taken from a horse-drawn tram, it contains a sequence with several others manoeuvring at a terminus like the beginning of *Ulysses*' 'Aeolus' chapter.[142] Mitchell and Kenyon also filmed a phantom ride from Cork as *Illustrated Tram Ride over Patrick's Bridge and Grand Parade* (1902). Their *Train Ride from Blarney* (1902) comprises several films taken on the Cork to Muskerry Light Railway, which ran from the terminus on the Western Road.[143] Although his family had strong Cork connections and might well have been drawn to films of that county, the most Joyceanly suggestive of Mitchell and Kenyon's phantom rides is *Panorama of College Green* (1902). It features prominent shots of central Dublin's 'street furniture' (as *Stephen Hero* dubs it) including statues around College Green and Foster's Place, the west side of the Bank of Ireland and former Irish Parliament House, as well as a random cross-section of perambulating Dubliners, some acknowledging the filming tram in various ways as it progresses through the streets like the viceregal cavalcade in 'Wandering Rocks'.[144]

Moreover, remediation of 'panoramic views' by film was internationally symptomatic and just as likely to have raised Joyce's awareness after leaving Dublin for the Continent. As Uricchio demonstrates, they constitute the single largest title group copyrighted in the United States between 1896 and 1912, preponderantly before 1906. Similarly, in France, Pathé's 1900 catalogue (covering production from 1896) lists '*vues panoramiques*' as one of nine genres, sub-divided into '*scènes panoramiques et de plein air*' and '*vues panoramiques circulaires*'. The genre utilised techniques especially developed to 'capture the grandeur' of the 1900 Paris Exposition, itself dominated by experimental forms of moving panorama as we have seen.[145] (It was also filmed by Edison's team as the phantom boat ride *Panorama of the Paris Exposition from the Seine* [1900].) This suggests that the panorama constituted one of the most popular and influential categories of early film production internationally. Given the ways in which its principles, as Uricchio puts it, 'found form in related technological constellations' throughout the nineteenth century, the specific manner in which the new medium thus positioned itself affords insight not only into how it remediated features of painted, architectural or moving panoramas, but also how its fundamental 'relationship to the world was imagined'.[146] Joyce's texts, especially *Ulysses*, show a parallel awareness of this further mutation in moving panoramas, as an inter-medial and discursive form, and also of what film added to them which was distinctive to its treatment of urban subjects.

Although the first film panoramas tended to replicate Barker's comprehensive *tour d'horizon* through lateral tracking movements, or camera 'pans' as they became known, these were sometimes composed of discontinuous shots edited together. Hence they initiated the process by which filmic mediation of cities became increasingly dependent on montage. Moreover, they rapidly departed from the familiar mode of horizontal panoramas and 'explored space in many different ways' (in Uricchio's terms). Panoramic films extended the immersive and scrolling effects of moving panoramas, which took audiences into, across or up and down painted scenes, in new and sometimes disorientating ways: 'horizontally, vertically, and by tracking shots that penetrated the depths of Albertian perspective'. Panoramic films became, in effect, a large-scale, highly mobile version of the stereograph, opening up cinematic space as if the eye travelled into and ranged around it three-dimensionally.[147] The forward tracking shot, in particular, undermined a fundamental characteristic of the original panorama: 'the image's fixed distance from the spectator'. Zooming into scenes themselves, it shifted the 'extensive relations' constituted by Barker into 'a set of intensive relations – an ever closer inspection of spaces'. Hence by foregrounding and multiplying 'the texture of movement itself' through combinations of techniques, panoramic films offered 'new pleasures and presences' which went beyond even the most ingenious moving panorama shows.[148] This was epitomised in screening modern cityscapes.

Thus films marketed as panoramas bore both significant formal continuities and differences from painted predecessors, attributable to technical innovations and the immersive mapping of space by the camera-eye's simulation of perceptual movement within it, often from moving vehicles, or by alternating 'low' and 'high' angles' from above on buildings and from down below on the street itself. Similarly, editorial excision, compression and linkage (already common in some panorama formats that switched between locations or subjects) became increasingly marked in the fragmentariness of multi-shot films presenting portions of the cityscape at different moments and from diverse points of view. Although early film panoramas 'maintained time and space relations in a rigorously continuous manner', as Uricchio puts it,[149] directors gradually exploited the possibilities of shifted viewpoints and editorial juxtaposition to experiment with montage, complementing the fractured visual planes and multi-perspectivism that characterised Cubist or Futurist treatments of urban subjects.

Film also corresponded to Huhtamo's three stages of discursive panoramic perspective, reprising them in a relatively short span of technical development: from the detached or elevated *tour d'horizon*, to immersion in street-level activity and into increasingly subjectivised viewpoints. As Uricchio points out, vehicle-mounted film panoramas already offered 'vestibular traces' of the texture of movement itself, upsetting the impersonal smoothness of their scanning by a sense of vicarious embodiment: 'The ambient rocking of boats, the bumping, halting, and pacing of wagons on rough city streets, the ebb and flow of traffic and its translation into the fabric of the shot we see, all served to modify the view presented.' Such perturbations revealed the camera 'as a "physicalised" entity', giving access to spaces in a particular way and resituating film panoramas 'within a world far less serene and contemplative' than that portrayed in the painted one. This subverted any illusion of detachment and implicated the viewer in the scene.[150]

Another factor leading to subjectification of point of view concerned 'camera movements as a response to the movement before the camera',[151] in a process related to what Griffith meant by 'objects of attention' for revealing character psychology. Paul's processional panorama of Victoria's 1897 Diamond Jubilee (as shown at the Rotunda) includes some of the earliest panning shots from a camera equipped with fully mobile head.[152] In Edison's Paris film *Champs de Mars* (1900), however, the camera begins to pick out and follow particular pedestrians from the crowd, motivating its panning movement 'on the basis of human interest'. Hence the notion of a view 'dominated by an agency with particular interests' is foregrounded.[153] This would appear to parallel the subjectivisation of perceived movement in Joyce's fiction, extended in *Portrait*'s effect of Stephen's continuously mobilised virtual gaze and multiplied in the focalisers of *Ulysses*' moving panorama, inviting readers to share in and ponder the feelings behind their individual visions at particular moments, but also the motivations of the invisible monstrator who switches between them.

Hence the ways film-makers explored the 'representational capacities' of the new medium by extending panoramic forms find striking parallels in Joyce's fiction. In the same way that the traditional panorama's impersonal 'mastery of a visual domain' is gradually 'subverted by the marks of a mediator' in early films,[154] Joyce's monstrative technique challenges a totalising, imperial overview of Dublin. *Ulysses* foregrounds the capacity to orchestrate points of view more democratically, inviting readers to construct a moving and immersive montage from multiple locations and perspectives. This subverts the seamless rendering of location or event in the original panorama by a more critically Modernist transaction with the reader's own capacity for responding creatively to switches in viewpoint (also marked by a dioramically shifting temporality, rather than 'frozen' in a three-dimensional instant). Thus, Joyce's reader cooperates in the process of assembling an alternative psychogeography of Dublin as lived by its inhabitants. In his own experimentally cinematic extension of the discursive panorama, Joyce opted instead for presenting the Irish metropolis from a critically anti-colonial viewpoint. He emphasises Dublin's universal, modernising possibilities as urban centre through *Ulysses*' inter-medial form, which focuses precisely on how both the perspectives of imperialism and internalised (self-) repression hold its citizens back. Hence, as moving panoramic novel, it laid down an influential, cosmopolitan template for Modernist representations of the city in both fiction and film. While distinctive to his home town, this proved eminently transferable into different national contexts and forms.

There was ongoing inter-mediality between panoramic representation of the metropolis in Modernist fiction exemplified by *Ulysses* and in film. This conceptual and discursive cluster of modernity/city/cinema seemed to be ultimately concerned not just with specific metropolises, but with creating a kind of 'cognitive mapping'[155] of the experience of urban modernity by exploring the potential of film for remediating the panoramic. If the original circular panoramas represented a whole city in an instant of time, seen from a rotational perspective, the diorama with its transformational effects began to mobilise urban time itself by representing diurnal changes in a span of the city's horizon. Both modernist documentary films and Joyce's *Ulysses* would merge and develop these forms into a dynamic montage of city space and time across roughly twenty-four hours, continually shifting between simultaneous activities and contrasting locations to constitute an impression of the city's physical and social totality as a narrative unfolding in text and on screen. Hence, as moving panorama, *Ulysses* emulates the critical juxtapositions achieved by parallel editing techniques in lanternism and early film, but also anticipates the large-scale orchestration of such devices in the editorial structures of the Big City Symphony genre.

ULYSSES AS MOVING PANORAMA: ANTICIPATIONS OF THE BIG CITY SYMPHONIES

The panorama quickly went from being one of the most common titles in film's first decade to disappear 'almost without a trace' during its second,[156] as narrative features replaced its attractions as a genre in their own right. Panoramic effects nonetheless remained part of the technical repertoire of films set in cities, whether sensational fiction or expositional documentary, climaxing in the Big City Symphony montage genre, which flourished from the mid-1920s and shared many characteristics with *Ulysses*.

In an essay published in 2003, I compared *Ulysses* – especially 'Wandering Rocks' – to these Big City Symphonies, focusing on their common 'cross-sectional' method; not only in cutting between geographical and social locations, but juxtaposing multiple perceptions of phenomena in the urban scene.[157] These 'day-in-the-life-of-a-big-city' films, particularly Alberto Cavalcanti's *Rien que les heures* (1925), Walther Ruttmann's *Berlin: Sinfonie einer Großstadt* (1927) and Dziga Vertov's *Man with a Movie Camera* (1929), are avant-garde screen panoramas of contemporary metropolises in France, Germany and the Soviet Union, respectively. Joyce considered Ruttmann a suitable alternative candidate to Eisenstein for adapting *Ulysses* because of *Berlin*'s achievement.[158] (*Berlin* even uses a kind of whirling spiral motif to signify the perceptual overload of the city in ways that seem to echo Joyce's metaphor of entrapment in Dublin's urban labyrinth.) However, had Joyce also known Vertov's work, he might have added him to his shortlist.[159] Interestingly, the Jerry Reisman and Louis Zukofsky scenario for adapting *Ulysses* (written in consultation with Joyce in the 1930s), although not treating 'Wandering Rocks' as a discrete episode as such, nonetheless intersperses its method between episodes across their whole scenario to widen the viewpoint panoramically. Thus it foregrounds Dublin as a 'principal character' in its own right throughout the day, cross-cutting for effects of simultaneity through Stephen and Bloom's urban milieu in ways that suggest the scenarists' own familiarity with the Big City Symphony genre.[160]

In Big City Symphonies, continuous dynamic cross-cutting between locations, social levels and activities creates the impression of a civic totality by prompting the spectator to make connections between them. Their counterpart Modernist literary fictions similarly enlist the reader in constructing connections from suggestive 'intervals', as Vertov called them in his theory of montage.[161] However, this chapter revisits my 2003 argument in ways informed by the pre-filmic history of panoramas to show how Joyce's apparent foreshadowing of the cinematic methods of Big City documentaries is in fact another indication of how his imaginative relationship with nineteenth-century visual media primed him to engage with film with extraordinary creativity and foresight; in this case, with its parallel capacity for remediating panoramic techniques to represent the city and its inhabitants in new ways.

Christie argues that the development of cinema and of urban modernity were coterminous: 'An appetite or habit was being created . . . an industry emerging to feed it. Movies had become the mirror of modern life – which meant city life.'[162] Similarly, Siegfried Kracauer argued that film's primary cultural function is to 'confront us with our visible environment', a project inherited from the panoramic tradition which helps explain focus on the city in both Modernist fiction and film-making as modernity's representative location.[163] Similarly, recognising affinities between cinema and the city, Benjamin asserted that changes in technology do not just affect culture in the abstract, but are linked to changes in our perception of experience in lived ways: 'The film corresponds to profound changes in the perceptive apparatus – changes that are experienced on an individual scale by the man in the street in big-city traffic.'[164] However, Benjamin also believed that this process began with the panorama, which marked an initial 'upheaval in the relation of art to technology'. Its dioramic and moving forms, which strove to produce naturalistic and highly sensory illusions of change, prepared 'the way not only for photography, but for film and sound film'.[165] In this context, the Modernist novel's critical engagement with panoramic mediation of the city in successive forms, questing models for reimagining the individual's ideological relationship with the social totality, is a key cultural development exemplified by Joyce.[166]

Association between film and Modernist representation of the metropolis was already thoroughly self-conscious by *Ulysses*, seventeen years after the Lumières invented the cinematograph. As Pound wrote in a 1921 review of Jean Cocteau's poetry, 'In the city, the visual impressions succeed each other, overlap, overcross, they are cinematographic.'[167] Consequently, for Pound, Ruttmann's City Symphony came to epitomise the modern metropolis's generic rhythm as cinematic space and convinced him that this could be simultaneously captured both on screen and in text by avant-garde methods:

> in the Grossstadt Symphony we have at last a film that will take serious aesthetic criticism: one that is in the movement, and that should flatten out the opposition (to me, to Rodker's *Adolphe*) with steam-rolling ease and commodity, not of course that the authors intended it [. . .] It would be simple snobism [*sic*] not to accept the cinema, on such terms, as being, on parity with the printed page . . .[168]

However, *Ulysses'* central chapter, 'Wandering Rocks', devised an influential literary-cinematic template for representing the city panoramically five years before Ruttmann. Joyce named 'mechanics' as its dominant art, and film was mechanical art *par excellence*, though other technological entertainments laid the basis for it and were remediated by it. His own emulation of its panoramic potentials helped break up the city's linear time and homogeneous space, coordinating events in different locations all over Dublin. As Ruth Frehner points out in her essay on simultaneism in 'Wandering Rocks', 'the new medium of film could extend the present moment, "the here and now", to a "here and now and anywhere"', breaking down Gotthold Lessing's famous distinction in his

Laocoon: An Essay on the Limits of Painting and Poetry (1767) between the temporal *Nacheneinander* of textual narrative and the spatial *Nebeneinander* of visual art.[169] Kern argues that *Ulysses* was '[t]he highpoint of simultaneous literature' and that Joyce's precocious fascination with film montage, *avant la lettre*, made this possible.[170] However, as we have seen, well before filmic models, diverse examples of episodic and elliptical presentation through editorial condensations of diegetic time and space were already available to Joyce in magic lantern and moving panorama shows; moreover, in forms that influenced film as well as textual equivalents evolving alongside them. Joyce's panoramic techniques showed 'the simultaneous activity of Dublin as a whole, not a history of the city but a slice of it out of time, spatially extended and embodying its entire past in a vast expanded present'.[171] Thus the imaginative effect of reading *Ulysses* is of 360-degree textual horizons fading to the distant vanishing point in space and time. With characteristic hyperbole, Joyce even boasted that the sheer accuracy and detail of its cognitive mapping would be so comprehensive that if the real Dublin were destroyed it would be possible to rebuild it from his textual replica.[172]

Hence in *Ulysses'* most explicitly panoramic chapter, Joyce intended to bring Dublin 'even more fully into the book by focusing upon it rather than upon Bloom or Stephen', in Ellmann's words.[173] In this sense, like the Big City Symphonies that followed, 'Wandering Rocks' breaks away from dependence on plot, protagonists and conventional narrative structure, into *Ulysses'* most radically 'synoptic' mode.[174] However, Joyce also manages to articulate the individual's often disorientating, lived experience of urban complexity through orchestrating Huhtamo's three developmental phases in the discursive panorama. His monstration constantly shifts between an implied all-seeing, Daedalian aerial perspective; zooming down to immerse the viewpoint in a close-up moving panorama of street-level action; then switching between various flows of lesser characters' streams of consciousness. In doing so, he not only anticipates the cross-sectional structure of Big City Symphonies, but also provides a democratically subjective psychogeography, which their synoptic methods – effectively limited to Huhtamo's first two phases only through a relative lack of focalising personae – do not tend to accommodate.

Panoramic Structure and Methods in 'Wandering Rocks'

Each of Joyce's nineteen cinematic segments shows a different facet of Dublin and its citizens, but also their parallelism and simultaneity. Kern argues that Joyce deploys five basic devices to achieve this: 1) multiple accounts of a character from different perspectives; 2) repetition of action in different episodes; 3) narration that begins repeatedly; 4) multiple appearance of objects in linear movement (e.g. the handbill and viceregal cavalcade), which unite Dublin spatially and also provide temporal markers; and 5) a final recapitulation – the cavalcade which 'cross-sections' the city by means of all the characters and places it passes by. This last motif in particular suggests spatial and social interrelatedness and provides a point of juncture for all the events that occur, leading to 'the final summation of the simultaneity of [the chapter's] movements'.[175]

Before unpacking the implications of Kern's five devices in detail, it is worth reminding ourselves of the connotations of Joyce's mythic parallel, in this case not Homer, but another Greek epic, the third-century BC *Argonautica*, as noted in the Gilbert and Linati Schemata. The Wandering Rocks or 'Symplegades' imperilled ships entering the straits of the Bosphorus by clashing together. Joyce's symbolic avatars are the mobilised spiritual and temporal powers of modern Dublin, personified by the 'very reverend John Conmee S.J.', on foot and by tram, and the British Viceroy of Ireland, in his state coach.[176] Significantly, just as moving panoramas often centred on the famous and powerful in civic processions, parades and gala events, so did many early films. Among Mitchell and Kenyon's Irish ones, shots of dignitaries in state coaches are prominent, particularly in the Cork Exhibition films of 1902, with crowds of locals reacting as individuals with varying levels of enthusiasm. For example, there may be no surviving footage of Dublin's historical Lord Lieutenant, William Humble Ward, Earl of Dudley (viceroy 1902–05), in his state coach, but there is of Dublin's Lord Mayor's (among other 'big nobs', as Stephen calls them) in films such as Mitchell and Kenyon's *Trade Procession at Opening of Cork Exhibition* (1902) (see figure 3.3). The viceroy nonetheless became a familiar figure at screenings of such prestigious events and was courted by the film industry as a patron. In a self-reflexive loop, he watched himself presenting medals to Irish troops returning from the Boer War, among other Thomas-Edison Electric Animated Pictures, as guest of honour at their Rotunda benefit programme on 24 April 1902. Accompanied by Lady Dudley, he patronised further programmes at the same venue in 1903 (*EIC*, p. 244). Similarly Father Conmee, while not appearing on film in person, nonetheless famously left a textual trace on a poster picked out by Mitchell and Kenyon's cameraman in *Congregation Leaving Jesuit Church of St. Francis Xavier* (1902), a venue mentioned frequently in *Ulysses* and adjacent to the presbytery from which Conmee descends at the beginning of 'Wandering Rocks' (*Ulysses* 10.1). To the right of the church door on screen is an advertisement for a forthcoming sermon on Sunday 11 January 1903, in aid of the Convent of our Lady of Charity, St Mary's Asylum, Drumcondra. The sermoniser is 'Revd. J. Conmee, S.J.'[177]

Joyce's moving 'hazards', representing theological and temporal powers, are tracked panoramically through Dublin's streets, on courses apparently unconnected but symbolically convergent, marking out a kind of ideological force field within which his cross-section of citizens' lives are played out, both physically and subjectively. It is characteristic of *Ulysses'* rich textuality that

Figure 3.3 Screengrab from Sagar Mitchell and James Kenyon, *Trade Procession at Opening of Cork Exhibition* (1902). Reproduced with kind permission of the BFI.

so many details are magnetised towards this danger of being symbolically crushed between two apparently conflicting powers circulating through the city. For example, Master Dignam's boyish enthusiasm for a poster advertising a boxing match, another popular film subject from kinetoscope loops onwards (boxing featured prominently in early Dublin film programmes),[178] contrasts with Stephen's pacifist scepticism about the spectacle and benefits of force (*Ulysses* 10.1131–49, 10.831–5), thus creating a kind of metaphor for the adversarial pattern of Irish history, whose central dynamic is a cult of 'heroic' masculinity (prominently celebrated on the imperial side in battle panoramas). Consequently, narrative strands from previous chapters continue to unspool through chapter 10, meshing in particularly suggestive ways both through physical contiguity and, in particular, visual cross-referencing. The 'title' thus also refers to Joyce's structural technique, both satirical and cinematic, based on ironic juxtaposition equivalent to the visual clashes of 'collision montage' produced by radical editing, with its roots in the deadly parallels of socially critical lantern shows and early films. Through this technique, Joyce's monstrator draws the reader actively into their moving subversion of the city's spiritual and temporal agencies and their attendant symbolic networks.

The chapter's Baudelairean *flânerie* is also related to 'wandering' more positively, particularly if emulating a roving camera-eye in the immersive panorama that Joyce presents at street level. This suggests that Joyce, like Benjamin, came to view the camera as the ultimate *flâneur*, whose defamiliarising gaze might render everyday modernity readable as a cultural, social and political text. Joyce's 'footage' of Dublin was edited to create a dynamically coordinated, multi-track narrative of overlapping, episodic shots rather than conclusive scenes. Indeed, 'Wandering Rocks' is realistic in a simultaneously panoramic, but also cinematic way by suggesting a virtually overwhelming contexture of potential narrative connections and visual details too numerous for any reader/spectator to follow up, which recede into its imaginary horizons, simulating a whole metropolis.

Joyce applied filmic techniques to refining his Flaubertian process of narrative impersonality, radiating subtle implications, rather than pausing for authorial comment. The alternating focalisers of 'Wandering Rocks' can be likened to mobile, intra-diegetic cameras. They record, but also impose, in that we 'see' aspects of street-level Dublin from their subjective and partial viewpoints, as it is 'thought through [their] eyes', to adapt Stephen's phrase about simultaneity of vision and cognition from 'Proteus'. But they are also 'caught on camera', presented as seen either by others or by Joyce's invisible third-person monstrator, orchestrating their implicit overview with editorial freehand.

Moreover, just as Stephen's mobilised gaze is enhanced by mechanised vehicles in *Portrait*, trams play a prominent part in traversing and mapping Joyce's panoramic cityscape. As director Patrick Keiller argues, Mitchell and Kenyon's stock typifies how the stability and ubiquity of the new electric tram (a key metonym for turn-of-the-twentieth-century modernity) developed in symbiosis with panoramic film-making, vastly expanding the Edwardian city's 'virtual landscape' both in terms of spatial amplitude and duration. Tram and film companies often collaborated to mutual advantage.[179] Hence the more than 48 hours of rediscovered actuality footage by Mitchell and Kenyon has literally expanded the virtual landscape of the British and Irish past c. 1900 partly due to how this is explored and reconstituted by films taken from trams as new, democratically 'Odyssean' vessels, navigating modernity's urban-capitalist nexus (albeit Dublin trams were less accessible than others, because unusually high fares meant that only better-off commuters could afford to ride them regularly from suburbs to centre, thus being insulated from poorer districts, like Father Conmee).[180]

'Wandering Rocks' cross-sections around an hour (2:55–4:00 p.m.) of Dublin life. It begins with explicit space-time coordinates, immersing readers at a precise point in Joyce's urban panorama as it starts to move: 'The superior, the very reverend John Conmee S.J. reset his smooth watch in his interior pocket as he came down the presbytery steps. Five to three' (*Ulysses* 10.1–3). First Conmee's progress is 'tracked' objectively, by third-person, extra-diegetic camera, as it were, alternating with Conmee's own stream of consciousness and sighting by others. (As noted, Joyce's characters are both subjective camera-eyes, seeing and being seen in brief encounters, but always framed by the implied panoramic overview of his anonymous monstrator.) Subtle thematic linkages are immediately initiated, through apparently random encounters: Conmee blesses in passing a 'onelegged sailor' instead of giving alms, snobbishly retaining the price of a fare so he can take the tram to avoid traversing the poorer quarters on foot. The same mendicant is seen singing by other characters at different moments and locations, as a linking motif repeated with variations throughout (buskers are similarly prominent in socially cross-sectional lantern shows and Big City Symphonies). Conmee's stream of consciousness also relates him to other pedestrians: for example, as director of Belvedere, the son of Paddy Dignam (whose funeral Bloom attended in 'Hades') is much on his mind; Master Dignam shows up in person in segments 9 and 18. The sailor is singing 'For England, Home and Beauty', which sets Conmee briefly thinking about men maimed fighting for national causes, but also subtly begins to align his viewpoint and movements with the 'temporal' power of the viceroy. The chapter's panoramic structure is thus symphonic, like Ruttmann or Vertov's films, in how it repeats and orchestrates particular images and themes first glimpsed in this 'overture' with variations in distance, duration, key and tone: its many wandering ecclesiasticals, for example, are a leitmotif of mobilised agency and ideological pervasiveness. As the Revd Nicholas Dudley (whose surname echoes the Lord Lieutenant's earldom) steps off an 'inward bound tram' on Newcomen Bridge, Conmee simultaneously boards an outbound tram (*Ulysses* 10.108–10). Repetition of this clerical motif also builds ironic sectarian-colonial connections and contrasts: the Revd Hugh C. Love and Father Cowley are later revealed as Protestant landlord and his impoverished Catholic tenant, threatened with eviction.

The chapter's many chance encounters vividly demonstrate how strands of different individual urban narratives continuously 'succeed each other, overlap, overcross' (in Pound's cinematographic terms), creating an overwhelming impression of panoramic scale and informational excess, which deliberately taxes both the reader's retrospective knowledge of the text and proleptic intuitions. Joyce emphasises the partialness of what we see when we randomly brush through mundane moments in others' lives, but also, unlike impersonal documentary films, how subjective history, memory and thought processes interact with present impressions in our urban environment. Thus he emphatically brings together Huhtamo's three levels of visualisation in the discursive panorama, connecting panoptic overview and moving street-level immersion with the inward image-track of individual streams of consciousness into a cinematic totality that only the reader can complete. To return to Conmee observed by Joyce's monstrator on the tram, we simultaneously see passengers through Conmee's eyes (implicitly cutting in through their own narratives as it were), but also with a tension between the external intimacy of close-ups in present time and the interiority of flashbacks triggered by Conmee's own 'remembering eyes' (to borrow *Portrait*'s expression):

> The gentleman with the glasses opposite Father Conmee had finished explaining and looked down. His wife, Father Conmee, supposed.
> A tiny yawn opened the mouth of the wife of the gentleman with glasses. She raised her small gloved fist, yawned ever so gently, tiptapping her small gloved fist on her opening mouth and smiled tinily, sweetly.
> Father Conmee perceived her perfume in the car. He perceived also that the awkward man at the other side of her was sitting on the edge of the seat.
> Father Conmee at the altarrails placed the host with difficulty in the mouth of the awkward old man who had the shaky head. (*Ulysses* 10.122–32)

Similarly to *Portrait*, Joyce creates a deft interplay of visual and verbal puns foregrounding the 'individuating rhythm' of Conmee's perceptions and thought processes. Having fantasised about being 'Don John Conmee', conducting lavish nobility weddings in a romanticised past while simultaneously relishing a *frisson* of forbidden eroticism, Conmee walks past a field full 'of cabbages curtseying to him with ample underleaves' (*Ulysses* 10.180–1). Then with farcical simultaneity, his peripatetic reading of the breviary is interrupted by an incident externalising the undercurrent flowing through his mind:

> A flushed young man came from a gap of a hedge and after him came a young woman with wild nodding daisies in her hand. The young man raised his cap abruptly: the young woman abruptly bent and with slow care detached from her light skirt a clinging twig. (*Ulysses* 10.199–202)

Joyce's next segment opens with another striking example of diegetic montage creating an impression of panoramic simultaneity, by switching back to Corny Kelleher in O'Neill's Funeral Parlour at the moment he sighted Conmee boarding his tram. Similarly, Kelleher's debriefing by Constable 57C is momentarily intercut through a visual match with a synedochic close-up of Molly Bloom. The contemptuous arc of hayjuice that the informant spits is juxtaposed with her 'generous white arm' flinging a coin from the window of No. 7 Eccles Street (10.221–3). Again it is only in the next section, when this

instantaneous and cropped image is expanded (in terms of both temporal duration, but also visual width), that we learn that Molly is bestowing charity on
the one-legged sailor passed up by Conmee, whereas the transaction between
Kelleher and the constable has a distinctly venal basis. This ironic connectivity
is reinforced by how the expanded image echoes Conmee's visual Freudian slip
about lingerie-like 'underleaves':

> The gay sweet chirping whistling within went on a bar or two, ceased.
> The blind of the window was drawn aside. A card *Unfurnished Apart-
> ments* slipped from the sash and fell. A plump bare generous arm shone,
> was seen, held forth from a white petticoatbodice and taut shiftstraps.
> (*Ulysses* 10.249–53)

With similarly panoramic coordination, the shot of the sailor's encounter
with Katy and Boody Dedalus in the following segment (4) is then expanded
as the narrative scene of the following one, which nevertheless keeps Conmee's
progress through Clongowes fields, 'thinsocked ankles tickled by stubble',
satirically in view by brief insert (*Ulysses* 10.264–5). Katy and Boody are
back home eating hand-out soup and listening to Maggy lamenting her failure
to pawn Stephen's books at McGuinness's (owned by the same well-heeled
woman who Conmee sucks up to in the opening section). But Joyce's panoramic connections can be prospective as well as retrospective, foretelling creatively 'asynchronous' sound in the talkies as Eisenstein argued.[181] The scene
in the Dedalus household is intercut with a bell-ringing lackey at Dillon's auc-
tion rooms, where their other sister Dilly begs their Micawberish father for
vital household expenses seven sections later. In an almost Chinese box-like
manner this leads into another cross-cutting sound effect: Dilly 'loitering by
the curbstone', listening to the bell and auctioneer shouting inside, is spliced
with the sound-match of the 'lastlap bell' for street-racing cyclists 'stretched
necks wagging' rhythmically, negotiating the bend by Trinity College library
(*Ulysses* 10.645, 651–3), yet another processional event tracked through town.
Throughout, Joyce's moving panoramic technique maintains a deadly parallel
between squalid poverty and public displays of religious sanctimony and colonial pomp, epitomised by continuous cutting back and forth both to Conmee's
progress and the viceregal cavalcade. It is also worth considering the possibility that if Griffith's prototype 'parallel editing' was the model most famously
available on film for this technique at the time Joyce wrote 'Wandering Rocks'
(as David Trotter argues), then Joyce deliberately subverts and repurposes it.[182]
Griffith used parallel editing to build melodramatic excitement towards violent
showdowns between hero and villain, which became known as the 'Griffith
climax'. His technique tended towards hysteria and ideologically dubious
ends, epitomised by the accelerating visual rhythm of the Ku Klux Klan racing

towards the plantation-owning Cameron family to rescue them from besieging ex-slaves in *Birth of a Nation* (1915). Alternatively, in the Jewish Bloom's pacifist avoidance of his rival Boylan, Joyce substitutes emotionally restrained and reflective non-confrontation (and thus more enlightened gender politics) for the macho and sometimes racist heroics of last-minute rescues of heroines in peril. Joyce's summative finale, repurposing such panoramic methods of parallel editing and processional tracking, also has a distinctly anti-climactic, even bathetic effect compared to Griffith's (as discussed below). There is no showdown between Bloom and Boylan. Instead both Bloom and Stephen quietly slip from narrative view and thus escape being caught in the clash of spiritual and colonial powers governing the city.

The current section (4) closes with another ironic parallel referencing Conmee's spiritual mission, a close-up 'tracking shot' of the handbill discarded by Bloom in chapter 8, publicising a rival tour by American evangelist Alexander J. Dowie, floating down the Liffey:

> A skiff, a crumpled throwaway, Elijah is coming, rode lightly down the Liffey, under Loopline bridge, shooting the rapids where water chafed around the bridgepiers, sailing eastwards past hulls and anchorchains, between the Customhouse old dock and George's quay. (*Ulysses* 10.294–7)

Joyce continuously cross-cuts to the progress of this 'throwaway' for the rest of the chapter (it is seen again at 10.752–4, 1096–9, etc.), perhaps parodying in miniature the river voyages typical of the moving panorama genre. Another avant-garde German city film, Berthold Viertel and Béla Baláz's *Die Abenteuer eines Zehnmarkscheins* (1924), features an impersonal object to intimately connect a cross-section of urban characters by the ironic economic interdependencies of poverty and wealth, as the ten mark note is progressively exchanged and tracked across Berlin. The bloodstream was the 'organ' Joyce assigned to chapter 10. Hence the handbill, along with the 'circulation' of other documents, newspapers, commodities and signs, lays bare multiple forms of ordinarily invisible contiguities, moral, social, economic, and so on, in much the same way that Ruttmann represents the workings of Berlin as a 'circulatory system' within a capitalist network of exchange. Other examples would be the sandwichmen advertising 'H.E.L.Y.S' stationer's, which anticipate Ruttmann's Surrealistic file of dummy negroes advertising 'Bullrich Magensalz' ('Bullrich's Stomach Salts') (see figure 3.4), ironically combining breadline labour for some with a temporary cure for over-consumption by others;[183] or the poster publicising 'Marie Kendall, charming soubrette', seen by many Dubliners in different locations and circumstances that invite inevitable comparison and contrast between them (for instance, 10.380–3 and 1141–4, among others).

Figure 3.4 Still from Walther Ruttmann (dir.), *Berlin: Sinfonie einer Großstadt* (1927). Courtesy of BFI National Archive, reproduced by kind permission of Eva Riehl.

The handbill 'laps' evocatively into the next section (5) through close-up visual matching with tissue paper in which luxurious accessories to seduction are being wrapped for Blazes Boylan (another man on a mission) for his rendezvous with Molly later that afternoon. Appropriately, Boylan's dishonourable intentions (and general caddishness) are monstrated by the silent innuendo of 'speaking objects' as the shopgirl prepares his basket of fruit: 'She bestowed fat pears neatly, head by tail, and among them ripe shamefaced peaches' (*Ulysses* 10.305–6). This motivates Boylan's own 'Carry On' double-entendre, which virtually cries out for invention of the soundtrack: 'May I say a word to your telephone, missy? he asked roguishly' (10.336).

In line with Joyce's declared intention to sideline his main characters in their panoramic urban environment and social milieu, a 'shot' of Bloom momentarily cuts into this segment, but only as a nameless silhouette at the periphery of its vision: 'A darkbacked figure under Merchant's arch scanned books on the hawker's cart' (*Ulysses* 10.315–16). Only five sections later is this enigmatic shot expanded into revealing close-ups of the *risqué* texts that Bloom is thumbing through, almost as if the monstrator's extra-diegetic camera zooms in to peep over his shoulder. Similarly, at the beginning of the next section (6), Stephen appears for the first time in the chapter, though even more truncated, all but cropped out of the frame through his singing teacher's focalisation: '*Ma!* Almidano Artifoni said. He gazed over Stephen's shoulder at Goldsmith's knobby poll' (i.e. the head of playwright Oliver Goldsmith's statue outside Trinity College, *Ulysses* 10.338–9). This exemplifies Joyce's highly cinematic metonymy (already rife in *Portrait*'s 'vivisective' method, as demonstrated above), cutting people up into moving body parts, clothing and functions. It is used to brilliant satirical effect in grotesque freeze-frame or snapshot-like close-ups in the chapter's elongated last sentence. The variable 'angling' of Joyce's shots also prefigures its bathos through potentially slapstick parallels with the hazards of the classical myth threatening his urban navigators: 'While he waited in Temple bar McCoy dodged a banana peel with gentle pushes of his toe from the path to the gutter' (*Ulysses* 10.512–13). A bookseller similarly defuses the slippery hazard of a 'gob of phlegm' (10.634–5).

In section 8, rackrent 'reverend Hugh C. Love' (appropriately to both panoramic theme and technique with recessive horizons in space and time) is researching a book on the Fitzgerald family, themselves powerful landlords from the Anglo-Irish Ascendancy. Moreover, Love is using a camera as a documentary aid on location. This cues Joyce's self-conscious reference to setting up multiple points of view and the camera's role as ubiquitous prosthetic to human sight, enhancing merely organic vision: 'Certainly, Ned Lambert said. Bring the camera whenever you like. I'll get those bags cleared away from the windows. You can take it from here or from here' (*Ulysses* 10.420–2). Joyce too, by continually 'taking it from here or from here', builds up a minute-by-minute, moving cross-sectional panorama, which challenges Dublin's dominant image in the imperial media of his time, but also creates a flexible template for subsequent representations of the living spectacle of the metropolis in both Modernist fiction and film. By means of meticulously coordinated and interlocking devices, he builds up a multi-perspectival montage taken from every possible defamiliarising angle.

Alongside screen panoramas, according to Stephen Bottomore, the genre of 'local films' taken wherever crowds congregated proliferated internationally in film's first decade, peaking around 1901–02. Some of these followed the typical genres of the Lumières' first programme, such as the 'factory gate film' (after *La Sortie des usines*) as in *Workers Leaving the Railway Works, Inchicore* (*MLP&MPS*, p. 242). Their chief attraction was the chance to recognise yourself or your locality, but also to see them in a new way. Gradually, fixed-camera factory gate and church porch scenes gave way to more panoramic films of organised local events watched by crowds, such as processions, parades and pageants.[184] Such mobile subjects doubled as topical attractions in themselves and signalled a shift from the mere appeal of seeing yourself or your milieu, although that remained a potential bonus even as the genre evolved into local newsreels and dramas. As Lumière panoramas and local topicals by others such as Mitchell and Kenyon built up a cinematic mosaic of Dublin around the time Joyce's novel is set, they also raised its population's awareness of their own potential visibility and mediation through increasing 'camera-mindedness'.

Similarly, 'Wandering Rocks' devises ingenious parallels for this cumulative, visual self-consciousness, which would be elaborated by Cavalcanti and Rutt-mann though the pervasive presence of photography and cinemas in their films, sometimes freezing moments into stills, then restarting the action or showing audiences watching screens-within-the-screen. This climaxes in the famously meta-cinematic structure of *Man with a Movie Camera*, in which subjects contin-uously interact with Vertov's roving camera and the material results are shown being edited as celluloid strips, and then projected. Joyce brilliantly foregrounds how Dublin's inhabitants, increasingly but ambivalently conscious of observa-tion in the public spaces of the modern city environment for both commercial and surveillance purposes, continuously perform versions of themselves as if in defensive expectation of being spotted and recorded. Many of his Dubliners con-struct themselves so as to be seen in 'Wandering Rocks', as if the street were a stage or film set, continually checking their external image in reflective surfaces, especially on this June day of organised civic spectacle for the opening of the Mirus bazaar. For example, in section 12, the same Tom Kernan who barred 'the magic-lantern business' in *Dubliners* nonetheless preens 'before the sloping mirror of Peter Kennedy, hairdresser', as if on the off-chance of being snapshot-ted as an extra in today's big production. He also tries to catch brief glimpses of others passing by, as if in the adventitious flash of a camera: 'Is that Ned Lambert's brother over the way, Sam? What? Yes. He's as like it as damn it. No. The windscreen of that motor car in the sun there. Just a flash like that. Damn like him' (10.757–60). Ironically, Kernan subsequently misses the moment of his own big photo-opportunity, as it were. Distracted by remembering a sentimental ballad from the failed 1798 Rebellion, the viceregal coach unexpectedly flashes past before Kernan has time to catch his Excellency's eye and be reciprocally acknowledged, like a fawning bystander picked out in a press photo or filmshot of the procession itself:

> A cavalcade in easy trot along Pembroke quay passed, outriders leaping, leaping in their, in their saddles. Frockcoats. Cream sunshades.
> Mr Kernan hurried forward, blowing pursily.
> His Excellency! Too bad! Just missed that by a hair. Damn it! What a pity! (10.794–8)

The pompous spectacle of British rule, visualised through Kernan's flustered focalisation, is nonetheless captured as a vividly cinematic impression by

Joyce's monstrator. His elastic syntax mimics the rising and falling rhythm of the cavalry escort in their saddles leading the way, while the precise sequencing of his nouns picks out key details from its mobile Gestalt as they enlarge in passing close by: outriders first, formal outfits of male dignitaries, then parasols obscuring female companions. As we have seen, *Portrait*'s genetics suggest Joyce's precocious and enduring interest in animal locomotion studies and the radically defamiliarising implications of close-up instantaneous photography which led to film. At the other end of the visual scale, Muybridge was also instrumental in transferring the immersive forms of the panorama into these new media. His composite photographic *tours d'horizon* of cities, such as his 13-section, 17-foot long wraparound image of San Francisco, are particularly significant in this respect.[185]

Ulysses is suffused with a desire to spot and exploit visual opportunities in its cityscape, epitomised not least through Bloom's fixation with catching moving 'flashes' of women's ankles and how this reveals Joyce's own fascination with what Mullin calls 'the erotics of everyday life', and hence a shared camera-mindedness between author and character.[186] Similarly, Georgina Binnie has recently historicised the increasing extent of covert photography for both amateur/voyeuristic and detective/political purposes on Dublin's streets at this time, and its likely influence on Joyce's visual awareness.[187] Spiegel also argues that the final section of 'Wandering Rocks', in its panoramic recapitulation, foregrounds the risks of being caught off guard as if by a kind of ubiquitous candid camera.[188] It displays the contingencies of being arbitrarily 'freeze-framed' mid-way through an action, in an ironic or embarrassing pose suddenly fixed in time forever or, conversely, of accidentally missing or even deliberately rejecting the decisive moment altogether. Similarly, the genre of local films, epitomised by Mitchell and Kenyon's, not only offered opportunities to recognise yourself on screen, but the complementary amusement of also seeing relatives or friends caught out (as Bottomore puts it) 'in a funny or grotesque posture'.[189] In a very Burnsian manner (also quoted by Bloom in 'Lestrygonians' and 'Nausicaa'),[190] Mitchell and Kenyon's films were advertised with the paradoxical slogan 'See Yourselves as Others See You'.[191] It even appeared directly in their filmed processions, reflexively planted on passing show floats like the one Bloom imagines in 'Lestrygonians' and picked out by their camera, as at the Llandudno May Procession of 1907: 'DON'T FAIL TO COME & SEE YOURSELF AS OTHER PEOPLE SEE YOU'.[192]

In 'Wandering Rocks', characters are variously motivated by a semi-colonial complex of desires and anxieties around seeing, being seen and even being recorded on Dublin's streets in the course of Joyce's processional panorama. However, in the final sequence, many are caught almost too candidly in attitudes responding to and subverting the moving spectacle of British rule as the viceregal cavalcade flashes past them.[193] What is officially intended as 'a parade of interpellative exchanges' (as Saint-Amour puts it),[194] in which loyal citizens duly heed the call to salute the passing embodiment of power, thus recognising and accepting their subordination as subjects in Althusserian terms, becomes something very different – a chaotic snapshot album of moments of bungled opportunity, tacit refusal and resistance. Any one could be missed in a blink. Instead they are captured for posterity in all their messy contingency by Joyce's panoramic, camera-eye technique. Similarly, in City Symphonies, the cinematic flow of images is sometimes temporarily stopped to arrest the movements of pedestrians and traffic on the busy streets and fix them in defamiliarised, split-second postures. This foregrounds film's material basis in the Muybridgian snapshot sequence, then blurs it back into life by the eye-con of persistence of vision as strip's flow restarts.

In Kern's terms, the final section of 'Wandering Rocks', by representing the viceregal cavalcade sighted through a whole spectrum of citizens, recapitulates the chapter's strategy for conveying a vividly moving and immersive, 360-degree impression of Dublin's extension in space over a one-hour segment of time:

> The viceroy was most cordially greeted on his way through the metropolis. At Bloody Bridge Mr Thomas Kernan beyond the river greeted him vainly from afar. Between Queen's and Whitworth bridges lord Dudley's viceregal carriages passed and were unsaluted by Mr Dudley White, B.L., M.A, who stood on Arran Quay outside Mrs M.E. White's, the pawnbroker's, at the corner of Arran street west stroking his nose with his forefinger . . . In the porch of Four Courts Richie Goulding . . . saw him with surprise. Past Richmond Bridge at the doorstep of the office of Reuben J Dodd, solicitor . . . an elderly female about to enter changed her plan and retracing her steps by the King's windows smiled credulously on the representative of his majesty. From its sluice in Wood quay wall under Tom Devan's office Poddle river hung out in fealty a tongue of liquid sewage . . . On Ormond Quay Mr Simon Dedalus, steering his way from the greenhouse for the subsheriff's office, stood still in midstreet and brought his hat low. His Excellency graciously returned Mr Dedalus' greeting . . . Gerty MacDowell, carrying the Catesby cork lino letters for her father who was laid up, knew by the style it was the lord and lady lieutenant but she couldn't see what Her Excellency had on because the tram and Spring's big yellow furniture van had to stop in front of her on account of it being the lord lieutenant . . . A charming soubrette, great Marie Kendall, with dauby cheeks and lifted skirt smiled daubily from her poster upon William, Humble, Earl of Dudley . . . (*Ulysses* 10.1182–222)

Beginning as a fawning news report like one of the inflationary parodies from 'Cyclops' or even an inter-title from an urban topical tracking a procession – 'The viceroy was most cordially greeted on his way through the metropolis' – the dignity of the colonial spectacle is systematically subverted by Joyce's monstration of individual reactions picked out from Dublin's crowded streets. The many incongruous gestures and situations recorded as it flashes past – vainly trying to attract attention, nose-stroking indifference, surprise, credulous smiling, doffing, frustratingly blocked viewpoint, and so on – are exactly like a succession of instantaneous photographs or short film inserts of reflex actions caught in *media res*. They democratically fracture the pomp of British rule and the evolving role of panoramas in mediating it. Even when the viceroy's interpellative gaze is actually reciprocated, the subject's reaction often cancels out the process of obeisance: for example, John Wyse Nolan 'smiled with unseen coldness' (10.1212). The satirical effect is amplified by characteristically Joycean visual puns such as Poddle river 'tongue-poking' in mid-flow; Marie Kendall's poster image beaming 'daubily' on everyone, irrespective of rank; the slapstick synchronicity of Master Dignam raising his greasy cap as 'His collar too sprang up' (1267–8); and the abrupt final metonymy of 'Almidano Artifoni's sturdy trousers' in ironic 'salute . . . swallowed by a closing door', before the chapter's 'screen' suddenly blacks out too (1281–2). For all the meticulous choreography of 'Wandering Rocks', Joyce's montage method emphasises awkwardness, tension, interruption and uncontrollably democratic excess rather than a smoothly panoramic, virtual tour of the Irish metropolis and its loyal population, leaving Dublin's officially mediated image within United Kingdom and Empire in distinct disarray.

Hence Joyce's final section replays the cavalcade's progress to simultaneously foreground and subvert how British rule maintains itself through combining 'public spectacle and covert surveillance', as Saint-Amour puts it.[195] This double-edged scopic objective explains Joyce's motive for incorporating a high-profile civic event that did not actually take place for the opening of the real Mirus bazaar, but that nonetheless plays a pivotal role. So significant is the viceroy's fictional procession to *Ulysses*' panoramic background and strategy, as a continuously mediated public event on which characters' viewpoints converge, that Joyce deliberately shifted the bazaar's real opening date (31 May 1904) to 16 June in order to coincide with Bloomsday. Normally obsessively accurate about historical details, Joyce makes this shift underpin other key events and motifs in 'Wandering Rocks'. Turning out on the street to watch simultaneously makes Dubliners available for watching by networks of informants and police, but also by the novel's own panoramic 'circuits of observation' (in Saint-Amour's phrase), which both mimic and subvert them.[196] Hence 'Wandering Rocks' opposes a city-wide, Bentham-like colonial system by opening up its own critical frame around such all-seeing authoritarianism, both real and internalised. In this process, Joyce's creative engagement with the tradition of panoramas and their formational role in the media-cultural imaginary of his time, as continued through the new technologies of photography and film, is crucial. Significantly, neither Stephen nor Bloom are sighted again in the final recapitulation of 'Wandering Rocks'. Does that mean that, like Jason's *Argo* (which sent a dove to test the hazardous straits ahead), they also slip unscathed and unsubordinated through the clash of spiritual and temporal power because Joyce's ruse directs attention elsewhere? Thus as 'a political anatomy of the late-colonial metropolis', as Saint-Amour puts it,[197] 'Wandering Rocks' arguably fulfils the panoramic social and aesthetic mission of the 'modern spirit' described in *Stephen Hero*, by 'examin[ing] the entire community in action and reconstruct[ing] the spectacle of redemption'.[198]

Certainly, 'Wandering Rocks' seems well aware of the formation of a modern media-cultural imaginary associated with an increasingly cinematised cityscape. Joyce foregrounds forms of communication though the inclusion of typists and telephones, cameras, newspapers and motor vehicles – all of which would also be leitmotifs in Big City Symphony films. As mentioned above, 'mechanics' was the art assigned to this chapter. Section 13 features the hum of powerhouse dynamos, alluding to the circulation of electricity and the avant-garde fascination with the role of technology in both sustaining urban civilisation and providing metaphors for its structure and functioning. However, Joyce particularly intermeshed the city's semiotic and technological networks with the power of colonial commerce, in a way that points towards *Berlin*'s visualisation of capitalism's all-determining cash nexus. There are striking parallels in the repeated use of shop windows, dummies, advertisements and commodities between *Ulysses* and such films. Stephen's view through a jeweller's window in section 13, for example, puns on the colloquial meaning of 'rocks' as fetishes of status and power, identifying the city's material and social space as one in which economic and ideological forces thwart modernity's liberating and democratising potential. Though the novel's monstration never makes Joyce's stance explicit, it is precisely its moving panoramic construction that should make us wary of concluding that it is politically indifferent, since *Ulysses*' representation of urban modernity visualises the effects of alienation so radically. Joyce's leitmotifs suggest both psychological contrasts and spatio-temporal contiguity. Overall, the novel's panoramic effect suggests almost mystical interconnectedness, despite the city's disjunctions and contradictions, close to his French contemporary Jules Romain's theory of *unanisme*, but distinctly cinematic in its terms.[199]

Joyce's creative engagement with evolving panoramic forms and techniques fed back into the genre of Big City Symphonies. *Ulysses* was a double influence: on *both* experimental textual *and* film montage. This seems especially the case in the intertwined cultural media of Weimar Germany, exemplified by the *Großstadt* films, on one hand, and fictions such as Alfred Döblin's panoramic novel *Berlin Alexanderplatz* (1929) on the other, dubbed by Walter

Laqueur 'a symphony of big city life', often considered the German *Ulysses* and promptly filmed by Piel Jutzi in 1931.[200] However, this was possible because Joyce's method also constituted the Modernist highpoint of the discursive panorama. This chapter has shown that 'Wandering Rocks' orchestrates a variety of strategies that can be understood in terms of Huhtamo's three-phase model of its development, shifting the imagined point of view from central overview to immersive moving panorama of street level, then internalising it through the imagistic flow of the Hodgsonian stream of consciousness. This makes *Ulysses* an uncannily inter-medial foreshadowing of the Big City Symphonies, but also enables it to reach beyond them into the presentation of the lived experience of the city through individual bodies and minds. It is precisely such extended psychological penetration that the virtually plotless and characterless method of Cavalcanti's, Ruttmann's and Vertov's documentaries precluded, by focusing more exclusively on the material contexture of the city environment and anonymous, mass life.

Significantly, no panoramic Dublin City Symphony reached the screen, due to the relative isolation of Ireland's film industry at the time and the predominant focus of Anglo-American films about Ireland on pastoral settings. Similarly, the refugee from Nazism and co-scenarist of *Berlin*, Carl Mayer, claimed that his attempt to transfer its principle to London was thwarted for lack of British producers willing to risk such an experimental and politically controversial project.[201] Only a small number of independent British films used montage more radically, but on generally less than panoramic scale as 'an interpretation of images' to reveal urban conditions.[202] Joyce's debunking montage technique did have a significant impact on other strands of the documentary movement through *May the Twelfth* (1937), Mass-Observation's panoramic and very 'film-minded', multi-perspectival account of the coronation procession of George VI and its similarly interpellative spectacle. As a 'democratic' form of social anthropology, Mass-Observation became particularly focused on the mediation of ideological spectacles and their role in generating the appearance of consensus, including by radio and early television.[203]

In Britain it is arguable that the most significant impact of Big City Symphony techniques fed back into fiction, made easier by writers' receptivity to film's remediation of panoramic form precisely through the influence of novels such as *Ulysses*. In 1929, for example, Graham Greene linked Joyce's template for representing urban modernity with Cavalcanti and Ruttmann.[204] Panoramic city fictions of the 1930s with montage structures and camera-eyed techniques, such as Greene's own *It's a Battlefield* (1933), John Sommerfield's *May Day* and James Barke's *Major Operation* (both 1936), Ashley Smith's *A City Stirs* and Christopher Isherwood's *Goodbye to Berlin* (both 1939), derive a great deal from *Ulysses*.[205] Hence commentators have oversimplified Greene's 1930s generation's apprenticeship to High Modernism in claiming that they forsook the 'obscurity' and experimentalism of their elders by emulating the most popular new medium for representing urban modernity. In fact, their creative inter-mediality with film was a legacy of the cinematic preoccupations of writers such as Joyce.

NOTES

1. See John Eglinton, W. B. Yeats, A.E. and W. Larminie, *Literary Ideals in Ireland* (London/Dublin: Unwin/Daily Express, 1899), pp. 42–3.
2. John Eglinton was the pseudonym of W. K. Magee. For Joyce's familiarity with Magee's critical essays, see Ellmann, *James Joyce*, pp. 118–19.
3. Cover blurb to Dolf Sternberger, *The Panorama of the 19th Century* (1938), trans. Joachim Neugroschel (New York: Urizen Books and Mole Editions, 1977). For Benjamin's review, see 'Dolf Sternberger, *Panorama oder Ansichten vom 19. Jahrhundert*', in *Gesammelte Schriften*, vol. 3: *Kritiken und Rezensionen*, ed. Hella Tiedemann-Bartels (Frankfurt-am-Main: Suhrkamp, 1991), pp. 572–9.
4. Available at <http://www.oed.com/view/Entry/136923?redirectedFrom=panorama #eid> (last accessed 4 March 2017).
5. William Uricchio, 'A "Proper Point of View": The Panorama and Some of its Early Media Iterations', *EPVC*, 9:3 (2011), pp. 225–38 (227).
6. Discursive evocations are the detailed focus of Huhtamo's chapter 11, pp. 331–59.
7. 'Specification of the patent granted to Mr. ROBERT BARKER', *The Repertory of Arts and Manufactures: Consisting of Original Communications, Specifications of Patent Inventions, and Selections of Useful Practical Papers From the Transactions of the Philosophical Societies of All Nations, &c. &c.*, vol. IV (London: Printer for the Proprietors, 1796), pp. 165–7.
8. Byerly, '"A Prodigious Map beneath His Feet"', p. 153.
9. Ibid., p. 153.
10. Anon., 'The Drama and Public Amusements', *Critic*, 9:218 (1850), pp. 229–30.
11. Letter to Stanislaus, 28 December 1904, *Letters of James Joyce*, vol. 2, ed. Richard Ellmann (London: Faber and Faber, 1966), pp. 74–6 (75).
12. Louis Althusser, 'Ideology and Ideological State Apparatuses' (1970), in *Lenin and Philosophy and Other Essays*, trans. Ben Brewster (New York: Monthly Review Press, 2001), pp. 85–126.
13. Denise Blake Oleksijczuk, *The First Panoramas: Visions of British Imperialism* (Minneapolis, MN: University of Minnesota Press, 2011).
14. David Cannadine, *Ornamentalism: How the British Saw Their Empire* (Harmondsworth: Penguin, 2001), p. 122.
15. Ibid., pp. 121–2.
16. Byerly, '"A Prodigious Map beneath His Feet"', p. 162.
17. Ibid., p. 165.
18. Michel Foucault, 'Panopticism', in *Discipline and Punish: The Birth of the Prison*, trans. Alan Sheridan (New York: Vintage, 1979), pp. 195–230.
19. For journalist Nathaniel Hazeltine Carter's comparison between panorama and Edinburgh's Bridewell panopticon, see *IiM*, pp. 339–40. Stephan Oetterman also points to Foucault's footnote, in *Discipline and Punish*, asking 'Was Bentham aware

of the Panoramas that Barker was constructing at exactly the same period(?)' (*The Panorama: History of a Mass Medium,* trans. D. L. Schneider [New York: Zone Books, 1997], p. 41, n. 108). Bernard Comment connects the omniscient perspective of both panorama and panopticon with other architectural manifestations of the 'Überblick, the gaze from above' (*The Panorama,* trans. Anne-Marie Glasheen [London: Reaktion, 2001], pp. 141–2).

20. Uricchio, 'A "Proper Point of View"', p. 228.
21. Alison Griffiths, *Shivers Down Your Spine: Cinema, Museum, and the Immersive View* (New York: Columbia University Press, 2008), p. 77.
22. Byerly, '"A Prodigious Map beneath His Feet"', p. 153.
23. 'Battle Scenes', in Thomas Greenwood, *Scripture Sketches: with Other Poems and Hymns* (London: Hatchard, 1830), pp. 95–100 (96, 99).
24. Ellmann, *James Joyce,* pp. 580–1 and note.
25. The recently restored Waterloo panorama is in a rotunda next to the 1815 memorial. Painted by Louis Dumoulin to mark the first centenary, it is 110 metres round and 12 metres high. For further details, see official website at <http://www.waterloo1815.be/index.php?page=the-panorama> (last accessed 4 June 2018).
26. Gernsheim and Gernsheim, *L. J. M Daguerre,* pp. 44–5.
27. Musser, 'Toward a History of Screen Practice', p. 59.
28. Kember, *Marketing Modernity,* pp. 44–83 (49).
29. For the diorama's evolution into numerous semi-immersive moving spectacles, see *IiM,* pp. 139–67.
30. The Rocketts reproduce contemporary lithographs representing the 'before' and 'after' effect in Daguerre's avalanche diorama (*MLP&MPS,* plates 35–6).
31. Quoted in *IiM,* p. 141.
32. For overlaps in technique and subject between dioramas and dissolving views, see *IiM,* pp. 268–70.
33. 'Advertisement', *Freeman's Journal,* 2 March 1839, p. 1.
34. See poster reproduced in *MLP&MPS,* p. 137.
35. 'Impromptu on Seeing Messrs Marshall's Peristrephic Panorama', *Freeman's Journal,* 8 April 1815, p. 4.
36. See Erkki Huhtamo, 'Penetrating the Peristrephic: An Unwritten Chapter in the History of the Panorama', *EPVC,* 6:3 (2008), pp. 219–38.
37. Byerly, '"A Prodigious Map beneath His Feet"', p. 154.
38. For a full account, see *IiM,* pp. 69–71. Huhtamo gives more detailed analysis of Pückler Muskau's account in 'Penetrating the Peristrephic', pp. 219–38.
39. For Smith's 1850 coinage, see *IiM,* pp. 179, 189. Richard Altick considers 'panoramania' the acme of the Victorian fascination with 'mimetic effects' produced by dioramas, clockwork figures, tableaux, waxworks and other simulations (*The Shows of London* [Cambridge, MA: Harvard University Press, 1978], p. 51).
40. Byerly, '"A Prodigious Map beneath His Feet"', p. 154.
41. Ralph Hyde, *Panoramania! The Art and Entertainment of the All-Embracing View* (London: Trefoil Publications in Association with Barbican Art Gallery, 1988), p. 133. Many surviving examples, sketches, plans, etc., collected for the Barbican Gallery's landmark 1988–89 exhibition are reproduced by Hyde.

42. Charles Dickens, 'The American Panorama', *The Examiner*, 16 December 1845, repr. in Dickens, *Journalism*, vol. 2, ed. Michael Slater (London: Dent, 1997), pp. 135–7 (136).

43. Ibid., p. 137.

44. Byerly, '"A Prodigious Map beneath His Feet"', p. 157.

45. 'Cyclopia', *Freeman's Journal*, 20 May 1896, p. 5.

46. McKernan, 'Appendix: Volta Filmography', pp. 189, 98.

47. Byerly, '"A Prodigious Map beneath His Feet"', p. 153.

48. Ibid., p. 152.

49. Ibid., p. 152.

50. Henry Mayhew, 'A Balloon View of London', *Illustrated London News*, 18 September 1852, repr. in Humphrey Jennings and Mary-Lou Jennings (eds), *Pandaemonium, 1660–1886: The Coming of the Machine Age as Seen by Contemporary Observers* (London: Pan, 1987 [1985]), pp. 264–7 (265).

51. James Glaisher, *Travels in the Air* (London: Richard Bentley, 1871), pp. 99–100.

52. See Byerly, '"A Prodigious Map beneath His Feet"', p. 159.

53. Mayhew, 'A Balloon View of London', p. 266.

54. Byerly, '"A Prodigious Map beneath His Feet"', p. 161.

55. Ibid., p. 162.

56. Charles Dickens, 'Moving (Dioramic) Experiences', *All the Year Round*, 23 March 1867, pp. 305–6.

57. David Herman, *Story Logic: Problems and Possibilities of Narrative* (Lincoln, NE: University of Nebraska Press, 2002), p. 305.

58. Byerly, '"A Prodigious Map beneath His Feet"', pp. 162–3.

59. See, for example, Greer, *A Modern Daedalus*, pp. 17–19, 71–4, 189–90, 227–30.

60. Anon., 'Triumphs of Photography', *Dublin Evening Mail*, 27 January 1896, p. 4.

61. Charles A. Chase, 'Stereopticon Cyclorama', *Optical Magic Lantern Journal*, 6:70 (1895), pp. 45–6 (46).

62. See further details in *IiM*, pp. 306, 317; see also David B. Clarke and Marcus A. Doel, 'From Flatland to Vernacular Relativity: The Genesis of Early English Screenscapes', in Martin Lefebvre (ed.), *Landscape and Film* (London: Routledge, 2006), pp. 213–43 (226–7).

63. See Hyde (ed.), *Panoramania!*, pp. 181–2; see also Thomas Kuchenbuch, *Die Welt um 1900: Unterhaltungs-und Technikkultur* (Stuttgart: Metzler, 1992).

64. Cf. Uricchio, 'A "Proper Point of View"', pp. 230–1.

65. Ibid., pp. 229–30.

66. Anon., 'Triumphs of Photography', p. 4.

67. Wolfgang Schivelbusch, *The Railway Journey: The Industrialization of Time and Space in the 19th Century* (Leamington Spa: Berg, new edn, 1986 [1976]), p. 64.

68. Sternberger, *The Panorama of the 19th Century*, p. 39. Compare Stephen Kern, *The Culture of Time and Space 1889–1918* (Cambridge, MA: Harvard University Press, 1983), p. 128; Lynne Kirby has historicised how symbiosis between moving panoramic perception and rail travel was extended by film in *Parallel Tracks: The Railroad and the Silent Cinema* (Exeter: University of Exeter Press, 1997), pp. 6–11, 42–8.

69. For details, see *IiM*, p. 8; also Huhtamo, 'Penetrating the Peristrephic', p. 231.

70. See Huhtamo, 'Aeronautikon! Or the Journey of the Balloon Panorama', EPVC, 7:3 (2009), pp. 295–306.

71. Michel Foucault, 'Of Other Spaces', Diacritics, 16 (1986), pp. 22–7 (25).

72. Byerly, '"A Prodigious Map beneath His Feet"', p. 157.

73. Anon., 'Gompertz's Panorama', Irish Times, 7 May 1859, p. 2.

74. Powell, Poole's Myriorama, pp. 9, 90–1; IiM, p. 292.

75. Hudson John Powell reproduces a typical poster showing Boer War era cavalry in action over the slogan POOLE'S MYRIORAMA FOR BRITISH SUPREMACY, in 'New Light on Poole's Myrioramas', The New Magic Lantern Journal, 8:1 (1996), pp. 12–15 (15).

76. For details of such programmes, see Powell, Poole's Myriorama, p. 198; see also MLP&MPS, p. 145.

77. Canvas dimensions for the 1891 New Eclipse Myriorama cited in Powell, Poole's Myriorama, p. 132. The account quoted below is from the Poole Scrapbook (compiled by Fred Mayer) in ibid., pp. 100–2 (101).

78. See Powell, Poole's Myriorama, pp. 132–4.

79. Quoted from the Poole Scrapbook in ibid., p. 102.

80. See ibid., Appendix II, p. 201.

81. Available on BFIPlayer at <https://player.bfi.org.uk/free/film/watch-factory-workers-in-clitheroe-1901-1901-online> (last accessed 6 July 2018). See also text and image in Tom Gunning, 'Pictures of Crowd Splendour: The Mitchell and Kenyon Factory Gate Films', in Toulmin, Russell and Popple (eds), The Lost Worlds of Mitchell and Kenyon, pp. 49–58 (56–7, respectively).

82. Byerly, '"A Prodigious Map beneath His Feet"', p. 152.

83. Ellen E. Kenyon, 'Teaching Literature', School Journal: A Weekly Journal of Education, 51:1 (6 July 1895), p. 10.

84. Grahame Smith, Dickens and the Dream of Cinema (Manchester: Manchester University Press, 2003), pp. 29–33, 83–6; also IiM, pp. 116, 272, 333, 341, 363–84 and passim.

85. J. D. Lewis, Our College: Leaves from an Undergraduate's 'Scribbling Book' (London: G Earle, 1857), p. 27.

86. James Stirling, Letters from the Slave States (London: John W. Parker and Son, 1857), p. 192.

87. See Maggie Dunn and Ann Morris, The Composite Novel: The Short Story Cycle in Transition (New York: Twayne, 1995), esp. pp. xiii, 39–42.

88. For examples of Waterloo panoramas, see Oleksijczuk, The First Panoramas, p. 159; IiM, pp. 2–3; Comment, The Panorama, pp. 129, 150, 241 and passim.

89. See IiM, p. 67; Huhtamo, 'Penetrating the Peristrephic', p. 232, n. 5.

90. See Powell, Poole's Myriorama, p. 100.

91. See photograph advertising a film show c. 1905 in Liam O'Leary, Cinema Ireland 1896–1950 (Dublin: National Library of Ireland, 1990), p. 9. The Rotunda is also mentioned in 'Ithaca', referring to Albert Hengler's circus, at which a clown jokes that Bloom is his lost father. This incident confirms that all three of Ulysses' protagonists are familiar with the venue's reputation for entertainment and fundraising for the attached maternity hospital (see 17.975–9).

92. For 'change pictures', see Powell, *Poole's Myriorama*, p. 96.

93. Anon., 'Poole's Myriorama', *Dublin Daily Nation*, 12 September 1898, p. 6.

94. Advertisement, *Freeman's Journal*, 12 September 1898, p. 5.

95. *Freeman's Journal*, 29 August 1898, p. 4.

96. *Freeman's Journal*, 12 September 1898, p. 6.

97. See Powell, *Poole's Myriorama*, Appendix II, p. 202.

98. Kember, *Marketing Modernity*, p. 58.

99. *Limerick Chronicle*, 1 October, 1901, quoted in Powell, *Poole's Myriorama*, Appendix II, p. 204.

100. For further details of Boer War films and Myriorama performances in Dublin and split audience reactions, see *MLP&MPS*, pp. 236–8; see also *EIC*, pp. 22–3, 61–73, and Condon, 'Receiving News from the Seat of War', pp. 104–6.

101. Slides 40 and 44 of the 52–54 slide set accompanying G. W. Wilson's lecture on *The Life of the Right Honourable William Ewart Gladstone* (in/before 1895) featured a portrait of Parnell, as well as a caricature with the atheist MP Charles Bradlaugh, the two pulling Gladstone in different directions. LUCERNA lists four similar lantern lives of the British Prime Minister.

102. John Simpson argues that the Freddy Mayer whom Molly refers to ('He was always on for flirtyfying too when I sang Maritana with him at Freddy Mayers private opera' [*Ulysses* 18.1292–4]) was Poole's general manager and showman, as referred to in the notice 'Amusements in Dublin [. . .] Round Room, Rotunda. – Mr Joseph Poole's myriorama opened here on Monday last. Mr Fred. Mayer is an able guide . . .', *Era*, 9 July 1892. Mayer regularly acted in this role for Rotunda shows until at least 1901; see <http://www.jjon.org/jioyce-s-people/mayer> (last accessed 13 June 2019).

103. Crary, *Techniques of the Observer*, p. 7.

104. Yvonne Whelan has historicised the symbolism of Dublin's built environment in Joyce's youth in 'City of Empire, Site of Resistance: The Iconography of Dublin before Independence', Part II of her *Reinventing Modern Dublin: Streetscape, Iconography and the Politics of Identity* (Dublin: University College of Dublin Press, 2003), pp. 33–111.

105. See Oleksijczuk, *The First Panoramas*, pp. 102, 151–4.

106. Carville, 'Mr Lawrence's Great Photographic Bazaar', pp. 275–7.

107. Greer, *A Modern Daedalus*, pp. 75–6.

108. See '12102. Sackville Street and O'Connell Bridge, Dublin', available at <https://commons.wikimedia.org/wiki/File:Flickr_-_%E2%80%A6trialsanderrors_-_Sackville_Street_%5E_O%27Connell_Bridge,_Dublin,_Ireland,_ca._1899.jpg> (last accessed 4 October 2018).

109. For such mid-century imperial panoramas, see *IiM*, pp. 191–201, esp. p. 194.

110. David Spurr, 'Monumental Displacement in *Ulysses*', in his *Architecture and Modern Literature* (Ann Arbor, MI: University of Michigan Press, 2012), pp. 187–203 (194). Spurr is quoting from M. Christine Boyer, *The City of Collective Memory: Its Historical Imagery and Collective Entertainments* (Cambridge, MA: MIT Press, 1994), p. 33.

111. Spurr, 'Monumental Displacement in *Ulysses*', p. 194.

112. Ibid., p. 195.

113. Baudelaire, 'The Painter of Modern Life' (1863). I have followed Charvet's translation (Baudelaire, *Selected Writings on Art and Literature*, p. 400), except where this unaccountably renders 'images' as 'energies'. See Charles Baudelaire, *Œuvres complètes*, vol. 2 (Paris: Gallimard, 1975–76), p. 692.

114. Benjamin, *The Writer of Modern Life*, p. 191.

115. See 'Kinoks: A Revolution' (1923), in *Kino-Eye: The Writings of Dziga Vertov*, ed. Annette Michelson, trans. Kevin O'Brien (Berkeley, CA: University of California Press, 1984), pp. 11–21 (17–18).

116. George R. Sims, *The Social Kaleidoscope*, 2 vols (London: J.P. Fuller, 1881), vol. 1, pp. vii–vii.

117. For Modernist 'psychogeography', see Giuliana Bruno, 'Haptic Space, Film and the Geography of Modernity', in Alan Marcus and Dietrich Neumann (eds), *Visualizing the City* (London: Routledge, 2007), pp. 13–30 (26).

118. 'The Stream of Thought', in William James, *The Principles of Psychology*, 2 vols (New York/London: Henry Holt/Macmillan, 1890), vol. 1, pp. 224–90 (239).

119. May Sinclair, 'The Novels of Dorothy Richardson', *The Egoist*, 5 (April 1918), pp. 57–9 (58).

120. See Shadworth H. Hodgson, *Time and Space: a Metaphysical Essay* (London: Longman, Green, Longman, Roberts and Green, 1865), p. 74.

121. H. Wildon Carr, 'I. - Shadworth Hollway Hodgson', *Mind*, 21 (1912), pp. 473–85 (478).

122. Ibid., p. 478.

123. Shadworth H. Hodgson, *The Relation of Philosophy to Science, Physical and Psychological: an Address* (London: Williams and Norgate, 1884), p. 19

124. Shadworth H. Hodgson, *The Metaphysic of Experience*, vol. 3: *Analysis of Conscious Action* (London: Longmans, Green, 1898), p. 97. Hodgson uses the term 'panorama' over twenty times in this volume alone. See also *IiM*, pp. 349–50.

125. Spiegel, *Fiction and the Camera-Eye*, p. 3.

126. Hodgson, *The Metaphysic of Experience*, vol. 3, p. 34.

127. Letter to Stanislaus, 7 December 1906, in *Letters of James Joyce*, vol. 2, pp. 200–4 (203)

128. Letter to Harriet Shaw Weaver, 27 June 1924, in *Letters of James Joyce*, vol. 1, ed. Stuart Gilbert (London: Faber and Faber, 1957), pp. 215–17 (216); letter to Harriet Shaw Weaver, 23 December 1924, in *Letters of James Joyce*, vol. 3, ed. Richard Ellmann (London: Faber and Faber, 1966), pp. 111–12 (112).

129. In Wells's 1898 'The Stolen Body', psychic investigator Mr Bessel's 'televisual' experiment in astral projection goes hideously wrong, because his temporarily vacated flesh is instantly hijacked by another consciousness craving physical embodiment, leaving his stranded in another dimension. Bessel tracks his body rampaging round London from a panoramic perspective of total mobility, zooming down into and out of street level. Simultaneously, the city's most intimate spaces are rendered transparent, as though by X-rays, 'like watching the affairs of a great glass hive'. *The Complete Short Stories of H. G. Wells*, ed. John Hammond (London: Phoenix Press, 2000), pp. 512–24 (519). Wells repeated this figure for

the panoramically surveilled city in his novel about London under globalised media dictatorship, *When the Sleeper Wakes*. Big Brother's prototype, Ostrog, surveys his metropolis with a system of CCTV cameras from his skyscraper HQ. Wells's glass-domed London of 2100 (itself a huge optical device) thus becomes a 'gigantic glass hive', a futuristic, totalitarian configuration of Bentham's panopticon on a city-wide scale. H. G. Wells, *When the Sleeper Wakes* (1899) (London: Dent, 1999), p. 63.

130. Paul K. Saint-Amour, 'The Vertical Flâneur: Narratorial Tradecraft in the Colonial Metropolis', in Duffy and Boscagli (eds), *Joyce, Benjamin and Magical Urbanism*, pp. 224–49 (238).

131. Ibid., p. 239.

132. Prologue to George R. Sims (ed.), *Living London*, 3 vols, with over 450 illustrations (London: Cassell, 1902), vol. 1, pp. 3–6 (3).

133. See also Monks, 'The Irish Films in the Mitchell and Kenyon Collection', p. 93.

134. Gunning, 'Pictures of Crowd Splendour', p. 50; Louis Lumière, 'Address to the Congrès à Lyon des Sociétés de Photographie de France' (1 July 1895), quoted in Gunning, ibid.

135. Ibid., p. 50.

136. Monks, 'The Irish Films in the Mitchell and Kenyon Collection', p. 101.

137. Ibid., p. 101.

138. Lindsay, *The Art of the Moving Picture*, pp. 67–8

139. For the many taken by Lumiére operatives and others between 1896 and 1897, see *MLP&MPS*, pp. 226–7; *EIC*, pp. 177, 182–3.

140. Warwick Trading Company's tourist series, *With the Bioscope through Ireland* (1900), were all films of rural locations or events. For further details, see Robert Monks, *Cinema Ireland: A Database of Irish Films and Filmmakers, 1896–1986*, CD-ROM (Dublin: National Library of Ireland, 1996); see also his 'The Irish Films in the Mitchell and Kenyon Collection', pp. 75–97.

141. Condon estimates that around seventy fiction films were made in Ireland before 1921, though again few were urban (*EIC*, p. 78).

142. For Mitchell and Kenyon's phantom rides, see Monks, 'The Irish Films in the Mitchell and Kenyon Collection', pp. 94–5.

143. Ibid., pp. 100–1.

144. Ibid., p. 95.

145. Uricchio, 'A "Proper Point of View"', pp. 231–2.

146. Ibid., p. 231.

147. Ibid., p. 231.

148. Ibid., pp. 234 and 231, respectively.

149. Ibid., p. 233.

150. Ibid., p. 234.

151. Ibid., p. 234.

152. See Tom Gunning, 'Camera Movement', in Abel (ed.), *Encyclopedia of Early Cinema*, pp. 92–5 (93).

153. Uricchio, 'A "Proper Point of View"', p. 234.

154. Ibid., pp. 234–5.

155. For the concept of 'cognitive mapping' and its extension to film theory, see Fredric Jameson *Postmodernism, or, The Cultural Logic of Late Capitalism* (London: Verso, 1991), ch. 1, esp. pp. 6, 18. See also his *The Geopolitical Aesthetic: Cinema and Space in the World System* (Bloomington, IN: Indiana University Press, 1992), esp. pp. 4, 114.

156. Uricchio, 'A "Proper Point of View"', p. 235.

157. Keith Williams, 'Symphonies of the Big City: Modernism, Cinema and Urban Modernity', in Paul Edwards (ed.), *The Great London Vortex: Modernist Literature and Art* (Bath: Sulis Press, 2003), pp. 31–50.

158. Ellmann quotes from Richter's account in *James Joyce*, p. 654 n., but cf. Werner, 'James Joyce and Sergej Eisenstein', p. 498; Marie M. Seton, *Sergei M. Eisenstein: A Biography* (London: Bodley Head, 1952), p. 149; and Patricia Hutchins, *James Joyce's World* (London: Methuen, 1957), pp. 245–6. Despite disagreement about details, Joyce's view that *Ulysses* could only be filmed by either Eisenstein or Ruttmann seems beyond dispute (see, for example, Yon Barna, *Eisenstein* [London: Secker and Warburg, 1973], p. 143). However, for consideration of the Irish-Americans Robert Flaherty and John Ford as candidates for directing a later screenplay, see Joseph Evans Slate, 'The Reisman-Zukofsky Screenplay of *Ulysses*: Its Background and Significance', *Library Chronicle of the University of Texas*, n.s., 20/21 (1982), pp. 106–39.

159. For comparison of Eisenstein and Vertov in relation to Joyce, see Thomas W. Sheehan, 'Montage Joyce: Sergei Eisenstein, Dziga Vertov and *Ulysses*', *JJQ*, 42–3:1–4 (2004/2006), pp. 69–86.

160. See, for example, Jerry Reisman and Louis Zukofsky, *James Joyce's Ulysses: Scenario and Continuity* (1935), p. 40, shots 133–7 (a rapid montage of Dublin industry); also pp. 59–62 and 71–2, shots 196–218 and 247–51 of the Dedalus home and various street encounters. Manuscript available for consultation at the Harry Ransom Humanities Research Centre (University of Texas at Austin); also in carbon copy at the Zürich James Joyce Foundation (Hans E. Jahnke bequest).

161. See Vertov, 'From Kino-Eye to Radio-Eye' (1929), in *Kino-Eye*, pp. 85–92 (90–1).

162. Christie, *The Last Machine*, p. 39.

163. Siegfried Kracauer, *From Caligari to Hitler: A Psychological History of the German Film* (Princeton, NJ: Princeton University Press, 1947), p. ix.

164. Benjamin, 'Work of Art in the Age of Mechnical Reproduction', p. 250, n. 19; see also 'Introduction: Previewing the Cinematic City', in David B. Clarke (ed.), *The Cinematic City* (London: Routledge, 1997), pp. 1–18 (2).

165. Walter Benjamin, 'Daguerre or the Panoramas', Part II of 'Paris, the Capital of the Nineteenth Century' (May 1935), in *The Writer of Modern Life: Essays on Charles Baudelaire*, ed. Michael W. Jennings, trans. Howard Eiland, Edmund Jephcott, Rodney Livingstone and Harry Zohn (Cambridge, MA: Harvard University Press, 2006), pp. 33–5 (33).

166. Colin MacArthur, 'Chinese Boxes and Russian Dolls: Tracking the Elusive Cinematic City', in Clarke (ed.), *The Cinematic City*, pp. 19–45, gives an overview of this quest.

167. Ezra Pound, *The Dial* (January 1921), p. 110.

168. Ezra Pound, 'Berlin', *The Exile*, 4 (autumn 1928), pp. 113–15. *Adolphe 1920* (1929), by John Rodker is a novella set in Paris, spanning eight hours in the life of its protagonist. It is similar both to *Ulysses* and Woolf's *Mrs Dalloway* in structuring its diegetic present across one day punctuated by spatio-temporal dilations through stream-of-consciousness technique.

169. Ruth Frehner, 'Warum ein Pater dunnbesockt durch eine fremde Küche läuft: Gleichzeitigkeit in den "Irrfelsen"'/'Why a Thinsocked Clergyman Walks through Other People's Kitchens: Simultaneity in "Wandering Rocks"', in Zeller, Frehner and Vogel (eds), *James Joyce: 'Gedacht durch meine Augen'*, pp. 157–87 (182).

170. Kern, *The Culture of Time and Space*, pp. 76–7.

171. Ibid., p. 77.

172. Joyce told Budgen, 'I want to give a picture of Dublin so complete that if the city one day suddenly disappeared from the earth it could be reconstructed out of my book.' According to him, Joyce wrote 'with a map of Dublin before him on which were traced in red ink the paths of the Earl of Dudley and Father Conmee', calculating to a minute the time necessary to cover distances. See Budgen, *James Joyce and the Making of 'Ulysses'*, pp. 69, 124–5. Clive Hart confirmed empirically that Joyce's characters 'move at rates consistent with physical life in Dublin in 1904'; see his 'Wandering Rocks', in Clive Hart and David Hayman (eds), *James Joyce's Ulysses: Critical Essays* (Berkeley, CA: University of California Press, 1974), pp. 181–216 (200–1). Joyce employed a huge range of documents and records, including spatio-temporal overviews from maps, tidal charts and street atlas information in *Thom's Official Directory of the United Kingdom of Great Britain and Ireland* for 1904, as well as employing friends to time distances on foot.

173. Ellmann, *James Joyce*, p. 452.

174. Blanche H. Gelfant emphasises the panoramic features of synoptic city fiction over the 'portrait', in which the city is explored through the experiences of a single character, and the 'ecological', centred on one neighbourhood, street or even house. Blanche H. Gelfant, *The American City Novel* (Norman, OK: University of Oklahoma Press, 1954), pp. 11, 133–6. Joyce combines features of all of these.

175. Kern, *Culture of Time and Space*, p. 77.

176. See Richard Ellmann, *Ulysses on the Liffey* (London: Faber and Faber, 1972), pp. 98–9.

177. For details and screenings, see Monks, 'The Irish Films in the Mitchell and Kenyon Collection', p. 95.

178. Dublin's *Evening Telegraph* explained the functioning of the kinetoscope using a boxing example, 6 April 1895, p. 5. As we saw in Chapter 2, sporting dynamics were a common subject of photographic analysis and the early films it influenced. One of the most popular exhibited in Dublin (appropriately by widescreen-format 'Veriscope' – literally 'truth seer') was the controversial outcome of the Corbett versus Fitzsimmons boxing match in Carson City, Nevada, in March 1897 (recalled by Master Dignam, Ulysses 10.1145–9). Film's reputation for being 'quicker than the eye' allowed audiences to make up their own minds about the foul allegedly missed by the referee (see *EIC*, pp. 20, 53–60).

179. Patrick Keiller, 'Tram Rides and Other Virtual Landscapes', in Toulmin, Russell and Popple (eds), *The Lost World of Mitchell and Kenyon*, pp. 191–200.

180. For Joyce and the Dublin tram system, see Liam Lanigan, 'Becalmed in Short Circuit: Joyce, Modernism, and the Tram', *The Dublin James Joyce Journal*, 5 (2012), pp. 33–48.

181. For an account of Modernist debate about the aesthetics of synchronised sound, see James Donald, Anne Friedberg and Laura Marcus (eds), *Close Up 1927–1933: Cinema and Modernism* (London: Cassell, 1998), esp. pp. 79–93.

182. See David Trotter, *Cinema and Modernism* (Oxford: Blackwell, 2007), pp. 88–9.

183. Appropriately to a modern urban culture increasingly based on stimulating consumption through publicity, Bloom is himself an advertising canvasser. Ruttmann's punning slogan is also uncannily close to the jingle that plays on Bloom's unconscious and becomes a symbol of his own dysfunctional sexuality: 'Kein Haushalt ohne Bullrich Magensalz' (No household without Bullrich's Epsom salts'); 'What is home without/Plumtree's potted meat? Incomplete./With it an abode of bliss' (*Ulysses* 5.144–7).

184. Stephen Bottomore, 'From the Factory Gate to the "Home Talent" Drama: An International Overview of Local Films in the Silent Era', in Toulmin, Russell and Popple (eds), *The Lost World of Mitchell and Kenyon*, pp. 33–48.

185. Hyde identifies Muybridge as the principal pioneer of photographic panoramas (see his chapter on the form in *Panoramania*, pp. 179–98, esp. p. 180).

186. See Katherine Mullin, 'Joyce, Early Cinema and the Erotics of Everyday Life', in McCourt (ed.), *Roll Away the Reel World*, pp. 43–56.

187. See Georgina Binnie, 'James Joyce and Photography', unpublished PhD thesis, University of Leeds, 2016, available at <http://etheses.whiterose.ac.uk/15993/> (last accessed 8 October 2018).

188. Spiegel, *Fiction and the Camera-Eye*, pp. 96–7.

189. Bottomore, 'From the Factory Gate to the "Home Talent" Drama', p. 35.

190. Bloom quotes 'See ourselves as others see us' from Robert Burns's 1786 satire of public appearance, 'To a Louse; On Seeing a Lady's Bonnet at Church' (*Ulysses* 8.662 and 13.1058).

191. Janet McBain, 'Mitchell and Kenyon's Legacy in Scotland – The Inspiration for a Forgotten Film-Making Genre', in Toulmin, Russell and Popple (eds), *The Lost World of Mitchell and Kenyon*, pp. 113–21 (114).

192. John Widdowson, 'Ceremonial Processions and Folk Traditions', in Toulmin, Russell and Popple (eds), *The Lost World of Mitchell and Kenyon*, pp. 136–49 (141)

193. Bottomore, 'From the Factory Gate to the "Home Talent" Drama', p. 35.

194. Saint-Amour, 'The Vertical Flâneur', p. 241.

195. Ibid., p. 239.

196. Ibid., p. 238.

197. Ibid., p. 238.

198. *Stephen Hero*, p. 167; see also Chapter 1 above.

199. For a discussion of Jules Romains's influential collection of poems about the interpenetration of self and city, *La Vie unanime* (1908), see Peter Nicholls, *Modernisms:*

A *Literary Guide* (London: Macmillan, 1995). Romains is also crucially associated with what he called the 'conte cinematographique' and *roman fleuve;* see, for example, P. E. Charvet, *A Literary History of France, 5: The Nineteenth and Twentieth Centuries 1870–1940* (London: Ernest Benn, 1967), p. 239.

200. Walter Laqueur, *Weimar: A Cultural History 1918–1933* (London: Weidenfeld and Nicolson, 1974), p. 133. For analysis of Döblin's 'Kinostil' montage and its affinity with *Ulysses,* see Peter I. Barta, *Bely, Joyce and Döblin: Peripatetics in the City Novel* (Gainesville, FL: University of Florida, 1996), esp. pp. 83, 98.

201. See Kracauer's account in *From Caligari to Hitler,* p. 246.

202. Dziga Vertov's cameraman's definition of montage; see 'A Kinok Speaks: Mikhail Kaufman in Interview', in Kevin Macdonald and Mark Cousins (eds), *Imagining Reality: The Faber Book of Documentary* (London: Faber and Faber, 1996), pp. 65–9 (67). For limited use of radical montage in British documentary films of the period, see Hogenkamp, *Deadly Parallels,* pp. 105–35, and Stephen G. Jones, *The British Labour Movement and Film 1918–1939* (London: Routledge, 1986), esp. pp. 24–5, 64–5.

203. See Keith Williams, 'Reportage in the Thirties', unpublished DPhil thesis, University of Oxford, 1991, pp. 241–2, available at <https://ora.ox.ac.uk/objects/uuid:e8ea296e-9b1b-4e60-a2da-6ced3f276617> (last accessed 24 October 2017). See also Keith Williams, 'Joyce's Chinese Alphabet: *Ulysses* and the Proletarians', in Paul Hyland and Neil Sammells (eds), *Irish Writing: Exile and Subversion* (Basingstoke: Macmillan, 1991), pp. 173–87 (183).

204. See 'The Film Society: *Riens que les heures*', *The Times,* 14 January 1929, in *Mornings in the Dark: The Graham Greene Film Reader,* ed. David Parkinson (Manchester: Carcanet, 1993), pp. 4–5 (4).

205. For discussion of Joyce's key influence on these, see Williams, 'Joyce's Chinese Alphabet', pp. 180–6, and Williams, *British Writers and the Media,* pp. 129–50.

CODA: THE MEDIA-CULTURAL IMAGINARY OF *FINNEGANS WAKE*

So how did Joycean literary cinematicity develop after *Ulysses*? The notion of 'hands-on' play is both integral to optical toys and to linguistic creativity in Joyce's next major work, *Finnegans Wake* (1939), based as it is on a ludic approach to language which kaleidoscopically deforms and reforms its graphic and phonic elements. Although a comprehensive examination of *Finnegans Wake* in cinematic terms is beyond the scope of this book, it clearly continues to reference and explore the by then well-established moving image technologies such as film, as well as emergent ones in the form of television broadcasting. Indeed it confirms that transformative visual and linguistic play were fundamental and ongoing to Joyce's artistic processes. As discussed in Chapter 2, the young Joyce performed a boisterous charade punning on the kaleidoscope's ability to produce moving patterns through symmetrical permutations of coloured shapes in combination and dispersal, by colliding with a partner, then flying apart.[1] This riddle reappeared in *Finnegans Wake* as: 'Answer: A collideorscape!' (143.28). Philip Kitcher treats Joyce's trope as the foundation for his method of reading the novel. It occurs in a passage in which a 'fargazer' seems to look back telescopically over the time and space of their own life, but also the text 'scape' of the novel itself, which continuously figures and refigures Irish and collective human history in a synaesthetic moving 'panaroma of all flores of speech' (143.26 and 3–4, respectively). Kitcher argues that Joyce's reference to 'a device in which the same elements constantly rearrange themselves in new patterns' is a prompt foregrounding the novel's own endlessly recirculating system of recombination and dispersal at thematic, motific and linguistically granular levels.[2] Consequently, in this coda, I want to show that, far from abandoning his fascination with the past and future of moving image media in *Finnegans Wake*'s linguistic turn, which has been seen as marking Joyce's reorientation towards the 'radiophonic', his last novel continues to express it in ingenious ways.

Finnegans Wake played on how film simulated reality as moving images with a virtualism unsurpassed in any medium before, punning it homophonically in the phrase 'roll away the reel world' (64.25–6). Joyce suggests both the rolling of the film through the camera as it duplicated the world, but also printed film reel passing through the projector which effaced – 'rolled away' – the reality that it merely counterfeited on screen. The *Wake* is replete with ongoing references to film, but also its predecessor cinematic technologies such as optical toys like the kaleidoscope, phantasmagoric shadow effects ('Sole shadow shows', 565.14) and lantern fade ups ('vigorously rubbing his magic lantern to a glow of full consciousness', 421.21–2), as well as the phantasmagoria and the panorama. Besides 'roll away the reel world', some of the most famous allusions, sometimes referencing specific techniques, include 'cinemen' (6.18); 'Shadows by the film folk, masses by the good people. Promptings by Elanio Vitale. Longshots, upcloses, outblacks ... ' (221.21–2); 'A phantom city, phaked of philim pholk' (264.19–20); 'the celluloid art!' (534.25); 'moving pictures' (565.6). One of the characters even appears as a 'Moviefigure on in scenic section' (602.27) and Mercius says 'thank movies from the depths of my innermost still attrite heart' (194.2–3), playing on the fundamental relationship between still and moving photographs.

Verbal Dissolves

With apparent inauspiciousness, the *Wake*'s completion coincided with faltering negotiations over the Reisman-Zukovsky treatment for adapting *Ulysses* and its eventual abandonment. If the *Wake*'s method is accounted for at all in terms of cinematic inter-mediality, it tends to be as 'mottage'. Joyce famously asks, 'When is a pun not a pun?' (307.02–3). A possible answer might be, when it's a 'mottage', as in the 'once current puns, quashed quotatoes, messes of mottage' (183.22) lining the walls of Shem the penman's 'Haunted Inkbottle' home (182.31). 'Mottage' plays on *mot*, the French for word, and 'montage', apparently directing attention to his text's formal affinities with Eisenstein's montage cinema, after Joyce met with the Soviet director. It proposes some equivalence between the collisions of images edited together in films such as *Strike* and *Battleship Potemkin* (both 1925) and *October* (1928) with the verbal collisions in Joyce's method of combining linguistic meanings and forms.

However, *Finnegans Wake* has also been recently viewed as marking the, by then all-but-blind Joyce's final turn away from film, as both popular cultural medium and ekphrastic narrative model, in his late experimentalism. Jane Lewty and others have argued that *Finnegans Wake*'s logos-focused method is more like a form of 'radiophony' than cinematicity, in which words, voices and languages rather than images and film techniques continuously shuffle, layer, clash and blend.[3] Joyce's radical exploitation of aural and semiotic multiplicity as the principal creative drive of his text often appears closest to a criss-crossing of wireless broadcasts on heterogeneous frequencies. Nonetheless, I would argue that the *Wake*'s processes and themes continued to be Janus-faced in relation to the history, present and future of moving images. In fact, it represents a further stage in Joyce's experimental *ekphrasis* and relationship with modernity's common media-cultural imaginary, expanded by the possibilities of broadcasting in both its aural *and* visual forms during the 1920s and 1930s. Far from splitting with cinematicity's roots, *Finnegans Wake* continues to creatively 'retrofit' pre-filmic technologies for his purpose and equally to engage with film's emergent successor in the form of early television. Though Joyce's eyesight was too dim to make out what was actually passing on screens big or small by this time, with an imagination saturated by the forms and effects of visual media since childhood he remained eminently capable of visualising moving pictures in the projection box of his mind and ingeniously translating their possibilities into words.

Joyce's self-reflexively 'palimpcestuous' text (as Anthony Burgess described it),[4] in which words, characters and scenes constantly overwrite each other, shifting back and forth, also displays his ongoing creative engagement with the legacy of lantern techniques in particular. Dissolving views can be regarded as 'visual palimpsests', one picture shimmering through the outlines and interstices of another. Arguably, Joyce's quest to devise and refine their verbal equivalent, far from being abandoned, could be seen as reaching its hypostasis in *Finnegans Wake*. At a macro-level above individual lexical components often *'verbivocovisual'* (341.18, Joyce's italics) in themselves, the *Wake*'s creative processes are arguably based on the principle of 'verbal-dissolves', a textual but also ekphrastic tissue, shimmering between motifs, characters, spaces and times. Through this, linguistic forms and meanings continually morph in and out of each other like the multi-layered images of dissolving views and their remediation in filmic cross-fades and superimpositions.

This process also seems to be foregrounded in Mary Ellen Bute's partial adaptation, *Passages from Finnegans Wake* (1965), which won her the Cannes Film Festival prize for a first feature-length film. Bute often meshes or layers characters, scenes and locations in diaphanous or montaged effects which are simultaneously auditory *and* visual, influenced by the deliquescent imagery of Surrealist films such as Germaine Dulac's *Le Coquille et le Clergyman* (1928), but also by Bute's own long-standing collaboration with cinematographer Ted Nemeth on numerous short abstract animations from 1934 onwards, influenced by the 'Absolute Film' work of Ruttmann and Hans Richter.[5] Just as Joyce's text references and emulates many new media technologies in *Finnegans Wake* such as Movietone machines for recording soundtracks onto film, as well as radio and television, Bute, originally a painter, was fascinated by how visual art could be revolutionised by new mechanical and electronic means (in the 1930s she worked with Leon Theremin to devise an optical instrument that would be the visual equivalent of the electronic musical device named after him). As she stated in an interview, 'There were so many things I wanted to say, stream-of-consciousness things, designs and patterns while listening to music. I felt I might be able to say [them] if I had an unending canvas.'[6] Her search for that 'unending canvas' for breaking down boundaries between media ultimately led to her attempt to adapt Joyce's moving textual dream panorama.

In this context, it is also illuminating to consider the work of Irish-American experimental film-maker Hollis Frampton. Under similarly *Wakean* inspiration, Frampton created films that, as Gunning puts it, 'redefined the nature of cinema by enlarging the limits of its possibility'.[7] This includes films which are endlessly layered cycles of words and pictures, but in which they are often deliberately asynchronous, as if taking their cue from Eisenstein's praise for Joyce's temporal decouplings of sound and image on the page. For example, *Gloria!* (1979) self-consciously reflects on Frampton's chief literary inspiration, while also resuscitating early films of ballads from the Irish wake cycle which Joyce drew on. It ends with the 1903 two-shot trick film *Murphy's Wake*, having begun with a similar one-shot film as yet unidentified. Like Joyce's novel, both quoted films 'stage a parody of the resurrection as thirsty and apparently dead Irishmen rise from their coffins to partake of the drink offered at their wakes'. Moreover, the dance sequence that ends *Murphy's Wake* reflects the originary theme of cinema itself: as a medium which counterfeits real movement or apparently brings back the absent or dead as living presences.[8]

Finnegans Wake and the Panorama

Following *Ulysses*, *Finnegans Wake* could also be explored as a phantasmagoric, moving dream panorama of Dublin, overlaid by global history and culture. It is also topographically wrapped round by Joyce's famously circumambient, *media res* opening and closing sentence about the river Liffey, which like the mythical worm Ouroboros has its tail in its mouth. The polyglot, inter-medial and multi-sensory tendency of the novel is hinted at as a synaesthetic 'panaroma of all flores of speech' (143.26), one that can be virtually heard and smelt as much as read or visualised. Joyce's reference to 'A phantom city, phaked of philim pholk' (264.19–20) could equally allude to the faking of urban locations in studio sets inhabited by actors for filming, as much as to the versions of real cities simulated by film panoramas and toured round by the camera as phantom rides.

As we saw in Chapter 3, Joyce had a particular interest in Waterloo and visited the historic site in September 1926 to secure location details for the Napoleon–Wellington struggle for chapter 1 of *Finnegans Wake*.[9] It is also very likely that as part of the tour he would have entered the Rotunda which houses the battle panorama nearby. In *Finnegans Wake*, we first zoom down into the battlefield – 'in some greenish distance, the charmful Waterloose country' (8.2–3) – from a kind of panoramic aerial perspective – 'Hence when the clouds roll by, jamey, a proudseye view is enjoyable' – as if swooping from a bird's-eye position like that atop the 'Wallinstone' monument built in Dublin's Phoenix Park to triumphalise what was in fact a close-run victory with enormous slaughter (7–8.35–1). Interestingly, the 'museyroom' around which we are then guided is first referred to as a 'museomound', echoing the Rotunda housing the Waterloo panorama itself. The moving exhibits and actions to which attention is drawn by Joyce's showman-like narrator as we pass through are a surreal parody of the immersive and highly detailed scenes depicted in battle panoramas on both large and close-up scales:

> This is Rooshious balls. This is a ttrinch. This is mistletropes. This is Canon Futter with the popynose. After his hundred days' indulgence. This is the blessed. Tarra's widdars! This is jinnies in the bawny blooches. This is lipoleums in the rowdy howses. This is the Willingdone, by the splinters of Cork, order fire. Tonnerre! (Bullsear! Play!) (9.18–24)

Battles down the ages from classical times are superimposed on the panorama by Joycean wordplay to emphasise the apparently endless and futile wastage of human life in the name of megalomanic ambition and empire: 'This is camelry [Camel, AD 656], this is floodens [Flodden Field, 1513], this is the solphereens [Solferino, 1859] in action [Actium, 31 BC], this is their mobbily [Thermopylae, 480 BC], this is panickburns (Bannockburn, 1314). Almeidagad! [Almeida, 1811] Athiz too loose! [Orthez and Toulouse, 1814]' (9.24–6). *Finnegans Wake* more or less opens with a subversive attack on panoramic media, their latest embodiment being recent propaganda films from the First World War and those to come from the next in 1939, which monumentalise and glorify armed conflict. *Finnegans Wake* thus continues Joyce's satirical targeting of the ideological functions of the panorama, in a way that complements how he appropriates and subverts its urban form as imperial spectacle in the cinematic structure and themes of *Ulysses*.

TELEVISION BROADCASTING IN THE *WAKE*

Finnegans Wake confirms that Joyce retained an interest in both the most ancient moving image media and the futuristic possibilities of the latest technologies in cinema and telecommunications. Joyce's recurrent motif of the shadow show inadvertently screened on a night-time blind, from his earliest 'Silhouette' sketch, through *Dubliners* to *Ulysses*, is also reworked in *Finnegans Wake*. By this means a sexual act is made blatantly visible on the street outside: 'O, O, her fairy setalite! Casting such shadows to Persia's blind! The man in the street can see the coming event. Photoflashing it far too wide. It will be known through all Urania soon' (583.14–16). However, here the Platonic allegory of deceptive moving shadows is updated within a new technological context. The climax is compared to a glimpse of something revealed by the illuminating power of flash photography; its 'coming event', like the 'money-shots' of porn films, is a much more explicit version of the 'flashes' of forbidden ankles that the camera-eyed Bloom constantly watches out for. It also suggests the broadcast transmissions which carry television pictures. Joyce knew that the new mass medium would one day be available to 'the man in the street', albeit BBC television was limited to a prototype network only accessible to the better off in south-east England in the 1930s. The passage is suffused with astronomical wordplay – 'setalite' suggesting erotically 'set alight', as well as 'satellite', Urania as the muse of astronomy, as well as a quibble on the planet 'Uranus' – but also alludes to the scientific theory that broadcasts continue out into space beyond Earth's atmosphere and might eventually even be picked up in other worlds. Perhaps Joyce even anticipates the concept of geostationary communications satellites, proposed by the science fiction writer Arthur C. Clarke in 1945, which would enable the first global broadcasts in the 1960s.[10]

As Donald F. Theall and others have noted, *Finnegans Wake* contains frequent allusions to television broadcasting, still in its relative infancy, as well as other modern communications technologies.[11] The recent shift in inter-medial focus towards the radiophonic in the novel is part of a broader reorientation in Modernist studies towards considering the influence of broadcasting, exemplified by pioneering research such as Timothy Campbell's *Wireless Writing in the Age of Marconi* (2006), and the essays in *Broadcasting Modernism* (2009), edited by Debra Rae Cohen, Michael Coyle and Jane Lewty, and *Broadcasting in the Modernist Era* (2014), edited by Matthew Feldman, Erik Tonning and Henry Mead. As they note, the Modernist epoch is synchronic with a vast expansion in electronic mass media. Alongside film, broadcasting constituted one of modernity's most demanding challenges – and opportunities – for writers across the cultural spectrum: low, 'middlebrow' and high. It was a key driver of change in practice and outlook, prompting adaptations in modes while offering potentially wider publics and transcending national borders. Its rival, cinemagoing, though still dominant, mostly depended on dedicated public venues and collective viewing. Conversely, radio became the new technological 'deity of the hearth' through cheap domestic sets. It brought 'ether-real' voices into listeners' own homes, opening 'soundscapes' in the theatres of their minds, producing a mediated experience that was simultaneously intimate, anonymous and dispersed. Above all broadcasting created a matrix in which writers rethought their relationship with technology, the state and 'collective consciousness'. Timothy Campbell calls this the 'radio imaginary'.[12]

Thus *Finnegans Wake* expanded Joyce's engagement with the overall media-cultural imaginary – with which he was already deeply preoccupied both critically and creatively – in new directions, both radiophonic, but also televisual. Moreover, radio added new resources to the ancient potential of *ekphrasis* as it interacted with the listener's own visualisation processes, enriched by the internalisation of images they have been exposed to from other media and summed up in the period cliché that 'the best pictures are always on the radio'. Hence this new trend in Modernist studies examines how writers strove to create 'radiogenic' forms and develop techniques and modes of delivery best suited to the medium's specific features, but also how, in turn, the new 'radio imaginary' informed their fiction.

Feldman et al.'s *Broadcasting in the Modernist Era* investigates how writers got to grips with 'wireless telegraphy' creatively, performatively and politically, before radio itself, like cinema, began to be displaced by the spread of mass television reception from the 1950s. Presciently, *Finnegans Wake* also offers one of the few case studies of Modernist literary encounter with a pre-war 'televisual imaginary' outside the genre of science fiction. From the mid-1930s until the outbreak of hostilities, its limited networks transmitted both moving images and synchronised sound, often 'live', into the home. Hence Finn Fordham's 'Early Television and Joyce's *Finnegans Wake*: New Technology and Flawed Power' combs through Joyce's 'Work in Progress' notebooks to show how they progressively inject his 'How Buckley Shot the Russian General' episode (*Finnegans Wake*, pp. 348–50) with 'geekish' levels of technical detail about the apparatus.[13] This corroborates David Trotter's conclusion in his *Literature in the First Media Age* (2013) that 'When Joyce termed the "bairdboard" televisor screen a "bombardment" screen he knew what he was talking about.'[14] Fordham also shows Joyce responding to contemporary debates: about TV's mind-expanding potential for bringing the outside world into domestic space, or 'bombarding' audiences everywhere with new forms of celebrity distraction or bellicose propaganda, just as electrons bombard TV screens to make pictures in what Joyce puns as 'the charge of the light barricade'.

Joyce's pantomimic episode, framed by banter between the music-hall double act Taff and Butt (derived in part from strip cartoon characters Mutt and Jeff, created by Bud Fisher in 1907 for the *San Francisco Chronicle* and animated by Charles Bowers and Raoul Barré from 1916), is set in a bar in which an audience are watching one programme interrupted by another, which fades up through it due to a technical malfunction. Hence a farcically scatological anecdote, about an Irish sniper from the Crimean War unable in common humanity to shoot a distant enemy with his trousers down, collides with a sensational confession transmitted live. The latter appears to satirise both public Catholic penitentialism and film footage of the recent Soviet show trials. The mediated character baring his soul, 'Popey O'Donoshough', 'is typically composite', as Fordham puts it, his name rolling into one the Pope, Irish and Russian aristocrats and Popeye for good measure.[15] The episode's comic layering and clash of audio-visual transmissions reflects the *Wake*'s characteristic superimposition and dissolving between scenarios, thus undermining monologically authoritative messages through wordplay. Moreover, Fordham argues that Joyce parodies extremes in contemporary attitudes towards the power of the new medium – naive utopianism on one hand and science-fiction alarmism on the other – taking a more open-minded position on television's potential future benefits and drawbacks. As he concludes, Joyce 'does not take sides in the debate for and against the new medium', showing instead 'strong engagement with its technical aspects and an inventive exploration of the metaphorical dimensions of these new techniques'.[16]

ANIMATING THE *WAKE*: STUART GILBERT'S TREATMENT OF 'ANNA LIVIA PLURABELLE'

Finnegans Wake's 'Mime of Mick, Nick and the Maggies' (pp. 219–59) is partly a parody of a sound film script, with its 'Shadows by the film folk, masses by the good people. Promptings by Elanio Vitale. Longshots, upcloses, outblacks . . . ' (221.21–2). This indeterminately inter-medial production – a 'celtelleneteutoslavsendlatinsoundscript' (219.7) – is on stage/screen/air from the 'Feenichts Playhouse' (219.2), alluding to Dublin's Phoenix Picture House, which had been showing films since the early 1910s, but also raising the question of how the *Wake* itself might be remediated before Bute and Frampton's efforts. Famously, Joyce was recorded reading the 'Anna Livia Plurabelle' episode himself in 1929.[17] This showcases its creative principles through the aural medium of the gramophone, but works equally well broadcast in the 'blind' medium of radio. However, recognising the episode's simultaneous affinities with cinema, Joyce also sanctioned a mid-1930s sample treatment by Stuart Gilbert for adapting *Finnegans Wake* as a sound film. This clearly brings out the text's ongoing influence from lantern transformations and their remediation by film animation through how it visualises Joyce's morphing and interfusion of characters, objects and situations.

Gilbert's treatment was undertaken around 1935, at Joyce's 'request' and 'encouragement', the writer even 'ma[king] a number of suggestions for its improvement' which Gilbert incorporated directly.[18] Gilbert's project seems particularly apt for a text sprinkled with punning references to contemporary animated figures, not just Mutt and Jeff, but Popeye and Olive Oyl (Olive d'Oyly, 279.F21), as well as popular strip cartoons such as Krazy Kat ('Kat Kresbyterians', 120.02), Hergé's boy reporter ('Tintin tintin', 235.32), and their avatars in Victorian characters such as Ally Sloper ('allysloper', 248.10) and Handy Andy ('handy antics', 229.02.), who also featured in lantern slides. Umberto Eco also identified multiple scenarios based on strip cartoons and animation woven into Joyce's 'meandertale', from Mandrake the Magician to Felix the Cat.[19] The early vogue for micro-photographic documentaries led to the surreal 'entomological animation' of Wladislaw Starewicz in Russia. Starewicz used real insects in a logical extension of the popular tradition of Victorian 'humorous Taxidermy', which often brought its narrative displays to life using electricity. In Starewicz's satirical masterpieces of the 1910s, insects acted out anthropomorphic roles. He made a version of Krylov's fable, *The Ant and the Grasshopper* (1911), one of the first Russian films to be exported and screened widely, which could have influenced *Finnegans Wake*'s 'Ondt and Gracehoper' section (pp. 414–19). Nicholas Miller has compared the Fleischer Brothers' *Out of the Inkwell* cartoons with the 'Haunted Inkbottle' in which Shem the Penman resides (182.31).[20] The Fleischers developed the Rotoscope technique for producing more realistic animated movement for their serial character Koko the Clown in the 1920s, who always emerges from a cartoonist's inkwell to wreak havoc around a live-action studio. (They also developed Popeye as one of the first sound cartoon characters in the 1930s.) Just as the cartoonist produces the 'polymorphous plasticism' of their animated screen world from the medium of ink, Shem as Joyce's writer-within-the-text is the proxy author of its polytropic play, which spills riotously into life out of his haunted inkbottle. Thus examination of Gilbert's scenario confirms that Joyce recognised the affinity between the methods of animation and his text at least strongly enough to take the project seriously.

Corresponding to the 'Anna Livia Plurabelle' episode's first seven pages (pp. 196–202), the script's layout also recalls 'Circe's' surreal 'stage' directions and visual trickery while displaying distinct cartoon influence in its morphing and interfusing of characters, objects, scales, situations and sounds. Arguably, those influences from the polymorphous plasticity of cartoons are themselves a technical extension of the capacity for almost infinite, protean transformation between projected images which Mrs Abdy celebrated in Victorian dissolving views. The transformations emerge from an initial context of live action and dialogue in Gilbert's script, as two Liffey washerwomen, scrubbing HCE's dirty linen in public, give a running commentary:

> No. 2 points to the horizon. Both women look upstream. The horizon rapidly approaches, showing a tall, triangular hill outlined against storm-clouds. Flashes of lightning. The mountain is gradually covered with clouds which condense into a man, the Big Man (H.C.E.). He is staggering down a rock road carrying a lantern. A close-up of the lantern shows that it is really a parrot cage. (pp. 10–12)

The horizon 'rushes' towards the viewer like a landscape mobilised by scrolling a panorama. HCE carries a transformative lantern, hinting equally at film's debt to this other technical predecessor. Moreover, parrots magically appearing in cages were a common subject of the cinematic combination of images achieved by spinning thaumatropes, one of the commonest eye-conning optical toys. HCE's parrot escapes this constricted visual space to metamorphose into an aeroplane, tracing a panoramic map of Dublin on the sky. Meanwhile, HCE pursues Anna Livia as a nymph materialising from a misty waterfall like a living statue from 'Circe' in *Ulysses*. Caressing her on his lap, HCE transforms back into a mountain in dioramically fading light, 'his knees . . . the ledge of rock on which Anna is sitting'; before she too dissolves back into waterfall (p. 14). Similarly, the ancient form of an invading Viking longship approaching the Liffey's mouth oscillates with a modern liner's; at which the estuary's sandbanks turn into raging bulls, tossing its waters with their horns (p. 14).

Taking full advantage of parallels between the synchronised soundtrack and the aural dimension of Joyce's text, Gilbert's script treats hearing as polymorphically as vision, echoing their creative interplay in the animated genre epitomised by Disney's *Silly Symphonies* at this time.[21] Popping back up from the water like Botticelli's *Birth of Venus*, Anna tosses away her fiddle, only for its strings to be matched by reeds 'swaying and rubbing together' which continue its tune for HCE, who now shimmers between sunbather and basking crocodile himself. Seasons change as instantaneously as popular set-piece summer and winter views in lantern shows: when Anna tosses bacon scraps from a pan they fall back as snow, initiating a bacchanalian ice carnival. Perhaps recalling the famous scene in Griffith's *Way Down East* (1920), the thawing river cracks into floes carrying away stranded dancers. They in turn dissolve into 'leaves of a tree, rustling in the wind', under which Anna sits, flirtatiously nuzzling its trunk, which becomes HCE's cheek through close-up (p. 16). Anna plunges through the pool formed by the uprooted tree to escape as he morphs into a forbidding priest. HCE finally captures and masters her elusive image by sculpting it from the pool's water in a moment of impossible plasticity which climaxes the episode's visual Pygmalionism (p. 18). Poignantly, Gilbert's concluding audio-visuals return to symphonic reeds and the floating violin abandoned by Anna over dialogue in Wakese:

> No 1: He gave her the tigris' eye!
> No 2: O happy fault! Me wish it was he!
> No 1: O wasn't he the bold bad priest!
> No 2: And wasn't she the naughty Liffey! (p. 19)

Gilbert's sample treatment is conclusive evidence that cinematic animation remained a significant form for Joyce, while nested within it are clearly many echoes of older forms which film remediated. It was undertaken as Joyce was negotiating with a Hungarian director about adapting the episode over-all. Though Gilbert later referred to it as an 'ideal', rather than practical, sce-nario, he agreed that it might have been finally realised using techniques like the 'Night on Bald Mountain' sequence of Disney's *Fantasia* (1940), based on Modest Mussorgsky's composition. This animated Russian 'Walpurgisnacht' famously features a mountain transforming into a devil and back again, among numerous phantasmagoric audio-visual metamorphoses.[22] With today's state-of-the-art computer-generated imagery, which can treat live footage of actors' bodies or any object on screen with all the polymorphous plasticity that was once the preserve of dissolving views and cartoons, Gilbert's treatment seems far from unfeasible now.

Hence *Finnegans Wake* in no way terminated creative inter-mediality with the cinematic in Joyce's work. It enriched his legacy for literary form by con-tinuing to face, Janus-like, into film's prehistory and future simultaneously. It confirms that no other Modernist writer was more imaginatively driven by moving images and their ever expanding role in modernity's media-cultural imaginary.

NOTES

1. See Ellmann, *James Joyce*, p. 53, note.
2. Philip Kitcher, *Joyce's Kaleidoscope: An Invitation to Finnegans Wake* (Oxford: Oxford University Press, 2007), pp. 3–4.
3. See Jane Lewty, 'Joyce and Radio', in Richard Brown (ed.), *A Companion to James Joyce* (Oxford: Blackwell, 2008), pp. 390–406; see also her '"What They Had Heard Said Written": Joyce, Pound, and the Cross-Correspondence of Radio', in Debra Rae Cohen, Michael Coyle and Jane Lewty (eds), *Broadcasting Modernism* (Gainesville, FL: University Press of Florida, 2009), pp. 199–220.
4. Anthony Burgess, *Re Joyce* (1965) (New York: W. W. Norton, 2000), p. 194. *Finnegans Wake* refers to 'piously forged palimpsests', 182.02.
5. See the special section on 'Mary Ellen Bute: "Film Pioneer"', in *Flashpoint Maga-zine*, including Kit Smyth Basquin on 'Mary Ellen Bute's *Passages from Finnegans Wake*', available at <http://www.flashpointmag.com/basquin.htm>. See also the in-depth article by Sheila O'Malley in *Film Comment* (May/June 2018) at <https://www.filmcomment.com/article/mary-ellen-bute-passages-from-finnegans-wake/> (both last accessed 8 June 2011).
6. Quoted in Wheeler Winston Dixon, *The Exploding Eye: A Re-visionary History of the 1960s* (Albany, NY: State University of New York Press, 1997), p. 37. See also Lauren Rabinowitz, 'Mary Ellen Bute', in Jan-Christopher Horak (ed.), *Lovers of Cinema: The First American Avant-Garde 1919–1945* (Madison, WI: University of Wisconsin Press, 1998), pp. 315–34.
7. Gunning, 'Waking and Faking: Ireland and Cinema Astray', p. 29.
8. Ibid., pp. 30–1.
9. Ellmann, *James Joyce*, pp. 580–1 and note.

10. See Arthur C. Clarke, 'Extra-Terrestrial Relays', *Wireless World* (October 1945), pp. 305–8.

11. Donald F. Theall, *James Joyce's Techno-Poetics* (Toronto: University of Toronto Press, 1997), esp. pp. 66–7, 148–50, 165–6.

12. See introduction to Timothy Campbell, *Wireless Writing in the Age of Marconi: Electronic Mediations* (Minneapolis, MN: University of Minnesota Press, 2006), pp. ix–xvii (xiii).

13. Finn Fordham, 'Early Television and Joyce's *Finnegans Wake*: New Technology and Flawed Power', in Matthew Feldman, Erik Tonning and Henry Mead (eds), *Broadcasting in the Modernist Era* (London: Bloomsbury, 2014), pp. 39–56 (46–7).

14. David Trotter, *Literature in the First Media Age* (Cambridge, MA: Harvard University Press, 2013), p. 13.

15. Fordham, 'Early Television and Joyce's *Finnegans Wake*', p. 51.

16. Ibid., p. 54. For an alternative view, see Louis Armand, 'JJ, JD, TV', in Andrew J. Mitchell and Sam Slote (eds), *Derrida and Joyce: Texts and Contexts* (Albany, NY: State University of New York Press, 2013), pp. 213–26.

17. See Ellmann, *James Joyce*, p. 617.

18. Stuart Gilbert, 'Sketch of a Scenario of Anna Livia Plurabelle', in *The James Joyce Yearbook*, ed. Maria Jolas (Paris: Transition Press, 1949), pp. 10–19 (19n). Subsequent references to this work are given in parentheses in the text.

19. Umberto Eco, *The Role of the Reader: Explorations in the Semiotics of Texts* (Bloomington, IN: Indiana University Press. 1994), pp. 67–72.

20. I am grateful to Nicholas Miller's unpublished paper, 'Joyce's Haunted Inkbottle: Early Animation and *Finnegans Wake*', delivered at the 2016 James Joyce Symposium in London. Joyce may also have based his character's name on a famous play about a forger, *Jim the Penman*, filmed twice in his lifetime, by Edwin S. Porter in 1915 and Kenneth S. Webb in 1921.

21. Cleo Hanaway-Oakley also makes some interesting suggestions about synergies between *Finnegans Wake*'s 'grapho-phonic' playfulness and the synchronised film soundtrack, which added another sensory resource to cinema from the late 1920s. Cleo Hanaway-Oakley, *James Joyce and the Phenomenology of Film* (Oxford: Oxford University Press, 2017), pp. 119–20.

22. See Patricia Hutchins, 'James Joyce and the Cinema', *Sight and Sound*, 21 (August–September 1951), p. 12.

CONCLUSION: BEFORE AND AFTER FILM

By placing Joyce's writing back into the context of nineteenth-century moving image media, I have provided an explanation for the paradox that his cinematicity seemed ahead of screen practice itself in the views of directors and theorists. I have demonstrated how Joyce's eye and imagination were so profoundly shaped by the late Victorian visual culture which film remediated that he was able to achieve what Bazin called 'ultracinematographic' effects. This explains Joyce's extraordinary receptiveness to projected film when it arrived, and as pioneers began developing its capacities by synthesising the diverse characteristics of its predecessors. Thus Joyce was instrumental in extending classical *ekphrasis* into the modernity of moving photographic images, broadcasting and telecommunications. Hence I have addressed the deficit in scholarship before the cinematograph on Joyce's cinematic Modernism,

We have seen how pre-filmic optical toys such as the kaleidoscope, stereoscope, zoëtrope and phenakistoscope, which exploited the 'persistence of vision effect', are central to how Joyce presented vision and consciousness in terms of technologically produced moving images. His fiction reveals a profound understanding that cinematicity was never solely inherent to the apparatus and institution that became known as cinema in the twentieth century, but was a set of evolving characteristics shared across a whole inter-medial ecology. Moreover, Joyce's ekphrastic experiments tell us much about how such cinematic forms interacted and shaped the media-cultural imaginary of his historical moment and after. My research confirms that his literary method was imaginatively primed and nourished through the connective tissue of a visual culture imbued with a sense of things to come. Alongside optical toys, Joyce references shadowgraphy, magic lanterns, panoramas and dioramas, instantaneous photographic analysis, as well as film peepshows. His fiction reflects how these media influenced, overlapped and continued to coexist with projected film for some time; and he emulates and critiques their effects in its pages, with a flair for ekphrastic cinematicity surpassing other Modernists.

The mutoscope, which mechanised the flipbook principle, is the only device for watching moving photographic pictures named in *Ulysses*, albeit what we commonly call cinema was nearly a quarter of a century old by its publication. By choosing this device rather than projected film shows, Joyce both looked into cinema's future and backwards into its prehistory in animated images. Similarly, this book has made the case for being more 'Janus-faced' in examining Joyce's influences before 1895 as well as after. Joyce showed ambivalent fascination with the seductive appeal of moving images, reaching back into the prehistory of film's eye-conning illusion. Hence he frequently reworked Plato's archetypal media parable to express wariness about the modern age of mechanised moving images. On the one hand, his teenage 'Silhouettes' are embryonic of camera-eyed visualisation and form in his published fictions; on the other, the latter continue to parallel how ancient shadow shows would be remediated by film and cartoon animation.

As a major progenitor of film, we have also seen how magic lantern shows were a key influence on Joycean cinematicity. Despite claiming to 'bar' their influence, *Dubliners* alludes to lantern motifs, genres and techniques in many stories, and Joyce continued to do this from *Portrait* to *Finnegans Wake*. The lantern's underlying presence explains key aspects of Joyce's experimentalism in making his writing cinematic before film developed equivalent methods through editing, particularly in 'dissolving views' transitioning through space, time and consciousness. This book confirms how such intimations in Joyce's style reached maturity in *Portrait* and *Ulysses*.

In *Portrait* Joyce also advanced the literary emulation of instantaneous photography, one of the primary scientific drives leading to film, extending such analysis of movement into the perceptual and cognitive processes of the subject through the mobilised virtual gaze of his protagonist. The novel's camera-eyed focalisation and 'montage' structure are rooted in speculations about a method for picturing a mind developing over time using photographic experiments as a guiding metaphor. The imagistic rhythm of Stephen's stream of consciousness continuously overlaps present perceptions and past memories, to trace a pattern moving dynamically towards his vocational future as an artist, revolutionising the *Bildungsroman* by adding a new cinematised temporality to it.

We have also seen Joyce engaging with another visual entertainment, comparable to the lantern in terms of its contribution to the modern media-cultural imaginary. I have drawn extensively on media archaeology into the lost history of the moving panorama as another large-scale, 'moving picture' event and immersive, virtual experience. Detailed references and effects confirm Joyce's familiarity with several forms of panorama show. I have shown how *Ulysses* is a Modernist extension of Huhtamo's parallel discursive panorama, which both plays on and critiques the imperial tendencies of the panorama itself by engaging with its key topoi and techniques. Joyce brought together every previous strand of his literary cinematicity in his Modernist epic, but also laid down a template for panoramic representation of the city that has been influential on both fiction and film. *Ulysses* implicitly occupies the narrative vantage point of the original panorama and its imaginary city overview, but also descends into mobile, street-level modes. Joyce's *flâneuring* Dubliners mimic the roving camera-eyes of urban 'phantom rides' and film montages which remediated panoramic principles. Joyce also extended Victorian figurations of the 'stream of consciousness' itself as a kind of moving panorama, switching interactively between external perception and internalised, involuntary memory and creating a kind of Modernist psychogeography. *Ulysses* reflects the inevitable updating from moving panorama to cinema screen as a key metaphor for the imagistic flow of consciousness after the cinematograph. Moreover, because Joyce's narrative techniques emulated methods of storytelling through moving images common in magic lantern and moving panorama shows, readers have the impression of an almost invisible agency working behind the structures of his texts. This is emphatic in his orchestration of sub-sections and implied linkages between them in 'Wandering Rocks'. If not absolutely identical with Gaudreault's filmic monstrator, there is significant convergence through intermedial resemblance.

Continuing the focus on Joycean cinematicity after film, my Coda has also challenged *Finnegans Wake*'s status as marking Joyce's final turn towards more radiophonic methods. I have shown that Joyce continued to be Janus-faced in relation to the history, present and future of moving images, expanded by the possibilities of broadcasting in both aural *and* visual forms. Far from splitting with cinematicity's roots, the *Wake* both retrofits pre-filmic technologies for its own creative purposes and engages with film's emergent successor in the form of television.

Throughout this book, I have stressed that it is vital to understand the conditions under which film shows finally arrived in Joyce's home city, leading to his symptomatic involvement with the industry as one of its first cinema managers. This typifies how Joyce's interest in cinematicity had deeper and wider roots in contemporary visual culture. As we have seen, before the cinematograph arrived in Dublin, reports raised expectations about its astonishing combination of the capabilities of its predecessors, so audiences could witness an illusion so virtual that it 'appears to be looking through a window at something actually occurring in the next street'. The effect of total movement and vicarious participation in events elsewhere in space and time seemed equally impressive. Projected film's ability to capture living urban scenes with a new kind of panoramic inclusiveness was also highlighted. As I have shown, such reactions quickened Joyce's aspirations towards rendering everyday life through ekphrastic moving images. Hence he emulated film's virtually stereoscopic and immersive simulation, but also expanded this effect to a similarly panoramic impression of Dublin's urban milieu. In particular, Joyce explored the ideological implications of how and why film panoramas mediated civic events. Hence 'Wandering Rocks' can be seen as a subversive response to choreographed colonial spectacles. The film camera had alternative potentials for defamiliarising everyday life, making its telling details visible in ways that were harder for propagandists to control than traditional media. This has demonstrable affinities with Joyce's scrutinising of visual contingencies for unexpected epiphanies through his literary lens.

Despite its failure, the Volta remains a significant landmark in the creation of cinema and the accompanying visual revolution, both in the popular media-cultural imaginary and the Modernist arts. It was undoubtedly more than a passing business opportunity, but was bound up with Joyce's long-held and intensely creative fascination with optics and moving images. This did not diminish after its demise, as his writing overwhelmingly testifies. I hope that this book has made a convincing case that to understand Joyce's response to the evolution of cinematicity properly we have to dig deeper into its role in his work both *before*, as well as *after* the coming of film.

SELECT VISIOGRAPHY

FILMS

Ambrosio, Arturo, and Luigi Maggi (dir.), *Nero: A Sensational Story of Ancient Rome* (1909).

Bertolini, Francesco, and Adolfo Padovan (dir.), *L'Inferno* (1911).

Blackton, J. Stuart (dir.), *Quo Vadis or the Way of the Cross* (1909).

Boggs, Francis, and Thomas Persons (dir.), *The Count of Monte Cristo* (1908).

Bowers, Charles, and Raoul Barré, *Mutt and Jeff* (1916–23 and 1925–26).

Buñuel, Luis, and Salvador Dalí (dir.), *Un Chien Andalou* (1929).

Bute, Mary Ellen (dir.), *Passages from Finnegans Wake* (1965).

Campbell, Colin (dir.), *Monte Christo* (1912).

Cavalcanti, Alberto (dir.), *Rien que les heures* (1925).

Clair, René (dir.), *Le Fantôme du Moulin Rouge* (1925).

Collins, Alf (dir.), *Murphy's Wake* (1903).

Deed, André (dir.), *Cretinetti che Bello! (Too Beautiful!)* (1909).

Deed, André (dir.), *Cretinetti ha ingoiata un Gambero (Devilled Crab?)* (Italy 1909).

Dickson, W. K. L. (dir.), *Pope Leo XIII* (1898).

Director unknown, *The Count of Monte Christo* [*sic*] (Challenge Film Company, 1910).

Disney, Walt (dir.), *Fantasia* (1940).

Disney, Walt (dir.), *Silly Symphonies* (1929–39).

Dulac, Germaine (dir.), *Le Coquille et le Clergyman* (1928).

Dupont, E. A. (dir.), *Varieté* (1925).

Edison, Thomas A., Company, *Champs de Mars* (1900).

Edison, Thomas A., Company, *Panorama of the Paris Exposition from the Seine* (1900).

Edison, Thomas A., Company, *Uncle Josh at the Moving Pictures* (1902).

Eisenstein, Sergei M. (dir.), *Battleship Potemkin* (1925).

Eisenstein, Sergei M. (dir.), *October* (1928).

Eisenstein, Sergei M. (dir.), *Strike* (1925).

Fleischer Brothers, *Out of the Inkwell* (1918–29).

Fleischer Brothers, *Popeye* (1933–42).

Frampton, Hollis (dir.), *Gloria!* (1979).

Golden, Joseph A., and Edwin S. Porter (dir.), *The Count of Monte Cristo* (1913).

Griffith, D. W. (dir.), *After Many Years* (1908).

Griffith, D. W. (dir.), *Birth of a Nation* (1915).

Griffith, D. W. (dir.), *A Drunkard's Reformation* (1909).

Griffith, D. W. (dir.), *Judith of Bethulia* (1913).

Griffith, D. W. (dir.), *The Drunkard's Child* (1909).

Griffith, D. W. (dir.), *Way Down East* (1920).

Griffith, D. W. (dir.), *What Drink Did* (1909).

Hepworth, Cecil (dir.), *The Late Queen's Visit to Dublin: Royal Procession Entering the City Gates* (1900).

Hickey, Kieran (dir.), *Faithful Departed* (1968).

Hickey, Kieran (dir.), *The Light of Other Days* (1972).

Irish Animated Photo Company, *Great Gordon-Bennett Motor Race* (1903).

Keaton, Buster (dir.), *Sherlock Junior* (1924).

Lang, Fritz (dir.), *Metropolis* (1927).

Lumière, Auguste and Louis (dir.), *L'Arrivée d'un train* (1895).

Lumière, Auguste and Louis (dir.), *Barque sortant du port* (1895).

Lumière, Auguste and Louis (dir.), *Démolition d'un mur* (1895).

Lumière, Auguste and Louis (dir.), *La Mer (Sea Bathing)* (1895).

Lumière, Auguste and Louis (dir.), *La Sortie des usines lumière à Lyon* (1895).

Lumière, Auguste and Louis (dir.), *Traffic on O'Connell Bridge* (1897).

Maggi, Luigi (dir.), *The Count of Monte Cristo* (1908).

Melbourne Cooper, Arthur (dir.), *Matches an Appeal* (1899 or 1914?).

Méliès, Georges (dir.), *L'Affaire Dreyfus* (1899).

Méliès, Georges (dir.), *Au Pays des jouets* (1908).

Méliès, Georges (dir.), *Les Aventures de Robinson Crusoe* (1902).

Méliès, Georges (dir.), *Cendrillon* (1899).

Méliès, Georges (dir.), *L'Escamotage d'une dame (The Disappearing Woman)* (1896).

Méliès, Georges (dir.), *L'Homme a la tête de caoutchouc (The Man with the Indiarubber Head)* (1901).

Méliès, Georges (dir.), *The Infernal Palace* (titled *The Bewitched Castle* in Volta's first programme?) (1903).

Méliès, Georges (dir.), *Jeanne D'Arc* (1900).

Méliès, Georges (dir.), *La Lanterne magique* (1903).

Méliès, Georges (dir.), *La Lune à un mètre* (1898).

Méliès, Georges (dir.), *Le Mélomane* (*The Melomaniac*) (1903).

Méliès, Georges (dir.), *Le Rêve de Noël* (1900).

Méliès, Georges (dir.), *Le Voyage dans la lune* (*A Trip to the Moon*) (1902).

Mitchell, Sagar, and James Kenyon (dir.), *Congregation Leaving Jesuit Church of St. Francis Xavier* (1902).

Mitchell, Sagar, and James Kenyon (dir.), *Diving Lucy* (1903).

Mitchell, Sagar, and James Kenyon (dir.), *Illustrated Tram Ride over Patrick's Bridge and Grand Parade* (1902).

Mitchell, Sagar, and James Kenyon (dir.), *Panorama of College Green* (1902).

Mitchell, Sagar, and James Kenyon (dir.), *Poole's Clitheroe* (1901).

Mitchell, Sagar, and James Kenyon (dir.), *Ride on a Tramcar through Belfast* (1901).

Mitchell, Sagar, and James Kenyon (dir.), *Trade Procession at Opening of Cork Exhibition* (1902).

Mitchell, Sagar, and James Kenyon (dir.), *Train Ride from Blarney to Cork on Cork & Muskerry Light Railway* (1902).

Mitchell, Sagar, and James Kenyon (dir.), *A Trip to North Wales on the St Elvies* (1902).

Mitchell, Sagar, and James Kenyon (dir.), *Wales v Ireland at Wrexham* (1906).

Montgomery, Robert (dir.), *The Lady in the Lake* (1946).

Morley, Harry T., and Sidney Olcott (dir.), *Ben Hur: A Tale of the Christ* (1907).

Murnau, F. W. (dir.), *Der letzte Mann* (*The Last Laugh*) (1925).

Nichols, George (dir.), *The Star Boarder* (1914).

Olcott, Sidney (dir.), *The Lad from Old Ireland* (Kalem, 1910).

Paul, R. W., and Birt Acres (dir.), *The Countryman and the Cinematograph* (1901).

Paul, R. W., and Birt Acres (dir.), *Queen Victoria's Diamond Jubilee* (1897).

Paul, R. W., and Birt Acres (dir.), *Rough Sea at Dover* (1895).

Paul, R. W., and Birt Acres (dir.), *Scrooge or Marley's Ghost* (1901).

Porter, Edwin S. (dir.), *Great Train Robbery* (1903).

Porter, Edwin S. (dir.), *Jim the Penman* (1915).

Porter, Edwin S. (dir.), *Life of an American Fireman* (1903).

Rawlence, Christopher (dir.), *The Missing Reel: The Untold Story of the Lost Inventor of Moving Pictures* (1989).

Rector, Enoch J. (dir.), *Corbett-Fitzsimmons Fight* (1897).

Reiniger, Lotte (dir.), *Die Abenteure von Prinz Achmed* (1926).

Robison, Arthur (dir.), *Schatten: eine Nächtliche Halluzination* (*Warning Shadows*) (1923).

Ruttmann, Walther (dir.), *Berlin: Sinfonie einer Großstadt* (1927).

Smith, G. A. (dir.), *Aladdin and the Wonderful Lamp* (1899).

Smith, G. A. (dir.), *Cinderella* (1898).

Smith, G. A. (dir.), *Santa Claus* (1898).

Starewicz, Wladislaw (dir.), *The Ant and the Grasshopper* (1911).

Stow, Percy (dir.), *A Glass of Goat's Milk* (GB, 1909).

Strick, Joseph (dir.), *A Portrait of the Artist as a Young Man* (1977).

Sullivan, Pat, and Otto Messmer (dir.), *Felix the Cat* (1919–32).

Tait, Charles (dir.), *The Story of the Kelly Gang* (1906)

Vertov, Dziga (dir.), *Man with a Movie Camera* (1929).

Viertel, Berthold, and Béla Baláz (dir.), *Die Abenteuer eines Zehnmarkscheins* (1924).

Warwick Trading Company, *With the Bioscope through Ireland* [tourist series] (1900).

Webb, Kenneth S. (dir.), *Jim the Penman* (1921).

Webb, Steve (dir.), *Holmfirth Hollywood* (BBC 4, 6 June 2006).

Williamson, James (dir.), *Remorse* (1903).

Zecca, Ferdinand (dir.), *Histoire d'un crime* (1901).

SLIDE SETS

The principal sources of information and/or images for these are:

LUCERNA: http://lucerna.exeter.ac.uk

MLS website: http://www.magiclantern.org.uk/

MLS, *Illustrated Bamforth Slide Catalogue* CD-ROM, compiled by Richard Crangle and Robert Macdonald for the Magic Lantern Society (London: MLS, 2009).

Bamforth, James, and Co., *Christie's Old Organ, Or, Home! Sweet Home!* (1892).

Bamforth, James, and Co., *Christmas Day in the Workhouse* (1890).

Bamforth, James, and Co., *The Drink Fiend* (1893).

Bamforth, James, and Co., *The Holy Shrine* (1897).

Bamforth, James, and Co., *In His Steps* (1899).

Bamforth, James, and Co., *The Lifeboat* (1899).

Bamforth, James, and Co., *Love's Old Sweet Song* (1899).

Bamforth, James, and Co., *The Matron's Story* (1890).

Bamforth, James, and Co., *Robin Adair* (1898).

Bamforth, James, and Co., *The Scent of the Lilies* (1903).

Bamforth, James, and Co., *The Signal Box* (1889).

Bamforth, James, and Co., *The Soldier's Dream* (1890).

Bamforth, James, and Co., *What Are the Wild Waves Saying?* (1898).

Boggs Beale, Joseph, *The Raven* (1894).

Catholic Truth Society, *Catholic Foreign Missions* (1897).

Catholic Truth Society, *Joan of Arc* (n.d.).

Chatham Pexton, *White Slaves of London* (c. 1894)

Cruikshank, George, *The Bottle* (1847; repr. in colour by York and Son, in/ before 1888).

Cruikshank, George, *The Drunkard's Children* (1848; repr. in colour by York and Son, in/before 1888).

Lawrence, William, *The Lakes of Killarney and Glengariff, via Cork and Bantry* (1894).

Maker unknown, *Buffalo Hunting in the Wild West* (in/before 1891).

Maker unknown, *Greece: Prehistoric, Legendary, Classical and Modern* (in/ before 1888).

Maker unknown, *In His Steps: Or, What Would Jesus do?* (n.d.).

Maker unknown, *Travels in the Holy Land* (1872).

Maker unknown, *The Vision of Hell by Dante Alighieri* [from Doré's illustrations] (n.d.).

Newton and Co., *Enoch Arden*, (in/before 1888).

Newton and Co., *Voyage Round the World* (in/before 1888).

Piggot, T. J. and W.F., *The Curtain: Or, A Peep into the Future* (1897).

Pumphrey, Alfred, *Dante's Inferno* (in/before 1888).

Pumphrey, Alfred, *A Railway Story with a Moral* (in/before 1888).

Pumphrey, Alfred, *Subjects from Dante's Inferno* (in/before 1895).

Riley Brothers, *Ben Hur: A Tale of the Christ* (1880).

Riley Brothers, *Street Life: Or, People We Meet* (c. 1887).

Riley Brothers, *A Strong Contrast* (1892).

Theobald and Co., *Handy Andy* (in/before 1903).

Theobald and Co., *Western Pioneers and Indian Warfare* (n.d.).

Valentine and Son, *Texan Cowboy: Through South-Western Texas with a Camera* (1885).

Wilson, G. W., *The Life of the Right Honourable William Ewart Gladstone* (in/before 1895).

York and Son, *Bunyan's Pilgrim's Progress* (in/before 1888).

York and Son, *Buy Your Own Cherries – A Tale of Real Life* (1885).

York and Son, *Curfew Shall not Ring Tonight* (in/before 1888).

York and Son, *Dan Dabberton's Dream* (c. 1887).

York and Son, *Enoch Arden* (1890).

York and Son, *Gabriel Grub, a Christmas Story: Or, The Sexton Who Was Stolen by Goblins* (c. 1875).

York and Son, *John Hampton's Home* (n.d.).

York and Son, *The Lifeboat* (1886).

York and Son, *Marley's Ghost: A Christmas Carol* (1884).
York and Son, *Mary, the Maid of the Inn* (in/before 1888).
York and Son, *Rambles about Rome* (1894).
York and Son, *Wanderings in Paris* (in/before 1888).

PANORAMAS AND DIORAMAS

The principal sources of information and/or images for these are Comment, *The Panorama*; *IiM*; Hyde, *Panoramania!*; and *MLP&MPS*.

Banvard, John, *Panorama of the Mississippi* (1851).
Barker, Robert (or Nelson's?), *Bay of Dublin*, exhibited at Leicester Square (1807–09).
Barker, Robert (or Nelson's?), *Panorama of the Battle of Waterloo* (1816).
Barker, Robert (or Nelson's?), *Panorama of Edinburgh* (1788).
Barker, Robert (or Nelson's?), *A View of London* (1794).
Burford, Robert, *Summer and Winter Views of the Polar Regions* (1850).
Chase, Charles, 'Stereopticon Cyclorama' (1895).
Daguerre, Louis-Jacques-Mandé, *The Inauguration of the Temple of Salomon* (September 1836).
Daguerre, Louis-Jacques-Mandé, *A Midnight Mass at the Church of Saint-Étienne-du-Mont* (1834).
Daguerre, Louis-Jacques-Mandé, *The Village of Alagna* (1836).
d'Alési, Hugo, *Maréorama, ou Illusion d'un voyage en mer à bord d'un paquebot* (1900).
Dibdin, T. C., *Diorama of the Ganges* (1850).
Dumoulin, Louis, *Panorama of the Battle of Waterloo* (1912).
Edwards, W. H., *Two Hours in the New World* (1862).
Gillard, Hardy, *Great American Panorama* (1872).
Gompertz, *Diorama of India* (1859).
Grieve, Thomas and William, *Aeronautikon! Or, Journey of the Great Balloon* (1836).
Grimoin-Sanson, Raoul, *Cinéorama* (1900)
Groves's Animated Dioramas (presented at the Rotunda from February 1839):
    Great St Bernard's Pass.
    Napoleon Bonaparte's Crossing of the Alps.
    Vision of Shakespeare.
Howorth's Hibernica (various, 1880s).
Jambon, Marcel, and A. Bailly, *Trans-Siberian Railway Panorama* (1900).
Maker unknown, *Grand Balloon Ascent from the Rotundo [sic] Gardens* (1854).
Marshall's, *Grand Peristrephic Panorama* (1815).
Marshall's, *Peristrephic Panorama of the Battle of Navarin* (1828).

Marshall's, *Peristrephic Panorama of the Battle of Waterloo* (1818).

Phillips, Knell, Connop, Louis Hage and Dudgeon, *Grand National Diorama of Ireland* (1865).

Poole and Young, *Myrioramas* or 'Dioramic Excursions':

Myriorama of the Soudan and Egyptian Wars (1885).

Myriorama of the Soudan, Egyptian and Boer Wars (1890).

New Eclipse Myriorama (1891).

Our Empire (1901).

Picturesque Trips Abroad and Latest Events (1898?).

Sights of the World (1892).

Trips Abroad (1886).

Smith, Albert, *Ascent of Mont Blanc* (1852–58).

Smith, Albert, *The Overland Mail* (1850).

Warren and Fahey, *Grand Moving Panorama of the Nile* (1849).

SELECT BIBLIOGRAPHY

PRIMARY SOURCES

Abdy, Mrs [Maria], 'Dissolving Views', *Metropolitan*, 38:149 (September 1843), p. 72.

Black, Alexander, *Miss Jerry, with Thirty-Seven Illustrations from Life Photographs by the Author* (New York: Charles Scribner's Sons, 1895; facsimile repr. London: Forgotten Books, 2018).

Catholic Truth Society, *Shrines of Our Lady: A Lecture for Use with the Magic Lantern* (London: Catholic Truth Society, 1896).

Dujardin, Edouard, *Les Lauriers sont coupés* (1888); Eng. trans. *The Bays Are Sere*, trans. Anthony Suter (London: Libris, 1991).

Eden, Fannie, *White Slaves of London* (London and Dublin: W. B. Horner, 1887) (also slide reading on MLS website no. 91139, in/before 1894).

Gilbert, Stuart, 'Sketch of a Scenario of Anna Livia Plurabelle', in *The James Joyce Yearbook*, ed. Maria Jolas (Paris: Transition Press, 1949), pp. 10–19.

Greenwood, Thomas, 'Battle Scenes, Upon Viewing the Peristrephic Panorama of the Battle of Waterloo', in Thomas Greenwood, *Scripture Sketches: with Other Poems and Hymns* (London: Hatchard, 1830), pp. 95–100.

Greer, Tom, *A Modern Daedalus* (London: Griffith, Farran, Okeden and Welsh, 1885; facsimile repr. Kessinger Publishing, 2015).

'J.B.C.', *Ireland in the Magic Lantern: The Lakes of Killarney and Glengariff, via Cork and Bantry: The Prince of Wales Route* (Dublin: William Lawrence, 1894).

Joyce, James, *Finnegans Wake* (London: Faber and Faber, 1939).

Joyce, James, *Letters of James Joyce*, vol. 1, ed. Stuart Gilbert (London: Faber and Faber, 1957).

Joyce, James, *Letters of James Joyce*, vol. 2, ed. Richard Ellmann (London: Faber and Faber, 1966).

Joyce, James, *Letters of James Joyce*, vol. 3, ed. Richard Ellmann (London: Faber and Faber, 1966).

Joyce, James, *Poems and Shorter Writings: Including* Epiphanies, Giacomo Joyce *and* 'A Portrait of the Artist', ed. Richard Ellmann, A. Walton Litz and John Whittier-Ferguson (London: Faber and Faber, 1991).

Joyce, James, *A Portrait of the Artist*, in *The James Joyce Archive: A Facsimile of Epiphanies, Notes, Manuscripts and Typescripts*, ed. Hans Walter Gabler (New York: Garland Publishing, 1978).

Joyce, James, 'A Portrait of the Artist' (1904), in Robert Scholes and Richard M. Kain (eds), *In the Workshop of Daedalus: James Joyce and the Raw Materials for* A Portrait of the Artist as a Young Man (Evanston, IL: Northwestern University Press, 1965), pp. 60–8.

Joyce, James, *A Portrait of the Artist as a Young Man*, ed. Jeri Johnson (Oxford: Oxford University Press, 2000).

Joyce, James, *A Portrait of the Artist as a Young Man*, ed. Hans Walter Gabler (New York: W.W. Norton, 2007).

Joyce, James, *Stephen Hero* (1944) (Frogmore: Granada, 1977).

Joyce, James, *Ulysses: The Corrected Text* (1922), ed. Hans Walter Gabler with Wolfhard Steppe and Claus Melchior (London: Bodley Head, 1993).

Langbridge, Revd Frederic, *Dan Dabberton's Dream, etc* [service of song] (London: UK Band of Hope Union, 1894), 'Temperance Stories with Song' series, no. 8 (also slide readings on MLS website nos. 90051 and 90052).

Mitchell, Thomas, *In His Steps, Or What Would Jesus Do? A Service of Song with Readings from the Popular Story by C.M. Sheldon compiled by Thomas Mitchell* (London: T. Mitchell, n.d.) (slide reading on MLS website no. 92038).

O'Brien, Edna, *Lantern Slides* (London: Weidenfeld and Nicolson, 1990).

Pepper, John Henry, *A Strange Lecture: An Illustration of the Haunted Man Ghost Illusion* (London: McGowan and Danks, 1863).

Pirandello, Luigi, *The Notebooks of Serafino Gubbio or (Shoot!)*, trans. C. K. Scott Moncrieff (1915) (Sawtry: Daedalus, 1990).

Plato, *The Republic*, trans. Robin Waterfield (Oxford: Oxford University Press, 1998).

Pope Leo XIII, 'Ars Photographica' (1868), trans. H. T. Henry (1902), quoted in James Joyce, *Dubliners: A Norton Critical Edition*, ed. Margot Norris, Hans Walter Gabler and Walter Hettche (New York: W.W. Norton, 2006), p. 242.

Proust, Marcel, *Du côté de chez Swann* (1913); Eng. trans. *Remembrance of Things Past*, vol. 1, *Swann's Way*, trans. C. K. Scott Moncrieff and Terence Kilmartin (Harmondsworth: Penguin, 1983).

Reisman, Jerry, and Louis Zukofsky, 'James Joyce's Ulysses: Scenario and Continuity' (1935), manuscript available at the Harry Ransom Humanities Research Centre (University of Texas at Austin); also in carbon copy at the Zürich James Joyce Foundation (Hans E. Jahnke bequest).

Romains, Jules, *La Vie unanime* (Paris: L'Abbaye, 1908).

Schnitzler, Arthur, *Leutnant Gustl* (Berlin: S. Fischer Verlag, 1901).

Sims, George R. (ed.), *Living London*, 3 vols, with over 450 illustrations (London: Cassell, 1902).

Sims, George R., *The Social Kaleidoscope*, 2 vols (London: J.P. Fuller, 1881).

Symons, Arthur, *Silhouettes* (London: Matthews and Lane, 1892).

Tiddeman, Lizzie Ellen, *Poverty's Pupil, or Jenny's Promise* (London: Religious Tract Society, 1908).

Walton, O. F., *Christie's Old Organ* (London: Religious Tract Society, 1874) (also slide reading on MLS website as *Christie's Old Organ, Or, Home, Sweet Home*, no. 91859).

Wells, H. G., 'The Stolen Body' (1898), in *The Complete Short Stories of H. G. Wells*, ed. John Hammond (London: Phoenix Press, 2000), pp. 512–24.

Wells, H. G., *When the Sleeper Wakes* (1899) (repr. London: Dent, 1999).

SECONDARY SOURCES

Articles, Essays, Reports and Reviews

Advertisement [for Solomon's], *Freeman's Journal*, 17 February 1890, p. 5.

Agamben, Giorgio, 'Notes on Gestures', in Giorgio Agamben, *Means without End: Notes on Politics*, trans. Vincenzo Binetti and Cesare Casarino (Minneapolis, MN: University of Minnesota Press, 2000), pp. 49–62.

Agee, James, Introductory Essay to Helen Levitt, *A Way of Seeing* (repr. Durham, NC: Duke University Press, 1989), pp. vii–xv.

Anon., 'The Analyticon at the Rotunda', *Freeman's Journal*, 7 October 1898, p. 5.

Anon., 'The Analyticon at the Rotunda', *Dublin Daily Nation*, 11 October 1898, p. 5.

Anon., 'The Cinematograph: A Startling Invention', *Dublin Evening Telegraph*, 26 February 1896, p. 4.

Anon., 'Cyclopia', *Freeman's Journal*, 20 May 1896, p. 5.

Anon., 'Edison's "Kinetoscope"', *Evening Telegraph*, 4 April 1895, p. 3.

Anon., 'The Ghost', *Freeman's Journal*, 16 September, 1863, p. 3.

Anon., 'The Kinetoscope at "Ierne"', *Dublin Evening Telegraph*, 6 April 1895, p. 5.

Anon., 'The Kinetoscope at "Ierne"', *Dublin Evening Mail*, 14 May 1895, p. 4.

Anon., 'The Mechanism of the Kinetoscope', *Dublin Evening Telegraph*, 6 April 1895, p. 5.

Anon., 'The Modern Marvel Co. – The Analyticon', *Dublin Daily Express*, 3 October 1898, p. 6.

Anon., 'The Photographic Society of Ireland', *Optical Magic Lantern Journal and Photographic Enlarger* (June 1890), p. 8 (also available on the DVD-ROM compiled by L. M. H. Smith and Martin Gilbert, *From the Magic Lantern to the Movies: the Optical Magic Lantern Journal 1889–1903* [Ripon: PhotoResearch, 2010]).

Anon., 'Star Theatre of Varieties', *Irish Times*, 22 April 1896, p. 6.

Anon., 'Star Theatre of Varieties', *Irish Times*, 3 November 1896, p. 6.

Anon., 'The Star Theatre: The Cinematographe', *Freeman's Journal*, 3 November 1896, p. 7.

Anon., 'Triumphs of Photography', *Dublin Evening Mail*, 27 January 1896, p. 4.

Anon., untitled article on Muybridge's lecture to the Royal Dublin Society, *Freeman's Journal*, 17 February 1890, p. 5.

Baron, Scarlett, 'Flaubert, Joyce: Vision, Photography, Cinema', *Modern Fiction Studies*, 54:4 (2008), pp. 689–714.

Baudelaire, Charles, 'The Painter of Modern Life' (1863), in *Selected Writings on Art and Literature*, trans. P. E. Charvet (Harmondsworth: Penguin, 1972), pp. 390–435.

Bazin, André, 'In Defence of Mixed Cinema', in *What Is Cinema?*, 2 vols, ed. and trans. Hugh Gray (Berkeley, CA: University of California Press, 1967; 2005), vol. 1, pp. 53–75.

Benjamin, Walter, 'Daguerre or the Panoramas', Part II of 'Paris, the Capital of the Nineteenth Century' (May 1935), in *The Writer of Modern Life: Essays on Charles Baudelaire*, ed. Michael W. Jennings, trans. Howard Eiland, Edmund Jephcott, Rodney Livingstone and Harry Zohn (Cambridge, MA: Harvard University Press, 2006), pp. 33–5.

Benjamin, Walter, 'Little History of Photography' (1931), in *Selected Writings*, 2: *1927–1934* (Cambridge, MA: Belknap Press of Harvard University Press, 1999), pp. 506–30.

Benjamin, Walter, 'The Work of Art in the Age of Mechanical Reproduction' (1936), in *Illuminations*, ed. Hannah Arendt, trans. Harry Zohn (London: Fontana, 1973), pp. 217–52.

Briggs, Austin, '"Roll Away the Reel World, the Reel World": "Circe" and the Cinema', in Morris Beja and Shari Benstock (eds), *Coping With Joyce: Essays From the Copenhagen Symposium* (Columbus, OH: Ohio State University Press, 1989), pp. 145–56.

Brooker, Jeremy, 'The Polytechnic Ghost', *EPVC*, 2:5 (2007), pp. 189–206.

Byerly, Alison, '"A Prodigious Map beneath His Feet": Virtual Travel and the Panoramic Perspective', *Nineteenth-Century Contexts*, 29:2–3 (2007), pp. 151–68.

Cahill, Mary, Andy Halpin, Carol Smith and Stephen D'Arcy, 'Have You Tried the Ash Pit?', *Archaeology Ireland* 28:1 (2014), pp. 30–4.

Carr, H. Wildon, 'I. – Shadworth Hollway Hodgson', *Mind: A Quarterly Review of Psychology and Philosophy*, 21 (1912), pp. 473–85.

Carville, Justin, 'Mr Lawrence's Great Photographic Bazaar: Photography, History and the Imperial Streetscape', *EPVC*, 5:3 (2007), pp. 263–83.

Cate, Phillip Dennis, 'The Spirit of Montmartre', in Phillip Dennis Cate and Mary Shaw (eds), *The Spirit of Montmartre: Cabarets, Humour and the Avant-Garde, 1875–1905* (New Brunswick, NJ: Jane Vorhees Zimmerli Art Museum, 1996), pp. 1–93.

Chase, Charles A., 'Stereopticon Cyclorama', *Optical Magic Lantern Journal*, 6:70 (1895), pp. 45–6.

Condon, Denis, '"Baits to Entrap the Pleasure-Seeker and the Worlding": Charity Bazaars Introduce Moving Pictures to Ireland', in Marta Braun, Charles Keil, Rob King, Paul Moore and Louis Pelletier (eds), *Beyond the Screen: Institutions, Networks and Publics of Early Cinema* (New Barnet: John Libbey, 2012), pp. 35–42.

Condon, Denis, 'Receiving News from the Seat of War: Dublin Audiences Respond to Boer War Entertainments', *EPVC*, 9:2 (2011), pp. 93–106.

Condon, Denis, 'Spleen of a Cabinet Minister at Work: Exhibiting X-rays and the Cinematograph in Ireland, 1896', in John Hill and Kevin Rockett (eds), *Film History and National Cinema: Studies in Irish Film 2* (Dublin: Four Courts Press, 2005), pp. 69–78.

Condon, Denis, 'The Volta Myth', *Film Ireland*, 116 (May/June 2007), p. 43.

Cullen, Fintan, 'Marketing National Sentiment: Lantern Slides of Evictions in late Nineteenth-Century Ireland', in Fintan Cullen and John Morrison (eds), *A Shared Legacy: Essays on Irish and Scottish Visual Art and Culture* (London: Ashgate, 2005), pp. 113–31.

Dickens, Charles, 'The American Panorama', *The Examiner*, 16 December 1845, repr. in *Journalism, 2: 'The Amusements of the People' and Other Papers: Reports, Essays and Reviews*, ed. Michael Slater (London: Dent, 1997), pp. 135–7.

Eisenstein, Sergei M., 'A Course in Treatment' (1932), in Sergei M. Eisenstein, *Film Form: Essays in Film Theory*, ed. and trans. Jay Leyda (London: Dennis Dobson, 1963), pp. 84–107.

Eisenstein, Sergei, 'Sur Joyce', *Change* (May 1972), p. 51.

Fordham, Finn, 'Early Television and Joyce's *Finnegans Wake*: New Technology and Flawed Power', in Matthew Feldman, Erik Tonning and Henry Mead (eds), *Broadcasting in the Modernist Era* (London: Bloomsbury, 2014), pp. 39–56.

Foucault, Michel, 'Panopticism', in Michel Foucault, *Discipline and Punish: The Birth of the Prison*, trans. Alan Sheridan (New York: Vintage, 1979), pp. 195–230.

Frehner, Ruth, 'Warum ein Pater dunnbesockt durch eine fremde Küche läuft: Gleichzeitigkeit in den "Irrfelsen"'/'Why a Thinsocked Clergyman Walks through Other People's Kitchens: Simultaneity in "Wandering Rocks"', in Ursula Zeller, Ruth Frehner and Hannes Vogel (eds), *James Joyce: 'Gedacht durch meine Augen'* = *'Thought through my Eyes'* (Basel: Schwabe, 2000), pp. 157–87.

Gaudreault, André, 'The Diversity of Cinematographic Connections in the Intermedial Context of the Turn of the 20th Century', in Simon Popple and Vanessa Toulmin (eds), *Visual Delights: Essays on the Popular and Projected Image in the 19th Century* (Trowbridge: Flick Books, 2000), pp. 8–15.

Gaudreault, André, 'Showing and Telling: Image and Word in Early Cinema', in Thomas Elsaesser (ed.), *Early Cinema: Space, Frame, Narrative* (London: BFI, 1990), pp. 274–328.

Gorki, Maxim, 'In the Kingdom of Shadows' (1896), trans. Leda Swan, Appendix 2 in Jay Leyda (ed.), *Kino: A History of the Russian and Soviet Film* (London: Allen and Unwin, 1960), pp. 407–9.

Greene, Graham, 'The Film Society: *Riens que les heures*', *The Times*, 14 January 1929, in *Mornings in the Dark: The Graham Greene Film Reader*, ed. David Parkinson (Manchester: Carcanet, 1993), pp. 4–5.

Gunning, Tom, 'The Cinema of Attractions: Early Film, its Spectator and the Avant-Garde', in Thomas Elsaesser (ed.), *Early Cinema: Space, Frame, Narrative* (London: BFI, 1990), pp. 56–67.

Gunning, Tom, 'Illusions Past and Future: The Phantasmagoria and its Spectres', *Media Art Histories Archive* (2004), pp. 1–17, <http://www.mediaarthistory.org/refresh/Programmatic%20key%20texts/pdfs/Gunning.pdf> (last accessed 5 June 2017).

Gunning, Tom, 'New Thresholds of Vision: Instantaneous Photography and the Early Cinema of Lumière', in Terry Smith (ed.), *Impossible Presence: Surface and Screen in the Photogenic Era* (Sydney: Power Publications, 2001), pp. 71–100.

Gunning, Tom, 'Pictures of Crowd Splendour: The Mitchell and Kenyon Factory Gate Films', in Vanessa Toulmin, Patrick Russell and Simon Popple (eds), *The Lost World of Mitchell and Kenyon: Edwardian Britain on Film* (London: BFI, 2004), pp. 49–58.

Gunning, Tom, 'Waking and Faking: Ireland and Cinema Astray', in Kevin Rockett and John Hill (eds), *National Cinema and Beyond: Studies in Irish Film 1* (Dublin: Four Courts Press, 2004), pp. 19–31.

Heard, Mervyn, 'Paul de Philipsthal and the Phantasmagoria in England, Scotland and Ireland', Part 2, *New Magic Lantern Journal*, 2 (October 1997), pp. 11–16.

Heard, Mervyn, 'Pearls before Swine: A Prurient Look at the Lantern', *EPVC*, 3:2 (2005), pp. 179–95.

Hershberger, Andrew E., 'Performing Excess/Signalling Anxiety: Towards a Psychoanalytic Theory of Daguerre's Diorama', *EPVC*, 4:2 (2006), pp. 85–101.

Huhtamo, Erkki, '*Aeronautikon!* Or the Journey of the Balloon Panorama', *EPVC*, 7:3 (2009), pp. 295–306.

Huhtamo, Erkki, 'Penetrating the Peristrephic: An Unwritten Chapter in the History of the Panorama', *EPVC*, 6:3 (2008), pp. 219–38.

Hunt, Verity, 'Raising a Modern Ghost: The Magic Lantern and the Persistence of Wonder in the Victorian Education of the Senses', *Romanticism and Victorianism on the Net*, 5:2 (2006), <https://www.erudit.org/en/journals/ravon/2008-n52-ravon2573/019806ar/> (last accessed 7 May 2018).

Lewty, Jane, 'Joyce and Radio', in Richard Brown (ed.), *A Companion to James Joyce* (Oxford: Blackwell, 2008), pp. 390–406.

Lewty, Jane, '"What They Had Heard Said Written": Joyce, Pound, and the Cross-Correspondence of Radio', in Debra Rae Cohen, Michael Coyle and Jane Lewty (eds), *Broadcasting Modernism* (Gainesville, FL: University Press of Florida, 2009), pp. 199–220.

McCole, Niamh, 'The Magic Lantern in Provincial Ireland, 1896–1906', *EPVC*, 5:3 (2007), pp. 247–62.

McKernan, Luke, 'Appendix: Volta Filmography', in John McCourt (ed.), *Roll Away the Reel World: James Joyce and Cinema* (Cork: Cork University Press, 2010), pp. 187–204.

McKernan, Luke, 'James Joyce and the Volta Programme', in John McCourt (ed.), *Roll Away the Reel World: James Joyce and Cinema* (Cork: Cork University Press, 2010), pp. 15–27.

McKernan, Luke, 'James Joyce's Cinema', *Film and Film Culture*, 3 (2004), pp. 7–20.

Mannoni, Laurent, 'Elbow to Elbow: The Lantern/Cinema Struggle', *The New Magic Lantern Journal*, 7:1 (1993), pp. 1–6.

Mannoni, Laurent, 'Lucien Bull', in Richard Abel (ed.), *The Encyclopedia of Early Cinema* (London: Routledge, 2010), p. 86.

Marsh, Joss, 'Dickensian "Dissolving Views": The Magic Lantern, Visual Story-Telling, and the Victorian Technological Imagination', *Comparative Critical Studies*, 6:3 (2009), pp. 333–46.

Marsh, Joss, and Francis Davis, '"The Poetry of Poverty": The Magic Lantern and the Ballads of George R. Sims', in Ludwig Vogl-Bienek and Richard

Crangle (eds), *Screen Culture and the Social Question*, KINtop Studies in Early Cinema 3 (New Barnet: John Libbey, 2014), pp. 64–81.

Miller, Nicholas, 'Joyce's Haunted Inkbottle: Early Animation and *Finnegans Wake*', unpublished paper delivered at the 2016 James Joyce Symposium in London.

Monks, Robert, 'The Irish Films in the Mitchell and Kenyon Collection', in Vanessa Toulmin, Patrick Russell and Simon Popple (eds), *The Lost World of Mitchell and Kenyon: Edwardian Britain on Film* (London: BFI, 2004), pp. 75–97.

Morus, Iwan Rhys, 'Illuminating Illusions, or, the Victorian Art of Seeing Things', *EPVC*, 10.1 (2012), pp. 37–50.

Mullin, Katherine, 'Joyce, Early Cinema and the Erotics of Everyday Life', in John McCourt (ed.), *Roll Away the Reel World: James Joyce and Cinema* (Cork: Cork University Press, 2010), pp. 43–56.

Mullin, Katherine, '"Something in the Name of Araby": James Joyce and the Irish Charity Bazaars', *Dublin James Joyce Journal*, 4 (2011), pp. 31–50.

Musser, Charles, 'Toward a History of Screen Practice', *Quarterly Review of Film Studies*, 9:1 (1984), pp. 59–69 (repr. in Charles Musser, *The Emergence of Cinema: The American Screen to 1907* [Berkeley, CA: University of California Press, 1990], pp. 16–54).

Pound, Ezra, 'Berlin', *The Exile*, 4 (autumn 1928), pp. 113–15.

Pound, Ezra, Review, *The Dial*, January 1921, p. 110.

Powell, Hudson John, 'New Light on Poole's Myrioramas', *The New Magic Lantern Journal*, 8:1 (1996), pp. 12–15.

Robinson, David, 'A Film Maker's Magic Lantern Years', *The New Magic Lantern Journal*, 7:1 (1993), p. 11.

Rossell, Deac, 'Chronophotography in the Context of Moving Images', *EPVC*, 11:1 (2013), pp. 10–27.

Rossell, Deac, 'Double Think: The Cinema and Magic Lantern Culture', in John Fullerton (ed.), *Celebrating 1895: The Centenary of Cinema* (Sydney, NSW: John Libbey, 1998), pp. 27–36.

Saint-Amour, Paul K., 'The Vertical Flâneur: Narratorial Tradecraft in the Colonial Metropolis', in Enda Duffy and Maurizia Boscagli (eds), *Joyce, Benjamin and Magical Urbanism*, European Joyce Studies 2:1 (Amsterdam: Rodopi, 2011), pp. 224–49.

Senn, Fritz, 'Hören und Sehen/Do You Hear What I'm Seeing?', in Ursula Zeller, Ruth Frehner and Hannes Vogel (eds), *James Joyce: 'Gedacht durch meine Augen'* = *'Thought through my Eyes'* (Basel: Schwabe, 2000), pp. 7–22.

Uricchio, William, 'A "Proper Point of View": The Panorama and Some of its Early Media Iterations', *EPVC*, 9:3 (2011), pp. 225–38.

Vertov, Dziga, 'From Kino-Eye to Radio-Eye' (1929), in Dziga Vertov, *Kino-Eye: The Writings of Dziga Vertov*, ed. Annette Michelson, trans. Kevin O'Brien (Berkeley, CA: University of California Press, 1984), pp. 85–92.

Vertov, Dziga, 'Kinoks: A Revolution', originally published in *Lef*, in Dziga Vertov, *Kino-Eye: The Writings of Dziga Vertov*, ed. Annette Michelson, trans. Kevin O'Brien (Berkeley, CA: University of California Press, 1984), pp. 11–21.

Vogl-Bienek, Ludwig, 'A Lantern Lecture: Slum Life and Living Conditions of the Poor in Fictional and Documentary Lantern Slide Sets', in Ludwig Vogl-Bienek and Richard Crangle (eds), *Screen Culture and the Social Question*, KINtop Studies in Early Cinema 3 (New Barnet: John Libbey, 2014), pp. 34–63.

Werner, Gösta, 'James Joyce and Sergej Eisenstein', trans. Erik Gunnemark, *JJQ*, 27:3 (1990), pp. 491–507.

Williams, Keith, 'Joyce's Chinese Alphabet: *Ulysses* and the Proletarians', in Paul Hyland and Neil Sammells (eds), *Irish Writing: Exile and Subversion* (Basingstoke: Macmillan, 1991), pp. 173–87.

Williams, Keith, 'Odysseys of Sound and Image: "Cinematicity" and the *Ulysses* Adaptations', in John McCourt (ed.), *Roll Away the Reel World: James Joyce and Cinema* (Cork: Cork University Press, 2010), pp. 158–73.

Williams, Keith, 'Short Cuts of the Hibernian Metropolis: Cinematic Strategies in *Dubliners*', in Oona Frawley (ed.), *A New and Complex Sensation: Essays on Joyce's Dubliners* (Dublin: Lilliput, 2004), pp. 154–67.

Williams, Keith, '"Sperrits in the Furniture": Wells, Joyce and Animation before and after 1910', in Matthew Creasy and Bryony Randall (eds), *Alternative 1910s*, a special issue of *Literature and History*, 3rd series 22:1 (2013), pp. 95–110.

Williams, Keith, 'Symphonies of the Big City: Modernism, Cinema and Urban Modernity', in Paul Edwards (ed.), *The Great London Vortex: Modernist Literature and Art* (Bath: Sulis Press, 2003), pp. 31–50.

Williams, Keith, '*Ulysses* in Toontown: Vision animated to Bursting Point in Joyce's "Circe"', in Lydia Rainford and Julian Murphet (eds), *Writing After Cinema: Literature and Visual Technologies* (Basingstoke: Palgrave, 2003).

Woolf, Virginia, 'The Cinema' (1926), in *Collected Essays*, ed. Leonard Woolf, 4 vols (London: Hogarth, 1964), vol. 2, pp. 268–72.

Woolf, Virginia, 'Reading Notes for "Modern Novels"' (Joyce), 1 volume (April 1918), in New York Public Library Berg Collection (also available in microform, Reel 11, M91).

Books, CD-ROMs and Theses

Abel, Richard (ed.), *The Encyclopedia of Early Cinema* (London: Routledge, 2010).

Altick, Richard, *The Shows of London* (Cambridge, MA: Harvard University Press, 1978).

Anon., *The Magic Lantern: How to Buy and How to Use it, By 'A Mere Phantom'* (London: Houlston & Sons, 1866).

Apollonio, Umbro (ed.), *Futurist Manifestos* (London: Thames and Hudson, 1973).

Barna, Yon, *Eisenstein* (London: Secker and Warburg, 1973).

Baron, Scarlett, *'Strandentwining Cable': Joyce, Flaubert, and Intertextuality* (Oxford: Oxford University Press, 2011).

Bergson, Henri, *Creative Evolution*, trans. Arthur Mitchell (New York: Henry Holt, 1911).

Braun, Marta, *Picturing Time: The Work of Étienne-Jules Marey* (Chicago: University of Chicago Press, 1992).

Brewster, David, *The Kaleidoscope: Its History, Theory and Construction* (London: John Murray, 1858).

Brewster, David, *Letters on Natural Magic* (London: John Murray, 1832).

Brooker, Jeremy, *The Temple of Minerva: Magic and the Magic Lantern at the Royal Polytechnic Institution, London 1837–1901* (London: MLS, 2013).

Brookman, Philip, and Marta Braun (eds), *Helios: Eadweard Muybridge in a Time of Change* (London: Tate, 2010).

Budgen, Frank, *James Joyce and the Making of 'Ulysses'* (London: Grayson and Grayson, 1934).

Burch, Noel, *Life to Those Shadows*, trans. and ed. Ben Brewster (London: BFI, 1990).

Cannadine, David, *Ornamentalism: How the British Saw Their Empire* (Harmondsworth: Penguin, 2001).

Chandler, Edward, *Photography in Ireland: The Nineteenth Century* (Dublin: Edmund Burke, 2001).

Christie, Ian, *The Last Machine: Early Cinema and the Birth of the Modern World* (London: BFI/BBC, 1994).

Clarke, David B. (ed.), *The Cinematic City* (London: Routledge, 1997).

Clegg, Brian, *The Man Who Stopped Time: The Illuminating Story of Eadweard Muybridge, Father of the Motion Picture, Murderer* (Washington, DC: Joseph Henry Press, 2007).

Coe, Brian, *Muybridge and the Chronophotographers* (London: Museum of the Moving Image, 1992).

Comment, Bernard, *The Panorama*, trans. Anne-Marie Glasheen (London: Reaktion, 2001).

Condon, Denis, *Early Irish Cinema, 1895–1921* (Dublin: Irish Academic Press, 2008).

Cook, David A., *A History of Narrative Film* (New York: W. W. Norton, 4th edn, 2004).

Cook, Olive, *Movement in Two Dimensions: A Study of the Animated and Projected Pictures which Preceded the Invention of Cinematography* (London: Hutchinson, 1963); repr. as vol. 3 of Stephen Herbert (ed.), *A History of Pre-Cinema*, 4 vols (London: Routledge, 2000).

Crary, Jonathan, *Techniques of the Observer: On Vision and Modernity in the Nineteenth Century* (Cambridge, MA: MIT Press, 1992 [1990]).

Crompton, Dennis, David Henry and Stephen Herbert (eds), *Magic Images: The Art of Hand-Painted and Photographic Lantern Slides* (London: MLS, 1990).

Crompton, Dennis, Richard Franklin and Stephen Herbert (eds), *Servants of Light: The Book of the Lantern* (London: MLS, 1997).

Dellmann, Sarah, and Frank Kessler, *A Million Pictures: Magic Lantern Slides in the History of Learning*, KINtop Studies in Early Cinema 6 (New Barnet: John Libbey, 2019).

Deming, Robert H. (ed.), *James Joyce: The Critical Heritage*, 1: *1902–1927* (London: Routledge and Kegan Paul, 1970).

Doane, Mary Anne, *The Emergence of Cinematic Time: Modernity, Contingency and the Archive* (Cambridge, MA: Harvard University Press, 2002).

Donald, James, Anne Friedberg and Laura Marcus (eds), *Close Up 1927–1933: Cinema and Modernism* (London: Cassell, 1998).

Ellmann, Richard, *The Consciousness of Joyce* (London: Faber and Faber, 1977).

Ellmann, Richard, *James Joyce* (1959) (Oxford University Press, rev. edn, 1983).

Ellmann, Richard, *Ulysses on the Liffey* (London: Faber and Faber, 1972).

Flint, Kate, *The Victorians and the Visual Imagination* (Cambridge: Cambridge University Press, 2000).

Friedberg, Anne, *Window Shopping: Cinema and the Postmodern* (Berkeley, CA: University of California Press, 1993).

Gaudreault, André, *Film and Attraction* (Urbana, IL: University of Illinois Press, 2011).

Geiger, Jeffrey, and Karin Littau (eds), *Cinematicity in Media History* (Edinburgh: Edinburgh University Press, 2013).

Geiger, Jeffrey, and Karin Littau (eds), '"Cinematicity" 1895: Before and After', a special issue of *Comparative Critical Studies*, 6:3 (2009).

Gernsheim, Helmut, and Alison Gernsheim, *L. J. M. Daguerre: The History of the Diorama and the Daguerretotype* (New York: Dover, 1968).

Grøtta, Marit, *Baudelaire's Media Aesthetics: The Gaze of the Flâneur and 19th Century Media* (London: Bloomsbury, 2015).

Gunning, Tom, *D. W. Griffith and the Origins of American Narrative Film: The Early Years at Biograph* (Urbana, IL: University of Illinois Press 1994).

Hanaway-Oakley, Cleo, *James Joyce and the Phenomenology of Film* (Oxford: Oxford University Press, 2017).

Hayes, Michael Angelo, *The Delineation of Animals in Rapid Motion* (Dublin: Royal Dublin Society, 1877).

Hayman, David, *Ulysses and the Mechanics of Meaning* (Madison, WI: University of Wisconsin Press, rev. edn, 1982).

Heard, Mervyn, *Dressed in Light: The Ancient Art of Projecting on People* (February 2014), <http://www.mervynheard.com> (last accessed 4 August 2016).

Heard, Mervyn, *Phantasmagoria: The Secret Life of the Magic Lantern* (Hastings: The Projection Box, 2006).

Hendricks, Gordon, *Eadweard Muybridge: The Father of the Motion Picture* (London: Secker and Warburg, 1977).

Herbert, Stephen (ed.), *A History of Pre-Cinema*, 4 vols (London: Routledge, 2000).

Herbert, Stephen, and Luke MacKernan, *Who's Who of Victorian Cinema: A Worldwide Survey* (London: BFI, 1996).

Hickey, Kieran (ed.), *The Light of Other Days: Irish Life at the Turn of the Century in the Photographs of Robert French* (London: Allen Lane, 1973).

Hodgson, Shadworth H[ollway], *The Metaphysic of Experience, 3: Analysis of Conscious Action* (London: Longmans, Green, 1898).

Hodgson, Shadworth H[ollway], *The Relation of Philosophy to Science, Physical and Psychological: An Address* (London: Williams and Norgate, 1884).

Hodgson, Shadworth H[ollway], *Time and Space: A Metaphysical Essay* (London: Longman, Green, Longman, Roberts and Green, 1865).

Hogenkamp, Bert, *Deadly Parallels: Film and the Left in Britain 1929–1939* (London: Lawrence and Wishart, 1986).

Holloway, Joseph, 'Joseph Holloway Diaries (1896–97)', Ms 1794–1797, National Library of Ireland.

Household, G. A. (ed.), *To Catch a Sunbeam: Victorian Reality through the Magic Lantern*, from the collection of L. M. H. Smith (London: Joseph, 1979).

Huhtamo, Erkki, *Illusions in Motion: Media Archaeology of the Moving Panorama and Related Spectacles* (Cambridge, MA: MIT Press, 2013).

Humphries, Steve, and Doug Lear, *Victorian Britain through the Magic Lantern*, illustrated by Lear's Magic Lantern Slides (London: Sidgwick and Jackson, 1989).

Hyde, Ralph, *Panoramania! The Art and Entertainment of the All-Embracing View: An Exhibition at the Barbican Art Gallery, Nov 3 1988–Jan 15*

1989 (London: Trefoil Publications in Association with Barbican Art Gallery, 1988).

Joyce, Stanislaus, *My Brother's Keeper: James Joyce's Early Years*, ed. Richard Ellmann (London: Faber and Faber, 1958).

Kember, Joe, *Marketing Modernity: Victorian Popular Shows and Early Cinema* (Exeter: University of Exeter Press, 2009).

Kenner, Hugh, *Ulysses* (London: Allen and Unwin, 1980).

Kern, Stephen, *The Culture of Time and Space 1889–1918* (Cambridge, MA: Harvard University Press, 1983).

Kershner, R. Brandon, *The Culture of Joyce's* Ulysses (Basingstoke: Palgrave, 2010).

Kitcher, Philip, *Joyce's Kaleidoscope: An Invitation to Finnegans Wake* (Oxford: Oxford University Press, 2007).

Lawrence, William, *Illustrated Catalogue: Magic Lanterns, Dissolving View Apparatus and Lantern Slides* (Dublin: Printed by Leckie and Co., n.d.)

Lawrence, William, *Ireland in the Magic Lantern: List of Photographic Lantern Slides* (Dublin: Printed by the Freeman's Journal, 1890).

Lindsay, Vachel, *The Art of the Moving Picture* (1915; rev. edn 1922) (New York: Liveright, 1970).

Loss, Archie K., *Joyce's Visible Art: The Work of Joyce and the Visual Arts, 1904–1922* (Ann Arbor, MI: UMI Research Press, 1984).

McCole, Niamh, 'Seeing Sense: The Visual Culture of Provincial Ireland, 1896–1906', unpublished PhD thesis, Dublin City University, 2005, <http://doras.dcu.ie/18053/1/Niamh_McCole.pdf> (last accessed 28 September 2018).

McCourt, John (ed.), *Roll Away the Reel World: James Joyce and Cinema* (Cork: Cork University Press, 2010).

Magic Lantern Society, *Illustrated Bamforth Slide Catalogue*, CD-ROM, compiled by Richard Crangle and Robert Macdonald for the MLS (London: MLS, 2009).

Marey, E. J., *Movement: The Results and Possibilities of Photography*, with 200 illustrations, trans. Eric Pritchard (London: Heinemann, 1895).

Molyneux, William, *Dioptricka Nova, A Treatise of Dioptricks in Two Parts* (London: Printed for Benj. Tooke, 1692).

Monks, Robert, *Cinema Ireland: A Database of Irish Films and Filmmakers, 1896–1986*, CD-ROM (Dublin: National Library of Ireland, 1996).

Mullin, Katherine, *James Joyce, Sexuality and Social Purity* (Cambridge: Cambridge University Press, 2003).

Münsterberg, Hugo, *The Photoplay: A Psychological Study* (New York and London: Appleton and Co., 1916; repr. as *The Film: A Psychological Study* [New York: Dover Publications, 1970]).

Nead, Lynda, *The Haunted Gallery: Painting Photography and Film, c. 1900* (New Haven, CT: Yale University Press, 2008).

Oetterman, Stephan, *The Panorama: History of a Mass Medium,* trans. D. L. Schneider (New York: Zone Books, 1997).

O'Leary, Liam, *Cinema Ireland 1896–1950* (Dublin: National Library of Ireland, 1990).

Oleksijczuk, Denise Blake, *The First Panoramas: Visions of British Imperialism* (Minneapolis, MN: University of Minnesota Press, 2011).

Parikka, Jussi, *What is Media Archaeology?* (Cambridge: Polity, 2012).

Pellerin, Denis, Brian May and Paula Fleming, *Diableries, Stereoscopic Adventures in Hell* (London: London Stereoscopic Company, 2013).

Powell, Helen, *Stop the Clocks! Time and Narrative in Cinema* (London: I.B. Tauris, 2012).

Powell, Hudson John, *Poole's Myriorama: A Story of Travelling Panorama Showmen* (Bradford on Avon: ELSP, 2002).

Quendler, Christian, *The Camera-Eye Metaphor in Cinema* (New York: Routledge, 2017).

Ramsaye, Terry, *A Million and One Nights: A History of the Motion Picture* (1926) (London: Frank Cass, 1964).

Robertson, David, Stephen Herbert and Richard Crangle (eds), *Encyclopaedia of the Magic Lantern* (London: MLS, 2001).

Robinson, David (ed.), *The Lantern Image: Iconography of the Magic Lantern 1420–1880* (London: MLS, 1993).

Rockett, Kevin, with Emer Rockett, *Film Exhibition and Distribution in Ireland* (Dublin: Four Courts Press, 2011).

Rockett, Kevin, and Emer Rockett, *Magic Lantern, Panorama and Moving Picture Shows in Ireland, 1786–1909* (Dublin: Four Courts Press, 2011).

Roe, Clifford G., *Horrors of the White Slave Trade: The Mighty Crusade to Protect the Purity of Our Homes* (London and New York: n.p., 1911).

Rossell, Deac, *Living Pictures: The Origins of the Movies* (Albany, NY: State University of New York Press, 1998).

Rouse, Sarah, *Into the Light: An Illustrated Guide to the Photographic Collections in the National Library of Ireland* (Dublin: National Library of Ireland, 1998).

Schivelbusch, Wolfgang, *The Railway Journey: The Industrialization of Time and Space in the 19th Century* (Leamington Spa: Berg, new edn, 1986 [1976]).

Seton, Marie M., *Sergei M. Eisenstein: A Biography* (London: Bodley Head, 1952).

Sexton, Sean, *Ireland, Photographs 1840–1930* (London: Calman and King, 1994).

Sinyard, Neil, *Filming Literature: The Art of Screen Adaptation* (London: Croom Helm, 1986).

Smith, Grahame, *Dickens and the Dream of Cinema* (Manchester: Manchester University Press, 2003).

Solnit, Rebecca, *Motion Studies: Time, Space and Eadweard Muybridge* (London: Bloomsbury, 2003).

Spiegel, Alan, *Fiction and the Camera Eye: Visual Consciousness in Film and the Modern Novel* (Charlottesville, VA: University Press of Virginia, 1976).

Spurr, David, *Architecture and Modern Literature* (Ann Arbor, MI: University of Michigan Press, 2012).

Sternberger, Dolf, *The Panorama of the 19th Century*, trans Joachim Neugroschel (New York: Urizen Books and Mole Editions, 1977) (originally *Panorama oder Ansichten vom 19. Jahrhundert* [1938]).

Theall, Donald F., *James Joyce's Techno-Poetics* (Toronto: University of Toronto Press, 1997).

Toulmin, Vanessa, Patrick Russell and Simon Popple (eds), *The Lost World of Mitchell and Kenyon: Edwardian Britain on Film* (London: BFI, 2004).

Trotter, David, *Cinema and Modernism* (Oxford: Blackwell, 2007).

Turim, Maureen, *Flashbacks in Film: Memory and History* (London: Routledge, 1989).

Usai, Paolo Cherchi (ed.), *The Griffith Project*, 1: *Films Produced in 1907–1908* (London: BFI, 1999).

Vertov, Dziga, *Kino-Eye: The Writings of Dziga Vertov*, ed. Annette Michelson and trans. Kevin O'Brien (Berkeley, CA: University of California Press, 1984).

Vogl-Bienek, Ludwig, and Richard Crangle (eds), *Screen Culture and the Social Question*, KINtop Studies in Early Cinema 3 (New Barnet: John Libbey, 2014),

Warner, Marina, *Phantasmagoria: Spirit Visions, Metaphors and Media into the Twenty-First Century* (Oxford: Oxford University Press, 2006).

Weedon, Brenda, *The Education of the Eye: History of the Royal Polytechnic Institution 1838–1881* (Cambridge: Granta Editions, 2008).

Whelan, Yvonne, *Reinventing Modern Dublin: Streetscape, Iconography and the Politics of Identity* (Dublin: University College of Dublin Press, 2003).

Williams, Keith, *British Writers and the Media 1930–45* (Basingstoke: Macmillan, 1991).

Williams, Keith, *H. G. Wells, Modernity and the Movies* (Liverpool: Liverpool University Press, 2007).

Williams, Keith, 'Reportage in the Thirties', unpublished DPhil thesis, University of Oxford, 1991, <https://ora.ox.ac.uk/objects/uuid:e8ea296e-9b1b-4e60-a2da-6ced3f276617> (last accessed 24 October 2017).

Zeller, Ursula, Ruth Frehner and Hannes Vogel (eds), *James Joyce: 'Gedacht durch meine Augen' = 'Thought through my Eyes'* (Basel: Schwabe, 2000).

Zielinski, Siegfried, *Deep Time of the Media: Towards an Archaeology of Hearing and Seeing*, trans. Gloria Custance (Cambridge, MA: MIT Press, 2008).

Zone, Ray, *Stereoscopic Cinema and the Origins of 3-D Film, 1838–1952* (Lexington, KY: University of Kentucky Press, 2007).

INDEX

Note: References to images are in italics; references to notes are indicated by n.

3-D images, 4, 57
1904 'A Portrait of the Artist' (Joyce),
    114–15

Abdy, Maria, 43–4
Abenteure von Prinz Achmed, Die
    (animation), 13
Acres, Birt
    Rough Sea at Dover, 45
actualities, 23–4, 46, 54, 209–12
adventure, 60–1
aeronautics, 186–8
Aeronautikon, 188, 191–2
Affaire Dreyfus, L' (film), 25
after-images, 3
Agamben, Giorgio, 126
Agee, James, 125
agitprop cinema, 72–3
Aladdin and the Wonderful Lamp
    (film), 25
alcoholism, 11, 38–9
Alice in Wonderland (slide show), 42

Ally Sloper's Half-Holiday
    (comic strip), 69
Althusser, Louis, 177
America *see* United States of America
Analyticon shows, 56, 57
animal locomotion, 4, 16, 17, 45,
    117–23, 228
    and horses, 109, 110–12
animation *see* cartoons
animatograph, 121–2
'Anna Livia Plurabelle' (Finnegans
    Wake), 251, 252–4
anti-colonialism, 203
Aquinas, Thomas, 124–5
'Araby' (*Dubliners*), 55, 75, 146,
    155, 209
    and panorama, 4–5, 60
    and railings, 83, 142
Argonautica, 218
Arrivée d'un train, L' (film), 22–3
art, 118–20
Art Nouveau, 58

Artist's Dream, The (lantern show), 87
Au Pays des jouets (film), 47
Aventures de Robinson Crusoe, Les (film), 25
aviation, 124, 186

Baláz, Béla
  Die Abenteuer eines Zehnmarkscheins, 224
Balla, Giacomo
  Dynamism of a Dog Leash, 119
balloon flight, 42, 61, 62, 183, 186–8
Bamforth, James, 53–4, 78
  The Holy Shrine, 75
Banvard, John
  Panorama of the Mississippi, 184, 185
Barke, James
  Major Operation, 232
Barker, Robert, 18, 175, 176, 179, 201, 212
Baron, Scarlett, 125–6
battles, 179–80, 184, 193–4, 198–9; *see also* Waterloo, Battle of
Baudelaire, Charles, 6–7, 19, 32n65, 204, 205
  Le Peintre de la vie moderne, 110–11
Bay of Dublin (panorama), 179
Bazin, André, 2
Belfast, 65, 210, 211
Benjamin, Walter, 110, 125, 174, 204, 216
Bentham, Jeremy, 178
Bergson, Henri, 126, 206
  L'Évolution créatrice (*Creative Evolution*), 134–6
Big City Symphonies, 215, 216, 217, 221, 229, 231–2
Bildungsroman, 59, 92, 136, 257
Binnie, Georgina, 228
binocular vision, 3
biophantic lantern, 46–7
birds, 124
biscenascope, 44
Black, Alexander, 55
Blake Oleksijczuk, Denise, 177
bodies, 142–4
Boer War, 181, 199

Bottle, The (slide show), 38, 39, 82–3
Bottomore, Stephen, 226, 228
Bouton, Charles Marie, 181
Brewster, David, 162
  Letters on Natural Magic, 2–3
  The Magic Lantern: How to Buy and How to Use it, By 'A Mere Phantom', 59, 89
Briggs, Austin, 14
British Empire, 177–8, 193
broadcasting, 2, 246, 249–50; *see also* radio; television
Brooker, Jeremy, 65
Budgen, Frank, 111, 112
Bull, Lucien, 118, *119*
Buñuel, Luis
  Un Chien Andalou, 156
Burford, Robert
  Summer and Winter Views of the Polar Regions, 177
Burgess, Anthony, 246
Bute, Mary Ellen
  Passages from Finnegans Wake, 246–7
Byerly, Alison, 18, 192
  and panoramas, 177, 178, 179, 184, 185, 186, 188, 195

camera-eye, 107
camera obscuras, 200–1
cameras, 52, 128–31, 176, 212–13
Campbell, Timothy, 249, 250
Cannadine, David, 178
Carpenter, Paul, 38
cartoons, 13, 69–70, 163, 251–2
Carville, Justin, 51, 201
Cate, Phillip Dennis, 12
Catholicism, 64, 65
Cavalcanti, Alberto, 227, 232
  Rien que les heures, 215
cave allegory, 13, 31n42, 84–5, 150, 153–4, 157
Cendrillon (film), 24–5
'change pictures', 182, 184
Chaplin, Charlie, 56, 70
Chapman, Alison, 85
Charles, Jacques Alexandre, 44
Chase, Charles A., 189, 190

Chat Noir, Le (Paris), 12
Childe, Henry Langdon, 43, 44
children, 59
Christianity, 63–4
Christie, Ian, 215
Christmas, 89, 91
Christmas Day in the Workhouse
   (slide set), 70
chronophotography, 4, 17, 114–15,
   116, 117–23
cinema, 26–7, 30n32
cinematicity, 7–8, 9, 106–9, 256–9
cinematograph, 4, 5, 7–8, 21–3
   and early films, 210
   and movement, 45
   and time, 122–3
Cinéorama, 189–90
'Circe' (*Ulysses*), 12, 13, 24, 38
   and apparition, 47
   and sight, 156
   and visual language, 136
circular panoramas, 176–7, 183–4
cities *see* Big City Symphonies; Dublin;
   London; Paris
civic processions, 185–6, 218,
   228–9
Clarke, Edward Marmaduke, 44, 182
Cocteau, Jean, 216
Collins, Wilkie
   The Frozen Deep, 79
colonialism, 60, 178, 184, 199, 229–31;
   see also anti-colonialism; British
   Empire
colour, 56, 57, 137–8
columns, 201–3
comic strips, 69–70
Condon, Denis, 22, 23, 26, 61–2, 75
   and actualities, 210
   Early Irish Cinema, 1895–1921, 5
   and religion, 64
   and X-rays, 156
Conmee, John, 218, 221, 222–3
consciousness, 109–10, 111, 137–8,
   205–7; *see also* stream of
   consciousness
Cook, David A., 7
Cook, Olive
   Movement in Two Dimensions, 6

Cooper, Arthur Melbourne
   Matches: an Appeal, 164
coronations, 185
Corsican Brothers, The (slide show), 42
cowboy slides, 60
Crangle, Richard, 15
Crary, Jonathan, 2, 3–4, 200
Cruikshank, George, 188
   The Bottle, 38, 39, 82–3
Cubism, 118, 119, 213
Curfew Shall not Ring Tonight
   (slide set), 54
Curtain: Or, A Peep into the Future,
   The (slide set), 79
cycloramas, 189, 190

Daedalum, 123
Daguerre, Louis-Jacques-Mandé, 6,
   181–2, 198
   A Midnight Mass at the Church of
   Saint-Étienne-du-Mont, 148–9
Dan Dabberton's Dream (slide set),
   81–2, 85
D'Arcy, Patrick ('Patrice'), 6
Davitt, Michael, 63
Deadly Parallel, The (periodical), 72
Delville, Gustave, 148–9
diableries, 160
Dibdin, T. C.
   Diorama of the Ganges, 203
Dickens, Charles, 71, 185, 196
   The Frozen Deep, 79
   Sketches by Boz, 188
Dickson, W. K. L., 45, 49, 58, 115
Diorama of India, 192–3
dioramas, 8, 19, 148–9, 181–3,
   192–3, 203
Disney, Walt, 253, 254
dissolving views, 37, 43–4, 47
Doane, Mary Ann, 4
Döblin, Alfred
   Berlin Alexanderplatz, 231
documentary, 51–3, 72–3
domestic abuse, 11
Donisthorpe, Wordsworth, 30n32
Dowie, Alexander John, 66
Drunkard's Children, The (slide show),
   38–9

Dublin, 20, 214
  and camera obscuras, 200–1
  and chronophotography, 117–18
  and dioramas, 182–3
  and dissolving views, 44
  and film, 21–7, 209–10
  and *Finnegans Wake*, 247–8
  and magic lanterns, 36
  and panoramas, 179–81, 183–4
  and photography, 49–50, 51–3
  see also *Dubliners*; *Ulysses*
Dubliners (Joyce), 10–11, 56, 70–1, 72
  and 'After the Race', 61, 132, 209
  and 'An Encounter', 60–1
  and 'The Dead', 50–1, 56, 80–2,
    89–92, 197
  and 'Eveline', 50, 68, 73, 76–7, 78,
    79, 83
  and film, 209, 211
  and flashbacks, 76–80
  and 'Grace', 15, 38, 39, 49
  and locomotion, 132–3
  and magic lanterns, 15–16, 74–6
  and objects, 83–5
  and panorama, 198
  and photography, 50–1
  and time, 140
  see also 'Araby'; 'Sisters, The'
Duchamp, Marcel
  Nude Descending a Staircase, No. 2,
    119, 120
Dudley, William Humble Ward, Earl
  of, 218
Dujardin, Edouard
  Les Lauriers sont coupés (*The Bays
    Are Sere*), 131
Dulac, Germaine
  Le Coquille et le Clergyman, 246
Dumas, Alexandre
  The Count of Monte Cristo, 146–7
Dupont, E. A.
  Varieté, 143
Dusty Rhodes (cartoon character), 70

Eco, Umberto, 252
Edinburgh, 176, 179
Edison, Thomas Alva, 8, 45, 58, 120–1
  Champs de Mars, 213

Uncle Josh at the Moving Pictures,
  177
education, 58–62
Eglinton, John, 174
Eifler, Karen, 72
Eisenstein, Sergei M., 2, 10, 30n38, 106
  Battleship Potemkin, 156
  and Joyce, 136, 215, 245
ekphrasis (verbal imitation of visual
  modes), 2, 8, 75–6, 246, 250,
  256–7
Ellmann, Richard, 4
emigration, 184
epiphany, 16–17, 125, 126–7, 158–60
eroticism, 55, 155, 228
Escamotage d'une dame, L' (*The
  Disappearing Woman*) (film), 47
Evans, Walker, 125
eye, the, 2–4, 144, 156

faces, 143
Fairview (house), 64–5
Faithful Departed (film), 51
Felix the Cat (cartoon), 13
film, 5–6, 8, 153, 245–7
  and Dublin, 21–7
  and literature, 71–2
  and local events, 226–7, 228
  and movement, 41, 45–6
  and panoramas, 208–14
  and time, 134–6
  and *Ulysses*, 113–14
Finnegans Wake (Joyce), 20–1, 44, 50,
  70, 244–54
fire shadows, 13, 150
fireplaces, 84–5
flâneurs, 19, 32n65, 204, 205, 220, 258
flashbacks, 16, 76–80, 102n155–6
Flaubert, Gustave, 125
  Madame Bovary, 9
Fleischer brothers
  Out of the Inkwell, 252
Flint, Kate, 4
Fordham, Finn, 250, 251
Foucault, Michel, 178, 192
Frampton, Hollis, 247
France, 211–12; *see also* Paris
Francis, David, 53–4, 71

Frehner, Ruth, 216–17
French, Robert, 51
Friedberg, Anne, 107
Friese-Greene, William, 47
frozen images, 113
Fuller, Loïe, 58
Futurism, 118, 119–20, 213

Gabriel Grub (slide show), 42, 53
'Galantees', 12
Gaudreault, André, 5, 9–10
gaze *see* virtual gaze
Geiger, Jeffrey, 7–8
geography slides, 60–1
George VI, King, 232
Gernsheim, Helmut and Alison, 181
Gessner, Robert A., 106–7
ghosts, 3, 16, 85, 86–92
Gilbert, Stuart, 251–4
Gladstone, William, 117, 198, 199
Glaisher, James, 187
Gloria! (film), 247
Gonne, Maude, 101n153
Gorki, Maxim, 55, 90
Great American Panorama, 185
Great Gordon-Bennett Motor Race
    (film), 132–3, 209
Greene, Graham, 90
    It's a Battlefield, 232–3
Greenwood, Thomas, 180
Greer, Tom
    A Modern Daedalus, 124, 188,
    201–2
Griffith, Alison, 179
Griffith, D. W., 39, 84, 102n155–6,
    213, 223–4
    After Many Years, 77–8
Grimoin-Sanson, Raoul, 189
Grøtta, Marit, 6–7
Groves, 182
Gunning, Tom, 209–10, 247

Halford, C. A. D., 112
Hansen, Miriam, 72
Hayes, Michael Angelo, 117
Hayman, David, 9–10
heads, 142–3
Hell, 156, 157, 160

Hepworth, Cecil, 42, 88, 209
Herman, David, 188
Hershberger, Andrew E., 148
Hickey, Kieran, 51
history, 62–3
Hodgson, Shadworth H., 20, 206
Holloway, Joseph, 9, 23, 24
Holmes, Oliver Wendell, 112
Home Rule, 62–3, 199, 202
Home! Sweet Home! (slide set), 67–9
Homer, 13, 174; see also *Odyssey*
Horgan Brothers, 54
Horner, William George, 6, 123
Household Words (magazine), 196
Howorth's Hibernica (panorama), 185
Huhtamo, Errki, 196, 207
    and discursive panorama, 188, 204,
    205, 213, 221–2
    Illusions in Motion: Media
    Archaeology of the Moving
    Panorama and Related Spectacles,
    2, 4
    and narrative panoramas, 191
    and panoramas, 18, 19, 20, 174,
    175, 176, 177, 178, 179, 181,
    183, 185
Humphries, Steve, 35
Hunt, Verity, 59
Huxley, T. H., 117
Huygens, Christiaan, 41

Iliad (Homer), 181
illusions *see* optical illusions
Illustrated London News (periodical), 4
imperialism, 177–8, 179–80, 184
In His Steps (slide set), 66–7, 69
India, 179, 192–3, 203
Inferno, L' (film), 156
Ireland, 5–6, 57, 62–3
    and actualities, 210–11
    and British Empire, 193
    and magic lanterns, 35–7, 39–40
    and panoramas, 175
    and travelogues, 61
    see also Dublin
Irish Animated Photo Company, 26, 209
Isherwood, Christopher
    Goodbye to Berlin, 232

James, William
  The Principles of Psychology, 206
Jameson, James Taylor, 26
Jameson, Storm, 72
Jeanne D'Arc (film), 25
Jesuits, 39
John Hampton's Home (slide set), 83
Johnson, Steven
  *Wonderland: How Play Made the
    Modern World*, 4
Joyce, James, 4, 10–11, 118
  and cinematicity, 1–2, 16–17, 256–9
  and film, 21, 23, 27
  and gazing, 55–6
  and magic lanterns, 15–16, 35–8,
    39–40, 64–5
  and music, 47–8
  and panoramas, 177, 180–1, 188,
    197–8, 207–8
  and phantasmagoria, 85–9
  see also *Dubliners*; *Finnegans Wake*;
    *Portrait of the Artist as a Young
    Man*; *Stephen Hero*; *Ulysses*

Kain, Richard M., 125
kaleidoscopes, 1–2, 7, 162–3, 244–5
Keaton, Buster
  Sherlock Junior, 147
Keiller, Patrick, 220
Kember, Joe, 54, 181
Kenner, Hugh, 9–10
Kenyon, Ellen E., 195–6
Kenyon, James, 24
Kern, Stephen, 217–18, 229
kinetoscope, 7, 8, 45, 120–1
Kircher, Athanasius
  *Ars magna lucis et umbrae
    (The Great Art of Light and
    Shadow)*, 39
Kirkton, James
  Buy Your Own Cherries, 71
Kitcher, Philip, 244–5
Knock visions, 38
Kracauer, Siegfried, 215–16

Lad from Old Ireland, The (film), 25
Lang, Fritz
  Metropolis, 143

Lange-Fuchs, Hauke, 41
Lanterne magique, La (film), 47
lanternism see magic lanterns
Lawrence, William, 36, 37, 39, 42–3
  and history, 63
  and life-models, 54
  and photography, 50, 51
  and stereoscopes, 56–7
  and travelogues, 61–2
Le Grey, Gustave, 112
Le Prince Augustin, 30n32
Lear, Doug, 35
Leo XIII, Pope, 39, 49–50
Leslie, Esther, 45
Lessing, Gotthold
  *Laocoon: An Essay on the Limits of
    Painting and Poetry*, 216–17
Levitt, Helen, 125
Lewis, J. D., 196
Lewty, Jane, 246
life-model melodramas, 53–7, 67–9,
    70–1, 82–3
Light of Other Days, The (film), 51
Lilienthal, Otto
  Bird-Flight as the Basis of Aviation,
    124
Lincoln, William F., 123
Lindsay, Vachel, 84
  The Art of the Moving Picture, 210
Literary Panorama, 175
literature, 71–2, 73–4, 146–7
  and broadcasting, 249
  and cities, 232–3
  and panorama, 195–7, 204–5
Littau, Karin, 7–8
Livesey, Joseph, 66
locomotion, 132–3; see also animal
    locomotion; transportation
Loiperdinger, Martin, 41
London, 36, 43, 47, 62, 179, 201
  and panoramas, 182, 187–8,
    193, 195
  and Sims, 12, 208–9
  and society, 72
  see also Royal Polytechnic Institution
Loss, Archie K., 119
Lover, Samuel
  Handy Andy, 70

Lumière brothers, 4, 8, 13, 189, 200, 211
  Barque sortant du port, 45
  Démolition d'un mur, 114
  Workers Leaving the Railway Works, Inchicore, 226
  see also cinematograph
Lune à un mètre, La (film), 25

McBratney Hoard, 64–70
McCole, Niamh, 36, 62
McCourt, John, 27
McKernan, Luke, 27
magic lanterns, 3, 5–6, 8, 15–16, 46–7
  and *Dubliners*, 74–6, 80–2
  and education, 58–63
  and *Finnegans Wake*, 246
  and genres, 57–8
  and Ireland, 35–8, 39–40
  and Joyce, 257
  and literature, 73–4
  and Modernism, 70–3
  and movement, 40–3
  and objects, 82–4
  and photography, 51–3
  and religion, 63–4
  and sound, 47–8
  and temperance, 38–9
  and time, 78–9
  see also phantasmagoria; slides
Malevich, Kasimir
  Knife-Grinder, 119
Man with the Indiarubber Head, The (film), 47
Mann, Thomas, 7
Mannoni, Laurent, 47
Marcellus, Percy S., 189
Marey, Étienne-Jules, 8, 17, 114, 115
  The Flight of Birds, 124
  Le Mouvement, 117
Marsh, Joss, 71
Marshall, 183–4
Martineau, Harriet
  Household Education, 59
Mass-Observation
  May the Twelfth (documentary text), 232
Matron's Story, The (slide set), 55

Maxwell, James Clerk, 56
May the Twelfth (film), 232
Mayer, Carl, 232
Mayhew, Henry
  London Labour and the London Poor, 186–7
Méliès, Georges, 12, 24–5, 47, 87
melodrama, 53–7
Melomaniac, The (film), 47
memory, 81–2, 126
  and *Portrait of the Artist as a Young Man*, 133–4, 138–9, 145–6, 147–8
  see also flashbacks
Mer, La (*Sea Bathing*) (film), 45, 46
Messmer, Otto, 13
Messter, Oskar, 88
Miller, Nicholas, 252
Miss Jerry (picture play), 55, 60
Mitchell and Kenyon, 24, 164, 210, 211, 228, 220
  Poole's Clitheroe, 195
  Ride from Blarney to Cork on Cork & Muskerry Light Railway, 133
  Trade Procession at Opening of Cork Exhibition, 218, 219
  Wales v Ireland at Wrexham, 128
Mitchell, Sagar, 24
Modernism, 7, 8, 9, 70–3
  and panorama, 191, 192, 195, 215–16
Molyneux, William
  Dioptricka Nova, 36
Monks, Robert, 210
monstration, 9–10
monumental viewing towers, 200
Morus, Iwan Rhys, 3
mottage, 245
movement, 16–17, 40–3, 45–6, 115, 181–3
moving panoramas, 4–5, 18–20
Mullin, Katherine, 75, 228
Münsterberg, Hugo
  The Photoplay: A Psychological Study, 153
Murnau, F. W.
  Der letzte Mann, 128–30
Murphy's Wake (film), 247
music, 47–9, 67–8

Musser, Charles, 15, 181
mutoscope, 8–9, 257
Muybridge, Eadweard, 8, 16, 17, 45, 117–18
  and horses, 109, 110–12
  and movement, 115
  and phenakistoscope, 123–4
  and *tours d'horizon*, 228
Myrioramas, 25, 61, 193–5, 198–200

Napoleon Bonaparte, 179, 180
narrative, 9–10, 82–3
  and episodic, 136–7
  and panoramas, 191–2
  and 'Wandering Rocks', 218–21
Nelson, Horatio, 201–2
Nelson's Column (London), 201–2
Nelson's Pillar (Dublin), 201, 202, 203
Nemeth, Ted, 247
Nero: A Sensational Story of Ancient Rome (film), 74
New World *see* United States of America
Notebook of Epiphanies (Joyce), 158

objects, 82–4
O'Brien, Edna
  'Lantern Slides', 80
O'Brien, William Smith, 201
O'Connell, Daniel, 23, 33n76
Ochtorloney, Maj Gen Sir David, 203
Odyssey (Homer), 25, 62, 78
Olcott, Sidney, 25
Ombres chinoises ('Chinese shadow') puppetry, 11–12
One Winter Night (slide set), 43
optical illusions, 2–3
Optical Magic Lantern Journal and Photographic Enlarger, 52
optical toys, 3–4, 6–7, 244–5
Ovid
  Metamorphoses, 123

Palmer, William, 72
Panopticon, 178
Panorama of Youth, The, 175
panoramas, 8, 18–20, 60–1, 174–9
  and aeronautic, 186–8
  and consciousness, 205–7
  and demise, 192–3
  and Dublin, 179–81
  and film, 208–14
  and *Finnegans Wake*, 247–8
  and Joyce, 197–8, 207–8, 257–8
  and literature, 195–7, 204–5
  and moving, 183–6
  and narrative, 191–2
  and *Ulysses*, 202, 203–4, 214–18, 221–4, 231–2
  see also dioramas; Myrioramas
panoramic perception, 190–1
Paris, 12–13, 182
Paris, John Ayrton, 6
Paris by Night (panorama), 176–7
Paris Notebook (Joyce), 126
Parnell, Charles Stewart, 63, 199, 202
parody, 250–1
Pathé, 211–12
Paul, R. W., 39, 54, 213
  The Countryman and the Cinematograph, 177
  Rough Sea at Dover, 45
peepshows, 4, 22, 49, 76, 144, 176, 257
  and kinetoscope, 7–9, 45
  and *Ulysses*, 55, 58, 74, 113
People's Popular Picture Palace, 26–7, 47–8
Pepper, John Henry, 3
'Pepper's Ghost', 86–8
peripheral vision, 3
persistence of vision, 3, 4, 6–9, 28n11
phantasmagoria, 3, 16, 85–8, 155–6
phantom rides, 132–3, 183, 211
phenakistoscope, 6, 7, 123–4
Philidor (Paul De Philipsthal), 43, 44, 85, 86
Photographie de Satan, La (*Satan's Photographic Emporium*), 160
photography, 6, 16–17, 49–53
  and colour, 56, 57
  and geography, 60
  and Joyce, 126, 257
  and panoramas, 192
  and writers, 196
  see also chronophotography
photoplays, 24–5
Photorama, 189

picture concerts, 47–8
picture plays, 55
Pilgrim's Progress (slide set), 66
Pirandello, Luigi
  Si, gira! (Shoot!), 130–1
Plateau, Joseph Antoine Ferdinand, 6
Plato, 10, 13, 257
  and cave, 84–5, 153–4, 155
pocket epics, 74
Political Panorama, The, 175
politics, 62–3; *see also* colonialism;
  imperialism
Poole and Young, 193–5
  The Strange Story, 88, 89
pornography, 55, 249
Porter, Edwin S.
  Great Train Robbery, 60
  Life of an American Fireman, 79
*Portrait of the Artist as a Young
  Man, A* (Joyce), 7, 13, 15,
    17–18, 57
  and 1904 sketch, 114–15
  and bodies, 142–4
  and cave allegory, 153, 154–5, 157
  and cinematicity, 91–2, 106–9
  and consciousness, 109–10
  and dreams, 78
  and education, 59
  and epiphany, 158–60
  and episodic narrative, 136–8
  and Hell, 156, 157
  and locomotion, 133
  and memory, 133–4, 138–9
  and panorama, 198, 199–200
  and phantasmagoria, 88
  and photography, 257
  and politics, 63
  and projection, 144–8, 149–50
  and religion, 64
  and shadow show, 38, 150
  and space-time shifts, 139–41
  and time, 135
  and trams, 220
  and *Ulysses*, 161–4
  and virtual gaze, 213
  and vision, 124–5, 127–30, 131–2
  and visual immersion, 150–3
  and waves, 46, 150

postcards, 53, 155
Pound, Ezra, 216
projection, 144–8, 149–50
Promio, Alexandre, 211
propaganda, 71, 86, 164, 175, 181,
  199, 209
props, 83
Protestantism, 64
Proust, Marcel, 7
  *Á la recherche du temps perdu,
    Du côté de chez Swann*,
    37–8
  Swann's Way, 109, 163
psychogeography, 20
psychology, 3
puns, 60, 162, 222, 230–1, 245,
  251–2
puppetry, 11–12, 47

Quendler, Christian
  *The Camera-Eye Metaphor in
    Cinema*, 107
Quo Vadis or the Way of the Cross
  (film), 74

radio, 249–50, 251, 258
railings, 83
Railway Story with a Moral, A (slide
  set), 69
Rains, Stephanie, 75
reflection, 3
refraction, 3
Reiniger, Lotte, 13
Reisman, Jerry, 215, 245
religion, 63–4, 66–7, 155–6
Rêve de Noël, Le (film), 25
Revivalism, 66–7
Richardson, Dorothy
  Pilgrimage, 206
Richter, Hans, 247
Riley Brothers, 73
  *Street Life: Or People We
    Meet*, 72
  A Strong Contrast, 83
Rivière, Henri, 12
'Robertson', 85
Robin Adair (slide set), 78, 84
Robison, Arthur, 14–15

Rockett, Kevin and Emer, 22, 25, 26, 64, 200
  Magic Lantern, Panorama and Moving Picture Shows in Ireland, 1786–1909, 5–6
  and magic lanterns, 35, 37, 38
Roe, Clifford G.
  The Horror of the White Slave Trade, 73
Roebuck Rudge, John Arthur, 46–7
Roget, Peter Mark, 3, 6
Romain, Jules, 231
Ross, Thomas, 45
Rossell, Deac, 42, 45, 112
Rotunda (Dublin), 24, 26, 48, 88–9, 236n91
  and dioramas, 182
  and panoramas, 176, 183–4
Rotunda (London), 179, *180*
Royal Panopticon of Science and Art, 182
Royal Polytechnic Institution, 3, 22, 44, 86, 87
Rubin, William S., 120
Ruttmann, Walther, 221, 227, 247
  Berlin: Sinfonie einer Großstadt, 215, 216, 224, *225*, 231–2

Sackville Street (Dublin), 36, 49, 176, 200, 201
Saint-Amour, Paul, 208, 230, 231
Salvation Army, 63, 72
Scent of the Lilies, The (slide set), 78
Schatten: eine Nächtliche Halluzination (film), 14–15
Schivelbusch, Wolfgang, 183, 190
Scholes, Robert, 125
science, 3, 4, 58
self-decapitation, 46–7
sexuality, 146, 249
Shadbolt, Cecil Victor, 62, 188
shadow plays, 12–13, 14–15, 248–9
shadowgraphy, 8, 11–12, 13
Siege of Delhi, The (slide show), 42
Sights of the World (Myriorama), 193, 194
silhouettes, 11–14
'Silhouettes' (Joyce), 10–12

Sims, George R., 71
  Christmas Day in the Workhouse, 70
  Living London, 12, 208–9
  The Social Kaleidoscope, 205
Sinclair, May, 206
Sinyard, Neil, 107
'Sisters, The' (Dubliners), 12, 13, 75, 89, 129, 142
  and camera-eye, 84–5
  and phantasmagoria, 145
Skeffington, Francis, 162–3
slides, 38–9, 41–3
  and documentary, 51–3
  and life-model melodramas, 53–7
  and McBratney Hoard, 64–70
  and memory, 78, 79
  and songs, 47–8
Smith, Albert, 184
Smith, Ashley
  A City Stirs, 232
Smith, G. A., 24–5, 54
Social Question, 11, 51, 65, 67, 70, 71–3
socialism, 72, 101n153
Soldier's Dream, The (dissolving view), 43, 79
Sommerfield, John
  May Day, 232
songs, 47–9, 67–8
sound, 47–9, 247
Spanish-American War, 198–9
special effects, 193–4
spectres *see* ghosts
Spiegel, Alan, 9, 10, 11, 206, 228
  and *Portrait of the Artist as a Young Man*, 107, 112
spooks *see* ghosts
sport, 128, 241n178
Spurr, David, 203
Star Boarder, The (film), 56
Starewicz, Wladislaw, 252
Stephen Hero (Joyce), 17, 23, 39, 40, 125–6, 175
Stereoramas, 193–4
stereoscopes, 56–7, 112–13
Sternberger, Dolf, 174, 190
still images, 113
Stirling, James, 196

Story of the Kelly Gang, The (film), 26
Stow, Percy
    A Glass of Goat's Milk, 160
stream of consciousness, 17, 20,
    106, 206
Strick, Joseph, 108–9
subjective camera, 128–31
Sullivan, Pat, 13
superimposition, 75–6
supernaturalism, 39
surveillance, 178, 207–8

Talbot, William Fox, 6
Taylor, A. J. P., 26
television, 20, 21, 50
    and *Finnegans Wake*, 246, 249–50,
    250–1
temperance, 38–9, 63–4, 83
Tennyson, Alfred, Lord, 117
    Enoch Arden, 77, 78
thaumatrope, 6, 121–2, 253
Theall, David, 50, 249
theatre, 79–80, 85
Théâtre des Ombres, 12–13
Theremin, Leon, 247
Thomas-Edison Electric Animated
    Pictures, 26, 91
Tiddemann, L. E.
    Poverty's Pupil, 73
time, 16–18, 115, 122–3, 134–6, 206
    and *Portrait of the Artist as a Young
    Man*, 126–8, 139–41
titling, 164
tours d'horizon, 176, 203, 212,
    213, 228
toys, 37; *see also* optical toys
Traffic on O'Connell Bridge (film), 23
transfer printing, 49
transportation, 183–5, 186–8, 211
    and trams, 220, 222
travelogues, 60–2, 176–8, 183, 193–5
Trewey, Félicien, 13, 23
trick films, 24, 25, 87
    Poole's Clitheroe, 195
Trieste, 27, 131
Triograph, 211
Trips Abroad (Myriorama), 193
trompe l'oeil, 176, 208

Trotter, David, 250
Turim, Maureen, 78, 79, 80
Two Hours in the New World
    (panorama), 185

Ulysse à Montmartre (shadow play), 13
Ulysses (Joyce), 9–10, 25, 57,
    111, 184
    and 'Aeolus', 202, 203, 211
    and cartoons, 69–70
    and exotic locations, 60
    and film, 113–14, 209
    and Futurism, 119–20
    and 'Ithaca', 7, 14, 48, 54
    and 'Lestrygonians', 66, 86,
    208, 228
    and mutoscope, 257
    and 'Nausicaa', 13–14
    and obscenity trial, 1–2
    and panorama, 19, 20, 174, 175,
    200, 201, 212, 213–17, 258
    and phantasmagoria, 86–7
    and *Portrait of the Artist as a Young
    Man*, 161–4
    and Reisman-Zukofsky, 245
    and religion, 64, 66
    and songs ('Sirens'), 48–9, 67, 68
    see also 'Circe'; 'Wandering Rocks'
uncanny, 16, 85, 90
United States of America (USA),
    184–5, 211
Uricchio, William, 175, 178, 211, 213

Van Dooren, Ine, 58
verbal-dissolves, 246
Verne, Jules
    Journey to the Centre of the Earth, 154
Vertov, Dziga, 205, 221, 232
    Man with a Movie Camera, 215, 227
Victoria, Queen, 57, 101n153, 199,
    209, 213
Viertel, Berthold
    *Die Abenteuer eines
    Zehnmarkscheins*, 224
View of London, A (panorama), 179
Village of Alagna, The (diorama), 182
virtual gaze, 107, 190–1, 213
virtual voyaging, 183–6

visualisation, 2, 125–6
  and *Portrait of the Artist as a Young Man*, 107, 108, 124–5, 127–30, 131–2
vivisection, 40
Vogl-Bienek, Ludwig, 15, 52
Volta Cinematograph, 21, 26, 27, 259
Voyage dans la lune, Le (film), 25
voyeurism, 55–6
vue panoramiques, 211–12

Walker, Henry, 42
Wallace, Lew
  Ben Hur: A Tale of the Christ, 73, 74
Walton, O. F.
  Christie's Old Organ, 67–9, 77
'Wandering Rocks' (*Ulysses*), 20, 72–3, 210, 217–21
  and cavalcade, 185–6, 227–31
  and close-ups, 224–6
  and panorama, 191, 203–4, 205, 208, 216–17, 221–4, 231–2
Waterloo, Battle of, 180, 197, 234n25, 248
wave motion, 45–6, 112

waxworks, 63
Wellington, Duke of, 197
Wells, H. G., 2, 30n39, 90, 106, 238n129
What Are the Wild Waves Saying? (slide set), 46, 78, 150
Wheatstone, Sir Charles, 112
'Wheel of Life' lantern, 45, 123–4
White Slaves of London (slide set), 73
Williamson, James, 54
  Remorse, 79–80
women, 73
Woolf, Virginia, 16, 90, 109, 111, 133–4
Woolsey, John M., 1–2
Wray, Cecil, 30n32
Wright, Orville and Wilbur, 124

X-rays, 156–7

Zecca, Ferdinand
  Histoire d'un crime, 79
zoëtrope, 6, 7, 45, 123
zoöpraxiscope, 17, 45, 111–12, 123–4
Zukofsky, Louis, 215, 245